# Activity-Based Management

# Activity-Based Management

## A Comprehensive Implementation Guide

**Edward Forrest**

Productivity Consulting Ltd.
Roslyn, New York

**McGraw-Hill**

New York   San Francisco   Washington, D.C.   Auckland   Bogotá
Caracas   Lisbon   London   Madrid   Mexico City   Milan
Montreal   New Delhi   San Juan   Singapore
Sydney   Tokyo   Toronto

**Library of Congress Cataloging-in-Publication Data**

Forrest, Edward.
    Activity-based management : a comprehensive implementation guide /
Edward Forrest.
       p.    cm.
    Includes index.
    ISBN 0-07-021588-X
    1. Activity-based costing.  2. Cost accounting.  3. Managerial
accounting.  I. Title.
HF5686.C8F584    1995
658.15'1—dc20                              95-45319
                                              CIP

## McGraw-Hill

*A Division of The McGraw-Hill Companies*

1 2 3 4 5 6 7 8 9 0  DOC/DOC  9 0 0 9 8 7 6 5


ISBN 0-07-021588-X


*The sponsoring editor for this book was Philip Ruppel, the editing supervisor was
David E. Fogarty, and the production supervisor was Donald Schmidt. It was set in
Century Schoolbook by Cynthia L. Lewis of McGraw-Hill's Professional Book Group
composition unit.*

*Printed and bound by R. R. Donnelley & Sons Company.*

McGraw-Hill books are available at special quantity discounts to use as premiums
and sales promotions, or for use in corporate training programs. For more information, please write to the Director of Special Sales, McGraw-Hill, 11 West 19th
Street, New York, NY 10011. Or contact your local bookstore.

 This book is printed on recycled, acid-free paper containing a
minimum of 50% recycled de-inked fiber.

# Contents

# Preface

We have a desire to provide both management and financial executives with the appropriate enablers to assist them in better understanding the activities that constitute an organization's work efforts. We believe that this book fulfills this wish by establishing the step-by-step methodology that can be followed by managers at every level.

Managers must initially accept a cultural transformation from a traditional hierarchical mentality to an activity-based view of the world. The business public provides an assortment of innovative solutions and inspired opportunities for learning, but the most productive environment in which to learn is our own.

When the idea for this book came to me in 1990, I wasn't sure who in the business community would be interested in this type of material. I began by doing some preliminary research as my idea turned into a passionate commitment, and my life hasn't been the same since. I discovered that there wasn't much available material on the activity-based methodology, and the material that was available didn't explain how to go about utilizing it.

In addition, our universities and colleges at the undergraduate and graduate levels aren't teaching the type of structured analysis that can be used throughout one's business career. The systematic approach described in this book provides an enormous return on investment and builds a manager's confidence in being able to understand how any business operation functions, and interfaces with either internal or external customers. The approach enables a manager to learn the most about his or her environment in the shortest possible time frame. It doesn't matter if cost cutting is given a fancy name like *downsizing* or *rightsizing*, because the process will not endure unless we eliminate non-value-added work. Random head count reductions won't cut it.

Our technique has been used successfully in many varied types of businesses, and virtually all those who have embraced its concepts have reaped rewards beyond their expectations. People often ask me how I can be so enthusiastic about this kind of subject. The response is simple, because I have experienced only positive results with the activity-based technique both as a line executive and as a consultant.

Knowledge is genuine power, and an objective, well-documented approach to understanding a business operation's activities is the way to achieve permanent cost reductions.

Now, after 4 years, I am pleased and proud to see this labor of love published so I can share my excitement with others. I am suggesting, not that you abandon everything you have learned—experience is a wonderful asset—but instead that you build on your background and business acumen by adding a new tool for success.

Some executives think they are different and may even feel that this methodology doesn't apply to them, but none of us can deny that the way we operate a business today has drastically changed. In order to remain competitive in this new world, we can no longer just say "cut 10 percent" and everything will be all right.

So let us all move down the yellow brick road together on this fabulous journey in learning a more realistic way to operate a business that more closely mirrors the way we perform our work. We can accomplish a great deal with dedication, passion, and commitment, while emphasizing our interactive relationship with colleagues and customers.

If we are able to respond to one another's needs in these changing times, there will be fewer moments of trauma and more time for joy and celebration. I believe if you utilize the contents of this book, you will become as enthusiastic as I am about the power it contains.

EDWARD FORREST
*President, Productivity Consulting Limited*
*Roslyn, New York*

# Acknowledgments

This book could not have become a reality without the assistance and encouragement of friends and family. The project became increasingly important to me as I continually read and heard about the downsizing and rightsizing of corporate America.

These shocking news items were followed by stories of how anticipated cost reductions didn't materialized or, if they did, failed to be permanent. The writing of this book is a result of personal experiences that I encountered during various implementations of the methodology presented in the pages that follow.

I must thank the exceptional individuals who made up the AT&T Network Services Division ABIP team: Robert J. Boylan, Hershel Le Grand, Richard Sciacchitano, Bob Casale and, Chris Prime. This high-level performing team succeeded beyond anyone's expectations and adopted the activity-based methodology as their own. Their courage and pioneering spirit have created a special bond between us.

In very different ways each team member took risks, kept his integrity intact, and was willing to say yes when traditional convention wasn't totally supportive. These fine individuals were supportive in reading early drafts, and they provided sincere constructive comments and suggestions.

I am also thankful and especially indebted to Robert Hill, a consultant's consultant, whose patience and coaching enabled me to hone my consulting skills. Bob provided support, encouragement, wise counsel, and friendly advice. He has been an inspiration in completing this project.

I appreciate the support and forward thinking of some of AT&T's senior managers—among them, Kevin J. Breen, Joan McManus Massey, Robert A. DiCarlo, and Henry J. Warren. Their belief in the power of this methodology has allowed me to validate the results of using it.

xii   Acknowledgment

A word of acknowledgment, delightfully, goes to Lori A. Rosenthal, who made up in spirit and enthusiasm what she lacked in hierarchical power. She had the courage to throw off political logic for what she believed in. I am also grateful to Lori Becker, who faced an ongoing barrage of notes and illegible scribbles and still performed the miracle of coverting them into literate sentences.

A special thanks to my editor, Jim Bessent, who helped organize and structure this neophyte's initial attempt at publishing and whose strong endorsement of the work carried me through. Danielle Munley, Jim's most valuable customer-focused assistant, administratively dotted the *i*'s, crossed the *t*'s, and kept everyone's spirits up throughout the process.

I must pay special tribute to my wife, Jill, a gifted writer who transformed the manuscript into a far more readable and effective work than it might have been. She could not have given more of herself if this book had been her own. Her insight, clear and objective thinking, and understanding of the English language are unsurpassed. Her critiquing and the innovative ideas she supplied from her own experiences can't be measured.

A special thanks goes to my father-in-law, Harry L. Rudes, Esq., for his continued confidence in my abilities and his unending giving of himself. He never asks what—only when—if his counsel or support is required. He has taught me what integrity means, and that honesty is definitely the only policy.

To my children, Courtney and Jonathan, a special thank you for your extraordinary patience and love during all those hours I spent working on this book. You made the project important to you because you knew it was important to me. I love you both.

# 1
# Introduction

## Purpose of the Book

The function of this book is to impart to managers at all levels of business the techniques and methodology for attaining and maintaining a high level of productivity within an organization regardless of its size. The approach we assert requires a high degree of patience and commitment to implement a program of this type. We use the term *program* rather than *project* because the methodology prescribed is an ongoing one that emphasizes a natural association to a total quality management philosophy.

The techniques we avow will provide a proven road map for success in achieving permanent cost reductions and higher throughput. The elimination of work is the only permanent modus operandi for an organization to reduce long-term costs. The traditional approach of decreasing expenses solely on the basis of head count—rightsizing—usually results merely in temporary relief, cosmetically displayed in financial statements. If you reduce head count without eliminating activities, you open an operational "black hole" with fewer people doing the same work.

An *activity-based management* (ABM) approach is more a management system than a financial system. We all need to understand its application as contained in this book in order to compete in today's business environment, which is heavily focused on customers. Remember that customers can be internal as well as external. The operational focus we emphasize centers on end-to-end processing of work, ignoring traditional hierarchical and departmental structures which build walls and are usually an impediment to performing work productively and efficiently.

This book is also designed to be an enabler for business managers by offering a step-by-step methodology—"how to proceed objectively"—in an orderly manner through the program. We have included all the necessary data collection tools which have been field-tested—describing each one in detail, how to fill them in, and the purpose each is used for. Figure 1-1 is a program map showing the ABM methodology and organization of the chapters in this book.

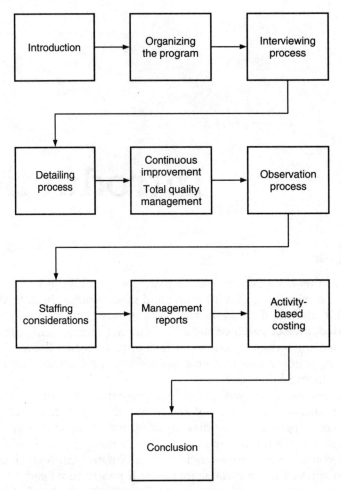

**Figure 1-1.** ABM program map.

We employ a standardized language throughout, clearly defining what each critical term means to avoid misunderstandings and misinterpretations of information once it is gathered.

The implementation process we describe, if applied correctly, will assist managers in managing their business process more effectively and confidently while increasing shareowner value. After reading this volume, some people may ask, "Why is there so much 'nitty-gritty detail' in a program of this type?" The answer is simple and direct.

Most managers need and want as much objective information as possible to understand how, what, where, when, and why work is performed. The field-tested, proven methodology we discuss is a thorough approach with built-in checks and balances to ensure accuracy and completeness. If what we dictate is properly implemented, the "nitty-gritty" work will have to be done only once rather than over and over again.

In the real world business processes change, and when an activity changes a manager should utilize our approach in his or her functional work area to reflect the change. The productivity improvement and reengineering processes are constructed to endure and are not crafted to be a one-shot quick fix. They involve analysis, understanding, creativity, and a pragmatic approach to performing work.

We accentuate flexible problem-solving techniques and have organized the material in the text as a guide for improving business operations. We believe that once a manager embraces these techniques, he or she can be confident in analyzing and improving any new or old business process. An executive, manager, or supervisor will, within a reasonably short period of time, know a business process as well as the people who have performed it for years, even though it may be new to that executive, manager, or supervisor.

When you conclude reading this book, you will be equipped with the tools for improving a company's competitive position by accomplishing the following tasks:

- Establish synergistic objectives between a specific functional work area and the corporation.
- Develop a detailed strategy to achieve those objectives.
- Prepare and present the positive aspects of an activity-based costing and management program to functional work areas.
- Emphasize the importance of every employee's support and buy-in if the program is to succeed.
- Acknowledge that shortcuts or quick-fix solutions will suboptimize the effectiveness of information.
- Stress that common sense, logic, preparation, planning, research, and objectivity are the essential ingredients for success.
- Standardize information available to everyone.
- Install a continuous improvement mentality and work ethic.
- Provide a common language and framework that facilitates communication and better decision making across processes, ignoring hierarchical rivalries.

## Critical Success Factors—The Chain of Success

There are seven critical success factors we term the *chain of success:*

- Management commitment
- Managing organizational resistance
- Multidiscipline ABM team
- Business segment versus entire business

- Evaluation of value-added versus non-value-added activities
- Business process stability
- Data gathering

## Management Commitment

Planning for an activity-based management effort, regardless of the complexity or size of an organization, is a courageous undertaking that sometimes involves a business culture change. The first link in the chain of success is the active participatory involvement of senior management. This commitment cannot be demonstrated solely by issuing and signing an initiative for the rank and file to blindly follow.

Senior management must show its resolve to ensure the success of an activity-based program by attending meetings on a regular basis, monitoring results, and motivating people in the organization. Senior management should initially explain the importance of the program and the expected results to be harvested by its implementation.

In addition, the management team must emphasize that this endeavor is a continuous, never-ending project, not just a one-shot effort that happens to be today's hot button. Senior management must play the role of Solomon when there are differences of opinion, and should clear all obstacles to progress.

## Managing Organizational Resistance

The quality of the planning process in the early phases of development is essential to the success of an activity-based management (ABM) program. The extent to which varying viewpoints and perspectives are considered in constructing the program's architecture could determine the long-term commitment of rank-and-file participants as well as senior management.

Many organizations that are currently entrenched in hierarchical management traditions will view an undertaking of this type as revolutionary. In a plethora of cases, hierarchy has negated the success of self-empowered teams once those teams reached a level of unexpected achievement—because control of fiefdoms was at stake.

A common revelation is the identification of a need for a cultural and behavior-patterns change within an organization. The Japanese spent almost 20 years in understanding and mastering the theory and practical application of reengineering and productivity improvement methodologies. The ABM program often acts as the catalyst for this type of transformation. Management must be convinced that ABM is important, must provide an efficient and effective mechanism for soliciting cooperation from the rank and file, and must link corporate goals to individual goals for improving company operations.

Once senior management is firmly leading this type of endeavor, the second key link in the chain of success is to have the rank-and-file employee buy into the program. This does not mean that every employee, supervisor, and/or manager has to buy into the new philosophy. It does mean that the pockets of resistance must be minimized and the number of pockets of support increased.

Buy-in can be accomplished through a bottom-up approach and through honest solicitation of ideas for improving operations from the people performing the work every day. They know what tools they need to improve their work, and if only lip service is given to their needs, the undertaking will fail. If senior management and its operations people work in harmony with mutual respect, a continuous improvement mentality and quality management philosophy will be adopted by all participants, ensuring success in the long run. The term *focus* can be defined as everyone working toward a clear, complete, and measurable set of goals. A focused organization has everyone pointed and moving in the same direction. Its goals are sufficiently clear that everyone understands them, and the goals represent a complete statement of where the organization wants to be. In addition, the goals are measurable so everyone knows when they are achieved.

Focus is crucial to activity-based management; without it, improvement efforts may not enhance performance and productivity. Achieving focus requires a vision, a clear mission, and a measurable set of goals based on that vision. The vision and goals must be shared and understood by everyone in the business process.

Focus also requires that everyone have a set of performance measures that are based on the business process's goals. These performance measures allow everyone to see how she or he contributes to the functional work area's performance, and provide the basis for establishing priorities for improvement.

This cooperative and collaborative approach to work activities will overcome any organizational resistance to change that may surface. An organization should drive decision making down to the worker level. In order to effectuate such a cultural transformation, the ABM team and senior management must exhibit a consistency of message combined with patience and persistence.

Senior managers cannot just wish for creativity, innovation, and quality. They must encourage it among their employees and reward them for it. It is important to maintain motivated employees to attain high levels of performance, high levels of productivity, and innovation that results in improved performance and productivity. Concurrently, management must instill a sense of commitment to the customer base in every employee.

A policy for ensuring that organizational resistance doesn't resurface once it is under control is to encourage interfunctional work area cooperation, coordination, and communication—emphasizing that "there are no secrets and/or hidden agendas; we are a team with a defined vision and mission."

Long ago Machiavelli wrote, "It must be remembered that there is nothing more difficult to plan, more doubtful of success, nor more dangerous to manage, than the creation of a new system. For the initiator has the enmity of all who would profit by the preservation of the institutions and merely lukewarm defenders in those who would gain by the new one."

## Multidiscipline ABM Team

The third link in the chain of success is the assembling of an ABM team to steward and facilitate the program. Although we are in the age of specialization, senior management must eliminate the individual-star reward system and introduce team effectiveness appraisals. The ABM team should be comprised of highly skilled professionals with varying backgrounds (accounting, engineering, operations, human resources, and so on). Educational and work experience are also important considerations.

Equally significant should be interpersonal skills to motivate people to do what you want them to do because they want to do it. *Team chemistry* is a term commonly associated with winning sports teams, and its value to an ABM program cannot be underestimated. There isn't any room for prima donnas on an ABM team, because each team member has to be able to jump in and assist another team member in a support role when required. Open and frequent discussions among team members as to what they are doing—their successes and failures—and identification of potential future problems are the order of the day.

All team members should have line experience as well as staff experience, and their business acumen should include the ability to analyze data and suggest alternative improvements. Each team member should possess strong administrative skills. The technical skills required will depend on the functional work areas involved and the type of analysis to be done.

The team approach has historically resulted in smoother implementation, superior communication, better transfer of knowledge, broader customer acceptance, and a cadre of disciples who are steeped in the methodology. The multidisciplined team should consist of cross-functional, experienced, respected, open-minded, dedicated, creative, and available individuals.

## Business Segment Versus Entire Business

A common query asked by senior management is, "How broad should the ABM program be?" The answer depends on several factors:

- Availability of resources
- Expected results
- Time frame in which results are to be achieved
- Senior management's familiarity with the program's methodology

If initially only limited resources are available and/or senior management isn't fully versed in reengineering, productivity improvement, and ABM techniques, it would be better to choose one business segment as a model. The sequencing of the remaining business segments within an organization should be crafted on the basis of return on investment, or on the criticality of the functional work area. If there is strong support and commitment from senior management, and if sufficient resources are available, an entire organization can be blanketed.

A useful way to augment the ABM team—thereby increasing available resources—is to enlist various business process members as adjunct members of the team to assist in the program. This technique has a twofold advantage: it involves experienced personnel who will be trained on the job in ABM methodology, and it expands the resource capability of the team.

In either case, the key events to be completed will be exactly the same, and the results will be generated at an earlier date. The size of the organization and the size of the ABM team are directly related to the completion date for implementation of the program.

## Evaluation of Value-Added Versus Non-Value-Added Activities

The fifth link in the chain of success is determining which activities are value added and which are non-value added. As the ABM program unfolds, the ABM team has to scrutinize each work activity to be certain it is worthwhile doing. If an activity isn't worthwhile, is redundant, or isn't necessary, eliminate or minimize it immediately. A *value-added activity* is defined as an activity required to produce a product or service and/or to improve a process. Conversely, a *non-value-added* activity is defined as one not required to produce a product or service and/or to improve a process.

An evaluation of these categories is part of the recipe for driving work out of a business process and thereby reducing costs permanently. The identification process is fully discussed in Chapter Four. Once an activity is identified as non-value added, do not waste time and resources attempting to reengineer it. Concentrate on improving the value-added activities.

## Business Process Stability

The ideal time to implement an ABM program is when a business process and/or organization is stable. This postulate, which is the sixth link in the chain of success, is important in order to fully understand what activities are performed in an organization or business process and how efficiently those activities are currently being executed.

If a business process is continually changing, the ABM team will not be able to establish a stake in the ground against which improvements can be measured as the program is implemented. It has been our experience that piecemeal changes done independently of one another often lead to rework and frequently cause a new problem somewhere else.

It is more efficient and cost-effective to build a fully planned and architectured set of changes to be implemented in the same time frame. You cannot reengineer a moving target effectively and expect long-term high-performance results. If a business process is undergoing change, temporarily place a moratorium on further changes until the prescribed methodology is completed and a full understanding of what should be altered is achieved.

Then and only then can an integrated solution be structured that will work effectively without disrupting other business processes. This approach is reinforced when activities cross traditional hierarchical structures, resulting in part of a process being fixed in one functional work area and the rest of the process remaining unchanged in another functional work area.

Reengineering only part of the business process could also result in negative morale and raise employee suspicion as to senior management's "real" motives. It is better not to start productivity improvement than to do it half-heartedly.

### Data Gathering

The seventh and last link in the chain of success involves the brain center of any ABM program: data gathering. The data-gathering process is discussed in detail in Chapters Three, Four, and Six.

A few high-level aspects of data gathering should be recognized. If the techniques and methodology discussed in this book are followed and thoroughly documented, you should feel secure that your data gathering is complete, checked and doublechecked, and obtained from the individuals who actually perform the activities.

There will not be surrogate allocation formulas—opinions of managers who believe they know the work performed in their functional work area but who may be out of touch with the manner in which current activities are completed. When you gather transaction volume, payroll, and work-hours data, be certain to choose a representative and appropriate historical time period to eliminate seasonal and unusual work pattern biases.

Lastly, be sure to avoid overkill with so much detail that it defeats the purpose of the overall program. Concentrate your data gathering on primary activities in which the greater portion of an employee's time is spent.

The seven links in the chain of success are the critical success factors for an ABM program and are overall guidelines in applying the techniques and methodologies described in subsequent chapters. The ABM process begins with the organization of the program.

## The True Meaning of Empowerment

"You are now empowered" is a phrase reverberating throughout the corporate world. Is this statement in line with today's management style? Yes. But do the majority of senior managers who know only a hierarchically structured culture really wish to relinquish what they have worked so carefully to achieve—power?

Empowerment can produce potent results, including increased customer satisfaction, lower operational costs, responsive decision making that doesn't include the manager, and highly efficient work teams. Employee empowerment excites staff members but, unhappily, unless senior management is willing to abandon its old ways of managing people and put forth the energy and investment of time required to learn new habits, employee empowerment could cause more harm than good.

Staff members who have never been empowered will be unsure how to conduct themselves or know what to expect if they make a wrong decision during the learning process. Empowerment, if implemented properly, entails giving all staff members the jurisdiction to make decisions, regardless of seniority. This delegation of authority allows problems to be handled and corrected immediately at the point of origin rather than navigating their way through bureaucratic channels while they become more serious.

Senior management cannot expect a paradigm shift overnight; it must invest the time needed to ensure empowerment's success. A good way to give senior management an appreciation of how the other half lives is to implement a "manager for a day" program. The executive would exchange jobs with each staff member for a day, thereby coming to understand what the individual who performs an activity is required to do in his or her job and what tools the employee needs to be truly empowered.

Management training courses should be afforded all employees so they can learn what elements go into objective, informed decision making. When a staff member begins making decisions, management should refrain from reviewing and/or overruling the decision. In this manner, a staff member can be allowed to exercise her or his own good judgment. Management must create an environment in which staff members feel secure in the knowledge that their decisions will be supported without fear of being berated or, even worse, fired. The functional work area manager should provide specific feedback and coaching to improve the quality of a staff member's decisions.

Staff members must insist on receiving the most complete and up-to-date data on which to base their decisions, eliminating the "need to know" syndrome. As President Franklin Delano Roosevelt said, "The only thing we have to fear is fear itself." The only impediments to the success of employee empowerment are the managers who must relinquish their power.

The key to this transformation is to show managers the benefits to be derived from managing their subordinates' work, not their subordinates' decisions, and to insist that managers be evaluated on their ability to improve staff performance and productivity. This will require some retraining. It is hard to conceive of anything more disconcerting to a staff member than to do a superior job and then see it wasted because some executive mismanaged his or her part in the process. All the elements for change could be present and still an organization could fail to implement them because a proper infrastructure was not in place to support the change.

The necessary elements to effectuate change are the capacity to visualize, produce, and adapt behavioral patterns into a different vision of an organization. Much has been written about how and why people resist change, but precious little has been said on the process of change itself, perhaps because it is difficult to measure accurately.

An activity-based management program does not involve merely the reconceptualizing and repackaging of activities; it also requires looking at the work in an entirely new way. It is similar to shaking a kaleidoscope. The set of fragments form a different picture each time. In reengineering work, we shake the activities and reform them in a new way. The overall change involves new policies, new behaviors, new methodologies, and most important, new ways of looking at things. The implementation of changes requires the design and formation of new habits to make new and hopefully more productive achievements possible.

It is a significant fact that companies alter their manner of doing business in a variety of ways, and not all the approaches are regarded by management as beneficial. Activity-based management programs can be either internally driven or externally driven. Internally driven programs are usually participative, based on volition and cooperation, whereas externally driven programs are usually based on coercion and opposition. Externally driven programs tend to be authoritarian and politically motivated. If senior managers feel threatened and not really certain that change would be good for them politically, they may be more inclined to restrict employee empowerment and participation in shaping the types of improvements that would be most beneficial to the company.

The external world or customer base that encircles an organization can be an important catalyst for stimulating productivity improvements. But since an organization's culture consists of numerous diverse groups and stakeholders, each with a personal agenda and varying degrees of power, it cannot be assumed that the issuance of an official initiative will lead to success. Sometimes, what the company wants may not always coincide with what the hierarchical management and/or staff member's culture wants.

A less obvious fact is that a change from a hierarchical environment to an end-to-end process environment can be brought to bear solely by pressure from outside sources. Perceptions often become reality; whether they are founded in fact or rumor is irrelevant. Senior management may make strategic choices on the basis of its own level of competence and political payoff, rather than on what's best for the company as a whole. Activity-based management looks for long-term innovations. Yet some senior managers might focus on short-term enhancements—because they may receive credit in the media or because the results are tied to their own personal contractual arrangements.

In devising a new approach to operating a business, you should be part historian as well. You must first understand what was done in the past, and why, in order to construct a scenario that will allow the future to evolve naturally out of the past. In reviewing the past, you may uncover several occurrences of broken promises to staff members by executives.

This substructure would foster distrust in any proposed new direction. The ABM team might have to alter its game plan by first fulfilling some earlier promises before moving forward, in order to establish the foundation for mutual trust. If this foundation is missing, it should be constructed quickly.

These positive underpinnings will enable changes to occur with a feeling of high self-esteem, mutual respect, and trust among all parties involved in the change. If a strong foundation already exists, it should be continually nurtured to provide security and stability for the program.

The factions within the management ranks who oppose an activity-based management program may be made to disappear or else transformed into allies, much as opposing forces in a war eventually reconcile and sign treaties of peace. What was a highly adversarial relationship at the time eventually gets resolved, and the tendency is to forget that conflict had existed.

## Let the Past Be Your Guide to the Future

Companies that have implemented successful ABM programs are graced with managers capable of seeing beyond an activity as it is currently being performed. Departing from tradition provides these managers with a basis of experience from which to replace existing routines with more productive ones. New strategies cannot be developed quickly without prior functional work area background. The ability to identify potential improvements facilitates the shift in the way an activity is completed and is a positive reinforcer for the participating staff member.

### The Unplanned Event

There are times when the change process is set in motion by an unplanned event, such as a lawsuit or a competitor's new product hitting the market. The significant characteristic for staff members involved in the incident is that it calls for a response. If the event cannot be handled by existing methods, or if external customers indicate that they will not be satisfied by the same old approach, then an innovative activity may be required to resolve the issue.

### Management Vision and Strength of Conviction

Strong leadership from senior managers in articulating direction can reduce non-value-added work. They project to others the clear-cut actions that must be taken. The more participatory ABM becomes in circulating new ideas, the more it enables managers to draw together many functional work areas. Through the integration of diverse experiences and exchange of ideas, ABM is able to promote forward planning instead of creating roadblocks to change, as does the hierarchical form of management.

The development of consensus and cooperative coalitions makes it easier to implement improvements.

## Choosing a Champion

Any new methodology, no matter how exciting or pragmatic it is, no matter how much support the creators muster for it, will stand a genuine risk of not being implemented without someone in senior management strongly driving it. We have all been part of a developing program that fails despite its excellent concepts. A consensus is built, but no one wants the responsibility and/or accountability for moving it forward. The change then dies by benign neglect.

The person of power must assign accountability to individuals and then make sure each person responsible lives up to completing the assignment on time. The senior executive is responsible for keeping the momentum of the ABM team moving forward, even when enthusiasm wanes. This individual is empowered as the program's *champion* who must continually push the new initiatives, concepts, or methodologies in every meeting, presentation, and/or internal publication.

It is critical not to adopt trite slogans or pat phrases, because many people tend to make fun of slogans and attribute or perceive a lack of sincerity on the champion's part. The key is to clearly demonstrate that the prime mover believes in the approach because it is good for the organization. The champion cannot show support only through verbal outlets; he or she should also physically demonstrate advocacy by visiting functional work areas.

In a corporation, none of the parties, hierarchical or activity based, can afford to bear grudges, especially in interactive processes. Each party gains cooperation by showing respect for those who were critical or opposed to change, not by embarrassing them with reminders of their opposition.

When the decision on a course of action has been made, it should be presented as if it were the only course of action, even though many people who were privy to the discussions knew that there were several acceptable alternatives. The champions must convey a convincing, unambivalent, and unequivocal belief that the chosen path is the only way to go. Such a stance signals to critics that the time for debate is over. A political friend who often ran for elective office once said to me that he always told the truth, just not 100 percent of it. The champion must do the same thing.

Activity-based management programs, and other innovative approaches that assist corporations in attaining improved productivity, are likely to evolve from several smaller changes that served as building blocks in constructing a strong foundation for success. Many seemingly major alterations in companies are likely to have their genesis in an accumulation of improvements built up over time and implemented prudently.

The drive for any change must become internalized, even if the work driver was external, so that everyone adopts the conviction that implementation of the program will meet the needs of both the organization and its staff members. In many companies, staff members spend an inordinate amount of time attempting to figure out what their management really wants, which programs are truly priorities, and which ones can be disregarded. Senior executives recommend several courses of action at the same time, and it becomes impossible to act on all of them simultaneously.

Therefore, it is incumbent upon the champion to be forceful in making her or his intentions clear so that enthusiastic staff members do not go in the wrong direction because they misinterpret their leader's statements. A handful of salient directives, regularly advanced, is all that it takes to alter an organization's culture and course.

## Performance Channels

A key component for inducing proactive innovation is providing performance platforms which allow alternative views to be communicated. All too often actions take place as a matter of policy while staff members in functional work areas scratch their heads, wondering what they should do.

There must be an infrastructure in place to support change. You do not want to fall into a trap that characterizes your concepts as faddism or "just another flavor of the month." In addition, staff members' actions are predicated on their perceived place within an organizational structure and on the activities they are to perform in support of a program. An ABM program cannot be isolated from the other activities in an organization's culture and structure, or it will never take hold and become institutionalized. Integration of the program's methodology into the mainstream will ensure that the full potential of benefits is realized.

Any new program that involves change needs to produce results in order for the change to become accepted. A variety of actions can assist in the process of implanting diversity into the routine of an organization's operation. New training techniques and mechanisms of communication can be important vehicles to incorporate new methods into an existing work environment. Training helps people learn new activities and makes the transition from old to new smoother. Do not be afraid to change the methods of rewarding staff members who support new methods and to openly publicize success stories.

The champion must promulgate a continuing series of reinforcing messages. Once individuals realize that utilizing new techniques benefits them, there will be no turning back. Additional paradigm shifts will be in order, as follows:

- The flow of information
- Division of responsibilities
- End-to-end processing
- The broadening of ABM practices beyond a few functional work areas to a wider universe

Constant pressure creates momentum and critical mass. As more and more functional work areas adopt the methodology, with an influx of converts to the new practices, an environment will be created in which it is embarrassing not to adopt them. The process becomes the norm—not out of sync, but rather "the way we do things around here." Carrying the entire linkage to its natural conclusion opens the door for a written or implied contractual guarantee to customers for the work to be performed on their behalf.

The ultimate goal of an ABM program is to keep an organization on course and to stimulate innovation, creativity, and collaborative interactions among functional work areas. All innovative concepts require a leap of faith, because they ask individuals to rally around the unknown, not yet experienced. People generally fear change, since it raises concern about loss or displacement of jobs, but the ABM team cannot overlook these issues and should take them into account.

The ABM team should work as the coordinating body that blends individual realities into a shared reality. The greater the shared reality is, the greater will be the success of the program. If we learn to ask questions rather than assume we know all the answers, and if we utilize varied experiences of all involved participants, we can open up several action possibilities. A high-performing team will be flexible and willing to reconceptualize if change assists in reaching the objective of shaping a more productive and successful future.

## A People-First Policy

The ideas and imagination that direct regeneration must be both insightful and substantive, based on a determination of a particular functional work area's strengths and history. Explicitly, there isn't any magical formula or potion for altering a company's way of doing business. It takes hard work and dedication to search for the innovations which fit the culture and vision of a specific corporation.

However, all organizations can create an atmosphere that empowers their people to carry out the search for a better way of doing work. Employees are the fuel that runs the engine of a company. Many senior executives forget that buildings, machinery, and even money are replaceable, but people who work well together are the organization's most important asset. A people-first policy is one of the keys to increased productivity and morale.

The methodology discussed in this book is centered around people: understanding their needs in order to generate the desire to be more productive. Cost reductions are the by-products of doing the job right the first time—because you satisfied the customer. Senior management needs to empower employees to be fair and honest and to utilize good judgment in harmony with established corporate goals. Each staff member should be made accountable and responsible for his or her actions. It should not be acceptable to use "just following orders" as the reason for implementing inferior courses of action.

The rank-and-file worker knows what should be done. Many managers think only they know what goes on in the trenches, when in reality they are suffering from organizational stupidity. All good coaches know that the players on the field should call the plays. When too many chiefs are in the boardroom, no one knows who is in control, work is stymied, performance drops, and ultimately customer service is nonexistent. ABM tries to impart to senior management the importance of letting go and allowing staff members to try, falter, fail, or deliver a qualified product or service.

If managers focus on placing blame, people will refrain from taking risks, and innovation and creativity will be stifled. It is essential to open a sincere, two-way communication between senior management and staff, so that employees can annually inform management of what they perceive to be good, bad, and ugly about the company without the threat of reprisal.

Senior management should respond to all the concerns in an open letter to employees. (This aspect of the ABM program is explored in Chapter Three.) The easiest and most efficient way of achieving corporate goals is by meeting employee goals. An organization cannot ask its employees to unselfishly support the organization's needs if the organization won't support their needs. It is simply unfair to expect staff members to give to the corporation if the corporation's senior management will not reciprocate and help its people meet the challenges in their lives. If you do not establish an environment that allows and rewards individual leadership, you are not going to be successful.

It has been documented that downsizing hasn't produced the increases in productivity that several companies expected. Most of these unsuccessful attempts to reduce costs simply took the nonanalytical approach of reducing staff, but not necessarily the work associated with those leaving the payroll. The result was fewer people to do the same amount of work.

## Leveling the Hierarchy

Activity-based management dictates that we disregard the pyramid in the hierarchy and turn our attention to a company's key business processes. In order to achieve significant gains in performance, we must refocus our thinking toward the way work gets done. In place of the traditional structure of departments, the organization should be built around its key business processes, with each process having a champion and its own performance goals. This newly conceived format eliminates the bureaucracy that impedes progress and innovation. Employees no longer have to pledge their loyalty and trust to the functional fiefdoms in which they once worked. Now their allegiance can be to the overall corporation, its mission and goals.

In other words, downsizing as it is generally practiced today doesn't alter the basic way activities are performed. The horizontal, end-to-end corporate structure is not solely a reengineering tactic; it is a cultural transformation that dissolves both hierarchical and departmental boundaries. It is similar to the Berlin Wall coming down in 1989 and Germany being reunified. You just can't dismiss people. You must reengineer the business process and drive unnecessary work out of the organization, or it will be back tomorrow.

By leveling the hierarchy, you can reduce management size, eliminate nonvalue-added activities, and keep staffing requirements to an absolute minimum. At the senior executive level, you require only a shell group of support processes such as finance or human resources.

Everyone else in the organization is assigned to one of the business processes. Within each business process established, self-empowered teams are the foundation of the newly structured organization. All performance criteria are created with the express purpose of meeting customer expectations rather than just profitability and/or shareholder value. The reward structure should be changed to be in line with team rather than individual performance. Encourage employees to learn multiple skills rather than be specialists.

The implementation of this new paradigm often can be complex and in some instances a strain. Identification of the important business processes in an organization can be an arduous process. The difficulty originates from staff members feeling threatened in venturing into the unknown. Many line and staff members know only the hierarchical culture and the behavior requirements within that environment.

Before embarking on the reorganization trip, clearly define and analyze the markets and customers you wish to service. Plan to bring customer service representatives onto each process team and empower them to have regular direct contact with the customer. Change the way information is disseminated. Provide staff members with all available data required to do their jobs and reach an informed decision, but be sure they are trained in analysis techniques so they can make their own decisions.

Every time you have an organizational boundary, you create the potential for a disconnect. The business process owner should focus on the day-to-day operation, while the champion should make sure the goals of the business process are in sync with the overall corporation's strategies and goals. The key word is *collaboration*.

# 2

# Organizing the Program

## Planning and Organization Overview

The initial step in an activity-based management program is the selection of ABM team members. The team configuration, as described under the chain-of-success factors in Chapter 1, should be diverse as to training, experience, and process familiarity, and strong in people and analytical skills. The ABM team should report to the chief executive officer who has made the decision to go forward. Reporting at this level will eliminate real-world political issues. When the CEO supports the program, political activists will be dissuaded from either impeding progress or filtering objective data that reach the chief executive.

It is an art to inspire confidence in individuals and a science to organize a program of this type into its elements. One aspect should not outweigh another; all are important. The operating problems of functional work area managers can provide valuable insight into their respective work activities, lack of tools to do an activity, and morale issues.

As a rule, most employees have a good attitude toward their job and their company. They want to do their best if they have the proper tools to perform their activities. They have good work habits and are more often than not following a prescribed method. The rank-and-file employee attitude is an important consideration in organizing the program.

Before the program is started, a schedule should be developed for communicating the scope, goal, and expected results to everyone involved. This is important in gaining employee confidence and cooperation. The entire effort should be a collaboration between operations and accounting, with operations as the owner of the business processes taking the lead and accounting providing its support.

In organizing an activity-based management program, you must consider long-range as well as short-range implications, especially in the construction of any productivity measurement strategy. This consideration can be the catalyst for refocusing management attention on what work they should be performing and an appropriate way to measure their performance.

There are a series of questions which every activity-based management team should ask prior to implementing the program in order to establish objective, well-documented measurement criteria:

- Who should be represented in developing a program?
- What do we want our activity-based management program to achieve?
- What are our explicit performance measurement preferences?
- What precise activities will be needed to effectuate the program?
- What is the cogent order and proper timing for each process or activity that comprises the program?
- How wide is the scope of the activity-based management program?
- At what level of detail do we wish to gather data?
- What are the intended results we wish to achieve?
- What are the important linkages between financial and operational requirements in our organization?
- What measures have been put in place to ensure that the gathered data can be converted into usable decision-making tools?

When measurement systems have been properly developed utilizing a bottom-up approach for gathering data, they tend to be more proactive in linking productivity improvement and performance measurement through synergy at the functional work area level.

Organizing a program is a distinctly different activity from implementing a program. Implementation involves putting things into motion, action, and involvement. Most of us would rather implement than organize. In fact, many managers like implementing so much better that they never organize to fail, they just fail to organize. Organization, on the other hand, is a critical function in activity-based management. If we take the time to execute it correctly, we will not have to spend the time to do it over again and/or accept a level of quality inferior to what it was possible to attain.

How does one become a better organizer? By taking an 8-hour course or seminar? Not likely! Organization is a proficiency that requires discipline, hard work, a commitment to excellence, and a great deal of practice. "Practice doesn't always make perfect; *perfect* practice makes perfect," said Vince Lombardi, Hall of Fame football coach of the Green Bay Packers.

Many managers overlook the importance of organization in their search for a magic formula, secret, or utopia. If senior management is truly committed to improving productivity, there is a price to pay. Properly organizing the activity-based management program is part of that price.

Each business process within the program must somehow be integrated into the development of any tactical and/or operational action plan. The organizational portion of the program develops the road map for where we want to or should go, while the implementation process specifies how we are going to get there (i.e., "follow the yellow brick road").

The components of a good organizational plan include objectives, activities, or key events, responsibilities and accountability, required resources to be consumed, and methodologies to be used. Many of the concepts involved in project management will pertain, such as monitoring and controlling the progress of the program. The goal is to be able to affirmatively answer these questions:

- Are we realizing what we planned to accomplish?
- Are the segments of the business we wanted involved actually cooperating?
- What specific performance measurements have evolved?
- Are we meeting the key events schedule on time?
- Is the scope of the program meeting our expectations?
- Is information being aggregated at the level at which it is meaningful?
- Are resources being consumed by activities within budgeted levels?
- Is there a performance measurement system which is compatible with other established systems currently being utilized?

The bottom line is that a program's management mechanism does not have to be complex or sophisticated; it just has to work. Figure 2-1 summarizes the components of performance measurement.

Good communication with the functional work units can achieve the following:

- Speedy your understanding of the processes in place.
- Surface hidden opportunities that you might not find.
- Develop relationships which foster a casual atmosphere.
- Partner with functional work area employees to exchange concerns and ideas with the ABM teams.
- Familiarize functional work area employees with ABM methodology, leading to smooth implementation of the tool.

Once the proper foundation for the proposed program has been laid, initial functional work area contact can be made well in advance of the start (Fig. 2-2).

**Measure Customer Satisfaction**

- Delivery lead time
- Order lead time
- Product availability
- On-time delivery
- Accurate invoice
- Number of product rejects
- Number of customer complaints

**Measure Flexibility**

- Lead time
- Setup/changeover time
- Cycle time
- Order turnaround time
- Performance to schedule
- Vendor performance
- Capacity utilization

**Measure Cost of Quality**

- Prevention
- Detection
- Internal failure
- External failure

**Measure Productivity**

- Return on assets
- Return on investment
- Inventory turnover
- Capacity utilization
- Overhead cost structure
- Net income per employee
- Trend non-value-added time and costs

**Figure 2-1.** Business performance measurement.

Measure Competitiveness

- Sales growth
- Market share growth
- New products' share of sales revenue (dollars and percentage)
  Order/order type
  Customer/customer type
  Product/product type
- Order turnaround time
- Order fill rate
- Performance to promise date
- Lost business

Measure Profitability

- By order, product, and customer
- At various levels
  After manufacturing costs
  After distribution costs
  After selling and marketing costs
  After R&D and G&A costs

**Figure 2-1.** (*Continued*) Business performance measurement.


# Initial Functional Work Area Contact

## General Announcement of the Program— Communication Bulletins

Create a corporatewide announcement about the impending ABM program (Fig. 2-3). The letter should be signed by the company chief executive officer and should direct the participating functional work area managers to begin to accumulate some important data. If the entire company isn't initially participating in the program, direct the announcement toward the participating functional work area(s). A sample program announcement is presented in Fig. 2-4.

Develop a series of general communication bulletins to herald the arrival of the ABM program. This series should begin approximately 30 days before program initiation and should directly follow the general announcement letter to

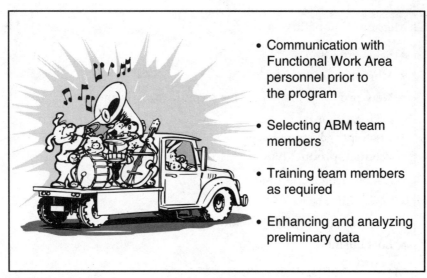

**Figure 2-2.** Planning and organization overview.

**Figure 2-3.** Announcement letter.

*Name*
*Street Address*
*City, State, Zip Code*

Dear_____,

I would like to take this opportunity to introduce you to the concept of activity-based management. Activity-based management (ABM) is an exceptional tool that can assist us in a number of functional work areas. _____ is currently involved in the ABM initiative that will span all functional work areas. Your functional work area has been chosen to be included in the ABM program. Information derived from your business process will guarantee that this ABM program will provide the necessary tools useful for managing our business more efficiently.

To ensure an organized and efficient program, there are a number of administrative matters that will need to be addressed. Before the program begins, we would like to collect and review a few pieces of organizational information related to your business process. Items such as the following will be helpful to you and the ABM team in managing the program:

- Mission statement

- List of work drivers

- List of activities and historical transaction volumes indicating any seasonal factors (i.e., 12 months)

- Organization charts with number of people indicated, including all full-time and part-time employees, contractors, and open requisitions

- Functional work area descriptions

- Job description for each employee

- Methods and procedures

- Data sources (e.g., MIS report names, frequency, manual logs)

- Employee phone listing and location that ties out to the organization chart

- Work process flows

**Figure 2-4.** Sample general announcement letter.

- Key performance indicators

- Functional work area schedule of hours

- Functional work area floor diagrams with employees' names filled in

- Official payroll data that indicates hours worked on specific activities and earnings for each employee over a given period (e.g., 12 months)

- Employee work and educational history

- Holiday, vacation, and sick time policies

Any information you feel may assist the team in better understanding the organization and its functions would be greatly appreciated.

The ABM team is tentatively scheduled to begin the program on _____. The team will also need access to a conference room and a secure cabinet to store laptop PCs and records if possible. We appreciate your cooperation and are looking forward to working with you. If you have any questions related to the program, please contact me at _____

Sincerely,


(Signature)

**Figure 2-4.** (*Continued*) Sample general announcement letter.

all employees. Two sample communication bulletins are presented below. Each organization should develop a set that is appropriate to its culture.

The participation and cooperation of all employees at all levels are important to the success of the program. The more informed and comfortable people are, the more likely we are to achieve the openness we seek in compiling an accurate and complete picture of the work we do.

An activity-based management program provides an objective platform upon which to make appropriate business decisions.

Expect some uneasiness as the program unfolds, because rumors will abound and people tend to become nervous when their work is scrutinized. Ask everyone to keep an open mind; keep people informed as to progress, and replace any preconceived notions with objective analysis.

Show visible physical support for the program by actively participating in ABM team meetings, training sessions, and status meetings. Each ABM core team should conduct a local ABM workshop for all functional work area employees to explain what is included in the program, build commitment, and emphasize the importance of the program to employees and the company.

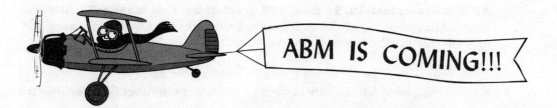

**ABM Communication 1: What Is ABM?**    Activity-based management is a methodology that assists everyone in understanding how the organization functions and interacts with other organizations. It is not only a financial methodology; it is also an operations-management-based methodology. ABM aims at turning traditional accounting data into decision-making information (Fig. 2-5).

**Figure 2-5.** Good information makes decisions easy.

> How will ABM help you manage?
> Look for next week's ABM communication!
> 30 Days to ABM...

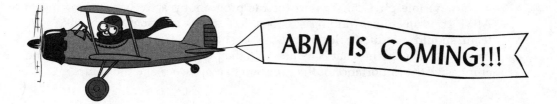

**ABM Communication 2: How Will ABM Help You Manage?**  Activity-based management provides everyone in an organization with a structure and focus to enhance the business decision-making process by

- Identifying *what* activities are performed in a given organization
- Scheduling *when* activities are performed in the work routine of an organization
- Determining *where* activities are performed within a given organization
- Evaluating *why* activities are performed within a given organization
- Associating *who* performs specific activities within a given organization
- Defining *work drivers* that cause activities to happen
- Categorizing and prioritizing activities
- Tracking and measuring the consumption of resources by activities against expectations
- Linking operational management and financial processes

Each participating functional work area should be visited after the general announcement is made to familiarize the ABM team with the logistics of work stations, types of documents processed, transaction volumes generated, and activities performed.

During the walk-through visit, each functional work area and/or business process should identify an ABM facilitator who will coordinate the program and functions as an adjunct member of the ABM team. The operations facilitator should recruit the resources needed to prepare and collect available data. The facilitator's team should be trained in the ABM techniques so it will be able to carry on the program after the ABM team leaves the functional work area following the program's implementation.

It is critically important that all functional work area and/or business process personnel have a clear understanding of what ABM is, why it is being implemented, and what the expected results will be. It is worthwhile to conduct a brief opening meeting with everyone involved and to articulate clearly and honestly what will happen during the ensuing weeks.

The more comfortable the people in an organization are, the more likely they will be open toward the ABM team. Once the team earns the respect of the functional work area and/or business process personnel, the easier it will be to compile complete data, the more accurate the data will be, and the more successful the program will be. A program of this magnitude cannot succeed without rank-and-file employee buy-in.

During the kickoff meeting do not be afraid to field questions, and be sure to answer them honestly and tactfully so as not to alarm anyone. Expect some uneasiness, because apprehension surfaces when people haven't been through a program of this type and do not know what to expect.

Request that each person keep an open mind as to what is about to unfold, and stress the fact that there are no secrets or preconceived notions either about the work that is currently being performed or the people doing the work. Once the announcement has been made and preliminary site visits have been completed, the ABM team should convene to establish a regular team meeting schedule.

## Team Meetings

It is advisable to establish weekly status review meetings with employees of each functional work area and/or business process, and to set up biweekly status review meetings with the entire ABM team (Fig. 2-6).

The ABM meeting is the forum for all those involved in the ABM program to let their hair down, be open, exchange ideas, raise questions, and propose solutions. It is intended to be a participating working session, not an agenda checklist to be carried forward forever. The team meeting should eliminate gridlock immediately. Attendance should be mandatory, not optional, and a top priority for all team members. The exchange of success stories as well as failures will

- Encourage members to speak their mind.
- Exchange ideas.
- Discuss findings and observations.
- Monitor progress of the study.
- Determine additional tasks that need to be performed.
- Prevent excessive documentation.
- Assign issues to team members to research and resolve.

**Figure 2-6.** The functions of team meetings.

encourage all team members to adopt techniques that work and to replace ones that do not work. If certain team members are having problems in completing their assignments, resources may have to be shifted to accommodate those special needs.

There should always be a planned agenda for each meeting, listing all the team member's names, and formal meeting notes should be taken and distributed to everyone. Indicate who was assigned a follow-up task to resolve by the next meeting in two weeks and have that individual present the results at the next meeting. Stress that each item must be resolved by the next session.

The ABM team members should continually interact informally with functional work area and/or business process management and employees, reviewing areas of work that might be discussed at the next formal team meeting. The informal discussions build a rapport with the functional work area and/or business process personnel, demonstrate a two-way dialogue, and emphasize the importance of working together toward a common goal.

There should not be any surprises and/or finger-pointing sessions either during team meetings or when interfacing with functional work area and/or business process personnel. If the ABM team is having difficulty in a functional work area and/or business process, seek senior management support in resolving the impasse. The ABM team should establish a Key Events Schedule at their first regular meeting and review the schedule at all future sessions.

## Key Events Schedule

The *key events schedule* (Fig. 2-7) provides the framework for the entire program. It lists all the milestones that have to be reached and estimates the time required to complete each event. In addition, it serves as a natural monitoring device for the ABM team's progress.

The key events schedule is constructed by listing all anticipated program events in a serial sequence and linking a calendar week-ending date to each event. Some events take several weeks to complete and are therefore shown transcending more than one week (e.g., observations are shown in weeks 3, 4, 5, and 6).

This is not to imply that more than one activity can't be going on at the same time. Several activities can occur in the same time period, with either similar or overlapping completion dates. When the key events schedule is discussed at the team meeting, each event should be highlighted as to its progress.

Do not get stuck working on one key event at the expense of other events, because work can be done concurrently while other work is slowed. A phrase used in the clothing industry applies here: "cut to fit" whenever you must stay on schedule.

The key events schedule should also be discussed at the weekly functional work area and/or business process meetings, delineating areas with problems as well as those events that are on schedule (Fig. 2-8). Once the organization of the program is finished, programs announced, site visits concluded, kickoff

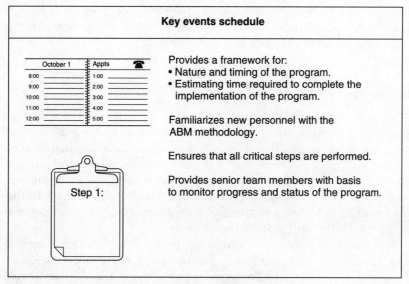

**Figure 2-7.** The functions of the key events schedule.

Date prepared:         **Key event schedule**         Department/Sect.:
        Area:

| Key events | Calendar week | 1 | 2 | 3 | 4 | 5 | 6 | 7 | 8 | 9 | 10 | 11 | 12 | 13 | 14 | 15 | 16 | 17 |
|---|---|---|---|---|---|---|---|---|---|---|---|---|---|---|---|---|---|---|
| | Month Day | 7 12 | 7 19 | 7 26 | 8 2 | 8 9 | 8 16 | 8 23 | 8 30 | 9 6 | 9 13 | 9 20 | 9 27 | 10 4 | 10 11 | 10 18 | 10 25 | 10 29 |
| Define job activities | | X | | | | | | | | | | | | | | | | |
| Sequence job activities | | | X | X | | | | | | | | | | | | | | |
| Savings evaluation | | | | | | | | | | | | | | | | | | |
| ID KVI's and base period | | | X | X | X | | | | | | | | | | | | | |
| ID vol.'s & units of meas. | | | X | X | X | | | | | | | | | | | | | |
| Observations | | | | X | X | X | X | | | | | | | | | | | |
| Systems design | | | | | X | X | X | | | | | | | | | | | |
| Write prelim. procedures | | | | | | | X | X | | | | | | | | | | |
| Dry-run system | | | | | | X | X | | | | | | | | | | | |
| Man loads | | | | | | | X | X | | | | | | | | | | |
| Present final recommen. | | | | | | | | X | | | | | | | | | | |
| Install project eval. | | | | | | | | | | X | X | | | | | | | |
| Wet-run sys. & train sup. | | | | | | | | | X | | | | | | | | | |
| Installation | | | | | | | | | | X | X | X | | | | | | |
| Procedures—final manual | | | | | | | | | | | | | | X | X | X | | |
| Progress meetings | | | X | X | X | X | X | X | X | X | X | X | X | X | X | X | | |
| Mail room reorganization | | | | | | | | | | X | X | X | | | | | | |
| Anal. for lockbox conver. | | | | | | | | | | X | X | X | | | | | | |
| Work control & methods | | | | | | X | X | X | X | X | X | X | | | | | | |

**Figure 2-8.** Key events schedule.

meeting completed, and key events schedule prepared, it is time to begin the data-gathering portion of the program. Competitive benchmarking should be used to accurately evaluate comparative data.

## Benchmarking

*Benchmarking* provides a sound basis from which to establish performance goals, and through which an organization can accurately and objectively measure progress against the competition (external) and against its own objectives (internal). This mechanism takes the emotion out of the evaluation process and the debate for the need to change. Today's business environment is increasingly competitive. Customer requirements seem to be altered all too frequently and expectations keep escalating, so the organization that can maintain high levels of quality will gain the advantage.

Benchmarking can be a simple process *if* senior management maintains enthusiasm for its importance. Management must clearly communicate that benchmarking isn't additional makework, but is the vehicle to achieve value-added productive work. Senior management must convey the results in an understandable manner so that the findings can be easily accepted by everyone at all levels in the organization (Fig. 2-9).

The data should be incorporated into company mission statements, objectives, goals, and business plans. A rewards program should be established that demonstrates progress toward benchmarking targets. Team recognition can be a powerful motivator for employees and leads to increased productivity.

Management should never use benchmarking as a negative motivator by tying it to downsizing an organization. It is a long-term commitment by senior management, which has to exhibit patience and restraint as benchmarking evolves and takes root. A company can tell that its benchmarking program has been successful when management institutionalizes the process. An organization that looks only at its own operations limits its ability to improve, and will not realize gains in performance, adaptability, or superiority over its competition.

Once senior management has decided to advance its performance to the next level and improve its competitive position by comparing its services and/or products against recognized industry leaders, it must determine whether to benchmark formally or informally. If formally, it would want to

1. *Develop a benchmarking plan.*
    a. Identify what you wish to benchmark.
    b. Determine your method of data collection.
    c. Select those primary activities that need upgrading, so improvements will be easily quantified and indicate significant results.
    d. Define the mission of the organization.
    e. Ascertain the objective of the business process or activity being measured.
    f. Be sure there is a necessity to change, and know what you are going to change.

There are three potential sources of information once comparative data are available:

- *Vendor quotes.* Like products may be available on the outside, or products defined in the analysis can be refined to resemble commercially available services.

- *Private survey.* Product managers are charged with contacting other companies that provide similar services internally, and with sharing information about costs.

- *Trade survey.* Some internal products are supported by trade associations that collect cost data to help numbers set standards.

Once this information is compiled, the following questions can be addressed:

- How do service levels compare?

- What pieces of data (indirect, overhead) are included in the benchmark?

- Will benchmark companies let us compare methods, if there are major differences?

**Figure 2-9.** Competitive benchmarking.

       *g.* Visualize the business process as it will be when the alteration is completed.
2. *Analyze the business process.*
       *a.* Detail and completely document the business process activity by activity, and within each activity task by task. This will assist you in recognizing patterns by developing activity work flows and will clearly show how you currently handle the selected process (Fig. 2-10).
       *b.* Quantify the gap between you and your competitor (external) or the current level of performance and the level you wish to attain (internal).
       *c.* Set goals.
       *d.* Ask yourself if your competitor is better and by how much. Is there any aspect of the competitor's process which you can and should adopt?
       *e.* Make site visits with high-performance organizations and meet with their employees to determine what they do and how they address problems. Ask for their coaching.
3. *Organize research.* Senior management should clearly communicate the research findings in an effort to gain consensus and obtain acceptance within the organization. Develop pragmatic action plans which will move the company in a new direction.
4. *Implement action plans.* When the action plan is accepted and implemented, monitor results, make any necessary adjustments to benchmarking parame-

- It is a work flow developed with vision by individuals who saw the true purpose of the work.

- It is a direct end-to-end process without sidetracks that are not absolutely essential.

- The work performed is within its own channel and assists in reaching its objective.

- Its productivity or throughput is equal to or exceeds its reasonable expectancy.

- The activity is performed the way management wants it to be and customers expect it to be.

- It is uncomplicated and straightforward.

- Management couldn't afford to spend additional analysis time on it, because any additional improvements wouldn't offer a suitable return on investment.

- The hierarchical organizational structure doesn't interfere with the activity, because the process structure has been set up correctly.

- Each task that makes up an activity, and each activity that comprises a business process, has been validated as to its value-added contribution.

- All staff members who participate in the business process know exactly what their role is and how their skills contribute to the process.

- The activity work flow is quick, efficient, simple, easy to administer, economical, and direct.

- The work flow is so well "thought out" that functioning is not dependent upon the performance of a single person.

**Figure 2-10.** Characteristics of an efficient activity work flow.

ters, and regularly report progress on the modifications to measure how you are doing. You should be careful to integrate total quality management and continuous improvement philosophies into the action plan to ensure a long-term success ethic.

In order to deploy a successful benchmarking process, companies should utilize both internal and external sources of data. Internal sources include financial data from accounting records, performance evaluations, business plans, payroll records, time sheets, billing records, and job assignment records. External sources of data include industry and/or trade publications, special reports, professional associations, general business periodicals, outside seminars and conferences, advertisements, competitors' brochures and newsletters, electronic databases, and professional industry experts.

Complete and precise benchmarking also requires some original research, such as customer surveys and assessments, focus groups, public opinion surveys, and information sharing with management counterparts at other organizations. Benchmarking should be looked at as one piece in a total quality management puzzle. During the organizational phase of an activity-based management program, it is important to determine what types of internal benchmarks should be used and what performance indicators are currently being used by functional work area managers and/or senior management.

Most corporations consider service efficiency to their customers as important as processing work. They realize it can cost two to three times more either to obtain a new customer or to retrieve an old customer instead of keeping a current customer. Competition also indicates that service rather than price can make the difference between a successful company and a troubled one.

The ABM team should meet with employees of a functional work area to discuss what they see as key indicators of work. Key indicators should have readily available, regularly generated data. The following are key performance indicator guidelines:

- *Historical hourly rate.*   An hourly rate figure is created by taking the regular annual earnings of all employees in a functional work area and dividing by the regular work hours. Regular work hours should include overtime hours and should exclude vacation, holiday, and sick hours.

- *Historical units per hour.*   A units-per-hour indicator is created by taking historical volumes for an activity in a functional work area and dividing by historical work hours. Historical work hours should include overtime hours and should exclude vacation, holiday, and sick hours. If volume data suddenly takes a permanent sharp upturn or downturn, use this information, because it indicates that the business has changed.

- *Timekeeping systems.*   Timekeeping systems provide records of the work done and the time spent on each activity. For example, the engineers in one company maintained records of their work and the products they were working on. This information was then used to develop an activity-based model for engineering.

Timekeeping can provide a reasonably accurate record of time spent. It's a low-cost source of data—at least to the ABM design team, to whom it's *free*. It's unusual, however, to find time records already available. The exception is direct labor, for which daily time recording is common. But there's no such timekeeping tradition for most nondirect labor, such as clerical-type activities. Consequently, a timekeeping system of some kind must be instituted.

This can be a problem. Functional work area managers and support staff aren't likely to be enthusiastic about filling in time sheets on a daily basis. Some may even look upon time sheets as being intrusive. Often time sheets won't be filled out properly through lack of attention or suspicion of their own purpose.

In such cases, the ABM team may need to use some other source for information. If timekeeping was not in place during the previous year, it's impossible to go back to re-create the records.

It is possible, however, to use timekeeping on a sample basis. One company instituted timekeeping for a one-week period, primarily to validate data obtained previously during interviews. The results from these time records were somewhat different from those obtained during the interviews. In some cases the differing records were discarded because their one-week coverage wasn't representative of the entire year. In other cases, the time records were used in the model in addition to the interview information.

In some areas, timekeeping may be an ideal source of ABM information. Keeping track of time spent on engineering projects is one example. For such areas, a request can be made to institute timekeeping as a future source of ABM information.

To summarize, the purpose of internal benchmarking is to obtain measurements that provide objective operating and financial information to support informed decision making.

# 3

# Interview Process

## Introduction

The interviewing process is a key element in collecting data during an activity-based management program. In the preceding chapter, it was pointed out that utilizing an organization chart as a checklist to ensure identification of the total universe of people in a company, division, and/or functional work area is a prerequisite to implementing the program. This checklist then becomes the interview schedule and control mechanism so that no individual is overlooked. Interviewing is more than just a data collection tool. It is the means that provide the platform for information and open the door for everyone regardless of position to become part of the process.

Interviews can be conducted in one of two major ways: (1) group interviews with several people from the same functional work area participating and feeding off one another's ideas or (2) one-to-one interviews. We prefer the one-to-one approach in a quiet, private location because it fosters candor, extracts personalized approaches to doing work, and is more relaxing for the interviewee (there is no peer pressure).

The individualized interview is the most effective approach in developing a confidential, anonymous suggestion list for improving a company socially, operationally, and financially. Users will learn about the ABM project—how it works and what it intends to accomplish. An informed user will become involved in a positive way and is therefore more likely to become an ABM supporter, using the program to promote positive change.

In short, interviewing has three key purposes:

- *Gathering information from reliable sources.* Interviewing is a tool for collecting much of the data used to build a dictionary of activities and their relationship to resources and cost objects.

- *Educating users.* The interview is an opportunity to teach potential users about ABM.

**Figure 3-1.** The first interview.

■ *Building ownership.* Interviewing is an opportunity to answer questions, address concerns, and build ownership and employee buy-in for the program.

Interviewing, however, is likely to be the most time-consuming information-gathering task—at least, the first time through (Fig. 3-1). Therefore, it is worth spending some time to learn how to do it well. The process begins with determining whom to interview. Interviews assist in understanding the relationships among work drivers, activities, performance measures, cost objectives, and resources.

There are six phases in the interview process:

■ Planning the interview

■ Conducting the interview

■ Preparing a fantasy list

■ Preparing an activity dictionary

■ Preparing a work distribution matrix

■ Classifying activities in preparation for the detailing process

These phases are not independent of one another. They are interwoven into the fabric of the ABM program in a checks-and-balances approach.

## Planning the Interview

When the ABM team receives the presite visit data it requested from the functional work areas (e.g., organization chart, employee list) in the program organization phase, it can establish an interview schedule.

Interviews should be held one to one in a quiet, private location, and should not exceed *30 minutes* in duration. The key to the interview process is to make certain that all activities are identified, whether they are primary or secondary. Primary activities are defined as those activities to which an employee devotes most of her or his time and effort. Secondary activities are defined as those activities to which an employee devotes time and effort sporadically (e.g., one hour every 3 weeks).

Assign a control number to each person to be interviewed, since it will be helpful in directing the interview process and in referring to interviewee data. The interviewer must prepare for the interview (Fig. 3-2), to increase the chances of gaining all the required data in the shortest possible time. As part of the planning process, a tour of the physical facility can be valuable (Fig. 3-3). Remember that people are busy and have to run their businesses. They may not have time to grant a second interview. The interview process will take several weeks to complete, depending on the size of an organization.

It is important to ask about vacation schedules and night-shift hours in preparing the interview schedule. Another important consideration is the length of time an individual has been with the company. Generally, it does not add value to interview people who have been with the company less than 3 months, because they will not know enough to contribute much data.

In preparing the interview schedule, be certain to include vice presidents, directors, and managers. It also makes sense to schedule their interviews first so you can explain the entire interview process to them and ask for their support. Staff members will follow the executive's lead. This approach is part marketing, part educational, and part informative. The executive interview will

**Planning the interview:**
- Understand purpose of interview.
- Review pertinent background material.
- Tour facility.
- Identify key topics to discuss.
- Develop interview plan and approach.

**Figure 3-2.** Hints for planning the interview.

- Day, evening, night, weekend.
- Identify unique off-tour activities.

**Figure 3-3.** Interview all employees on all workshifts.

usually take about an hour, rather than the 30 minutes for an employee interview, because of the aforementioned objectives.

The interviewer can prepare to conduct an interview by doing some advance research. For example:

- Learn as much as possible in advance about the functional work area's operations.

- Make sure to formulate questions in advance to secure the required data.

- Know what level of detail to ask for. Be careful not to get too detailed during the interview because the next phase, detailing, will be a more in-depth process.

- Understand the program's objectives and scope so it can be clearly expressed to all interested parties.

- Be familiar with the concepts of reengineering, productivity improvement, total quality management, and activity-based management. The interviewee needs to know what ABM is, what the project is to accomplish, and what information is required for the program to be successful.

- Make sure to compile a fully representative list of activities.

**Kickoff meeting.**    A kickoff meeting is a good forum for presenting information to interviewees. For example, the ABM team should invite all interviewees to a presentation that covers basic concepts, discusses the program, and describes the purpose of the interview process. The kickoff meeting eliminates the need to individually brief each interviewee at the start of the interview.

**Interviewee orientation.** An alternative to the kickoff meeting is to conduct the orientation during the interview itself. Although this may take more time, *it is a private meeting,* and the interviewee may be more willing to express concerns about the program. Also, the orientation can be tailored to the particular background of the interviewee. If the interviewee has attended an ABM exposure program or has participated in the planning or design process, orientation will be quite short.

**Material distribution.** Distributing materials in advance of the interview process can be valuable, if the interviewee reads the information. A brief executive summary of ABM concepts, the program, and the interview guidelines is most likely to be read. Articles, books, and videotapes are useful sources for those wiling to take the time. One company, for example, circulated a videotape entitled *An Introduction to Activity-Based Costing* to each manager prior to the interview.

Here are some other materials that may be helpful:

- *A preinterview to-do list for the interviewee.* Preparation may include assembling or copying relevant material such as a staff list, organization chart, and data source list.

- *A preinterview questionnaire.* The questionnaire should be filled out and returned to the design team prior to the interview. Ask human resources to provide a brief educational and work experience profile for each individual to be interviewed.

- *A notice stating the time and place of the interview.* If possible, arrange to meet in the interviewee's office, where the interviewee will be more relaxed. A second alternative is the safe, neutral ground of a conference room.

When the planning phase of the interview process is completed, it is time to conduct the interviews.

## Conducting the Interview

The interview process should be relaxed. The interviewer should exchange introductions with the employee and state clearly the purpose of the ABM program, explain the objectives of the interview process, address any concerns the interviewee may have, review the benefits to be derived, and indicate how activity-based information can help focus strategic planning and improve operations.

- *Describe the program.* Talk about the ABM program and its importance to the company. What will be the deliverables? What's the scope? Who is involved? What is the role of the interviewee? Who is giving support? What progress has been made?

- *Explain the process.* Tell the interviewee about the data requirements of ABM. Go over the ABM process, emphasizing its dependence on the knowledge and input of the interviewee. Make it clear that you are looking, not for absolute precision, but simply for good-quality information, information that meets the needs of the ABM user (such as the interviewee).

To assist in conducting the interview, it is beneficial to use an *activity dictionary worksheet* that records interviewee data in a structured manner (Fig. 3-4). Identify all the activities the interviewee performs. In doing so, it may be necessary to aggregate certain tasks under one activity instead of defining the task as a separate, distinct activity. For example:

> What is an activity and what is a task?
> An activity is repetitive in nature, consumes substantial resources (i.e., material, labor, technology) and converts them into outputs (i.e., products, services). A task is a step within the activity.

There is a business function hierarchy which will assist the interviewer in explaining how work is performed and by whom (Fig. 3-5).

The interviewer must be alert in identifying a unit of work as an activity, so as not to defeat the purpose of the ABM program by identifying so many activities that the program becomes unmanageable. Write a brief description of each defined activity, covering the high-level tasks involved in completing the specific activity from inception to completion. These notations should be entered in the comments section of the activity dictionary worksheet (Fig. 3-6).

Ask a set of key questions designed to yield all the data you need about each process. What work is done? What resources are required? How should the use of resources be measured? Why is work done? How well is it done? Which cost objects or other activities benefit from the work, and how should this be measured? Where can the data be found?

- *Who?*

  Interview representatives from key areas within the functional work area.
  Ask whom they rely on to perform their job.

- *What?*

  What is the purpose of their functional work area?
  What distinct, significant activities do they perform?
  What resources are used (e.g., computers, systems)?
  What are the "inputs" and "outputs" of each activity?

- *Where?*

  Where do inputs and outputs from each activity come from or go to?

- *When?*

  When are these activities performed?

| Interviewee 1 | Functional work area 2 | Prepared by/date 3 | Approved by/date 4 | Sheet #___ of ___ |
|---|---|---|---|---|

| Work driver 5 | Activity type P or S 6 | Activity name 7 | % of time spent 8 | Cost object 9 | Performance measure 10 | O/E 11 | Comments 12 |
|---|---|---|---|---|---|---|---|
| | | | | | | | |
| | | | | | | | |
| | | | | | | | |
| | | | | | | | |
| | | | | | | | |
| | | | | | | | |
| | | | | | | | |
| | | | | | | | |
| | | | | | | | |
| | | | | | | | |
| | | | | | | | |
| | | | | | | | |
| | | | | | | | |
| | | | | | | | |

**Figure 3-4a.** Activity dictionary worksheet.

| Line # | Title or Term | Is Used to Indicate |
|--------|---------------|---------------------|
| (1) | Interviewee | The name of the person interviewed in order to quantify that person's activities. |
| (2) | Functional work area | The name of the work unit in which the person interviewed resides. |
| (3) | Prepared by / date | The name of the interviewer and date of interview. |
| (4) | Approved by / date | The signature of the person interviewed, indicating the accuracy and completeness of the worksheet and date of interview. |
| (5) | Work driver | The reason we do work. |
| (6) | Activity type P or S | P for primary, S for secondary activity. |
| (7) | Activity name | Name of the activity performed by the interviewee. |
| (8) | % of time spent | The percentage of time spent on the activity performed by the interviewee. |
| (9) | Cost object | The reason for performing the activity (e.g., products, services, projects, control) |
| (10) | Performance measure | The unit of output to measure the activity. |
| (11) | O/E (observed or estimated) | Whether the activity will be observed or estimated as to the time consumed regarding the frequency of its occurence. |
| (12) | Comments | Brief description of the activity. |

**Figure 3-4b.** Activity dictionary worksheet key

- *Why?*

  Why is the activity performed (i.e., in response to what stimulus)?
- *How?*

  How much time is spent on each activity?

  How does the activity start and stop?

Facilitate the answers by helping the interviewee answer the questions. Ask follow-up questions if you sense that an answer is incomplete or reflects misunderstanding of the original question. Provide technical assistance if the interviewee cannot respond because of a lack of ABM knowledge. Keep the interview on track (it's easy to go off on a tangent).

Provide feedback to the interviewee on what you have learned about each key discussion area. This gives the interviewee clarification on what has been communicated and a chance to change his or her mind.

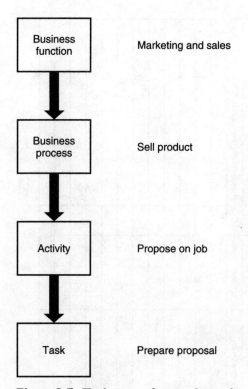

| | |
|---|---|
| Business function | Marketing and sales |
| Business process | Sell product |
| Activity | Propose on job |
| Task | Prepare proposal |

**Figure 3-5.** The business function hierarchy.

## Interviewing Hints

1. *General Questioning Strategies*
   a. Ask yes/no questions.
   b. Ask open-ended questions—who, what, when, where, and why.
   c. Focus on positive appraisal, not controversial questioning.
   d. Restate.
   e. Accept.
   f. Reflect.
   g. Summarize.
   h. Be silent and listen.
2. *What to Watch For*
   a. Check nonverbal clues.
   b. Try to read between the lines.
3. *Valuable Dos*
   a. Do avoid these attitudes: coyness, superiority, uncertainty.
   b. Do be positive, friendly, and sincere.
   c. Do establish the interview objective early.
   d. Do get the interviewee's full attention.

| Interviewee 1 | Functional work area 2 | Prepared by/date 3 | Approved by/date 4 | Sheet #1 of 1 |
|---|---|---|---|---|
| Joan Smith | Accounting Accounts receivable | Ed Forrest 02–Feb–94 | Joan Smith 05–Feb–94 | 126 |

| Work driver 5 | Activity type P or S 6 | Activity name 7 | % of time spent 8 | Cost object 9 | Performance measure 10 | O/E 11 | Comments 12 |
|---|---|---|---|---|---|---|---|
| Customer check | P | Cash application | 50 | Cmpltd cash application | # of checks | O | Apply cash to AR from customer cks received |
| Mail delivery | P | Mail sort | 21 | Cmpltd mail sort | Timelines | O | Sort incoming mail by dept |
| Customer check | P | Encoding endorsing | 20 | Cmpltd ck encode/endorse | # of checks | O | Prepare applied cash for bank deposit |
| Credit card slip | S | Bank chgs—amex, mc, visa | 1 | Cmpltd entry of cc slip | # of cc slips | E | 3x/week, review charge sales to gen. ledger acct |
| Bank memos | S | Bounced checks | 2 | Cmpltd investigation | # of checks | E | Rare—2–3 transactions/month |
| Inquiry | S | Credit memo research | 6 | Cmpltd investigation | # of credit memos | E | Research CMs check if applied to customer accts |

**Figure 3-6.** Activity dictionary worksheet.

   *e.* Do give your full attention to the interviewee.
   *f.* Do make the interviewee feel that she or he is part of the program.
   *g.* Do phrase questions to get more than a one-word response.
   *h.* Do use simple words.
   *i.* Do be sure the interviewee understands you.
   *j.* Do stay flexible.
   *k.* Do rewrite notes immediately after the interview.
   *l.* Do have the interviewee review rewritten notes, sign, and date them.
4. *Valuable Don'ts*
   *a.* Don't use long, complicated words.
   *b.* Don't use jargon that is unnecessary or that cannot be easily understood.
   *c.* Don't use clichés or abstract terms.
   *d.* Don't ask long questions.
   *e.* Don't let half-understood concepts pass. All points should be clear to all parties.
   *f.* Don't allow the conversation to be interrupted.
   *g.* Don't color a conversational point with your own view.
   *h.* Don't overpower, or be overpowered. Channel the discussion in a positive manner.
   *i.* Don't assume.
   *j.* Don't ask opinion-oriented questions.
   *k.* Don't finger-point.
   *l.* Don't forget to say thank you.
5. *Guidelines to Good Interviews*
   *a.* Identify appropriate sample of candidates.
   *b.* Formulate survey and interview questions in advance.
   *c.* Use interviews to determine the questions to be asked in a survey.
   *d.* Try the questions out first (on peers, candidates, and management).
   *e.* When you have fewer than 25 people to survey, *ask everyone.* You need to have responses from virtually everyone to be sure your results are accurate.
   *f.* Increase response rate with follow-up telephone calls.
   *g.* The way that questions are asked can influence answers. If you are going to bet your business on the answers, get (unbiased) professional help.
   *h.* Review and interpret interview data as soon as possible (while still fresh in your mind).
   *i.* Explain the purpose of the interview.
   *j.* Gather only information you can use. If you aren't sure why you are asking the question, it would probably be best not to ask it at all.
   *k.* Stick to timetables and deadlines.
   *l.* Use questions to help probe.
      - Why?
      - In what way?
      - Could you elaborate?
      - What do you mean by...?

    *m.* Use questions to test assumptions.
- If I provided you with XYZ, would you be satisfied?

    *n.* Use questions to ensure that you aren't missing anything.
- You said that accuracy is important. What about time lines or ease of use?

    *o.* Don't allow your knowledge to drive the interview or override the results of the survey. *Listen!*

    *p.* During the interview, avoid lengthy conversations.

6. *Concluding Strategies*
   *a.* Summarize.
   *b.* Thank the interviewee.
   *c.* Leave the door open for further questions.
   *d.* Field questions.
   - Am I going to lose my job?
   - Why did you pick me?
   - Is my supervisor going to know about this?

During the identification of activities exercise, you will be able to obtain the following additional information for each identified activity.

- *Work driver.* This term is defined as "What causes the activity to be performed?" The source can be either internal (from another functional work area) or external (from a customer and/or vendor). Ask the interviewee what causes him or her to perform an activity (e.g., telephone call, purchase order, repair order, claim).

- *Cost object.* This term is defined as "What is the reason the activity is performed?" It is often synonymous with output resulting from the activity being completed. Ask the interviewee what is completed as a result of performing an activity.

- *Performance measure.* This term is defined as "the unit of output" to measure the activity performed. Ask the interviewee if this is usually an input, output, or physical attribute of an activity. There is a measure or measures for an activity (e.g., number of telephone calls, purchase orders, repair orders, claims).

When all the activities performed by the interviewee have been identified, ask the interviewee to estimate the amount of time spent doing each activity (as a percentage of 100) until the employee's time is fully represented and quantified.

Next, classify each activity as primary or secondary, utilizing the parameters described in the "preparing for the interview" section of the interview process. The percentage of time spent performing a given activity is an excellent indicator of the activity's importance.

You are now armed with data that allows you to classify activities as either primary or secondary. This classification determines which activities will be detailed (i.e., primary activities) and which will be estimated (i.e., secondary activities) without being detailed.

If there is time, the following useful additional data can be obtained:

- Estimated time to complete an activity from beginning to end
- Frequency of the activity performed
- Volume of transactions processed historically (daily, weekly, monthly) for a full year

If the interviewee's time is equally divided among several activities, it is not always clear-cut as to which ones should be classified as primary or secondary. When such a dilemma presents itself, we recommend that you initially classify the activity as primary. Once the functional work area interviews are completed, review the number of identified primary activities and reclassify them if necessary.

When the activity dictionary worksheet is completed, ask the interviewee to review the data for accuracy and completeness. Have the interviewee sign and date the activity dictionary worksheet in the approved by/date box at the top of the form. Let the interviewee know what the approval indicates: that the interviewee has met with the interviewer and has told the interviewer what he or she does, not that the interviewer has made up the activities. This process eliminates misunderstandings (Fig. 3-7).

There is some support for starting with a prepared activity dictionary (see below) prior to the interview process and updating it as necessary in order to avoid getting into too much detail up front. We recommend preparing the activity dictionary after the interview process, because the dictionary will then be based on speaking to the people who actually do the work. It is pure and unfiltered, and as long as the interviewer properly controls the interview process, there isn't a real risk of securing too much detail up front. In addition, the after-the-fact approach is a built-in control to be certain that all work is accounted for, not what some executives and/or functional work area managers believe is done.

**Conducting the interview:**

- Introduce yourself.
- State objectives of the interview.
- Always put the interviewee at ease.
- Do not convey a sense of urgency.
- Show interest; listen.

**Figure 3-7.** Hints for conducting the interview.

## Prepare a Fantasy List

The final portion of the interview is the *fantasy exercise.* In it, you say to the interviewee, "Suppose the president of the company showed up at your desk and announced, `You have an open checkbook. How would you spend the money to enhance your job, make it easier, and/or improve the work environment in the overall company?' What would you do?"

Give the interviewee a few moments to think, and during this quiet time clearly state that all responses are strictly confidential and no employee names or functional work area names will be used. Explain that the list of responses will not even be prepared until the entire interview process is completed. Compile responses for the fantasy list on a separate piece of paper for each interviewee.

On the basis of interviews with thousands of respondents, we believe that the fantasy exercise can be one of the most abundant and reliable sources for reengineering and productivity improvement ideas. This exercise, which is geared to involve the people who perform the daily work, increases the chances that the ABM program will succeed on a continuous improvement basis, since grassroots support is fostered along with executive support. The involvement by each employee assists in developing a total quality management culture.

The fantasy responses can be business related, socially related, automation related, or related to any subject matter that an interviewee wishes to bring forth. Encourage the interviewee. If he or she seems hesitant, coach the interviewee by saying that any issue raised may affect many individuals. As a last resort, you may facilitate a response by offering this scenario: "You are out with a friend (husband or fiancée, as the case may be) and announce, `If I were in charge, this is what I would do.'" This statement has crossed the minds of all of us at one time or another in our business careers, and it usually breaks the silence. The fantasy list is derived from the aforementioned responses of the interviewees and alerts the interviewer to other potential reengineering opportunities that might not have been discovered in the first part of the interview.

Sample fantasy lists for operational, human resources, and social issues are presented in Appendix 3A, at the end of this chapter.

Emphasize to each interviewee that this confidential exchange is meant to be not just a gripe session, but a positive solicitation to improve what the organization does and perhaps make some activities more meaningful. The goal is to make the interview a positive experience. It's an opportunity to ensure the quality of the ABM program *and* to pave the way for positive change. If employees buy into the program and believe change can happen, you have assembled an army of doers.

Success is most likely when the interviewer plays the role of coach. The ABM coach is a teacher, motivator, and facilitator of the ABM program. Playing the role of a coach helps communicate to interviewees their ownership of the ABM process, their responsibility for its success, and the help they can expect to receive from the ABM team. A coaching role creates an atmosphere in which open two-way communication is possible without fear of reprisal.

Extend your support and make it clear that the interviewees are not alone in carrying out their responsibilities. Offer them software and information systems support. Offer technical support to resolve issues, and describe how you can help train their staff. Express your appreciation and don't forget to thank the interviewees for the time and support they are providing the ABM program. Remind them of how important they are to the success of the program. Congratulate them on their contributions to the improvement of the organization.

## Prepare an Activity Dictionary

Documentation serves as reference material (Fig. 3-8). Interview documentation (i.e., the activity dictionary worksheet) is a summary of what was learned during the interview and serves as the basis for the activity dictionary, the detailing process, and an observation routine.

When all the interviews are completed in a functional work area, prepare a comprehensive listing of all activities performed, whether they are primary or secondary. The activity dictionary, defined in Fig. 3-9, will begin the process of separating activities into value-added and non-value-added (i.e., rework, waste, inspection) categories.

1. Consolidate data into one activity dictionary per functional work area.

2. Ensure that all functions, levels, and tours are accounted for, including second and third shifts.

3. Review the activity dictionary with the employees interviewed to ensure completeness and accuracy. Include the manager of a functional work area in the review so he or she doesn't feel left out of the process. The manager's support for an ABM program is important to its success.

An activity dictionary form is shown in Fig. 3-10. The dictionary is prepared from the data included in the activity dictionary worksheets that were assem-

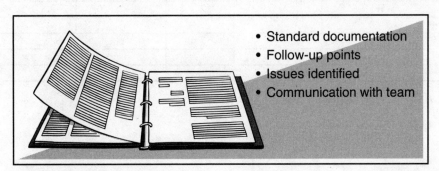

- Standard documentation
- Follow-up points
- Issues identified
- Communication with team

**Figure 3-8.** Documentation.

A comprehensive listing of all the activities performed by all personnel

**Figure 3-9.** What is an activity dictionary?

Activity dictionary

| | | | | Functional work area | |
|---|---|---|---|---|---|

| Activity name | Activity type P or S | Work driver | Cost object | Performance measure | Comments |
|---|---|---|---|---|---|
| | | | | | |
| | | | | | |
| | | | | | |
| | | | | | |
| | | | | | |
| | | | | | |
| | | | | | |
| | | | | | |
| | | | | | |
| | | | | | |
| | | | | | |

**Figure 3-10.** Activity dictionary form.

bled during the interview process. The completed dictionary (Fig. 3-11) will indicate the following information:

- Functional work area
- Activity name
- Activity type—primary or secondary
- Work driver(s)
- Cost object(s)
- Performance measure(s)

When the interviewing process is completed, a status report of the initial interview findings should be compiled by functional work area. We have included a typical status report for consideration by senior management in Appendix B, at the end of this chapter.

In addition, a typical action plan prepared by functional work area is presented in Appendix 3C to demonstrate how recommendations might be addressed by operations management. There aren't any hard-and-fast rules as to format and/or how a functional work area might respond to recommended changes in the work routine.

It has been our experience that when there is an open atmosphere with continuous routine two-way communication, most recommendations will not be a surprise. If the rank-and-file worker believes some concrete action will be taken to improve the work routine, most of the recommendations will be gratefully received and supported.

Remember that at this early stage of an activity-based management program, initial recommendations will be undocumented. When the detailing process is completed, these recommendations will be validated and a more thorough analysis will be completed. Also, other reengineering and productivity improvement opportunities will be identified.

## Prepare a Work Distribution Matrix

When the interviewing process is completed for a functional work area, the data obtained can be converted into a *work distribution matrix* (Fig. 3-12) that indicates which employees perform what activities. When the matrix is completed, compare the activities against the activity dictionary to make sure that all activities have been accounted for.

The purpose of the work distribution matrix is to link activities to individuals, define activity workloads, identify potential cross-training opportunities, and target potential activities for future elimination, especially if they are deemed non-value added. In addition, this matrix will assist in determining which employee performs a specific primary activity in a functional work area.

## Activity Dictionary—Functional Work Area: Claims

| Activity name | Activity type P or S | Work driver | Cost object | Performance measure | Comments |
|---|---|---|---|---|---|
| Supervision | P | Policy | N/A | N/A | Coaching, training, appraisals, create guidelines |
| Meetings | P | Policy | N/A | N/A | Committees |
| Training | P | Policy | Completed training | N/A | N/A |
| Coordination of Benefits Review | P | Requests | Completed investigation | Timeliness Type of request | Internal/external questions to process claims |
| Collection Agency Interface Subrogation | P | Legal action | Completed investigation | Number of investigations | Subrogation claims to recover monies paid out; call collection agencies, attorneys |
| Develop Methods and Procedures | P | Policy | Completed procedure | Timeliness | Procedures for home care claims, internal tracking |
| Claims Analysis— Hot Issues | S | Request | Completed analysis | Type of claim Number of claims | Management review |
| Problem Solving | P | Request | Resolved problem | Type of problem Number of problems | Contract questions about benefits, MIS problems |
| Departmental Reports | P | Policy | Completed report | Timeliness | Production volumes, quota analysis, production logs by type of claim, prescription, benefit reports |
| Claims Analysis— All Types/All Lines of Business | P | Claim form | Completed claim | Type of claim Number of claims | 100 per day is required; telephone physicians for data, track by lines of business, routing to the depths for reevaluation (batch of 50) |
| Contact Sheet Analysis | P | Telephone call | Resolved problem | Number of problems | Blue contact sheet for missing patient treatment codes for service (batch of 20), white contact sheet from marketing, member services, provider relations |

**Figure 3-11.** Filled-out activity dictionary.

| Activity | P/S | Trigger | Completion | Measures | Description |
|---|---|---|---|---|---|
| Emergency Room Denials Review Appeals | S | Letter | Completed review | Number of claims<br>Type of reason | Pull copy of claim and prepare for final review by appeals for payment |
| Claims Analysis—Anesthesiology | P | Claim form | Completed claim | Number of claims | Longer to process than regular claims; calculate units, look up formula, par/nonpar review |
| Distribution Mail/Claim Forms | P | Claim form | Completed distribution | Number of claims<br>Number of letters | Prepare log of what is given to analysts |
| Reconsideration Fees/Benefits | P | Request | Completed review | Number of requests | Members asking for payments for non-par services, physicians asking for fees - non-par; prepare log investigation claim |
| Issue Claim Document Numbers | P | Claim form | Document number issued | Correct control | Issue and void claim numbers |
| Member Appeals | S | Letter | Completed appeal | Type of appeal<br>Number of appeals | Investigate members appeal for payment for a denied service; claims analysis fills out review form |
| Coding—Hospital Bills | S | Hospital bill | Completed coding | Number of hospital bills | Hospital bills that are missing CPT code |
| Claims Analysis—COB | P | Claim form | Completed claim | Number of claims | Responsible for secondary coverage of Medicare claims—investigate copay and benefits to be paid |
| Claims Analysis—$3500 plus VIP Claims | P | Suspended claim | Completed claim | Type of claim<br>Number of claims | Analyze for payment other analysis submit claims for review, review employer VIP claims |
| Claims Analysis—Employees | P | Employee claims | Completed claim | Type of claim<br>Number of claims | Analyze employee claims for privacy |
| Claims Analysis—Podiatry | P | Claim form | Completed claim | Number of claims | Prepare log, enter claim count, code claims for Dr. review |

**Figure 3-11.** Filled-out activity dictionary (*Continued*).

## Activity Dictionary—Functional Work Area: Claims

| Activity name | Activity type P or S | Work driver | Cost object | Performance measure | Comments |
|---|---|---|---|---|---|
| Claims Analysis—Chiropractor | P | Claim form | Completed claim | Number of claims | Review with Dr. for extended benefits |
| Provider Set-ups/Data Entry | P | Applications | Completed set-up | Number of setups | Data-enter new physicians into database |
| Claims Analysis—Dermatology | P | Claim form | Completed claim | Number of claims | Review with Dr. difficult claims |
| Claims Analysis—Multiple Surgery | S | Claim form | Completed claim | Number of claims | Review with Dr. |
| Suspended 500 Claims | S | Claim form | Completed claim | Number of claims | Providers not entered in database but claims come in |
| Filing | P | Claim forms | Completed filing | Number of claims | Filed by lines of business; analyst pulls sheets, correspondence |
| Xeroxing | S | Request | Completed copies | Number of copies | Indicate how many claims to xerox for quality review (usually 5% of number processed) |
| Pull Sheets | P | Request | Completed pull | Number of requests | Customer Service requests copies of claims (30 per day) |
| Offsite Storage File Transfer | P | Request | Completed transfer | Timeliness | Storage |
| Suspended Claims (Night Team) | S | Claim form | Completed claim | Number of claims | Team members give suspended claims to team leader |
| Data Entry | P | Claim form | Completed entry | Number of entries | Nonpar providers from suspended 500 claims |
| Statistical Analysis | S | Claim form | Completed analysis | Type of claim Number of claims | Claims over $10,000 with a diagnosis code of 800 (fractured skull) |

**Figure 3-11.** Filled-out activity dictionary (*Continued*).

| Activity | P/S | Output | Completed | Measures | Description |
|---|---|---|---|---|---|
| Recoveries | P | Claim form | Completed investigation | Number of claims / Dollars recovered | Recover money paid in error for claims that were work-related, auto, accident, other medical coverage; send collection letters; overpayment calls to providers and members |
| Reissue Checks | S | Letter | Completed investigation | Number of claims / Dollars recovered | Payments that should have been made as a primary care payer but originally were not |
| Coordination of Benefits Investigations | P | Note pad printout | Completed investigation | Number of investigations / Dollars recovered | Weekly report giving names, workers' comp insurance for recovery investigation |
| Questionnaire—COB | P | Questionnaire | Completed entry | Number of entries / Number of questionnaires | Sort questionnaires into yes / no piles, data-enter into member file, research paid claims |
| Suspend Claims | P | Claim forms | Completed investigation | Number of claims / Claims by dollar level | Suspended claims; investigate claims over $10,000 first |
| Contact Sheet Count | P | Contact sheet | Completed count | Number of contact sheets / Aging/backlog count | Document stamp, prioritize, count |
| Tracers—Inquiries | P | Inquiry sheet | Completed investigation | Number of inquires / Number of tracers / aging | From provider relations, physicians claim not paid correctly or need data about a claim from member services/customer services |
| Claims Analysis | P | Claim form | Completed claims | Number of claims / Quality | Radiologist with a special contract |
| Incoming Checks | S | Checks | Completed entry | Number of entries | Recalculate claim, send checks to accounting; can repeat process several times for installment payments |

**Figure 3-11.** Filled-out activity dictionary (*Continued*).

Activity Dictionary—Functional Work Area: Claims

| Activity name | Activity type P or S | Work driver | Cost object | Performance measure | Comments |
|---|---|---|---|---|---|
| Return Check Investigation | P | Checks | Completed investigation | Number of investigations | Physician or member returns a payment, investigate and resolve, accounting receives checks, send copies to claims, data enter |
| Typing | P | Request | Completed letters/memos | Number of letters/memos | Form letters, stuff envelopes over payment letters, team leader reports, trainer reports |
| Sorting—Routing | P | Claim form | Completed sort | Number of claims | Blue Cross hospital claims; sort by lines of business, send claim to hospital to send to Blue Cross |
| Letter Review | P | Letter | Completed review | Type of letter Number of letters | Research analyst attaches letter request to claims to get missing data |
| Claims Coordination | P | Request | Completed request | Type of request Number of requests | Other departments ask questions |
| Claims Review—All Lines of Business | P | Claim form | Completed review | Type of review Number of reviews | Analyst prepares cover sheet and backup material; prepare manual log and enter in "D" word. Advantage, etc. |
| Claims Analysis—$10,000 Plus | P | Claim form | Completed review | Type of review Number of reviews | Review after analyst completes work to be certain data is OK |
| Benefits Maintenance—MIS Coordination | P | Claim form | Completed review | Type of review Number of reviews | MIS suspended claim, couldn't process claim; batch-entry for MIS to correct defect |
| Return Checks | P | Check | Completed review | Number of checks Dollar amount | Investigate why overpaid; accounting prepares credit memos, MIS problems |

**Figure 3-11.** Filled-out activity dictionary (*Continued*).

| | | | | | |
|---|---|---|---|---|---|
| Capacity Code Change | S | Claim form | Completed change | Number of changes | PCP code change when members can't visit their own PCP for some reason |
| Benefit Accumulators | S | Telephone call | Completed review | Number of reviews | Members say they met deductible, rep processes claim and reverses out; sometimes there is a carryover from a prior company |
| Quality Review— All Lines of Business | P | Claim form | Completed review | Number of claims Number of correct claims Types of errors | Review 5% of claims analyst work for correctness, prepare write-up, log in claims pulled for review |
| Multiple Surgery Review | P | Claim form | Completed review | Number of claims | Review surgeons' charges over $2000 and multiple surgeries; suspend claims and key in service to go through program |
| Claims Routing— Other Depts. | S | Claim form | N/A | Number of claims | N/A |

**Figure 3-11.** Filled-out activity dictionary (*Continued*).

| Functional work area | Accounting<br>1<br>Accounts receivable | Prepared by:<br>2<br>Date: | Approved by:<br>3<br>Date: |
|---|---|---|---|

| Activity type 4 | Activity name 5 | Employee name 6 | | | | | | | | | | | | | | | |
|---|---|---|---|---|---|---|---|---|---|---|---|---|---|---|---|---|---|
| | | | | | | | | | | | | | | | | | |
| | | | | | | | | | | | | | | | | | |
| | | | | | | | | | | | | | | | | | |
| | | | | | | | | | | | | | | | | | |
| | | | | | | | | | | | | | | | | | |
| | | | | | | | | | | | | | | | | | |
| | | | | | | | | | | | | | | | | | |
| | | | | | | | | | | | | | | | | | |
| | | | | | | | | | | | | | | | | | |
| | | | | | | | | | | | | | | | | | |
| | | | | | | | | | | | | | | | | | |
| | | | | | | | | | | | | | | | | | |
| | | | | | | | | | | | | | | | | | |
| | | | | | | | | | | | | | | | | | |
| | | | | | | | | | | | | | | | | | |
| | | | | | | | | | | | | | | | | | |
| | | | | | | | | | | | | | | | | | |
| | | | | | | | | | | | | | | | | | |

**Figure 3-12a.** Work distribution matrix.

| Line Number | Title or Term | Is Used to Indicate |
|---|---|---|
| (1) | Functional work area | The name of the functional work area unit in which the work is performed. |
| (2) | Prepared by / date | The signature of the ABM team member who did the interviewing, and the date the interviews for the functional work area were completed. |
| (3) | Approved by / date | The signature of the functional work area manager, indicating the accuracy and completeness of the worksheet. |
| (4) | Activity type | P for primary activity, S for secondary activity. |
| (5) | Activity name | Name of the activity which the interviewee performs. |
| (6) | Employee name | Name(s) of the employees who perform an activity. |

**Figure 3-12b.** Work distribution matrix key.

The information will provide the ABM team with possible choices of which employee to work with during the detailing process.

The matrix data is derived from the activity dictionary worksheets. When the work distribution matrix is completed (Fig. 3-13), review it with the functional work area manager for correctness and ask the manager to sign off that it is complete and accurate.

## Summary

The table of organization described at the outset of this chapter provides the controlled checklist to ensure that every employee is identified. The interview process utilizes the employee list to make sure all activities are identified and classified as primary or secondary. These two phases of the program identify the total universe of people and the total universe of work performed in an organization.

It is a controlled checks-and-balances methodology. The classification of activities into primary and secondary and the matrix of who does each activity create the basis for the next phase of the program: detailing activities.

The ABM team has identified the primary activities to be detailed. Each phase of the program connects with the others and feeds off the previous phase. This affords the ABM team with a methodology to control, administer, and begin to interpret what some of the data means. A secondary benefit of the interview process is that it gives a functional work area manager a job description created by the individual doing the work.

| Functional work area | Accounting 1 Accounts receivable | | Prepared by: Ed Forrest 2 Date: January 24, 1994 | | Approved by: 3 Date: |
|---|---|---|---|---|---|

| Activity | Activity name | Employee name 6 | | | | | | | | |
| type 4 | 5 | Robyn | Marc | Jon | Bob | Glen | Emily | Jen | Tom | Joan |
|---|---|---|---|---|---|---|---|---|---|---|
| P | Cash application process | | X | X | | X | | X | X | X |
| P | Mail sort | X | X | | X | | X | | X | X |
| P | Encoding-endorsing | | X | X | | X | | X | X | X |
| S | Bank charges-AMEX, VISA, MC | X | | X | X | X | X | | | X |
| S | Bounced checks | X | | X | | X | X | | | X |
| S | Credit memo research | | X | | | | | | | |
| S | Faxing | X | X | X | X | X | X | X | X | |
| P | Aging statistics | | | | | | X | | | |

**Figure 3-13.** Example of a completed work distribution matrix.

In addition, since the productivity improvements identified require minor effort to implement, the functional work area manager can do so immediately without waiting for the remainder of the program to be completed. The result is a living process which improves as it goes on and conveys to all employees that changes are happening because they opened the door with their ideas.

## Appendix 3A. Fantasy Lists

### Operational Issues

- Complete management information system (MIS) overhaul.
- Checks for new application are kept in enrollment, sometimes for days. Should deposit all incoming checks. Checks should go directly to finance.
- Use microfilm for reports instead of binding them and storing. Slow if we have to look for items. Stored off site. Wastes time.
- Create an automated enrollment report for newborns to alert quality assurance to authorize services.
- No reports on outgoing calls.
- All nurses should handle their own home-care cases, not one person as a specialist.
- Transplant guidelines should be in system, including a checklist of lab values and other data required for the procedure to be completed and benefits approved.
- Training in answering the telephone. Could there be a checklist for questions to ask?
- Increase filing area, because we have to purge the files too often.
- Shuffle paper to secretary when an analyst can't find a Medicare fee.
- Have customer service handle some items directly, because members keep calling back asking, "Has my problem been fixed?" Telephone and address changes.
- More printers in work areas so MIS doesn't have to stop running reports when the subrogation report must be run.
- Telephone system has a great deal of static.
- Log in claims in the mailroom.
- Benefits pager screen (HC124) should include benefit information like copayment amount ($8) and durable medical equipment percentage coverage.
- Provider service guidelines for in-office services should be in the system by provider instead of having to search for the data.
- Uniform procedures manual to be used throughout the company.

- System is slow and people have to stay extra hours until MIS prints to complete job because there is another full process the next day.

- Member eligibility screen sequence is too cumbersome—must back out, enter nurse identification number, enter password each time you want to go to another screen.

- Preexisting condition warning statement or flashing flag as part of the member eligibility screen for code 5, small business and code 6, individual—e.g., for student verification.

- Too many fires.

- Eliminate preexisting condition waiting periods—leads to outlays of cash later on.

- Enforce penalty on primary-care physician (PCP) for referral abuse, penalty on withhold.

- System track referrals by physician for out of plan or in plan.

- Desk calculators with paper-tape-printing capability instead of small calculators currently being used.

- Authorization screen sequence is cumbersome.

- Computer system should have home-care guidelines for medical necessities, custodial care. Medical review area should look at these cases.

- Do not receive executive support, only lip service to get things implemented.

- Improve system so you can find PCP; if address is missing, lab bills often only have PCP name.

- PCs are slow and the cursors freeze without moving.

- Uniform screens in all departments for benefits, DME. Currently customer service can give a member one interpretation and health services another.

- Do not begin a new service or plan until the system is updated and everyone on staff knows about it.

- Information dissemination should be uniform to everyone and system updated quickly.

- Automate approval and denial letters instead of typing form letters.

- Photocopy machines break down frequently. Should secure a workhorse machine.

- Weekly production report is not automatically accumulated.

- Approximately 2 hours of every 8 hours spent waiting for MIS to complete a job.

- So many meetings that you can't follow up on items.

- Process rules are changed frequently, so people tend to make errors.

- Review the preexisting condition policy—cost to eliminate the protocol and just pay the claim.

- Train a nonnurse to research physical therapy referral documentation.
- Train a nonnurse to data-entry physical therapy referrals.
- Have each nurse do his or her own physical therapy cases, not one specialist.
- Inappropriate referrals could be handled by a nonnurse.
- Member eligibility screen should contain the primary-care physician's telephone number on it. Currently have to look up in a book while member is on the telephone.
- Training class for PCP office managers—one-day workshop on what they should know with a takeaway field guide. Could be part of the credentialing process. Many calls must be answered by nurses that office managers should handle.
- Training in WordPerfect and operation of a Paradox system.
- Better photocopy machines, uniform service, more machines, complete supplies, 11" × 17" paper.
- More laser printers, possibly with A/B switches. People get backed up waiting to use the printers. There are only two machines in health services.
- All contracts by length-of-benefits data should be in the system. Focus papers do not do the job and errors are created because of the lack of computer support.
- Telephone for each employee.
- Voice-activated system referral module would also provide the physician with number of authorized visits, the referral number to use for a claim, physician's ID number, specialist ID number, and member eligibility.
- Create a utilization management department to assign length of stay in a hospital, primary-care physician who is referring to a specialist, how often in network, out of network, different trends and patterns. Currently, we do not go back to review cases to benchmark against other companies.
- Process Medicare claims electronically.
- Automate emergency room process.
- Put medicine codes in computer.
- Have a price for every patient-treatment code—doctors wait 3 months to get paid while fee is developed.
- Company lacks leadership to assign accountability to each department for doing the work it is supposed to do. Not putting the onus where it belongs.
- System requires too many keystrokes, and there is too much back-and-forth in using screens.
- Work at home with a PC and modem during the day instead of working in the office at night.

- Provider searches—system should allow you to find a group name, individual physician name, tax ID number. Can cross-train so all analysts can do this activity.

- Computer system is cumbersome and not friendly. For chiropractor, claims must back out of claims screen, reenter in system with ID into authorization screen. Very slow. Should be able to go directly from one screen to another.

- Automate chiropractor guidelines to pay claims. Too much room to deviate from the rules. Can extend expiration dates, etc. Rules are gray.

- Title is data entry, but we are doing claims analysis and not getting paid for the equivalent work.

- Automate authorization and denial letter process.

- Claims analyst should do capacity code changes.

- Process rules should be consistent. Team leaders tell an employee how to process claims and the quality auditors give the analyst an error—many guidelines are ambiguous.

- System should account for a covering PCP so we can eliminate paper shuffling.

- Purchase additional copy machines and typewriters. Medical record letters need to be typed for entering the hospital name, address, date of service, member name, member number. Automate this process because all other letters can be done on a word processor.

- Automate approval and denial letters instead of typing them.

- Increase number of ports for PC use; many users and some PCs go on hold.

- Uniform out-of-plan guidelines for authorizations to eliminate case management duplication between nurse coordination and medical review.

- Uniform policy for payments.

- Update the system to include anesthesiology calculation so any analyst can process the claim, not just one expert. This would spread the work and not rely on one person.

- Additional PCs and printers to be able to print claims.

- Eliminate the claims review manual log to back up the computer in case it goes down or someone wipes off a line in "D" word.

- Customer service reps should be trained better to handle all calls instead of coming to claims for an answer.

- Establish a manual control log for team leaders to control work by claim and analyst.

- Suspended claims disappear when sent out to other areas. Use a transmittal form from team leader, with number of documents and document numbers listed, and sign off by receiving area, with the original going back to the sending team leader.

- Improve system protocol to make it user friendly and to be able to correct an error immediately. Currently, we must go back through all the steps to process a change. (One day of service is correct but entered as 3 days of service.)

- PC screen should be set up to look like the claims form. Claims analyst should be able to use one screen for missing data instead of one screen for a missing diagnosis and another for something else.

- Credentialing—to provider rep to credentialing, back to rep. One area should complete the entire process. Train reps in credentialing process.

- Laptops to use with portable printers or a fax machine.

- Eliminate benefits manuals—automate by member number, covered/not covered.

- Mental health should be able to enter all data into PK Harmony system instead of entering a second time into Paradox.

- Larger monitor to do artwork—view is better to do work.

- New printer to utilize graphic elements. Current printers are inadequate and break down.

- Member provider issues—out-of-plan labs, calling doctors—someone other than rep should make the call.

- Ergonomically correct chairs that can be adjusted to correct height and back fit.

- Wristpads.

- Pull-out shelves for keyboards for correct height for typing.

- Use a call distribution reporting system for weekly and monthly production reports.

- Areas use the rap codes for monthly reports.

- Automated contact sheets, E-mail instead of waiting 12 days.

- Blue Cross liaison is time-consuming.

- Fill out a form to get anything done.

- Intercom system with music playing when not paging. ILC Data Device Corp. did a study and found that productivity improved when music was played.

- Should have a transmittal sheet that shows claims number sequence and total number of batches and claims delivered by line of business. Claims should sign transmittal acknowledging receipt of document.

- Need disaster recovery plan, fully insured. Complete fireproof safe, adhere to policy.

- Complete each call, with paperwork to follow sometime later in the day.

- Purchase order on same screen as invoice number instead of separate screens.

- Credit analysis screen should show state, to ease telephoning.
- Contact information is inaccurate or nonexistent. Salespeople should secure this data when taking an order.
- Sales should get approval for charging freight at time of contract.
- Secure purchase order numbers when sales takes an order.
- Sales should properly code COD orders or bounce back; would help if sales department screens indicated COD clearly.
- Centralized filing area.
- One screen for all customer basic information, perhaps like credit application format.
- Allow more than one person to look into an account in system when using the customer maintenance screen.

## Human Resources Issues

- Summer hours.
- Work abundant numbers of hours but never get done. Late hours every night, not just end of month.
- Incentives—don't receive overtime, so after many months receive bonus. Not being absent, receive a gift certificate.
- Would like to know what each department does to determine if I would like to work in that area.
- Don't receive coaching from supervisor on how to grow.
- When 3 months' probation is over, should receive some type of raise.
- Salaries not competitive with industry standards.
- Human resources not responsive to issues.
- Vacation time increased by one week after 5 years and another week after 10 years of service.
- Should not be penalized for taking a personal day, or working overtime but only being paid at straight time instead of at time and a half.
- Employee-of-the-month award.
- Organized training program of definite duration with manuals.
- Car allowance—tax too high.
- Workshops and seminars on self-esteem, peak performance, stress management.
- More paid holidays—Veteran's Day, Columbus Day, day after Thanksgiving.
- Vacation—3 weeks after 2 years.
- Do not understand how other areas of the company work, interact with health services.

- Cross-training.

- Team leader salaries are not substantially higher than those of claims analysts.

- New employee orientation program needs to include a computer training class for the company system. People feel stupid in using the system.

- When job openings are posted, human resources should list not only the qualifications for the particular job but also the salary. Most times you have no idea what the salary would be for another position and cannot make a decision if it would be worthwhile going through the interview process for it.

- More thorough training for newly hired employees, explaining interdepartmental relationships.

- Give employees a choice—bonus or Christmas party.

- Bring back annual bonus.

- Establish a competitive salary structure, because we are losing good people.

- Low morale.

- Decisions at the executive level are based on emotion, not business judgment.

- On-site day care for employees' children.

- Larger and more frequent raises.

- Overtime hours should not be penalized if you take personal or sick time during that same week.

- Training classes—in-service workshops on illness, diagnosis, medication, treatment—to keep nurses up to date.

- Should not have to use personal days as snow days; offer employees one or two discretionary days.

- Tuition reimbursement.

- Go to seminars for education.

- Empower individuals at all levels to make decisions without fear of being fired.

- Tuition reimbursement—nontaxable to employee up to $5280, deductible to company.

- Have summer hours so employees can spend more time with their families.

- Increase salaries to be competitive with marketplace.

- Easy conversion of sick time into vacation time.

- Too many management layers.

- Employee medical plan handled outside for privacy purposes.

- Workshops and seminars.

- Training in case-management techniques, when or when not to case-manage. Is the responsibility the company's because it's our member or is it the hospital/Blue Cross responsibility?

- Raises are low (4 or 5 percent) even if you are rated highly.
- Training on PC and other systems.
- Increase vacation, sick, and personal days with pay.
- Would like to make extra money working weekends when it's busy. Told can't do so because salaried individuals aren't allowed.
- Official breaks because people talk while working.
- Unused sick days can be used as vacation days.
- Develop a promotion-from-within policy for executive positions.
- Salary level structure should be commensurate with the job. If someone is promoted, he or she should receive the salary an outsider would receive instead of a minor increase.

## Social Issues

- Morale is bad in the company.
- Open-door policy really doesn't exist—words have no substance.
- No appreciation for a good job—half-day off, dinner, ballgame.
- No job security.
- Eliminate company fear.
- Take more interest in the employees and the job they are doing. Snowstorm—didn't want people to take lunch even though they made an effort to come in.
- Can't speak openly.
- Better office air quality—more sickness than normal. How often are filters changed?
- More professional managers who know how to treat their staff.
- Free aerobics program once a week downstairs in the health club.
- Kick-the-habit program for smokers.
- Quiet room when you do not feel well.
- Warmer relationship with director; availability and relaxed comfort level to discuss issues. Afraid to go in and talk.
- More personable boss to discuss business questions because we are afraid to ask anything. Hard on staff during work, tense.
- Executives should empower managers and let them manage.
- Don't put money into spiral staircase but into your people.
- If there are labels to run in the printer, you can't run other work.
- Treat people humanly, not like robots.

- People are fired on a regular basis.
- Improve lighting.
- Lounge area to rest and relax.
- No one says "Thanks" or "You did a good job."
- Form over substance—office appearance over work produced.
- Do what our goals say. We do not adhere to them. Not a mission or goal organization.
- Top-down approach; run by one person.
- Set up more coffee pots in more office areas.
- Hold company functions so people can get to know one another.
- Office cold in the winter.
- Improved cafeteria facilities.
- Bathroom facility for women is not adequately supplied.
- Lounge area that is quiet, to rest and unwind.
- Company activities and outings.
- Establish a company-subsidized cafeteria. Coffee shop is too expensive.
- Company is broken up into teams, with little interaction between teams.
- Allow plants on desk, pictures so the office isn't antiseptic and has a warmer feeling.
- Empowerment instead of fear as a management philosophy.
- Silly things are criticized, like items on the desk.
- Company activities to humanize the company—dress-down day, bowling.
- Personalize work station areas so the office isn't antiseptic.
- Production emphasis creates stress, resulting in employees not completing the claims process but just moving paper off their desks to another department.
- Music system for news and weather.
- Garbage dumpster pickups are noisy and disruptive.
- Frustrated—ideas submitted for productivity improvement are denied.
- Morale-boosting—congratulations, newsletter for items of exceptional work.
- Company activities so people can get to know one another—every 2 months.
- Women's softball team.
- Dress code is too strict.
- Create an employee lounge with television.
- Enlarge employee cafeteria area with more amenities.
- Increase employee morale with team sports, company functions, boat rides.

- Most people come in for a paycheck.
- Improved office lighting. Fluorescent lights are too bright.
- Company attitude is "Everyone is replaceable"; they do not care about people.
- There isn't a communication dialogue between directors/managers and staff.
- It's who you know, not what you know. Establish a set of guidelines for promoting from within.
- Lunchroom is too noisy, small, no windows.
- Improve kitchen facilities with microwave, toaster oven, stove.
- Clean parking lot.
- Enclosed smoking area.
- Company is too pretentious.
- Cafeteria for company employees, vending machines or a regular service.
- Night shift doesn't get the same respect as the day shift. Do not attend meetings and aren't kept up to date.
- Happy to have a job.
- Vending machines with food and soda for the night shift.
- Sick people who leave early must make up the time—not fair.
- Restore Christmas bonus.
- Outdoor lounge in good weather.
- Food service for night shift.
- No appreciation from managers after they ask you to give 200 percent.
- No incentives to remain with the company—vacation, retirement.
- No loyalty and/or job security.
- Do not feel support from executives.
- Staff meetings should not begin before regular hours or after regular hours because we do not get paid for it.
- Atmosphere is tense. Come to work not knowing if I will have a job at the end of the week.
- No privacy—new area just squeezed together.
- No morale because people feel the company isn't loyal to them. Everyone is replaceable.
- People don't want to extend themselves—no team players, cutthroat atmosphere, people don't trust one another.
- No one has authority to make a decision.
- Corporate social worker or psychologist whom employees can speak to in order to relieve stress.

- Heavy stress.
- If you use sick days, should not have to write them up. If you don't use them, should be able to carry over or get paid for them.
- Turnover.
- Bottled water dispensers throughout the office.
- No rules—book of what's not allowed. Can't have Christmas cards.
- No one wants to be blamed.
- Management blames lower-level people for mistakes.
- Each department is working against the other. People don't work as a team to resolve problems.
- No one listens to good ideas.
- Need a wider vision; run like mom-and-pop operation.
- Show employees they care—don't close at 4:30 after asking employees to take a half-hour lunch.
- Decisions made at the last minute and staff must react and stay late. No advance planning.

## Appendix 3B. Claims Interview Status Report

---

### MEMORANDUM

**DATE:** February
**TO:** Gordon Scott
**FROM:** Edward Forrest
**RE:** Initial Interview Findings—Status Report, Claims Area

**************************************************************************

We concluded all the interviews for the claims department by January. The following are some of the issues we believe to be relevant to the improvement of this area. These issues are considered important to your staff and if addressed, should increase productivity, eliminate non-value-added work and increase throughout.

We will better understand the significance of these preliminary findings as we move through the "detailing" phase of the program. We will continue our efforts and keep you abreast of developments as they surface.

---

- Automate the coordination of benefits (COB) claims process. Currently, the manual process creates many sources of errors—lookup, math calculation, and benefit errors.

- Automate a coordination of benefits credit savings methodology to create an accurate, clear-cut performance measure.

- Link database with prescription plans to ensure that the other company's primary coverage is used before your company has to pay. Currently, you have approximately 200,000 members with two primary-care companies. This would reduce workload and increase cash flow.

- Update line-of-business database to include complete benefit guidelines. This would eliminate time-consuming manual lookups and reduce error rates in processing claims.

- Install a voice-activated telephone system which will provide a physician with the member's eligibility status. This would save time and increase productivity.

- Review your agreements with all employer groups. Renewals and all new agreements should have a clause having the employer group responsible for all claims paid by your company because they weren't notified of a member's disenrollment status. This would improve cash flow and place the onus in the proper place to inform you in a timely manner of a member's change in status.

- Create a voice-activated referral module which provides the physician with the number of authorized visits and issues the referral number to use for a claim, the physician's ID number, specialist ID number, and the member's eligibility.

- Establish and/or renegotiate contracts with hospitals to include all associated physicians, ancillary services, labs, and tests to reduce disputes involving fees.

- Establish one clear-cut surgical fee policy, having nonparticipating physicians receive reasonable and customary fees. Inform a member and/or physician up front to eliminate multiple handling of a claim.

- Enforce a protocol in which marketing fills in completely the group data form, and understands what it takes to set up and administer a new customer. A customer should not be given a turn-on date before the infrastructure is in place to support that new account.

- Install a microfilm process as soon as a claim comes into the mail room. This would reduce misfiling, lost documents, and office space for filing cabinets. In addition, it would greatly speed up processing, because copies could be retrieved quickly. (At this time, three people pull, copy, and refile documents.)

- Eliminate the form preparation step when routing claims because the point of entry determines what department a claim is supposed to go to. In addition, you can track a claims number in the routing log.

- Cost-justify physician consultant expense versus money saved through their reviewing claims. Analysts should not have to spend time with the consultant—it is non-value added. The process also tends to accumulate claims rather than processing claims.

- Enhance and simplify the system protocol for correcting errors immediately. Currently, you must go back through all the same steps a second time to make a change.

- Set up a claims processing screen to mirror the claims form so the analyst has to utilize only one screen for missing data. Currently, the analyst uses one screen for a missing diagnosis and another screen for some other piece of missing data.

- Modify the system to automatically do the anesthesiology calculation. This would allow the analyst to process this type of claim instead of one expert.

- Instruct and enforce incoming laboratory bills to have the physician's name, group, address, and tax ID. If data is missing, bounce the invoice back to the lab. The system makes it difficult, if the primary-care physician (PCP) address is missing, to find the correct physician, and wastes time.

- Change the system to recognize nonpar calculations and OOP referrals.

- Enhance the system to include full podiatry guidelines.

- Postoperative services should be automatically calculated instead of manually doing the function.

- Eliminate paper shuffling for suspended claims. The analyst should handle the entire process to release the claim. Currently, the analyst sends the claim to the technical assistant, who then returns the claim to the analyst. An alternative would be to release the claim and not return it to the analyst.

- Focus papers are inadequate as a substitute for the system having complete line-of-business guidelines in its database. There are too many random facts to remember, which results in process errors.

- Establish a transmittal control protocol for suspended claims that are sent to other departments. Include number of documents, document numbers listed, receiving departments sign-off, and a copy retained by the sending team leader in a tickler file until documents are returned. Currently, documents for suspended claims disappear.

- Update the system to have it include the complete dermatological guidelines. This would reduce the number of suspended claims.

- Provide additional copies of manuals like the ICD-9 diagnosis and physician codes so there is a set for every two people instead of every seven people. This would increase productivity and reduce wait time to use a manual.

- Stabilize process rules. Currently, rules are changed frequently, which causes additional errors. Rules should be consistently applied. Team leaders instruct analysts to process claims in a certain way, and then quality auditors cite the analysts for errors when they are only doing what they have been told. Many guidelines are ambiguous.

- Eliminate the night shift and hire additional day people to work at home with a PC and modem. Negotiate an arrangement without benefits, reducing expenses by 26 percent. In addition, have a reserve crew that can be called upon on an "as needed" basis when there is a heavy inflow of claims. A secondary benefit would be increased morale in not having to share desks and at-home workers being able to ask questions of the better-trained day staff. In addition, payment could be made on the basis of claims processed, within quality tolerances, so production would be tied to salary.

- Reduce the number of keystrokes when using the system. Provider searches could be made easier if you could access an individual name, physician name, group name, address, and/or tax IB number.

- Adjust the screen sequence procedure to be more direct. Chiropractor claims require that you back out of the claims screen and then reenter the system with entering ID to get to the authorization screen. Why not use F stops to go directly, or update the claims screen with an authorization line (yes or no, etc.)?

- Enhance the database with full chiropractor guidelines. The guidelines currently leave too much room to deviate—extend expiration dates, and so on.

- Currently, the production area is assigning claims numbers by stamping them on the claims forms. Production should be instructed to stamp the number in an open space, not on written or typed material, because the numbers are hard to read and result in errors.

- Establish a paper recycling program. This would be an environmental plus and good publicity, but would also bring in some revenue.

- Provide additional sets of telephone books in each work area and/or have all departments enter telephone numbers in the system whenever they can. This would reduce the number of information call requests.

- Improve system response time and servicing when the system goes down. Members become annoyed because response time is slow.

- Eliminate claims analysts and health services personnel reviewing claims together. Double non-value-added work. Claims analysts or health services people should be able to complete the claim.

- Automate member and provider letters. Currently they are manually typed, and it could take a week before a manager can sign them.

- Eliminate the override capability for provider inquires; otherwise, your reason for having a controlled system is voided.

- Automate medical record letters so an analyst can directly enter the hospital name, address, date of service, member name, and member ID number. Currently, these items are typed on a typewriter (and there is an insufficient number of typewriters).

- Eliminate the manual claims review log which most analysts keep because they don't trust the computer. The system goes down or someone using "D" word wipes off a line. This is non-value added. Make the system secure and reliable.

- Claims analysts, instead of just team leaders, should enter capacity code changes.

- The system should include data for a nonlisted covering PCP. Currently, health services enters an authorized PCP in "D" word; the analysts don't look at "D" word and deny the claim. So you get the claim back for double handling.

- Accounting should immediately deposit returned checks instead of holding them. This would increase cash flow and generate interest.

- Automation of the referral system would eliminate the double handling of documents. Currently, the manual process is to receive a white sheet from a provider, enter the data, and then discover that the referral doesn't get into the system before a claim comes in.

- The system's coding structure is too broad—it was set up more from a financial perspective than from an operations view. The system assigns a specific service to a general ledger code-OPT code 9300 for an EKG and also assigns the same general ledger code for a treadmill EKG. This coding structure can be misleading to operations.

- Establish a central reference library to include medical directories, magazines, and other data on the health-care industry.

- Purge the system of useless statements. One message you are told to ignore, and another message you should act upon. Confusing signals.

- Time is wasted looking up items in books because the system database is not complete. Increases investigation time substantially.

## Appendix 3C. Claims Area Action Plan

---

**MEMORANDUM**

**TO:** Gordon Scott, Vice President—Claims Service
**FROM:** Jill Lindner, Director—Claims Service
**DATE:** March
**RE:** Action Taken on the Basis of Comments by Productivity Consulting Limited (Ed Forrest) in his February Status Report

---

- *Automate the coordination of benefits (COB) claims process. Currently, the manual process creates many sources of errors—lookups, math calculation, and benefit errors.*

  We agree with this determination. These problems have already been identified, and a project is underway to provide automation of mathematical calculations. The project will be implemented upon completion of HPR. We estimate that the COB project will begin sometime in August or September.

- *Automate a coordination of benefits credit savings methodology to create an accurate, clear-cut performance measure.*

  The credit savings methodology will be addressed as part of the COB automation project mentioned above.

- *Link database with prescription plans to ensure that the other company's primary coverage is used before we have to pay. Currently, we have approximately 200,000 members with two primary-care companies. This would reduce workload and increase cash flow.*

  We agree that this is an excellent idea, and it will be investigated.

- *Update line-of-business database to include complete benefit guidelines. This would eliminate time-consuming manual lookups and reduce error rates in processing claims.*

  We agree with this determination. For the present time, the staff will utilize manual binders until the database is updated and completed. The process of updating our database will be brought through the technical unit for investigation and implementation. In addition, the imaging system that has been approved for implementation will inevitably enhance the integrity of our database. Finally, the newly created position, benefit design and maintenance administrator, will ensure that all benefits are automated, and working properly.

- *Install a voice-activated telephone system which will provide a physician with the member's eligibility status. This would save time and increase productivity.*

  Voice-activated telephone systems, such as DIVA, are already being investigated by a committee for possible utilization at ChoiceCare.

- *Review our agreements with all employer groups. Renewals and all new agreements should have a clause having the employer group responsible for all claims paid by our company because they weren't notified of a member's disenrollment status. This would improve cash flow and place the onus in the proper place to inform us in a timely manner of a member's change in status.*

  We agree with this determination. Because of retroactive disenrollments and reenrollments, we may deny or approve claims inappropriately, and there is no procedure for advising the claims area to reprocess any payments when retroactive procedures are done. However, since implementing such a project would cross several departments at the company, we should consider forming a cross-functional team to review this opportunity.

- *Create a voice-activated referral module which provides the physician with the number of authorized visits and issues the referral number to use for a claim, the physician's ID number, the specialist ID number, and the member's eligibility.*

  DIVA, as mentioned above, would also provide us with this capability.

- *Establish and/or renegotiate contracts with hospitals to include all associated physicians, ancillary services, labs, and tests to reduce disputes involving fees.*

  We agree that this approach would greatly benefit from renegotiations such as these.

- *Establish one clear-cut surgical fee policy having nonparticipating physicians receive reasonable and customary fees. Inform a member and/or physician up front to eliminate multiple handling of a claim.*

  The problems associated with our fee policy regarding nonparticipating physicians has already been identified. We feel that a QIT should be formed to bring resolution to this problem.

- *Enforce a protocol in which marketing fills in completely the group data form, and understands what it takes to set up and administer a new customer. A customer should not be given a turn-on date before the infrastructure is in place to support that account.*

  The benefit design and maintenance administrator will be responsible for working with the marketing department, to ensure that the group data form is completed and that all benefits are automated as soon as a new account is implemented.

- *Install a microfilm process as soon as a claim comes into the mail room. This would reduce misfiling, lost documents, and office space for filing cabinets. In addition, it would greatly speed up processing, because copies could be retrieved quickly. (At this time, three people pull, copy, and refile documents.)*

  As previously stated, implementation of the recently approved imaging system will address these issues.

- *Eliminate the form preparation step when routing claims because the point of entry determines what department a claim is supposed to go to. In addition, we can track a claims number in the routing log.*

  We are unsure of what process this comment is referring to, and therefore cannot provide a response without further explanation.

- *Cost-justify physician consultant expense versus money saved through their reviewing claims. Analysts should not have to spend time with the consultant—it is non-value added. The process also tends to accumulate claims rather than process claims.*

  The newly formed claims policy committee is currently reviewing the necessity of utilizing physician consultants. The committee will determine whether it is more efficient, cost-effective, and consistent to utilize HPR versus the consultants. We are performing a cost/benefit analysis of this process.

- *Enhance and simplify the system protocol for correcting errors immediately. Currently, we must go back through the same steps a second time to make a change.*

  Although this process is time-consuming and redundant, system inadequacies are preventing changes to enhance the system protocol for correcting errors. A technical committee should be created to investigate other systems that would better suit present and growing needs.

- *Set up a claims processing screen to mirror the claim form so the analyst has to utilize only one screen for missing data. Currently, the analyst uses one screen for a missing diagnosis and another screen for some other piece of missing data.*

Through our current projects of benefit automation and imaging, all data fields will be provided under one screen.

- *Modify the system to automatically do the anesthesiology calculation. This would allow any analyst to process this type of claim instead of one expert.*

  We agree that all analysts should be trained to process all types of claims. However, because of our numerous, different contracts with various anesthesia groups, it would be difficult to automate the processing of anesthesia claims.

- *Instruct and enforce incoming laboratory bills to have the physician's name, group, address, and tax ID. If data is missing, bounce the invoice back to the lab. The system makes it difficult to find the correct physician if the PCP address is missing, and it wastes time.*

  We are unsure of what process this comment is referring to, and therefore cannot provide a response without further explanation.

- *Change the system to recognize nonpar calculations and OOP referrals.*

  In Phase II of benefit automation, the system will automatically utilize any fees negotiated with nonparticipating providers by linking the claims processing screen with the referral screen. The negotiated fee will automatically be pulled once the analyst enters the CPT code.

- *Enhance the system to include full podiatry guidelines.*

  The podiatry guidelines are currently being reviewed and enhanced by the claims policy committee. Once these guidelines are established, they will become automated through the system.

- *Postoperative services should be automatically calculated instead of manually doing the function.*

  The claims policy committee is currently reviewing these services also. Once guidelines are established, they too will become automated through the system.

- *Eliminate paper shuffling for suspended claims. The analyst should handle the entire process to release the claim. Currently, the analysts send the claim to the Technical Assistant, who then returns the claim to the analyst. An alternative would be to release the claim and not return it to the analyst.*

  The imaging process will virtually eliminate all paper shuffling associated with suspended claims, since the system itself will automatically send the claim to the correct individuals electronically. Eventually, the entire process will be "paperless."

- *Focus papers are inadequate as a substitute for the system having complete line-of-business guidelines in its database. There are too many random facts to remember, which results in processing errors.*

  We agree that the system's database should contain complete line-of-business guidelines. The benefit design and maintenance administrator will be responsible for providing such enhancements and ensuring that all new account information is promptly automated.

- *Establish a transmittal control protocol for suspended claims that are sent to other departments. Include number of documents, document numbers listed, receiving departments sign-off, and a copy retained by the sending team leader in a tickler file until documents are returned. Currently, documents for suspended claims disappear.*

  As previously stated, the imaging system will virtually eliminate all paper shuffling. This includes claims that require assistance from other departments. The system will control the flow of all documents associated with claims, and will also eliminate their disappearance.

- *Update the system to have it include the complete dermatological guidelines. This would reduce the number of suspended claims.*

  The dermatology guidelines are being addressed by the claims policy committee along with podiatry. Once these guidelines are established, they will become automated through the system.

- *Provide additional copies of manuals like the ICD-9 diagnosis and physician codes so there is a set for every two people instead of every seven people. This would increase productivity and reduce wait time to use a manual.*

  Coding books were provided to each analyst individually. The books are kept on the desk so they can be used by any evening personnel who share the office space. Extra books are available to everyone.

- *Stabilize process rules. Currently, rules are changed frequently, which causes additional errors. Rules should be consistently applied. Team leaders instruct analysts to process claims in a certain way, and then quality auditors cite the analysts for errors when they are only doing what they have been told. Many guidelines are ambiguous.*

  The claims policy committee will be responsible for reviewing and enhancing existing and new policies to determine appropriateness and consistency. This should reduce and eventually eliminate any ambiguous guidelines.

- *Eliminate the night shift, and hire additional day people to work at home with a PC and modem. Negotiate an arrangement without benefits, reducing expenses by 26 percent. In addition, have a reserve crew that can be called upon on an "as needed" basis when there is a heavy inflow of claims. A secondary benefit would be increased morale in not having to share desks, and at-home workers being able to ask questions of the better-trained day staff. In addition, payment could be made on the basis of claims processed, within quality tolerances, so production would be tied to salary.*

  In conjunction with the plans for implementing imaging technology, the current priority of the claims department is to shift the workload of the night staff from analysis to data entry. After these changes have been effectively implemented and evaluated with a throughput analysis, these suggestions will be revisited.

- *Reduce the number of keystrokes when using the system. Provider searches could be made easier if we could access an individual name, physician name, group name, address, and/or tax ID number.*

  The system has already been enhanced to provide easier access to information that is not readily available when processing a claim. Analysts are already able to utilize searching mechanisms while the claim is in process. These searches include locating provider and member information, diagnostic and procedural codes, tax identification numbers, addresses, and so on. Therefore, this recommendation has been implemented.

- *Adjust the screen sequence procedure to be more direct. Chiropractor claims require that we back out of the claims screen and then reenter the system with entering ID to get to the authorization screen. Why not use F stops to go directly, or update the claims screen with an authorization line (yes or no, etc.)?*

  The processing of chiropractic claims is being addressed as part of Phases I and II of benefit automation, thereby eliminating the need to bounce from screen to screen. The system will search for the authorization and link it to the claim being processed.

- *Enhance the database with full chiropractor guidelines. The guidelines currently leave too much room to deviate—extend expiration dates, and so on.*

  Benefit automation will also eliminate this problem, since the guidelines will be available on the database of the claims processing system.

- *Currently, the production area is assigning claims numbers by stamping them on the claims forms. Production should be instructed to stamp the number in an open space, not on written or typed material, because the numbers are hard to read and result in errors.*

  The imaging system will automatically print a claims number on each form. Since the system will be designed with individualized specifications for each type of claims form, the system will not print the claims number over important information.

- *Establish a paper recycling program. This would be an environmental plus and good publicity, but would also bring in some revenue.*

  Although we agree with the advantages of such a program, at the present time our efforts are concentrated on projects that are absolute priorities. Once these projects are complete, this type of program should be addressed.

- *Provide additional sets of telephone books in each work area and/or have all departments enter telephone numbers in the system whenever they can. This would reduce the number of information call requests.*

  This issue should be reviewed after the reorganization is completed. Each team will provide its own means of obtaining any missing information.

- *Improve system response time and servicing when the system goes down. Members become annoyed because response time is slow.*

  We agree that this is an extremely important issue. However, the MIS department can address the issue more effectively.

- *Eliminate claims analysts and health services personnel reviewing claims together. Double non-value-added work. Claims analysts or health services people should be able to complete the claim.*

  The imaging system will provide personnel with the capability of "sending" claims to other employees electronically. This will eliminate the need for personnel reviewing claims together.

- *Automate member and provider letters. Currently they are manually typed, and it could take a week before a manager can sign them.*

   Automatic letter generation is an ongoing process. To date, several of the routine letters normally sent to members and providers have been automated, and we expect to be fully automated in the near future.

- *Eliminate the override capability for provider inquiries; otherwise, our reason for having a controlled system is voided.*

   We are unsure of what process this comment is referring to, and therefore cannot provide a response without further explanation.

- *Automate medical record letters so an analyst can directly enter the hospital name, address, date of service, member name, and member ID number. Currently, these items are typed on a typewriter (and there is an insufficient number of typewriters).*

   Requesting the release of medical records is not a claims processing function, but part of claims review/appeals. An actual "claim" is not the driving factor for sending this letter, and therefore it cannot be automated. However, these requests are no longer individually typed. A template which utilizes a word processing system provides a faster means of requesting this letter.

- *Eliminate the manual claims review log which most analysts keep because they don't trust the computer. The system goes down or someone using "D" word wipes off a line. This is non-value added. Make the system secure and reliable.*

   An additional use of the Claims Review Log, which is kept by the two Claims Review Analysts, is for tracking and reporting purposes. However, the reorganization will absorb the Claims Review/Appeals process with each separate team, and this duplication of work will be eliminated.

- *Claims analysts, instead of just team leaders, should enter capacity code changes.*

   The reorganization will address the productivity issues associated with claims processing.

- *The system should include data for a nonlisted covering PCP. Currently, health services enters an authorized PCP in "D" word; the analysts don't look at "D" word and deny the claim. So we get the claim back for double handling.*

   This issue was resolved through the addition of a CD (covering doctor) authorization. When health services authorizes a nonlisted covering PCP, it will enter a CD authorization. Upon entry of the claim, benefit automation will search for the authorization, and automatically add it to the claim if a match is found.

- *Accounting should immediately deposit returned checks instead of holding them. This would increase cash flow and generate interest.*

   This is an issue that should be addressed by the accounting and/or finance departments.

- *Automation of the referral system would eliminate the double handling of documents. Currently, the manual process is to receive a white sheet from a provider, enter the data, and then discover that the referral doesn't get into the system before a claim comes in.*

The authorization/referral QIT will be responsible for reviewing this process and determining a solution. Also, projects currently under investigation such as DIVA and EDI (electronic data interchange) would alleviate many of the paper problems associated with this process.

- *The system's coding structure is too broad—it was set up more from a financial perspective than from an operations view. The system assigns a specific service to a general ledger code OPT code 9300 for an EKG and also assigns the same general ledger code for a treadmill EKG. This coding structure can be misleading to operations.*

As we proceed with benefit automation, we are reviewing the benefit structure and will make adjustments as deemed necessary.

- *Establish a central reference library to include medical directories, magazines, and other data on the health-care industry.*

Although we agree with the advantages of establishing a central reference library, at the present time our efforts are concentrated on projects that have been given priority. This idea will be revisited in the future.

- *Purge the system of useless statements. One message you are told to ignore, and another message you should act upon. Confusing signals.*

We are unsure of what process this comment is referring to, and therefore cannot provide a response without further explanation.

- *Time is wasted looking up items in books because the system database is not complete. Increases investigation time substantially.*

As previously mentioned, the benefit design and maintenance administrator will be responsible for ensuring that the system database is enhanced to include adjustments to existing accounts and design the benefits for new accounts.

# 4
# Detailing Process

## Introduction

During the interview process, activities are classified into primary and secondary as a preparatory step for the detailing process. Primary activities are those that the ABM team will detail by meeting with the appropriate staff members who perform the activities.

The detailing process includes a discussion and recording of the basic tasks required to complete the activity, the estimated elapsed time to complete the activity, how often the activity is performed, whether any seasonality factors must be considered, and the staff member's estimate of the volume of transactions processed daily, weekly, or monthly.

If the functional work area has historical transaction volume data that is easily accessible, attempt to obtain this data, which will be more precise than someone's estimate. If similar data is available for secondary activities, request this material as well, since all historical data collected will be useful as a comparative reference or stake in the ground.

Collect and identify exhibits, whether they be printouts of PC screens, forms, or documents, and relate them to each task within the activity. In selecting the staff member with whom the detailing process is to be completed, rely on the functional work area manager to identify the most experienced individual.

A few skeptics might ask about the need for detailing. Why can't the data collected during the interview process be used? What is the "value added" of this approach? The interview process data is high level in nature, while the detailing process is thorough. The detailing process serves two main purposes. First, it identifies opportunities for automation and elimination of paper shuffling. Second, it provides the documentation for the development of a procedures manual for a functional work area.

There are seven phases in the detailing process:

- Detail planning
- Detailing

- Activity work flows
- Activity analysis
- Refinement of work drivers
- Refinement of performance measurements
- Refinement of cost objects

These phases are not independent of one another. Each is a refinement of the preceding phase, drawing on explicit data to better analyze work content.

## Detail Planning

When the interview process and identification and classification of activities is completed, the ABM team must identify the individual who is most knowledgeable about an activity and who regularly performs it.

1. Prepare a list of functional work area employees and activities to be detailed (Fig. 4-1).
2. Schedule working sessions for each activity that is to be detailed. Unlike the interview, this working session doesn't have a specific time frame for completing the process. Notify employees in advance of what you expect and the actual data you want them to have so an activity can be documented from inception to completion.

   A word of caution: Be certain the transaction data is representative, that it includes not just easy transactions or difficult transactions but a good mix of both.
3. Think about the end result of what should be accomplished by the detailing process.

- Review interview data
- List activities
- List open issues

**Figure 4-1.** Review notes.

## Guidelines to Good Activity Detailing

The following list of questions can be used as a starting point in the detailing process.

1. What event or events (i.e., work drivers) cause you to start working?
2. For each of the events above, where does it originate and through what channels does it go to reach you?
3. For each of the events above, describe the activities you take to process the event. Whom do you hand off the process to after you are through? Is this person or group internal or external to the functional work area?
4. In processing these events, which activities take a lot of time? What causes these activities to be so time-intensive? Are interactions with other functional work areas and groups necessary? (Include only time actually worked; do not include waiting time.)
5. What systems are used to perform your activities? During which activity in processing each event do you use these systems? (Ask the interviewee to demo the systems.)
6. What types of exceptions are there and how often do they occur? How is the processing of these exceptions different from normal processing?
7. Are any special supplies (e.g., postage, machinery, forms) necessary to perform certain activities? (Get copies of the forms used.)
8. Do you track the volume of each event you process in a given period, by week or month? (If yes, get copies of the volume reports/logs for several periods; if no, how could the volumes be obtained?) Are any seasonal factors involved?
9. Do the volumes of events vary significantly from month to month, or from season to season?
10. What changes to the system, procedures, forms, inputs, or outputs of the processes would make your activity easier?
11. How long does it take to complete an activity?
12. How often is the activity performed?

# Detailing

The next step is to meet with the functional work area employee and explain the process to be followed during the detailing process (Fig. 4-2).

1. Observe each primary activity.
2. Record the tasks involved in performing an activity from beginning to end.

**Figure 4-2.** Objectives of detailing.

3. Collect and associate exhibits for each detailed activity relating to the work performed. Sequence the exhibits in line with the tasks that comprise an activity (e.g., forms, PC screen printouts).

4. Review each completed procedure with the functional work area employee. Ask the individual to make any necessary revisions to the text material.

5. Have the functional work area employee sign and date the final version of each procedure to signify its accuracy and completeness. The attention to detail in the documentation of tasks and activities will prevent potential disagreements about work content from arising at a later date.

The detail interview is summarized in Fig. 4-3. The detailed procedures will be helpful during the next phase of the ABM program, the observation process to make sure all tasks within an activity are seen.

Secondary activities do not have to be detailed, but should be noted as to their existence and frequency (daily, twice a week, monthly, and so on). Secondary activities can be estimated (e.g., 15 minutes once a month). The responsibility for estimating should fall to the functional work area manager, not the employee performing the activity.

Estimating should follow strict guidelines to establish uniformity in the development of usable estimates. The end product of estimating (determination of the required time to complete an activity) is essentially a reflection of individual judgment. That is, different functional work area managers will determine different estimates for an activity.

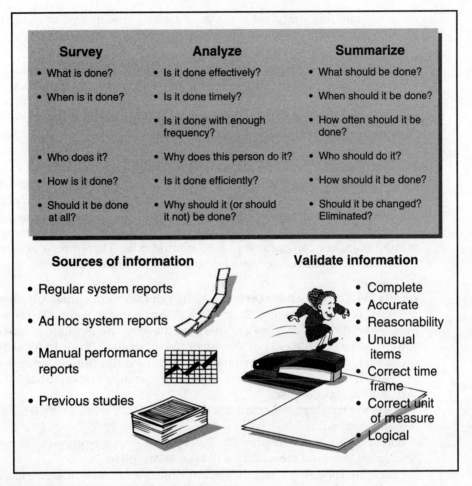

**Survey**

- What is done?
- When is it done?
- Who does it?
- How is it done?
- Should it be done at all?

**Analyze**

- Is it done effectively?
- Is it done timely?
- Is it done with enough frequency?
- Why does this person do it?
- Is it done efficiently?
- Why should it (or should it not) be done?

**Summarize**

- What should be done?
- When should it be done?
- How often should it be done?
- Who should do it?
- How should it be done?
- Should it be changed? Eliminated?

**Sources of information**

- Regular system reports
- Ad hoc system reports
- Manual performance reports
- Previous studies

**Validate information**

- Complete
- Accurate
- Reasonability
- Unusual items
- Correct time frame
- Correct unit of measure
- Logical

**Figure 4-3.** The universal detail interview.

## Definition of Estimated Time

Estimated time represents the amount of time it should take a qualified staff member, working consistently and conscientiously at a normal pace with available tools and materials, to accomplish an assigned activity.

The key words in the above statement are explained below.

**Qualified Staff Member.** It is recognized that individuals possess varying degrees of skill and knowledge. That is particularly true with respect to the specialized skill of today's industry. To be realistic, not all people would approach or perform a given activity in the same manner or in the same amount of time. Therefore, it is the *activity* that is to be estimated, not the person who might be assigned to perform it. The estimate must reflect the functional work area manager's professional, objective judgment of the specific activity—and this judgment is not to be altered or tempered to fit the personality or capacity of a specific staff member.

**Consistently and Conscientiously.**   These qualities refer not only to maintaining a steady pace in performing an activity but, just as important, to taking pride in one's skill so that the finished product is within the levels of acceptable quality standards. Activity estimating is concerned with obtaining quality levels, utilizing common sense, that are suited to the activity.

**Normal Pace.**   It must be recognized that normal pace is a factor of judgment by management personnel. The two extremes of pace are very fast and very slow, and every manager has staff members whose work matches both extremes. However, the activity estimate that is developed is geared to reflect moderation and balanced fairness to the employee. We cannot expect a 4-minute mile, nor can we accept a 60-minute mile. Therefore, a normal pace is subject to the manager's experience and activity knowledge.

**Available Tools and Material.**   Although this point would appear to be elementary, it is too often neglected when determining an estimate. The employee must have the proper tools required for the job. The estimate is based on the activity to be completed, not the talent to be assigned. Prior to focusing on the mechanics of establishing estimates, it must be thoroughly understood that they are a result of a functional work area manager's specialized knowledge, skill, and common sense.

There are two types of estimates that a functional work area manager should be concerned with.

*Total Person-Hours Required.*   Total person-hours required is an estimate of how long (in hours) an activity will take to complete.

*Calendar Time Required.*   Calendar time is a function of crew size. It is concerned with the sequencing of the skills and their respective person-hours to determine, from the start time, when the activity will be completed. In developing estimated person-hours for a multiskill job, the manager also needs to preplan the sequencing of the skills and to determine when each skill will begin and complete a particular phase of the activity. By doing so, the manager prevents "overassignment" of staff, which results in lost time as one skill waits on another to complete a portion of the work. In addition, preplanning will establish proper calendar time for activity completion and provide the functional work area manager with the basic elements of activity control. The functional work area manager must control each segment or task in order to ensure "on time" completion of the entire activity.

Once the functional work area manager has chosen the type of estimate to use, he or she will follow four major steps in developing reliable estimates (Fig. 4-4).

**Analyze the Activity.**   The activity must be examined to properly determine the nature and priority of the work to be done in relation to either backlog or

*"Estimating is a reflection of the functional work area manager's expertise and experience."*

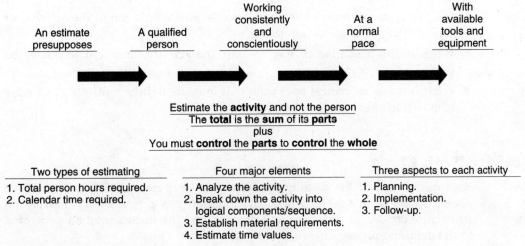

| An estimate presupposes | A qualified person | Working consistently and conscientiously | At a normal pace | With available tools and equipment |

Estimate the **activity** and not the person
The **total** is the **sum** of its **parts**
plus
You must **control** the **parts** to **control** the **whole**

| Two types of estimating | Four major elements | Three aspects to each activity |
|---|---|---|
| 1. Total person hours required.<br>2. Calendar time required. | 1. Analyze the activity.<br>2. Break down the activity into logical components/sequence.<br>3. Establish material requirements.<br>4. Estimate time values. | 1. Planning.<br>2. Implementation.<br>3. Follow-up. |

**Figure 4-4.** Estimating summary—facts of major importance.

scheduling needs. In analyzing the activity, three basic questions must be answered:

1. Is the activity within the scope of the functional work area manager's expertise?

2. Does the functional work area manager need to contract and/or consult with another manager for assistance or technical advice?

3. Does the functional work area manager have a thorough understanding of the problems and the corrective action required?

**Break Down the Activity into Tasks and Sequence.** There are three aspects to each activity, and material and time requirements are determined for each:

- Planning
- Implementation
- Follow-up

**Establish Material Requirements.** Materials and/or special equipment needs must be determined for each task within an activity. In addition, the availability of these materials must be established.

**Estimate Time Values.** Time estimates are applied to each task within the activity and total time is determined. In scheduling the work, the following questions should be considered:

1. Can some of the phases be performed simultaneously to reduce calendar time?

2. Will assignment of more personnel accelerate completion of the activity, or will the people be in one another's way?

3. When is the best time of day to start the activity, and will resources be ready?

4. What is the most critical operation that must be tightly controlled to ensure completion as scheduled?

## Activity Work Flows

An integral part of the detailing process is to prepare a *work flow diagram* for each primary activity. The work flow diagram is a pictorial that translates a procedure created in the interview process, and the documentation generated in the detailing process, into a stream of activities.

### Process Documentation

Each activity in the work flow diagram must be documented as to process. The process documentation should include:

- How the activity is performed, and by whom
- What input the activity receives
- What other activity or supplier organization provides input to the activity
- What output the activity produces
- What other activity or customer organization receives output from the function
- What support system or resource (not related to head count) is used to perform the activity

Activity work flows assist in capturing patterns of work and begin the process of understanding how work is performed in a functional area, how that work interacts with other functional areas, and what decision process is involved in completing the work performed. The activity work flows are the foundation for identifying what an organization does through the use of activity analysis.

Some authorities recommend preparing activity work flows prior to the detailing process rather than afterward. We believe it is more advantageous to prepare the activity work flows after detailing, because they will be based on completed first-hand data. In addition, the data is compiled and reviewed by the staff members who actually perform the activity day in and day out.

Predetailing work flows tend to be too high level and are often prepared by functional work area managers, not by the people who are responsible for performing the activity. The staff member is the only person who knows what it takes to complete an activity and the most expeditious way to do so. The staff member can impart his or her knowledge, particularly if activities cross hierarchical departmental lines.

Examples of a work flow diagram and related pictorial analyses are given for a warehousing operation in Figs. 4-5 and 4-6. Examples of work cycles for labor procurement and order fulfillment are given in Figs. 4-7 and 4-8.

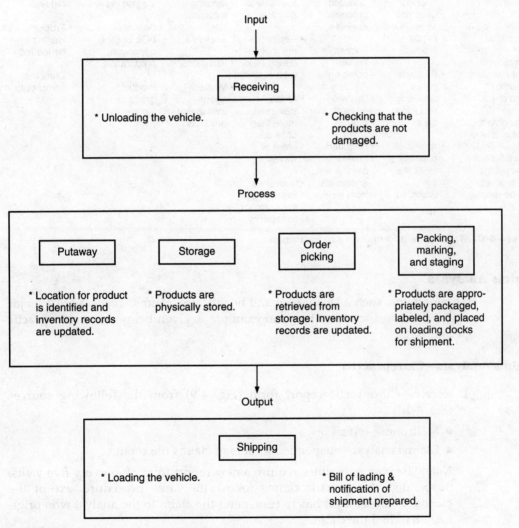

**Figure 4-5.** Work flow diagram of warehouse activities.

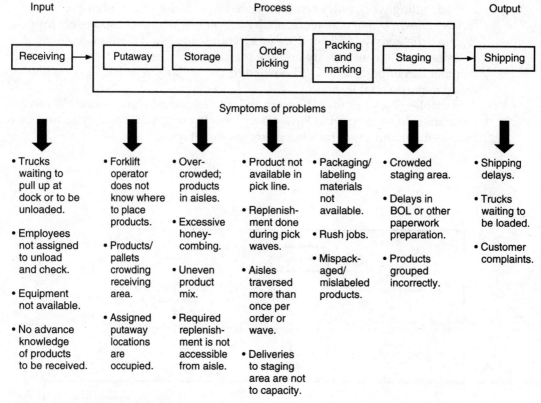

**Figure 4-6.** Warehouse information gap symptoms.

## Claims Analyses

In many fields, such as insurance and health care, claims analyses are a major part of process documentation. An example is given below for a chiropractic operation.

### Claims Analysis—Chiropractic

1. Receive chiropractic report form (Fig. 4-9) from the following sources (Fig. 4-10):

   ■ Mailroom—letters

   ■ Claims analyst—suspended folders in claims file room

   *Note:* The plan guidelines require a new report form after every five visits. Suspended chiropractor claims follow the same procedure, except the claims review analyst has to resuspend the claim to the analyst who originally handled the claim.

2. Select C12 screen (member background).

3. Enter the following data to update existing referral in C12 screen:

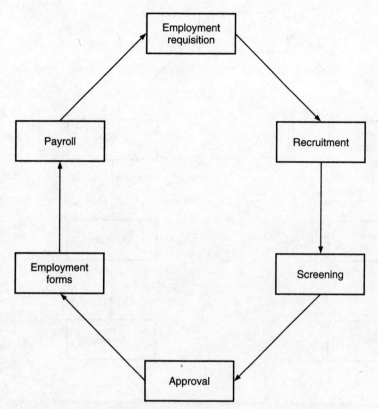

**Figure 4-7.** The labor procurement cycle.

- Member ID—subscriber 140-38-6214, MEM-01
- Date—1/1/92
- Option line—RG

4. Select C31 screen (Fig. 4-11).

5. Enter the following data:
   - Authorization number—A0093762
   - Type—CH
   - Change field—REF

6. Select C31.4 screen (Fig. 4-11).

7. Enter on line 1 the number of visits allowed (12 for an acute condition). Save.

8. Select C31 screen (Fig. 4-11).

9. Enter authorization comments (Fig. 4-11).

   *Note:* Delete old comments and enter new comments ("Don't exceed 120VS"). Incomplete reports—3/8/94. Change field F to exit AC field (Control E)—file.

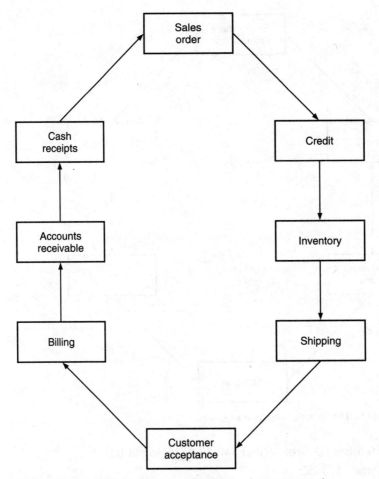

**Figure 4-8.** The order/billing/shipping/cash receipts cycle.

10. File chiropractor report forms alphabetically by member.
11. Receive physician's update report.
12. Prepare chiropractor reconsideration form (Fig. 4-12).
13. Select C12 screen.
14. Enter the following data:
    - From date of service (1/1/92 is the group enrollment start date)
    - Enter RG

    *Note:* Check to see if the consultant physician recently reviewed the case. If so, file the update report.
15. Forward chiropractor reconsideration form and backup document to consultant for review, determination, and comments.

Claim #A00943762

Report # _____ 1 _____     Visit # _____ 8 _____          Date _____ 4/8/94 _____

**Member name** ___ JOHN SILVERSMITH ___      ID __ 140-38-6214*01 __
**Chiropractor name** _ ROBERT BROWN _         ID __ 043-65-3597 __

        Was member referred?    ☐ Yes    ☐ No
        Source _____
                                                                                  ICD-9

**Diagnosis:** _____ 723.3, 728.85 _____

**Secondary
diagnosis:** _____

**Condition:**                                     **Severity**
        Acute        ☐           Mild        ☐
        Chronic     ☒          Moderate   ☐
        Trauma related ☐          Severe     ☐
        Onset of condition _____

**History:**
        ☐ Past history of similar condition
        ☐ Previous chiropractic treatment
        ☐ Contradictory or complicating factors for chiropractic care
        Comments _____

**Level of disability:**
        ☐ Mild                     ☐ At work
        ☒ Moderate              ☐ Not at work because of condition
        ☐ Severe                   Estimated return _____
        Comments _____

**Treatment level:**
                     **Current**               **Future**
        1x/2wk        ☐                ☒
        1x/wk        ☐                ☐
        2x/wk        ☐                ☐
        3x/wk        ☒                ☐
        Daily        ☐                ☐

**Estimated recovery time:**
        ☐ 1–2 weeks
        ☐ 3–6 weeks
        ☒ More than 6 weeks
        Comments _____

**Reason for continued treatment/comments:** _ Patient continues to have stiffness requiring
        continued Rx at 2x/wk _____
_____
_____

**Figure 4-9.** Chiropractor report form.

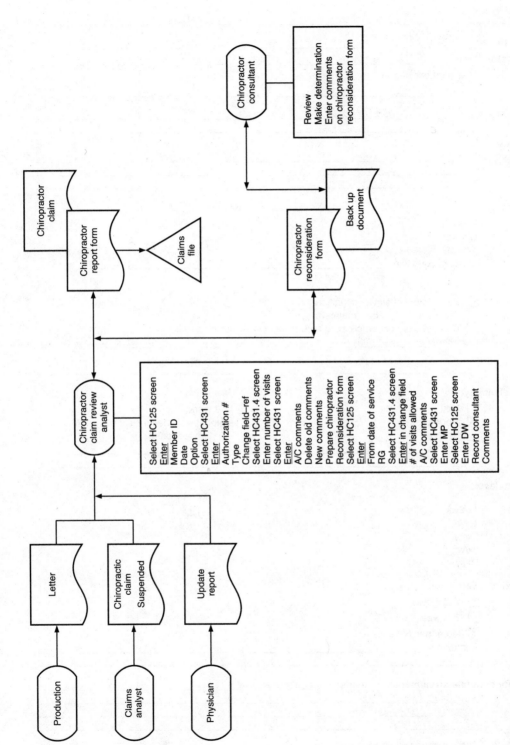

**Figure 4-10.** Claims analysis—chiropractic.

C–31          **Enter/update referral authorization**          Date 3/2/94

**Auth No.** A00943762      **Type** CH     **LOB** 20      **Reg Sci** PCP

| | | | | |
|---|---|---|---|---|
| 1. | **Subscriber** 140–38–6214 | **Mem** 01 | **M/R** | **Name** Silversmith, John |
| | **Group** 44462*01 | **SM** 04 | **Plan Com** | **Insurance** None |
| | **Age** 40 | **Sex** M | **DOB** 08–08–54 | |

**\*\*AC\*\***

| | | | |
|---|---|---|---|
| 2. | **Admission/service date** 02–24–94 | 11. | **Transportation type** |
| 3. | **Expiration date** | 12. | **Interviewer**   NAW |
| 4. | **Referred by**   55 Brown, Robert | 13. | **Int. date**   03–02–94 |
| 5. | **Prov/ref to P chir** 55 Brown, Robert | 14. | **Estimated amount**   86.00 |
| | **Vendor**   48188 Philip R. Paris | | |
| 6. | **Att. prov** | 15. | **General ledger code**   6215 |
| 7. | **Diagnosis (1)**   **MSO DA** | 16. | **Status** |
| | 723.3 Cervicobrachial syn | | |
| | 728.85 Muscle spasm | 17. | **COB (W/A/O/N)** |
| 8. | **Type of service** | 18. | **SSD waiver/concur (W/C)** |
| | | | **Waiver code** |
| 9. | **Place of service**   5   Doctor's office | 19. | **Authorize prov or vend (P/V)** V |

| | CPT code | Description | Qty | Copay | TP | AMB | AR | SSO | Benefit |
|---|---|---|---|---|---|---|---|---|---|
| 10. | C998 | Chiro limited V | 1 | 8.00 | $ | N | N | N | SCBI5 |
| | 97139 | Physical med | 0 | | | | | | Allow |
| | 97260 | Regional manipu | 2 | 16.00 | $ | N | Y | N | Used |

**Change field**    **Ref**    **F=file**    **DEL=delete**    **R=redisplay**    **O=other options**

**Figure 4-11.** Chiropractic report data sheet authorization screen.

16. Consultant enters comments on chiropractor reconsideration form.

17. Consultant forwards reviewed claims to claims review analyst.

18. Select C31.4 screen (Fig. 4-13).

19. Enter the following in change field REF (this will bring you to C31.4):

   ■ Number of visits allowed—change and save; this will return you to C31

   ■ A/C comments ("authorization was created from C41"); control E to exit A/C file

20. Select C31 screen (Fig. 4-13).

21. Enter MP—this will bring you to C12.

22. Enter DW and record consultant's remarks.

23. File claims.

24. Pull or print claims previously denied and reprocess if number of visits has been extended.

**C31.4**                    **Enter/update referral authorization**                    **Date 3/2/94**

**Auth No.** A00943762        **Type** CH      **LOB** 20        **Reg Sci** PCP

**Subscriber** 140–38–6214    **Mem** 01       **M/R**          **Name** Silversmith, John

**Group** 44462*01            **SM** 04        **Plan Com**     **Insurance** None

**Age** 40                    **Sex** M        **DOB** 08-08-54

1.  **# Visits allowed** 12   **Claimed** 4          8.  **Ref updated**              **Date**

2.  **Serv auth (S/C/O)**                            9.  **Remarks**

3.  **Date received**

4.  **Issue (UR/QA/B)**

5.  **UR/QA corresp**         **Date**

6.  **Med rel recd**          **Date**

7.  **Office rec req**        **Date**
    **Prov**
    **Remark**

**Change field**      **S=save**      **X=exit**      **R=redisplay**      **O=other options**


**C–31**

**Comments**

        **Authorization comments**



1.  **Comments**

    Don't exceed 12 OVs. Incomplete report. EFZ 3–8–94



**Change field F**        **F=file**              **R=redisplay**
                          **DEL=delete**          **P#=page**
                          **X=exit**

**Figure 4-11.** Chiropractic report data sheet authorization screen. (*Continued*)

Patient name __RICHARD JOHNSON__     Ref # __A 46253174__
Patient ID# __45 4136247__

                          **Auth** __5__     **First DOS** __9/7/93__
                          **Used** __5__      **Last paid** _____
**DX** __8460__

**Previously reviewed?** __NO__

**Doctor's name** __ROBERT BROWN__     **Phone #** __625-7645__
                      #55

**Problem:**
__Need additional visits to be authorized. Report attached__

**Response:**

**Figure 4-12.** Chiropractic reconsideration form.

C–31                    Enter/update authorizations                    Entry date: 10/7/93

**Auth No.** A 46253174         **Type** CH       **LOB** 18         **Reg Sci** PCP

1.  **Subscriber** 454136247      **Mem** 01      **M/R**            **Name** Johnson, Richard
    **Group** 444462*01          **SMU** 4                          **DOB** 06–10–48

                                     **\*\*AC\*\***

2.  **Admission/service date** 09–07–93
3.  **Expiration date**
4.  **Referred by N/P**   Non-par
5.  **Prov/ref to P chir** 55 Brown
    **Vendor**            48188 Philip R. Paris
6.  **Att. prov**
7.  **Diagnosis (1)**    **MSO DA**
    846.0 Lumbosacral sprain
8.  **Type of service**
9.  **Place of service**   3    Doctor's office

|     | **CPT code** | **Description** | **Qty** | **Copay** | **TP** | **AMB** | **AR** | **SSO** | **Benefit** |
|-----|--------------|-----------------|---------|-----------|--------|---------|--------|---------|-------------|
| 10. | 0997         | Chiro office    | 1       |           |        |         |        |         |             |
|     | 0999         | Chiro subseq    | 4       |           |        |         |        |         | Allow       |
|     | 0999         | Chiro subseq    | 0       |           |        |         |        |         | Used        |

11.   **Transportation type**
12.   **Interviewer**           SAP
13.   **Int. date**             10/07/93
14.   **Estimated amount**      0.00
15.   **General ledger code**   6215
16.   **Liability (Y/N/S/V)**   Y    Adj
17.   **Status**
18.   **COB (W/A/O/N)**
19.   **SSO waiver/concur (W/C)**
      **Waiver code**
20.   **Authorize prov or vend (P/V)** V

**Change field**    **?MP**    **F=file**    **DEL=delete**    **R=redisplay**    **O=other options**

**Warning—Procedure code 0999 is not a covered procedure— <Return>**

**Figure 4-13.** Chiropractic report data sheet authorization screen.

# Validation Tools

Two significant paths to work flow improvement can be used as validating tools after the interview and detailing processes are completed. These are the classic route and storyboarding.

## Classic Route

Experts in the field of productivity improvement vary in their approaches to improving an activity work flow. The common denominator found in the meth-

**C31.4**  **Enter/update referral authorization**  Date: 10/07/93

**Auth No.:** A46253174  **Type:** CH  **LOB:** 18  **Reg Sci PCP**

**Subscriber:** 454136247  **Mem:** 01  **M/R**

**Group:** 444462*01  **SC-MUNC**  **Plan Com**  **Insurance:** None

**Name:** Johnson, Richard  **Age:** 45  **Sex:** M  **DOB:** 6/10/48

1.  # Visits allowed  5  Claimed  5

2.  Serv auth (S/C/O)

3.  Date received

4.  Issue (UR/QA/B)

5.  UR/QA corresp  Date

6.  Med rel recd  Date

7.  Offic rec req  Date
    Prov
    Remark

8.  Ref updated  Date

9.  Remarks

Change field  REF  **S=save**  **X=exit**
  **R=redisplay**  **O=other options**

**Figure 4-13.** Chiropractic report data sheet authorization screen. (*Continued*)

ods used most often is some type of "efficiency" or "cost cutting" element. These approaches have some merit, but the most consistently successful courses of action are simple and, therefore, more reliable in achieving their desired results. This approach is deemed the *classic route*.

**Problem Identification.**  Once a problem has been identified, the ABM team member needs to determine its complexity and decide if it must be resolved immediately or if it can be deferred. The problem should be prioritized as to importance.

**Problem Description.**  The ABM staff member involved in uncovering the problem should prepare a brief description of the problem, explain its impediment to doing work, and suggest alternative solutions.

**Data Gathering.**  The ABM team member should begin gathering data, including procedures, forms, PC screen printouts, and/or written policies as to

**Comments**                              **Authorization comments**

1.  **Comments 1**
    Authorization was created from C41




2.  **Comments 2**

- •
- •
- •
- •


**Change field**          **F=file**              **R=redisplay**            **DEL=delete**
                          **P#=page**             **X=exit**

**Figure 4-13.** Chiropractic report data sheet authorization screen. (*Continued*)

how an activity should be completed. The data gathering includes talking with other staff members who perform the same work to document what they do in handling the problem that has arisen.

**Data Analysis.**    At this point, a great deal of facts have been gathered from documents and from staff members in the functional work area. Check the data for accuracy and completeness, and do not accept assumptions or opinions. Sift through the data and arrange it into meaningful groups. Some of the data collected will not be relevant, and should be discarded. Study the gathered data and begin a redesign exercise.

**Systems Requirements.**    When analyzing all the material, the ABM team must consider what kind of systems redesign will be required to support a change and whether the existing infrastructure is of sufficient size and speed. In addition, an analysis should be undertaken to determine if a mainframe or PC-based system is required by the user. User requirements should be thoroughly documented. Once the new work flow is designed, test the system—new screens, new forms, new procedures, and output reports against actual data—to be certain that it will perform as it is intended to do.

**Reengineering.**    When the reengineering has been completed and tested, present senior management with the full implementation plan—including what the original problem was, what the new alternative will accomplish, how much it will cost, what the expected return on investment will be, and how long it will take to implement.

**Implementation of Change.**    Finally the time arrives to stop all the data gathering and analysis and begin working with the newly reengineered activity. Staff members should be trained in how to process their work, and a new, detailed procedure with its associated activity work flow should be issued. Track and report the results for 6 months, and be sure to include how much of the anticipated benefits were realized and whether the original problem was eliminated. Quantify the changes in output, costs, customer service, and/or control.

In many organizations well-meaning individuals have undertaken reengineering and productivity improvement initiatives, and found out they haven't worked or achieved any benefits worth mentioning. Some initiatives actually proved to create more problems than they solved.

Changing any work routine is costly and serious business. The classic route is the best insurance a functional work area can have against failure. It works equally well for senior management and rank-and-file employees. It is the surest way to gain productivity improvement because it is thorough.

## Storyboarding

An especially effective alternative to the classic route for validating information is a technique called *storyboarding*. This approach involves all the people in a business process and/or functional work area. Activity-based costing, reengineering, and productivity improvement are the data-gathering vehicles that feed activity-based management, which provides the platform to utilize that data for meaningful decision making.

This technique is used extensively in the advertising field for creating ad campaigns and can be equally effective in assisting functional work area managers in selling productivity improvements. The methodology includes:

- Identifying activities
- Identifying tasks within activities
- Organizing and grouping activities into business processes
- Determining activity work flows
- Setting the stage for the observation process by defining where the most time is spent in performing work
- Assisting in classifying activities into value-added and non-value-added categories
- Uncovering work drivers that cause work to happen
- Educating staff members in cross-functional work area activities
- Initiating a common language to enable all staff members to more easily communicate with one another
- Replacing beliefs and opinions with objective, fact-based information
- Pictorially displaying the way work flows
- Pinpointing duplication of effort and redundancies

- Continuing and expanding the bottom-up approach with amplified work force involvement
- Reinforcing work force empowerment
- Providing a platform to decide what work should be done
- Clearly focusing the roles of suppliers, customers, and operational personnel
- Emphasizing activities that involve quality-of-work issues, such as rework and verification
- Setting the stage for the development of work-to-time relationships
- Objectively measuring costs in order to expose those activities with the highest cost
- Identifying root causes of work so management can become proactive by asking "Why are we doing these activities?"
- Organizing activities into meaningful associations, aggregating tasks into activities, and merging activities into business processes
- Assisting in transforming hierarchical structures into end-to-end processing entities
- Encouraging a new paradigm in which total quality management and continuous improvement philosophies influence the formulating of action plans to solve problems
- Training and educating the work force in understanding how their work affects their peers and the part it plays in reaching organizational goals
- Providing a strong foundation for rendering informed business decisions which meet customer needs and expectations

The data to be used in storyboarding is usually developed by functional work area staff members, with the ABM team acting as the facilitator. Each team creates storyboards displaying information about its activities and the direction in which work flows. The process focuses everyone toward a distinct, total, and measurable set of objectives.

The team also identifies a set of performance measures and gains an appreciation of how their contributions integrate into overall organizational performance. Storyboarding is a "shared experience" which fosters cooperation, promotes usage of a common language, and develops a common understanding of how all the parts working as a team can collectively improve productivity in the company.

Communication and functional work area barriers are eliminated, disorder is replaced by clarity, dissension is supplanted by agreement, and everyone shares accountability for the success or failure of the company. Storyboards are like bulletin boards, activity work flows, and procedures rolled into one. With them, the teams can visually represent data about the activities performed.

These pieces of information are enablers to help document and arrange activity information, and they serve to assist the functional work area staff members in brainstorming issues and correcting problems. Storyboards are simple, easy-to-use, and flexible tools that are well suited to demonstrating a clear understanding of how work is done and how it flows. Appreciating their value does not demand exhaustive training, and storyboards can be utilized by workers with a narrow educational background as easily as by highly trained MBAs or other extensively educated employees.

An ABM team member should lead the group process as facilitator to maintain forward progress. The facilitator's role includes encouraging and eliciting contributions from group members. The storyboarding process is as easy to begin as "once upon a time" by simply asking the question "What activities do we perform?" This basic opening should inspire functional work area members to begin identifying the work they do.

As the activities are identified, someone in the group should be assigned the task of writing the activities on index cards, and another individual should be given the responsibility of pinning the cards on the storyboard. This process is repeated until all the required activities are on the storyboards. If the interviewing process has been completed, the ABM team member can prepare the index cards from the activity dictionary.

The group can then move cards around to organize them in end-to-end process flows representing the work as it is currently performed. The cards should mirror the activity work flows completed during the "detailing process." Each index card should include the activity, a unit of measure in terms of outputs (e.g., checks applied, number of work orders), customers (internal and/or external), and work drivers (what causes the activity to commence). If reasonable expectancies have been developed, they should be included on the index card.

Once this information is organized, it can be used as the basis for setting priorities to improve productivity and develop action plans. The storyboarding technique usually has a favorable effect on a functional work area and its staff members, for several reasons:

- It engages those individuals who actually do the work, who are the most knowledgeable about the activities they perform, and who are best able to suggest improvements.

- It is a bottom-up approach that places responsibility for and ownership of the data with the operating employees, increasing the probability that they will use the data to improve the performance.

- It is a "participatory experience." All functional work area employees participate; therefore, they practice communicating and problem solving together using a common language. The interaction assists in breaking down hierarchical and functional work area, barriers creating an environment for cooperation and communication.

- It encourages customers and suppliers to work together to effectuate improvement with the greatest return.
- It is simple to learn and is an enabler that does not intimidate individuals.
- It allows each staff member to function as her or his own total quality manager, eliminating the need for specialized project teams.

Storyboarding is a fact-based process that uses activity-based information which can explain why work is done and establish performance measures to quantify how well that work is performed. It pictorially describes interactions between customers and suppliers. It can identify inputs from suppliers, which in turn helps disclose the causes of waste, and identifies the functional work area that has to be involved to eliminate that waste.

When performance measures are introduced, they can be used to establish an internal benchmark for productivity improvement to be measured against. Customers are important elements in this technique, because they are the recipients of any alterations in the content of work performed.

Activity-based management attempts to focus everyone's attention on an unimpeded, comprehensive, and quantifiable set of intentions. A focused, functional work area has all staff members working as a cohesive team. Its objectives are clearly defined so every member of the organization understands them, and they can be easily measured so everyone is aware of when (or if) they are realized. Storyboarding provides this focus for everyone. It is necessary to focus on performance measures to attain maximum improvement in the work that is done. This simple technique is a catalyst for change, since it promotes employee empowerment, accountability, responsibility, role definition, decision making, and organizational realignment.

The new paradigm for companies in today's competitive business arena is to empower their work force at all levels in order to improve productivity. Empowered staff members have a sense of proprietorship, control over what and how activities are performed, recognition for their accomplishments, and the realization that they are important to the company and to themselves. Empowerment builds self-esteem. The team approach fosters the conviction that work can be changed if individuals bury petty differences, and clearly indicates how individuals at all levels can contribute to achieving the objectives of the organization.

The "shared experience" with cross-functional colleagues, customers, suppliers, and other team members enhances the family atmosphere of being a part of an organization. The process assists in altering attitudes of "I follow orders and do what my boss tells me to do" to attitudes of empowerment. Employees now can say, "I know how my actions affect company performance, and I will share responsibility for that performance." Employees who are accountable are proactive, because they know what they do, why they do it, and how well they do it. They are fully involved in the success or failure of their company.

Storyboarding also breaks down the traditional role of a hierarchical manager who is used to making all the decisions and giving directions to staff members. These roles were appropriate when managers were the only individuals who possessed the knowledge, experience, and data to make decisions, while staff members did not have the information base to do anything but take orders.

These traditional roles change with storyboarding, because the staff member both has the required information and participates in the process. The employee can comfortably accept responsibility, participate in decision making, and develop his or her knowledge base, in addition to performing the activity. The manager's role shifts to one of coach, facilitator, and communicator for the team. The decision-making process can now be completed at any level, because the staff member has access to the information needed to make an informed decision.

The degree to which decisions can be dispersed depends on the depth of the empowerment initiative for staff members to take on responsibility for business performance and how well trained they are to accept this new role. If all the pieces are in place, the impact on the organization can be significant.

The overall quality of decisions improves because of the accuracy and completeness of the underlying data on which the decisions are based. Response time increases because the decisions are being made by those doing the work, eliminating the bureaucratic process of shuffling paper as a proposed change winds its way through the approval process.

Storyboarding offers some unexpected surprises when it pinpoints the hierarchical structure as the heart of shoddy performance. The traditional approach of organizing work into separate functional work areas constructs artificial barriers which stifle communication, increase costs, and lower quality. The reengineering and productivity improvement of activities into end-to-end processing work groups is a direct result of applying the basic storyboarding technique.

This approach to validating data gathered through the interviewing and detailing processes adds strength and support to continuous improvement and total quality management thrusts. All the participants understand how they can impact activities in order to take business performance to the next level. Each individual is accountable for her or his actions with a distinct difference from traditional management roles in that the employee is now "empowered" to succeed. The employee buy-in is real and commitment to excellence is assured when the work force takes ownership of a business process and/or activity.

The open availability and exchange of information rather than "the need to know" practices of traditional management provide a platform for improvement, because employees understand how their actions affect their peers' performance as well as the overall performance of the organization. An additional benefit is the expanded learning capacity of staff members, which in turn enhances their value to the organization.

The bottom line is that the realignment of the organization meshes with the way work is performed.

## Activity Value Analysis

Activity analysis is the method of identifying what an organization does by understanding all the processes and identifying how those processes fit into the organization's overall business strategies (Fig. 4-14).

Activity analysis decomposes a large, complex organization into processes and activities which are understandable, actionable, and relevant. A skeptic might suggest that no one will admit that his or her job is non-value added. The reality is that most staff members know what portion of their activities are unnecessary and/or redundant.

Staff members will generally volunteer ways to remove non-value-added activities and/or tasks because they would like to make their work more interesting. Activity analysis is done by the ABC/ABM team, supported by the staff member who performs the activity at any level in the organization.

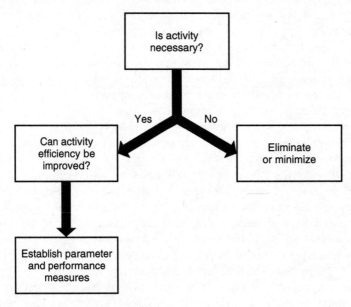

- **Value**
  Why is the activity performed?
  What is the impact of not performing?
  What alternatives exist?

- **Quality**
  What is the error/defect rate?
  How frequently do deviations occur?
  What causes errors/deviations?

- **Cycle time**
  How long does it take to perform activity?
  Are resources associated with processes/activities balanced?
  Is workload uniform?

**Figure 4-14.** Activity value analysis.

## Activity Evaluation and Assessment

Several indicators can be used in evaluating and assessing activities:

- Value-added analysis
- Non-value-added analysis
- Fixed activity assessment
- Variable activity assessment
- Activity level indicators
- Work flows and detail procedures analysis
- Performance measurements analysis
- Financial implications assessment
- Operational implications assessment

We will take a look at each of these indicators to examine their relative value to the activity analysis methodology.

**Value-Added Analysis.**   A value-added activity is defined as one that is required to produce a product or service and/or improve the process (e.g., work flow).

- Can an activity be improved (cost-justified, simplified, or reduced in scope)?
- Is the activity a world-class benchmark that cannot be improved?
- Does the work contribute to the production of the product or service?
- Does the activity create value in the customer's eye?
- Is the activity being performed somewhere else?
- Is the activity in direct support of the work area mission?

**Non-Value-Added Analysis.**   A non-value-added activity is defined as one that is not required to produce a product or service or improve the process.

- Eliminate unnecessary activities by challenging the appropriateness of the activity.
- Identify the source or work driver for non-value-added activities (e.g., result of a process breakdown).

Improvement of the overall process will minimize, reduce, or eliminate the non-value-added activity over time.

**Fixed Activity Assessment.**   A fixed activity is defined as one that cannot be changed or modified over a specified period of time and that must be done.

- Can the fixed activity be improved?
- Can the frequency of the activity be altered?

**Variable Activity Assessment.**    A variable activity fluctuates as a result of a business need, condition, or volume.

- Is there a pattern, randomness, or seasonality to the activity?
- Is there any predictable aspect to the occurrence of the activity?
- Is there any mechanism in determining where and when work will be performed?

**Activity Level Indicators.**    Analyze each activity's characteristics to determine what type of activity it is. Proceed with assessment, detection, correction, and/or prevention. The results of the analysis will show what portion of the work area process is inefficient.

**Work Flows and Detail Procedures Analysis.**    Determine redundancies, duplications, process inefficiencies, flow interruptions, system weaknesses, data sources, and the work performed and where work goes. Prepare work sequence plans.

**Performance    Measurements    Analysis.**    Define capacity (reasonable expectancies) for each activity. Compare actual volumes against planned capacity for variances (e.g., in time, volume, dollars). Compare actual performance results against reasonable expectancies.

**Financial Implications Assessment.**    Identify assignable costs to activities.

- Employee-related costs (e.g., travel, education)
- Wages and salaries
- Pensions and benefits
- Utilities (rent, heat, light, power, telephone)
- System changes
- Contractual services

Understand total costs for those activities and develop a unitized cost for one unit of volume of the activity. Also identify nonassignable costs.

**Operational Implications (Time and Staffing) Assessment.**    An operational assessment will provide work areas with the ability to adjust the work force to handle fluctuations in workload in a more precise manner rather than on intuition.

Activities can be aggregated into business processes that cut across hierarchical organizations for a common purpose, such as marketing. A business process is defined as a network of related activities linked by the output they generate.

A business process such as selling describes what gets done in a business. An activity such as making sales calls—and its related tasks (e.g., preparing a proposal)—is what the company does to accomplish the business process of selling (Fig. 4-15).

The more activities that are aggregated into a business process, the less a work driver is able to accurately trace the resources consumed by that activity. Therefore, it is important to determine the level of detail to be used in reporting resource consumption by an activity as it affects the decision-making process. In some instances, the procedure should be reversed by disaggregating the

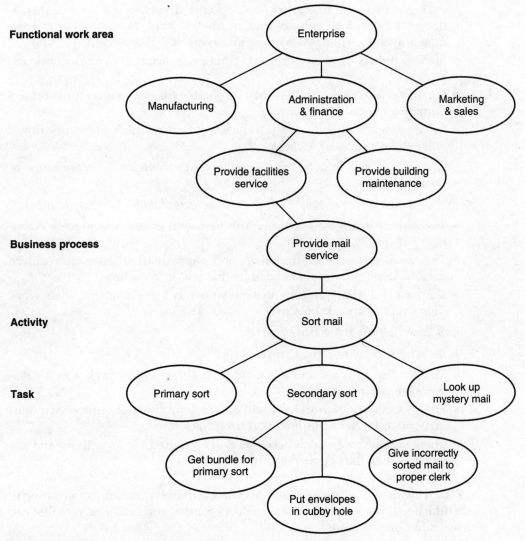

**Figure 4-15.** Activity analysis can be done at any level in the organization.

business process to determine the manner in which resources are being consumed by those activities which make up the process. Thus a receiving and shipping department may be considered one business process in a functional work area, but it may be appropriate to separate receiving and shipping in analyzing the work performed.

There are five basic questions to be asked in analyzing activities:

1. *Can I stop doing some or all of this activity?*
   - Some activities can be performed elsewhere for little or no additional cost.
   - Some activities can be eliminated for a given set of circumstances. For example, in a mail operation, look up only first-class mail that is misaddressed; discard all second- and third-class mail. Hand-deliver express mail only to functional work area managers and above.
   - Some activities can be prioritized, giving enhanced service to critical customers.
   - Quality assessment activities may be eligible for elimination if the underlying process can be improved.
   - Elimination of value-added activities, without restructuring work flows, will result in service cutbacks.

2. *Can I contract this activity less expensively, either outside the organization or within?*

3. *Can the activity itself be simplified, or can it be merged with another activity?*
   - The activity work flow diagram can be useful in revising process activities.
   - The functional organization chart and work distribution matrix can be used to identify multiple hands-offs that add to cycle time.
   - Contract and oversight activities can be reduced or eliminated when work flow simplification is effective.

4. *Can the activity be automated effectively?*

5. *Is the activity being performed productively?*
   - The activity volumes and work effort levels should be reviewed for reasonableness of output.
   - High variability of workload will decrease productivity unless activities are structured to be fill-in work during slack times.
   - There should be a match between skills required for an activity and the experience of the people performing it.

Following the initial analysis of individual activities there are organizational, interfunctional work area, and service-level comparisons and analyses that can reveal additional benefits.

## Organizational Activity Analysis

After individual activities and their work flows have been reviewed for process improvements, organization charts can be reviewed for organizational improvements.

- The activities performed by each position should use similar skill sets.
- Each activity should be performed by enough people to allow cross-training for backups.
- The activities performed by each position should have different patterns of variability to allow workload leveling.
- The time spent in managing the functional work area should be consistent with the skill levels of the group and with the complexity of the activities.

Once the organizational analysis is complete, functional work areas can be compared with one another to develop additional improvement opportunities.

- Do certain activities appear in one functional work area but not another? What are the service implications of eliminating the activity?
- Are usage factors for like activities different? What does this say about effectiveness of the functional work area? About service?
- Are differences caused by external factors (like building design), or can a change in methods improve one functional work area?
- Do the functional work areas use resources the same way?
- Are there advantages to duplicating features of functional work areas?
- Are there efficiencies that could be gained?
- Do functional work areas apply similar skill levels to similar activities?
- Does one functional work area show better efficiencies than another?
- Is progress being made in achieving objectives?
- Are improvements identified?
- Are usage factors improving, or are activities being eliminated?
- Do work driver differences explain part of the differences?
- Which activities should be studied further to reduce the effect of adverse work drivers?

Once comparative data is available, the following questions can be addressed:

- Are different service levels reflected in differing amounts of work? If not, how are additional services provided?
- Can trade-offs be made between activity and service level?

- Do differences in client requirements or attitudes give rise to different service levels? Refine service requirements to accommodate opportunities for improvement.
- Can resources be freed up for additional value-added activities?

## Sources of Comparative Data

Another source of output in the activity value analysis methodology involves best practices and competitive benchmarking. Larger organizations have a plethora of external sources to draw upon for data; smaller organizations sometimes have to be creative in obtaining comparative data.

A few potential sources of information are as follows:

- *Vendor quotes.*   Quotes are valuable to the extent that like products are in the marketplace.
- *Private survey.*   Product managers can be charged with contacting other companies that provide similar services and inquiring about sharing information and costs.
- *Trade survey.*   Trade associations often collect cost and other data (e.g., on service levels) to assist members.

Activity value analysis affords an organization and its management with several benefits:

- It provides managers with a clear view of their functional area's workload.
- It clarifies the customer/supplier relationship, including cross-functional work area dependencies leading to process management.
- It enables a review of existing processes, systems, procedures, organizational structures, and responsibilities.
- It supports the development of improvement plans.
- It provides a basis for improved planning and budgeting.
- It provides the basis for tracing costs and activity-based accounting.
- It minimizes or eliminates work by managing work drivers and non-value-added activities.
- It provides a basis for continuous improvement.
- It creates the platform for activity-based management decisions.

During the detailing process in each functional work area, several reengineering, productivity improvement, and work flow redirections become evident. The selective primary activities are worked task by task until the entire activity is completed, documented, and detailed. This thorough analysis of the activity and its associated work flow identifies redundancies, work drivers that cause work, paper-shuffling exercises, lack of appropriate information, services support, and the resulting cost objects.

A status report should be prepared, with recommendations for implementing improvements. An example of this document is presented in Appendix 4A, at the end of this chapter. In addition, a functional work area action plan for addressing the issues raised as a result of the detailing process should be developed. (See Appendix 3C for an example.)

Generally, the recommendations suggested are fresh issues and not recycled ones defined during the interview process. Only when the activity is worked in its entirety can non-value-added endeavors be seen, and discussed with the staff member performing the activity. In discussing options while working the activity, you can search for different approaches to completing an activity and educate the staff member to the merits of the total quality management/continuous improvement philosophy.

## Refinement of Work Drivers

In the interview process work drivers were superficially identified for each activity. The detailing process affords the ABM team an opportunity to more precisely identify the work driver(s) for each activity in the activity dictionary.

Work drivers cause activities to be performed and measure the frequency of activities (Fig. 4-16). Examples include:

Receipts

Production runs

Setup hours

Setups

**Figure 4-16.** Work drivers.

Applications

Repair orders

Attempts

Claims

Policy

It is crucial that a set of activities and work drivers reflect the physical activity or work that takes place in a functional work area and that they be easily recognizable by others.

ABM methodology requires that the number of work drivers correspond to the desired accuracy or complexity of the product or service mix. As the number of work drivers increases, the accuracy of product or service data increases. Products or services are considered diverse when they consume activities in different proportions, or when there is batch-size diversity. Review dollar values to determine if smaller values can be combined with larger values and not traced separately.

In practice, identifying how many work drivers to use calls for both judgment and analysis. Activity-based costing systems utilize more types of work drivers than do traditional management costing systems. Specific workload types are illustrated in Fig. 4-17.

### Selecting Work Drivers

Several factors come into play in selecting work drivers:

■ Utilize readily available data that is maintained within the organization. If data for a work driver is not easily obtainable, you can substitute another work driver. Validate the data as to accuracy, relevance, and up-to-dateness.

| Workload | Additional information |
|---|---|
| • Calls | • Call type—adjustment, inquiry |
| • Service orders | • Order type—new start, change disconnect |
| • Trouble tickets | • Reason Code—circuit dead, noise/errors |
| • Claims | • Customer—GBS, BCSv, BCSy |

**Figure 4-17.** Specific workload types.

- Correlate an activity's consumption of resources to the work driver causing the work. For example, actual inspection hours should be used instead of number of inspections if inspections vary as to time to complete.

- Carefully evaluate the work driver to make sure it induces positive behavior. People sometimes become apprehensive when they feel their performance will be evaluated in some way on the basis of a work driver.

Once a work driver has been identified, analyze it in order to associate it to the appropriate activity. An activity can have multiple work drivers, and a work driver can lead to more than one activity. Next, categorize the types of work drivers:

- Volume (e.g., trouble ticket, work order)
- Policy (local procedures and standards)
- Direct (service-specific)

Work drivers can also cause negative behavior, such as rework and checking the work of other functional areas.

### Identifying Indicators of Waste

The less time it takes to complete an activity, the greater the flexibility, the higher the quality, and the lower the cost (because elapsed time is reduced). Look for situations that force completion of nonessential activities or cause performance to fall below expectations. An organization can improve areas that matter to either internal or external consumers/customers by asking:

- What external factors cause high consumption of resources in performing an activity?
- What can be done differently?
- What causes waste of materials, time, space, or labor?
- Can performance measures for each activity be developed that indicate how each activity contributes to the overall company mission?

An organization can become more competitive and efficient by eliminating waste in operating activities, not by managing recorded costs associated with waste. An organization should consider eliminating any activity that does not contribute identifiable value to its customers (Fig. 4-18).

## Refinement of Performance Measurements

During the interview process cursory performance measurements were identified. The detailing process offers the ABM team the occasion to revalidate each activity's associated performance measurements.

- Misdirected calls
- Database discrepancies
- Order entry errors
- Amended service orders

**Figure 4-18.** Indicators of waste.

A performance measurement is defined as a quantifiable measure for the output of an activity. It describes how many times the activity was done (e.g., number of claims processed, length of a post office run, number of repair orders). In effect, performance measurements "count" the performance of an activity and how well it is performed. A prerequisite to establishing an appropriate performance measurement is understanding the factors that influence an activity. Performance measurements must be able to be expressed as or converted to a consumption of resources related to a product, service, and/or customer.

Performance measures play a prominent role in creating work-to-time relationships, as discussed in Chap. 6. Many organizations can take historical transaction volumes and convert them into what the organization is producing, but this does not address the question "What should production be?"

## Refinement of Cost Objects

The interview process identified potential cost objects. A cost object is defined as the reason for performing an activity and is the final point to which cost is traced. Examples are completed projects, completed applications, completed purchase orders, and completed service.

Cost objects can sometimes be equated to outputs of an activity and can be used as a basis for developing unit costs. The detailing process presents the ABM team with the chance to validate the cost objects preliminarily identified during the initial interview of each employee.

## Summary

The detailing process provides the ABM team with the means to thoroughly document all primary activities. The documentation becomes a procedures manual that functional work area managers can utilize in training new employees and cross-training current staff members.

Detailing provides all staff members with reference guidelines for primary activities that include forms, printouts of PC screens, and so on. The activity work flows can be used as the basis for developing an integrated work flow for a functional work area depicting redundancies, rework, and interactions between staff members and other functional work areas.

All staff members will understand where their work comes from, what causes it, and where work goes when an activity is completed. The detailing process identifies in clear and precise terms opportunities for reengineering an activity and/or process as well as validating initial impressions received during the interview process.

The staff member performing the activity that is being detailed will begin to become a believer that change can happen—that ideas for improvement will be listened to—and will buy into the program to make it a success. The detailing process is an extension of the interview process and a bridge to the continuous improvement/total quality management process discussed in the next chapter.

## Appendix 4A. Claims Detailing Status Report

---

**MEMORANDUM**

DATE:    April
TO:       Gordon Scott
FROM:  Edward Forrest
RE:       Detailing Process—Status Report—Claims Area

\*\*\*\*\*\*\*\*\*\*\*\*\*\*\*\*\*\*\*\*\*\*\*\*\*\*\*\*\*\*\*\*\*\*\*\*\*\*\*\*\*\*\*\*\*\*\*\*\*\*\*\*\*\*\*\*\*\*\*\*\*\*\*\*\*\*\*\*\*\*\*\*\*\*\*\*\*\*\*\*\*\*

We concluded all the detailing of selected primary activities for the claims department by March. The following are some of the issues we believe to be relevant to the improvement of this area. These issues are considered important to your staff and, if addressed, should increase productivity, eliminate non-value-added work, and increase throughput.

We now better understand the significance of these findings as we went through the step-by-step performance of these activities during the detailing phase of the program. We will continue our efforts and keep you abreast of developments as they surface.

---

**Executive Summary**

We have found an alternative source to complete the typing of activity work flows. We have completed the detailing of selected primary activities in customer service and enrollment services. We have completed the typing and sign-off of the health services detailing, and as soon as all the corresponding individual activity work flows are typed, we will distribute the entire health services detailing package. We will then attempt to prepare an integrated activity work flow for health services as an entire functional work area.

Claims detailing procedures are either in typing or in final review, and immediately after sign-off, the corresponding individual activity work flows will be created.

1. *Claims Analysis*
   a. *PCP Par Referral.* When entering data from a claim into the system, the data element identification on the claim form (i.e., authorized date) differs from the terminology on the screen (i.e., admit date/DOS). We should use uniform terminology on forms and in the system. There are several of these inconsistencies throughout the company. When diagnosis code is missing, the analyst looks in the system for a diagnosis code, and in some cases it isn't in the system. He or she must then go to a diagnosis list to find one. This slows the process. All diagnosis codes should be in the system, not on various lists. Procedure codes follow a similar time-consuming process. Recommend that all procedure codes be loaded in the system instead of manually looking them up.
   b. *New Referrals.* If a referral doesn't go to health services, it ends up in claims, where it is entered. If there isn't a referral entered in the system, a claim will be paid as a major medical claim instead of paying regular fees. This process can create additional work when the referral arrives later, resulting in double processing. A reversal is required which is done by a team leader, who forwards the claim to an analyst who reenters the claim. The reentry process could result in an overpayment letter, adjustment, and so on. This all comes about because of timing differences in entering referrals and claims, and because two separate areas are completing a part of the process.

      The recommendation is to have referrals come in from the specialists, not the PCP, and entered by claims all at once with the claim in one area.
   c. *Claims Letter Generation.* Most letters should be automatically generated by entering a code into the system rather than manually filling in a claims letter request form and forwarding it to a secretary for typing.
   d. *Provider Data.* Add a field for the system to capture a physician's license number so an analyst can locate a physician if a tax ID number is not on incoming documents.
   e. *Reconsideration of Benefits.* Currently, when a par physician requests more money, we enter the request like it is a new claim, suspend the claim, prepare a reconsideration of benefits form, and forward it to the director of claims for disposition. In almost all cases, the physician

receives a letter stating that we are not granting him or her more money. We recommend eliminating the processing time and paper shuffling and automatically sending the letter.

f. *Psychiatric Nonpar Claims.* Currently, the control of these psychiatric claims is not complete. They are assigned to an analyst in batches. The analyst signs out for specific claims by number. The claims are handled by the analyst and then turned over to a team leader to review them with a medical consultant. Claims find their way back to the file room. No one knows where the claims are after they leave the analyst.

We recommend that the claims analyst return the batch and sign in the batch as being returned. Batch control can check that all the claims in the batch are returned. Batch control can then have a team leader go through the same control procedure. This process would minimize lost documents and there would be specific accountability for claims throughout their life cycle.

g. Currently, the claims area enters nonpar providers into the system and provider relations enters par providers into the system. This creates inconsistencies and erroneous entries, which causes multiple vendor numbers and therefore multiple checks when paying claims.

We recommend that all providers, whether they be par or nonpar, be entered by provider relations. One functional work area should complete the process. This would result in uniformity, fewer errors, fewer vendor codes, and increased productivity.

2. *Customer Service Inquiry—Contact Sheets, Members.* Claims service reviews member/provider inquiries which originate as a telephone call or letter. Many of these arise because a claims analyst wasn't thorough in the initial review in his or her haste to make the expected production numbers for the day. We recommend that the service area just make a determination and complete the process. We waste time pulling claims, copying claims, and preparing a quality review form, all as non-value-added work.

If claims service determines an analyst made an error, place that error in the quality statistics for the original claims analyst handling the claim. You can set a dollar limit that any claim under $100 should just be corrected.

The claims service reviewer should update "D" word with the corresponding error code, original claim number, new contact sheet number, original claims analyst's initials, and the system should automatically produce a weekly report for training's review.

We recommend the elimination of the quality review process. System enhancement should allow the customer service representative to research and make spot corrections while on the telephone. If the inquiry results in a change, the claim must be reprocessed for a second time, instead of just correcting the incorrect fields. This is another instance of doing double work.

3. *Customer Service Inquiry—Provider Issue Forms*
   a. *25 Suspends.* The system should automatically generate 25 statistical reports, instead of provider relations preparing manual statistics, and eliminate copying of claims. Currently this type of suspend moves from

customer service to provider relations to claims service, back to provider relations and back to customer service to telephone the physician. We recommend that the paper shuffling end. Have provider relations make the calls to the physician instead of customer service.

b. The company can save money by making the provider issue form a three-part form instead of a four-part form. The company can save additional money by combining the provider issue form and contact sheet form into one, with a box to check as to the source of the inquiry.

c. *27 Suspends.* The system should automatically generate the 27 reports, so copying of claims can be avoided.

4. *Claims Routing.* Each claims analyst signs out a batch of work but never signs it back in when completed. We recommend that each analyst return completed batches back to the sign-out control desk. Furthermore, a control log should be kept including sign-out time, sign-in time, and elapsed minutes.

5. *Claims Production Statistics*

a. Several claims analysts take work home to work on during the evening, using a modem and PC. A study should be made comparing each analyst's units processed per production hour in the evening at home to the unit per production hour during the day.

We recommend having the PC equipped, at home as well as in the office, to have a log-on time and a log-off time with a unit accumulator. In addition, the system should time out if a minute goes by without any work being performed. If the system times off, the analyst must log on again. This eliminates the PC being left on without any tangible work being performed, and would provide a better statistical base of work performed and time to process each type of claim.

6. *Team Leader Authorization.* Currently team leaders are the only people allowed to make high-level authorizations, which consist of approximately 50 claims per week being handled per team leader. We recommend giving the claims analyst line 5 access capacity in the authorization screen so they can handle these type transactions.

The team leader codes the lines and adjudicates the claim. Then the team leader suspends the claim back to the analyst to approve the claim. We recommend that the complete process be completed by the analyst. We would eliminate paper shuffling and multiple handling, and increase the response time in processing this type of claim. These types of claims usually involve another PCP, not the member PCP, or a member not being covered at the date of service because he or she was disenrolled.

The analyst enters the claim, the system indicates a warning, the claim is suspended after being fully entered, is sent to a team leader, and finally goes back to the analyst. All this is non-value-added handling.

7. *Production—Mail Sort and Julianne Numbering Date Stamp.* Currently, production sorts the incoming mail during the day and date-stamps the mail. Several documents are numbered when they shouldn't be; other docu-

ments aren't numbered when they should be, requiring manual preparation of the daily claims numbered form in claims.

This manual operation could be reduced by having the mail room sort the mail by line of business and then have claims personnel date-stamp the mail. There are clerks available in the claims area who could handle the work, and who understand what documents should be numbered.

8. *Claims Analysis—Podiatry*

    a. The podiatry specialist currently reviews claims that an analyst has already completed work on, and redoes the work the analyst did. This double work is done so the reviewing analyst doesn't receive a quality demerit if the claim is processed with an error. We recommend that the review analyst just make the specific change and process the claim, eliminating the double effort. If there is an error, it belongs to the original analyst who suspended the claim. An alternative approach is to have the original analyst trained to complete the process. A third alternative is to simply give these claims to the podiatry consultant for review and determination and then have an analyst process the claim.

    b. Currently, the podiatry claims analyst reviewer manually prepares a denied savings report. We recommend that the system automatically generate a denied savings report and an overpay report. The analyst could enter a special code that the system utilizes to produce the statistics. The actual savings of claims dollars is an excellent performance measure.

9. *Claims Specialists.* If the appropriate data elements were contained in a relational, table-driven database, there wouldn't be a need for specialists. All analysts could process any type of claim.

10. *Reconsideration of Fees.* Currently the reconsideration-of-fees analyst does all the research and preparation when a CPT code and/or fee is not in the system, but must forward all the material to business operations to enter a fee into the system. We recommend that the complete process be done in one place—either business operations or claims. This would eliminate the paper shuffling and speed up the process of entering missing CPT codes and fees. It should also improve accuracy and place accountability with responsibility.

11. *Claims Review—Date Entry.* Currently, all the preparation and research work is completed by a claims team leader, who sends the claim to claims review, which reviews all the same material. We recommend elimination of the duplication of work and paper shuffling. One area should complete the entire process. This would reduce the response time to members, enhance customer service, and link accountability with responsibility.

12. *Claims Analysis—Employees/Hospital-Inpatient*

    a. We recommend that the system contain fee tables for each hospital. The tables are accessed by entering the appropriate CPT code, and the system would automatically populate the dollars in the authorization screen on the maximum amount line.

    b. Main Street Hospital doesn't have a DRG code for a burn so the analyst must do a manual calculation to arrive at a fee. We recommend an adjustment in the system logic that would direct the DRG calculation used in the screen methodology to be automatically calculated and to populate the calculated dollars in the screen on the maximum amount line.

c. Anesthesiology calculations are predominantly manual. We recommend that all provider groups have negotiated discounts rather than the manual unit accumulator base. Load all contact discounts in the system. Customary fees can also be loaded into the system, and if the calculated fee exceeded the customary fee by some set percentage, the system would kick out the claim, flash a warning, and so on. This would eliminate some suspends because no manual calculation would have to be completed before finishing the processing of the claim.

d. We recommend that employee claims be handled by a select number of people for confidentiality reasons, perhaps even by human resources. A special PO box number to which employee claims mail is sent to be segregated would be effective. At the back end, a separate file cabinet containing employee claims organized alphabetically by employee would add to the privacy of an employee. An alternative would be to outsource employee claims.

13. *Claims Analysis—Anesthesiology.* Currently, the anesthesiology analyst is checking data as if she was entering the claim for the first time. This is double non-value-added work. We recommend that the rechecking steps be eliminated and that only the calculation-of-fees process be completed until full automation is possible. This would allow the analyst to do other work, improve customer response time, and place accountability for errors on the entering of data.

14. *Claims Analysis—COB Dual Coverage*

a. Currently, the COB review analyst goes through all the steps to enter a COB claim just like the original analyst who handled the claim. Then the review analyst prepares a claims-to-print-or-pull form, claims are pulled or screens printed, a new document number is requested from the claims routing desk, and then a second claim is processed all over again.

   We recommend the elimination of the double non-value-added work by the COB review analyst just to avoid being given a demerit if something was entered in error. The review analyst should make only the correction needed and process the claim.

b. The dual coverage aspect and the processing of a second claim can be eliminated by using the copay par process, under which a code is entered to pay $8.00; print under a new member number and new document number. The system then populates the member profile, with the vendor receiving $46.00 and the member $8.00.

   In place of reentering data, change line 25 of the screen from $46.00 to $8.00, enter subscriber number and document number, and automatically process. The system currently has the ability to give $8.00 to the family and $46.00 to the vendor under the copay par process. This process should be adopted for dual coverage COB claims.

This adjustment would have an analyst process a COB claim once, eliminating all other manual interventions.

15. *Claims Analysis—Chiropractor*

   a. Chiropractor claims which are suspended by an analyst go to a review analyst, who researches the claim as if it was never entered and suspends the claim back to the analyst.

   We recommend that the review analyst complete the claim to eliminate the paper shuffling and speed up the response to the member. We also suggest that all analysts, not just a specialist, handle their own chiropractor claims. Alternatively, the flow of claims might be rerouted to initially go to the medical consultant for determination and then directly into the system by an analyst.

   b. If 25 visits have been authorized, why require a report for every 5 visits? The system should keep track of the visits and produce a report when the maximum number of authorized visits has been reached. Just attaching reports to a claim and going through the procedure is non-value-added in most cases. If the medical consultant initially reviews the case and decides on the appropriate number of visits, the process is complete.

   c. The system currently enters chiropractor claim comments twice in "D" word and in authorization comments. Eliminate the duplication of work by entering the comments once in authorization comments and have the system populate "D" word for customer service utilization. An alternative is to notify customer service to access authorization comments only and use only one comments section for everyone in the company.

16. *Claims Analysis—HMO Hospital*

   a. We recommend that a PCP attach a filled-in referral form to the associated claim form so it can be data-entered. If data is missing, deny the claim and send it back to the physician for completion. Providers should be instructed to enter their provider number on all claims, eliminating look-up time by an analyst.

   b. We recommend redesign of a four-part form that combines the referral form with the primary care service and billing form. Provide a box at the bottom of the form to check if it is a referral, and to insert specialist name and specialist ID number.

   c. The claims entry screen should be a mirror image of the claims form, and the system would populate all other screens. This would facilitate entry.

17. *Claims Analysis—PCP*

   a. Currently, the PCP sends in a referral to health services, which performs several clerical activities, including a data entry function. We recommend that the PCP forward the referral with all the PCP data filled in to the specialist. The specialist fills in the specialist data and forwards both the referral form and the claims form into claims. The claims analyst enters all data at one time in one place without a timing difference for entering a referral and a claim.

This would eliminate non-value-added work, including contact sheet preparation, telephone calls, customer service involvement. If the package comes in with missing data, the claim should be denied and sent back to the physician and his holdback reduced for extra administrative handling. Currently, health services use nurses to call the physician for missing data.

    *b.* We recommend adding the patient's ID number box to the PCP claims form, the primary care service and billing form, and the referral form.

    *c.* There are universal codes: 11 = physician's office for place of service, while the company uses its code 3 = physician's office for place of service. We recommend adopting one set of codes. In addition, physicians should be educated to use company forms, not their own, to speed up the handling of their claims. Conversely, the company's forms could be changed to look like universal billing forms.

18. *Claims Analysis—Preexisting Condition.* Currently, enrollment services places a flag in the system for each new member who has a waiting period. The flag causes all claims to be suspended. Health services is supposed to have the capability to remove these flags but is unable to because of a system problem. Therefore, claims for members who do not have preexisting conditions are suspended and require additional non-value-added handling. The dollar values in many instances aren't worth the administrative work and cost.

    We recommend that a table-driven list of high-priced conditions be created and any claims for these items for members with waiting periods be caught by the system. All other items should be processed. The health history questionnaire process should be either totally dropped or, if deemed important, made part of the enrollment and reenrollment process up front.

19. *Claims Analysis—Physical Therapy.* We recommend that the system monitor the number of visits used versus the number authorized, and when the limit is attained a warning should be displayed alerting the analyst that the claim cannot be paid.

20. *Claims Review—Appeals.* We recommend that entries into "D" word should not be able to be deleted. This would eliminate copying entries in the claims review log. Currently, the team leaders receive the claims review forms from the claims review group just to do a data entry function. We recommend the complete process be completed by claims review, including the data entry, or by the team leader who already did most of the work.

21. *Investigation Returned Check*

    *a.* Currently, the company goes through a great deal of paperwork, in preparing letters to get money back from physicians. We recommend the elimination of this non-value-added work and charging back the physician's holdback immediately for par physicians. For nonpar physicians, go after collection immediately.

    *b.* There is a physician in the system for which there is an arrangement to pay 80 percent of his fees. The system automatically calculates the fee.

Create a table for other physicians and contract with them for similar discounts and handling.

22. *Hospital Claims—Blue Cross.* The company currently goes through several manual procedures to determine if it pays certain bills or Blue Cross pays the bill. We recommend that the claims analyst be able to enter a service code so that the system determines whether the company or Blue Cross pays the bill. This can be accomplished by loading hospital coverage tables. In addition, when the analyst enters a service code, the place of service code is entered as well. The system automatically generates a hospital EOB. This would eliminate letters, labeling, stapling, stuffing, and mailing costs for the majority of these claims.

23. *Letter Request Review.* Currently, the company has an individual checking the work done by an analyst who prepared a letter request. We recommend the elimination of this double non-value-added work. The analyst who prepares a letter should have his or her name on the letter request form.

24. *Claims—Quality Review*
    a. Quality review has determined that suspended claims are a very high percentage of total claims processed with the data entry clerks. We recommend that data entry be eliminated for most claims and the analyst be allowed to do the complete process. This would end the double work created by the high percentage of suspends, therefore increasing throughput.
    b. We recommend the automation of claims review statistics. Currently, a page in a ledger book is prepared manually for each team, and the data is then entered into a PC to calculate a percentage of accuracy. This is time-consuming.

25. *COB Questionnaire/Investigation.* Currently the COB investigation unit sends a letter to members asking them to fill in a questionnaire. We recommend that enrollment include the COB questionnaire in each new member enrollment process package. This would ensure that the member's phone number, social security number, address, and COB indication get entered into the system. The capturing of this data up front will eliminate calls by customer service to members requesting missing information and the suspension of claims. The COB mailing dispersed 16,000 letters and received 3500 responses. The up-front approach should also enhance the number of responses received.

26. *COB Recoveries*
    a. This screen currently indicates three pieces of data. We recommend that the system contain individual insurance company data to populate this screen and report when needed. It would eliminate wasted time going to telephone books, rolodexes, and so on.
    b. The insurance report screen isn't currently used. We recommend the usage of this screen and a report to monitor COB recoveries. The report should be by the insurance company, member within the insurance company, total dollar amount to be recovered, dollar amount actually recovered, balance still to be recovered, and an aging of the balance.

27. *Miscellaneous.* The data entry function in claims doesn't appear to be harvesting the benefits initially expected. The percentage of suspends is still high according to the quality audit group, resulting in multiple handling of the same claim. We recommend eliminating the data entry thrust, and using only analysts who are responsible for their own work from beginning to end.

We will continue to proceed with the detailing activities process and recommend other immediate productivity improvements. The items discussed in this report should be implemented now and do not require further research.

# 5

# Continuous Improvement/ Total Quality Management

## Introduction

The aim of total quality management (TQM) and continuous improvement is to create and sustain a customer-oriented culture of high performance throughout an organization. Achieving such a culture is a complicated and difficult process. Success, however, can provide any producer of goods and/or services with a powerful, sustainable competitive advantage. TQM and continuous improvement are options that should be evaluated seriously by every organization and adopted immediately. Both of these disciplines are a set of guiding principles as well as a philosophy for improving an organization. These two approaches integrate fundamental management techniques, pro-

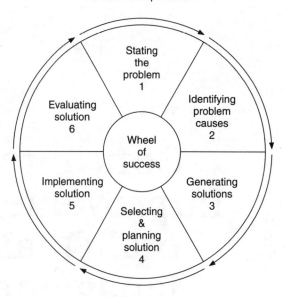

**Figure 5-1.** The wheel of success.

ductivity improvement efforts, and technical applications under a disciplined structure (Fig. 5-1).

The United States economy has been besieged by serious concerns that threaten the foundation of its existence. Our need to reverse the trade deficit, our overpowering budget deficit, and continued erosion of our preeminent standing in technological and economic fields have focused our attention on and made it increasingly important to change our method of doing business.

In the 1980s, we became preoccupied with quick-fix solutions—mergers—and we concentrated our efforts on short-term profits. We ignored our customers, overlooked the quality of our products, and employed various gimmicks to generate sales, profits, and increased market share. Businesses looked upon quality as an unnecessary cost and disregarded the contributions of their workers to productivity improvement. The result was loss of pride in work, abandonment of a proper work ethic, indifference to product quality, increased leisure time, and adoption of a "not my job" mentality.

Management and the rank-and-file worker grew to distrust each other, resulting in finger-pointing and hidden agendas. Bureaucracy reared its ugly head, which caused increased administrative costs in order to install intricate controls so everyone could check everyone else and pass off blame when something went badly. We spent precious little time training our managers to lead; failed to educate, motivate, and train our employees to be productive; and set up roadblocks that prevented workers from contributing to the full extent of their abilities.

Our management style emphasized damage control with intricate methods and procedures to measure failure. The result was an attitude of seeing how much one could get away with rather than a system that focused on incentives for success and rewarding people on the basis of achievement. In organizations where quality practices were tolerated, such practices were geared to stopping defective products after they were manufactured. This left a road strewn with inefficiency, increased costs, waste, repair, and rework.

The vision was blurred so management couldn't see the pluses of building quality into every activity from design through distribution. The placing of inspection teams at the end of a process was too little too late, and the adherence to faulty requirements resulted in poor-quality goods and services. Businesses have finally come to realize they must blend resources, people, and environment to add value to each activity involved in producing a product or service.

The utilization of inspectors will not vanish. They will now be strategically placed and the emphasis of their role will change. The quality-focused inspector will concentrate on the "how to" requirements, monitoring the controls of activities and ensuring that the end product or service meets performance and customer requirements. Emphasis must change from relying on inspection to designing and building quality into up-front processes that positively affect product quality.

TQM concepts were pioneered by such visionaries as Deming, Juran, and Friegenbaum and employs not just statistically based problem-solving techniques, but the more modern approaches of Ishikawa, Taguchi, and others. The active idea behind TQM is continuous process improvement. This belief enlists everyone in an organization from the presidents, vice-presidents, directors, and managers to the workers in a totally integrated effort to improve performance, and therefore productivity, for every process and activity at every level in the organization.

The transcendent focus of business to process improvement has increased customer user satisfaction whether that customer be external and/or internal to the organization. It isn't by accident that businesses seek out their customer's views in developing their process activity improvement methodology.

TQM should be directed toward awakening the creativity of every manager and worker to continuously improve the quality of their activities. This is accomplished by encouraging new concepts and approaches to better manage and by developing and implementing change, whether it be cultural and/or procedural.

Several American corporations have already embarked on the TQM path, and are not doing it for unknown reasons. Many have been burned by heavy rework costs, customer complaints, and return of merchandise—in addition to increased competition and price sensitivity that threaten the very existence of their business. They have come to recognize that quality resulting from continuous improvement retransmits into reduced costs, increased employee morale and productivity, customer satisfaction, and increased shareowner value. TQM should not be considered just another fad or program.

TQM—in conjunction with reengineering, productivity improvement, and activity-based costing/management—is a collective manifestation based on the premise that these practices are a never-ending process. This means that senior management must focus on the organization's culture, business processes, and activities in totality, including administrative support and functions.

The bottom line is that an organization can't tread water. Either quality is improving or it is deteriorating, and there isn't any gray middleground. The objective of TQM and continuous improvement is to alter the idea that quality means *correcting* defects to one of *preventing* defects by strictly conforming to appropriately defined user/customer requirements.

Important ingredients in TQM are the commitment of management and the effectiveness of its leadership in reaching the goal of total customer/user satisfaction. It is important to emphasize that total adherence to an incorrect user requirement will result in a consummate inferior product or service. TQM is an evolving process which cannot be accomplished overnight, because it involves retraining, rethinking, and redirecting of a work force. It involves the teaching of a new habit.

Once TQM is embraced, it can remove communication barriers, provide objective information about cost and performance, clearly show everyone in an organization how he or she contributes to the organization's process goals, provide an opportunity for employees to accept financial responsibility for the success of the organization, and foster fact-based decisions about improvement priorities.

An organization should disseminate a "corporate level" policy statement that attaches the highest priority to the principles of TQM. The policy statement should be supported by a TQM implementation plan that establishes persistent and long-range goals, and identifies norms for implementing TQM. Every employee regardless of level participates in the implementation and has a defined role in executing the plan.

## Establishing a Continuous Improvement/Total Quality Management Program

Total quality management establishes a framework for managing business processes to meet customer requirements. Through executive guidance, interpretation, and employee feedback, an organization is able to continually improve service and process quality so that it meets the expectations of both internal and external customers. There are several "articles of command" which communicate the critical characteristics desired in all managers to achieve a cultural change in an organization.

Businesses should design and continuously improve their work processes to deliver quality products and/or service to customers. Establishing a program of this type provides senior management with a comprehensive way to improve quality by examining the way work gets done in a systematic, integrated, consistent, organization-wide perspective.

Businesses should also adopt a "responsive prevention approach" to the management of data and information—whether it be customer data, internal operations and process data, competitive benchmark data, supplier quality data, or overall quality results. The data should be examined and reexamined to evaluate its support of the organization's key quality leadership objectives:

- Reducing defects and rework
- Reducing cycle time
- Managing the business by process and activity

Human resources should assist by attracting, developing, motivating, and retaining high-performance teams and individuals, and by coupling individual needs and expectations with organizational needs and expectations.

The bottom line—the reason we exist—is to meet and exceed customer expectations, to *not only satisfy but delight our customers*, external as well as internal.

We must know our current and future customer requirements and expectations, and cross-compare them with other key data such as customer complaints, losses and gains of customers, and performance data that may yield information on customer requirements and expectations relating to key products or services. Continuous process improvement is the key to performance improvement and should be pursued with all the resources required to achieve its implementation. We should endeavor to improve processes from within rather than wait for complaints and/or demands from internal or external users.

Begin the process of establishing a continuous improvement TQM implementation with these initial steps:

- Become acutely aware of the principles, practices, techniques, and tools associated with TQM.
- Obtain TQM-related training for key personnel and their subordinates.
- Open a dialogue with suppliers and customers to encourage self-initiation of a TQM effort.
- Examine the programs and processes associated with the activity, and identify ways to improve them using TQM principles.
- Establish process improvement teams within functional work areas and supplier organizations to pursue improvements aimed at increasing customer satisfaction, improving performance, reducing cycle time, and reducing cost.
- Ensure that the TQM implementation efforts encompass improving the processes that involve knowledgeable workers, including management, technical staff, and other specialty personnel.
- Begin TQM organizational planning.

- Identify for functional work area managers and senior executives involved in the program those suppliers and customers that are qualified and receptive to the intensive application of TQM principles.

- Enable employees to become the driving force for improvements (i.e., bottom-up approach).

- Involve suppliers in the improvement process as responsive partners, not as adversaries.

Knowledge of the customer's needs and expectations (internal and external) is a prerequisite to satisfying them. If product or service specifications do not properly define customer requirements, blind adherence to specifications can easily become counterproductive.

Responsibility for ensuring that customer requirements are thoroughly understood rests with both the customer and the supplier. The earlier in the process this is done, the more cost-effective and efficient upstream business processes will be. The quality payoff is maximized when both customer and supplier requirements are considered during the early phases of the development of a product or service. It is at this time that many problems can be prevented.

Thereafter, the leverage of prevention is reduced as correction of problems— a more costly procedure—becomes the dominant mode. Much of the high cost of poor quality comes from business processes that are allowed to be wasteful. Waste can be defined as any activity that does not add value to the product or service. Waste is often chronic and is accepted as a normal cost of doing business. The traditional approach to continuous improvement and quality improvement is not to get rid of chronic waste, but to prevent things from getting worse by "putting out the fires" or enlisting more people to do the job.

Chronic waste of time and resources can be driven out of a business process by implementing a continuous improvement/total quality management program.

The Japanese place a high priority on continuous, incremental process improvements (called *kaizen*) that, over time, leapfrog the competitors who depend solely on the "Hail Mary touchdown pass." By practicing continuous improvement, functional work area managers demonstrate leadership and commitment to quality. Additionally, the rank-and-file worker, supported by functional work area managers, becomes the major resource for business process improvement. The "articles of command" provide functional work area managers with the framework for ensuring the success of a continuous improvement program.

## Articles of Command

1. *Revitalizing and Authorizing Others.*   The capacity to create and convey a vision in a way that strengthens staff members and provides employees with responsibility and accountability to implement business strategies.

2. *Framing and Guiding Teams.* The capacity to organize, gain the buy-in from, and manage dissimilar functional work groups to achieve specific functional work area and/or business process objectives.

3. *Interpersonal Elasticity.* The capacity to accommodate varying people's behavior in different situations, while acknowledging and addressing hierarchical, political, and interpersonal sensitivities.

4. *Designing and Executing.* The capacity to forecast functional work area and/or business process resource needs and then create a plan which prioritizes and focuses activities to meet your customer needs.

5. *Implementation.* The capacity to perceive what determinations must be made and to execute multiple implementation plans simultaneously in a quick-paced, unstructured, and changing environment.

6. *Widespread Comprehension.* The capacity to critically assess data and to forecast and comprehend the potential outcomes of judgments and actions on functional work areas and/or business processes and their people.

7. *Business Acumen.* The capacity to comprehend both the technical nature of your business and its competition, while utilizing that acumen to satisfy customer requirements.

8. *Bottom-Line Focus.* The capacity to attain business goals while concentrating on quality, customer satisfaction, and profitability.

9. *Constructing Information Highways.* The capacity to identify and secure necessary information by requesting the appropriate data and effectively transforming the data into usable information that is accessible by many people in different locations.

10. *Persuading Others.* The capacity to verbally and through writing communicate and influence individuals and functional work areas.

## Revitalizing and Authorizing Others

- Establish and communicate the functional work area mission in a manner that awakens and stimulates an employee's imagination.
- Provide employees with a high level of accountability and responsibility for attaining goals.
- Identify and utilize any specialized skills an employee possesses.
- Establish a career development path for all employees, and facilitate their pursuit of their personal goals.
- Create an environment of mutual trust and support.
- Provide real-time objective feedback to employees, and recognize outstanding accomplishments immediately.
- Reinforce employees' self-esteem by frequently telling them how important they are for the functional work area's success.

- Listen to employees' thoughts and/or concerns and address them promptly.
- Administer company policy consistently and fairly with staff members regardless of their rank.
- Demonstrate energetic drive and leadership qualities to attain a high level of performance.
- Institute lofty expectations and performance measures for everyone.

## Framing and Guiding Teams

- Convey team goals in a manner that builds a strong sense of ownership by team members of the goals to be attained.
- Direct and stimulate team members, keeping them focused on the shared goals of the team.
- Foster and facilitate team member contributions regardless of hierarchical rank.
- Monitor signs of overwork, burnout, and mental blocks in the team and take corrective action to relieve tension.
- Identify, recognize, and reward team performance, and compliment individual successes as helping to facilitate the team's achievements.
- Diffuse intragroup discord by surfacing conflicts and effectively negotiating win-win solutions.
- Nourish a sense of togetherness and a high level of morale within the team so that members' energies and skills are centered on team execution.

## Interpersonal Elasticity

- Recognize and utilize distinctive team member strengths and interests.
- Comprehend each team member's effect on other members' incentives, attitudes, and actions in order to blend the best characteristics of each into a high-performing team.
- Accommodate varying management styles to accomplish the goals of the team and of the employees who participate in making the team a success.
- Promote, embrace, and utilize all suggestions from all sources without looking for hidden meanings or agendas of the contributor.
- Uphold a team member's self-esteem when providing feedback.

## Designing and Executing

- Assign people, equipment, and capital resources to an activity on the basis of need.
- Blend divergent points of view into an alliance of shared goals and objectives.

- Anticipate events outside your immediate control and responsibility which may impact your team's performance and/or timeliness of deliverables.
- Identify appropriate stakeholders and secure their buy-in.
- Persistently communicate with stakeholders to ensure their continued commitment and support.
- Alter program key events if required in order to attain established goals.
- Prepare and distribute to stakeholders regular status reports acknowledging each key event and its progress to date.

## Implementation

- Anticipate potential reactions and consequences from customers and/or stakeholders that could surface as a result of a particular decision.
- Establish structure and order in an indistinct or chaotic environment to be able to make competent decisions.
- Encourage educated risk taking when appropriate.
- Cultivate alternative courses of action that could result as an outcome of a significant decision.
- Shoulder responsibility for a dilemma created by the decisions taken on the basis of the best available data at a given time.
- Visualize several approaches to solving a given problem.

## Widespread Comprehension

- Recognize how pieces of the puzzle or of an issue interrelate. Do not lose sight of the "big picture" or team objective.
- Integrate various sources of pertinent information to paint a distinctive picture of a discrete problem.
- Secure information about a functional work area and/or business process and attempt to build a common language so that communication and interrelationships between organizational units can be established.
- Employ data about the complete universe and its markets as a basis for making significant decisions.
- Energetically question existing assumptions, using the latest data relevant to a changing environment, to be sure that modifying any situation does not alter established priorities.
- Perceive future urgencies in order to be able to shift priorities when appropriate in response to new information that could change results.
- Show evidence of continuous and insatiable intellectual curiosity.

## Business Acumen

- Possess a functional understanding of the industry involved.

- Comprehend and routinely track key business indicators.

- Decipher, analyze, and draw inferences from business data in order to make informed decisions.

- Critically evaluate customer and supplier implications of technical advances within the industry.

- Identify and track the competition.

## Bottom-Line Focus

- Construct an implementation cooperative that includes peers, subordinates, senior management, suppliers, and customers. The customers can be both internal and external.

- Accentuate both short- and long-term business goals.

- Demonstrate an inveterate and strong focus on quality and productivity.

- Foresee and satisfy customer requirements.

- Identify and capitalize on business opportunities when they present themselves.

- Create suitable schemes for attaining targeted bottom-line results, and monitor progress toward meeting those goals and objectives.

## Constructing Information Highways

- Encourage and facilitate information flow across hierarchical organizational units.

- Investigate alternative sources of information both within and outside the organization.

- Establish and sustain a wide web of information sources.

- Do not be afraid to share information.

- Solicit additional information by asking open-ended questions.

- Motivate and encourage others to seek out information and effectively utilize a variety of sources of information to make informed decisions.

- Earn the trust of colleagues across functional work areas and business processes through a free exchange of information.

## Persuading Others

- Tailor the terminology of the communication to the audience so the message can be comprehended by divergent groups.

- Be sensitive to sentiments of the audience and tailor communications to accommodate them.

- Influence others on why a certain piece of information is relevant and significant.

- Paint recognizable images that capture the audience's imagination.

- Portray a true and direct course in conveying a message to the audience.

- Involve audience members by helping them identify with the subject matter involved.

- Emphasize to others that positive possibilities exist, even in the midst of seemingly negative circumstances.

- Portray a very positive image of the organization when representing it externally.

## The Continuous Improvement Philosophy

Activity-based costing (ABC) provides the critical information that is necessary to support a total quality/continuous improvement approach in an activity-based management (ABM) program. An organization should solicit comments, criticisms, and complaints from its customers, suppliers, and employees and be prepared to implement their suggestions.

The ABM team should communicate corporate objectives to all company personnel so that each employee understands the importance of the mission and receives regular feedback from them on how the ABM program is progressing. A functioning continuous improvement program allows managers to pinpoint operational changes and resource requirements, and provides the platform for choosing alternative courses of action to keep costs to a minimum without compromising quality. It enables managers to achieve the following objectives:

- Design services or products with common components that meet customer requirements at the lowest possible cost.

- Reduce time or effort to complete an activity so that required resources are reduced.

- Eliminate activities by challenging the need for an activity.

- Quantify cost of eliminated activities.

- Improve the sequence of the way work is performed.

- Ensure that services or products share activities to reach economies of scale.

- Redeploy or eliminate unused resources.

- Develop employees' business acumen by increasing their skills, morale, and productivity.

- Institute training, essential for increasing and monitoring quality.

To achieve continuous improvement, both the ABM team and rank-and-file employees must be kept fully informed as to the way work is performed. The need is for accurate and timely information about the work (activities) being done and the cost objects of that work (products, services, and customers). That is how the techniques of activity-based management can contribute in a program of quality improvement. The following examples provide excellent graphic displays, in different ways, of how a quality management/continuous improvement methodology is used in a typical organization (Fig. 5-2).

An organization's management should use customer complaint data for quality improvement efforts and the prevention of future customer problems. Managers must set service standards and track how they are being met. They must effectively manage their customer relationships and continuously improve them. Employee feedback highlights the important influence that employee attitudes and morale have on the ability to provide world-class service to customers. Monitoring performance provides the checklist to assess the effectiveness of continuous improvement efforts (Fig. 5-3).

If an activity doesn't make a difference in your ability to serve your customer (internal, external), it's probably not required. A value orientation focuses your company on success. It shifts your orientation toward your revenue source and insinuates a new customer-driven philosophy into virtually everything your organization does.

The role of the supervisor is reinterpreted from someone who is there to catch you when you misbehave—much like a traffic cop—to someone who is there to help you perform better—like the coach of a team—and therefore provide enhanced service to your customers.

Activity-based management and activity-based-costing are made for each other. ABC supplies the information needed to manage activities for business improvement. ABM uses the information in various ways to yield this improvement. Activity-based management draws its power from the ABC database. ABM aims directly at two goals—ones that are common to any company. The first goal is to improve the value received by customers. The second is to improve profits by providing this value. These goals are reached by focusing on management of activities.

Activity-based management starts with a simple realization—customers have very direct wants. They want products and services that fit a specific need. They want quality. They want service. They want affordable prices. They want to be delighted. And they want it *now*!

Meeting customer wants is one thing. Meeting them profitably is quite another. It's not enough to tell stockholders that your products and/or services have the highest quality in the industry. Or that customers consistently rate you the highest in customer satisfaction. You must also provide an adequate return on stockholder investment. There's really no conflict between these two objectives. In the long run, your profitability is important to your customers—because customers want you around for the "long haul" (which you won't be if you're unprofitable).

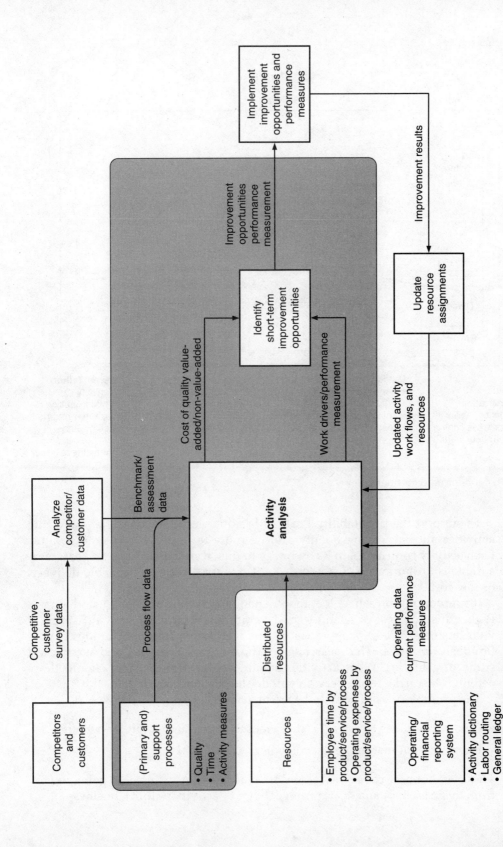

**Figure 5-2.** Continuous improvement program.

141

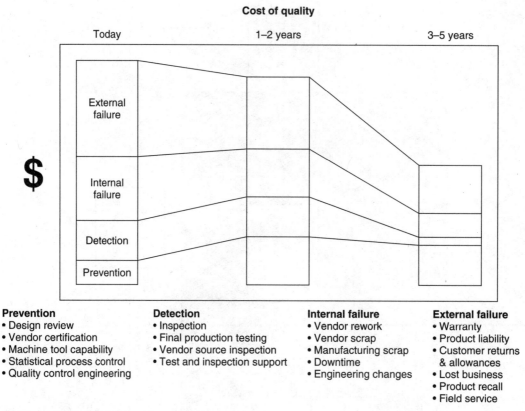

**Cost of quality**

| Prevention | Detection | Internal failure | External failure |
|---|---|---|---|
| • Design review | • Inspection | • Vendor rework | • Warranty |
| • Vendor certification | • Final production testing | • Vendor scrap | • Product liability |
| • Machine tool capability | • Vendor source inspection | • Manufacturing scrap | • Customer returns |
| • Statistical process control | • Test and inspection support | • Downtime |   & allowances |
| • Quality control engineering | | • Engineering changes | • Lost business |
| | | | • Product recall |
| | | | • Field service |

**Figure 5-3.** Monitoring performance.

To support the profitability goal, ABM adheres to the belief that managing activities and improving quality are the route to improving customer value. Each activity contributes in its own way to this overall goal. Each makes a measurable contribution to customers—be it quality, timeliness, reliable delivery, or low cost.

It's important to realize, too, that managing activities is not a custodial task. Rather, it's a process of relentless and continuous improvement of all aspects of your business. The effort involves an ongoing search for opportunities to continuously improve. That search, in turn, involves a careful and methodical study of activities. What activities should be performed? How should those activities be carried out? How do you define customer value?

The primary rules of activity-based management are:

■ Deploy resources to activities that yield the maximum strategic benefit.

■ Improve what matters to the customer.

These are not new concepts. What does matter to the customer is going to vary from business to business and from activity to activity within a business.

If quality is what matters to your customer, you would want to understand your customer's criteria for quality. What are the trends for key indicators? What activities are responsible for the indicators? How much cost is associated with poor quality? ABC can supply much of this information. It points out which functional work areas have large detection and correction activities.

Information on work drivers and performance measures reveals opportunities for improvement and helps monitor progress. There are many costly activities associated with detailing and correcting quality problems (e.g., inspecting, appraisal, rework).

Customer value is about what customers get (the realization) and what they give up to get it (the sacrifice). Subtract sacrifice from realization and you have customer value. Realization comes in a bundle. Included in the bundle are the features of the product or service. For a car, features include interior space, engine size, type of transmission, and front, rear, or all-wheel drive. For a checking account, features include electronic bill paying, access to automatic teller machines, and 24-hour verification of your account balance.

But realization goes well beyond features. Whether they are buying cars or checking services, customers value above all else good quality and service. In some cases, quality *is* the primary purchase consideration. In all cases, quality affects the cost of using the product or service. Customers also buy future costs when they purchase a product or service. Future costs are incurred to use and service a car. Fees are incurred for services associated with a checking account. Some products (such as nuclear fuel) also have disposal costs.

There's no realization without sacrifice. Many products and services require time and effort, both in the initial purchase of the product and/or service and in learning how to use it. It takes time, for example, to master a new software program.

A continuous improvement/total quality management program should encompass all functions, including administrative activities, research, accounting, and human resources activities. These functions all generate a product or service, which by definition means a business process exists and can be improved. In fact, "white collar" areas often represent the greatest opportunity for productivity improvement.

Some functional work area managers often think that 95 percent quality is good enough. However, at this level there would be approximately 6000 incorrect surgical operations per week and 3 short or long landings at most major airports each day—not an encouraging prospect if you require surgery or need to fly.

The continuous improvement philosophy emphasizes the importance of people in the total process. Considerations such as culture, incentives, teamwork, and training are typical. The optimum effectiveness of the program results from the correct blend of social and business process issues. It is common practice for organizations to emphasize the technical aspects of improvement—new tools, computers, and so on—with less emphasis on the people and their role in the process.

Improving quality and productivity to achieve competitiveness reemphasizes the need for an enterprise to capture the potential inherent in its work force by enabling each employee to do his or her job right the first time. Management must ensure that employees

- Receive proper training
- Get feedback on their performance
- Are empowered to make changes necessary to improve the process (with all barriers to employee contributions removed)

Quality improvement also requires that senior management demonstrate personal involvement to all employees. Management must provide an environment in which all employees will voluntarily cooperate to achieve organizational objectives. This requires that management accept the idea that employees can and want to contribute and encourage the flow of ideas up. Reducing the hierarchical levels in an organization can facilitate this process.

Employees will expend the necessary effort when they perceive that their performance will lead to desired rewards. Rewards are both extrinsic (salary, bonuses, recognition, and work security) and intrinsic (meaningful work, responsibility for outcomes, and feedback on the results of work activities).

Employees model their behavior on how management acts. Management must demonstrate by its actions that quality is extremely important and must lead and manage employee involvement in quality improvement efforts. Group activities are an effective way to tap the people resource to achieve quality improvement. Through teamwork, employees gain pride in their work and develop a personal stake in the achievement of excellence in quality and productivity.

Group activities are also an effective way to bridge the interface between functional disciplines and to reduce hierarchical influence and interference. In group activities, the integration of design, quality / reliability, and production is an effective way to achieve the synergy necessary for quality excellence. Some organizations are now using teams as the basic building block for organizational structure.

## Building Blocks for a Continuous Improvement/Total Quality Management Program

1. Identify the appropriate cultural environment.
2. Define the purpose of the business process.
3. Establish productivity improvement objectives.
4. Set productivity improvement action plans.
5. Implement action plans and methodologies.
6. Analyze improvement efforts.
7. Review and reemphasize the continuous improvement process.

## Identify the Appropriate Cultural Environment

The continuous improvement/TQM process is a complete approach which demands that functional work area management provide the leadership to create the climate in which the program can thrive. Senior management is responsible for establishing a new, more tractable setting that will foster the acceptance of change. This changed culture is uncovered and nourished so that all levels of the business process populace, functioning together as a team, can maximize their contributions to the organization's mission of excellence.

Management must be prepared to accept an initial investment in time and training before the new approach is accepted and becomes productive. Management must demonstrate a long-term commitment, even if improvement is initially difficult. Change at any time is difficult and is especially disruptive because it may negate values and behavior patterns that are ingrained in various functional work areas.

A simple idea that the customer sets the requirements could be considered reactionary in an organization that is used to having the individual in authority dictate what is wanted. A shift to a customer-focused universe is a difficult one.

Persistence and the disciplined application of continuous improvement methodology are a must. Senior management must exert its influence day after day so that continuous improvement becomes a new habit and way of life. This is a key factor for success. The establishment of a structured setting will enable

- Regular application and use
- Elimination of indefinite concepts
- Cooperation among functional work areas

A structured direction would seem easy to achieve at first glance, but it is extremely difficult to implement. For example, most of us understand that physical fitness can be maintained through proper eating habits and regular exercise, but when it comes to execution, we cannot sustain the discipline necessary for well-being in our daily routine. Many organizations attempt various quick-fixes and end up in worse shape than before. There is no substitute for the day-to-day discipline of continuous improvement and TQM.

You will recognize an absence of discipline when

- Activities within a business process become delayed
- Operating procedures and work flows remain unchanged
- Hierarchical authority and structure remain intact
- Activities that workers perform are not questioned
- Efficient ways to meet and exceed customer needs are inconsistent and lack continuity of purpose
- Day-to-day behavioral patterns continue unaltered

Implementation of continuous improvement necessitates a fusion of educational training and developmental strategies. When the participation and roles of employees begin to change, it is mandatory to communicate clearly and effectively to avoid counterproductive reactions. Training should be tailored both to support senior management's vision and goals and to closely relate them to employees' visions and goals. The closer these sets of goals are to each other, the greater the chances are for success.

## Define the Purpose of the Business Process

There must be established feedback between operating groups and their customers and suppliers. All employees in a functional work area must understand the objectives of their jobs, who their customers are, and their relationship to other functional work areas if they are to achieve customer satisfaction.

Defining the business process means identifying

- Customers served, including internal customers
- Customer requirements
- Products and/or services that the functional work area provides to meet customer requirements
- Resources required to satisfy the customer
- Performance measures geared to ensure that the functional work area adheres to customer requirements
- Mutual areas of discussion with customers to adjust activities if necessary
- Principal inputs, work drivers, and cost objects
- Supplier requirements and participation in developing functional work area demands and the supplier's conformance to them
- A clear-cut mission statement and a determination of whether established policies, procedures, and activities are in line with that statement

## Establish Productivity Improvement Objectives

In order to significantly improve performance, an organization must alter its processes and reassess its performance goals. Improvement objectives should first be established at the senior management level. They should mirror strategic alternatives centered around significant business processes and customer needs which are critical to survival. Productivity improvement objectives are then propelled by the desire to furnish value to the customer, whether that customer be internal or external.

It is then incumbent upon functional work area management to establish activity and business process improvement objectives to satisfy the overall strategic objectives set by senior management. This linking of both senior management and functional work area objectives sets the framework for improvement endeavors that transcend functional and hierarchical organizational boundaries. Thus, an entire organization will be productively intertwined to create the ideal environment in which to improve productivity and quality.

## Set Productivity Improvement Action Plans

Once the productivity improvement objectives are established, with each level of productivity improvement defined, teams can create their action plans.

**Executive Team.** The action plan of the executive team should include these objectives:

- Create philosophical parameters and identify goals.
- Demonstrate steadfastness of intention.
- Set guidelines for disposition of the methodology.
- Concentrate on significant business processes which impact customer satisfaction and/or involve large areas of non-value-added waste.
- Identify the "owner" of each significant business process.
- Eliminate all hierarchical barriers and begin to think end-to-end processing.
- Furnish necessary training, rewards, and resources.
- Set performance measures for objectively evaluating whether cost objects and customer satisfaction have been achieved.
- Monitor program progress against established objectives.
- Assign individual productivity improvement teams to resolve specific problems and to evaluate progress.

**Productivity Improvement Team.** The action plan of the productivity improvement team should focus on these objectives:

- Establish objectives which correlate with executive team parameters.
- Commence business process activity and system analysis.
- Train productivity improvement teams in the reengineering/productivity improvement methodology, and involve them incrementally.
- Create performance requirements to monitor progress against stated objectives.
- Provide facilitators to support operational business process teams.

## Implement Action Plans and Methodologies

The analysis and improvement of a business process are dependent on a well-configured life cycle that includes identifying improvement opportunities, analyzing the activities involved, implementing the change, and assessing the benefits derived from the improvement through objective performance measures to be sure that results conform to customer needs.

In identifying an improvement opportunity, you must know the business process owner and define the activities that make up that business process. In determining these key activities, be certain to consider supplier involvement and customer requirements. Create an open communication environment between customers and suppliers that provides regular feedback.

Performance measures should be able to evaluate the quality, cost, and timeliness of inputs, work drivers, outputs, and cost objects. Document improvement—the solutions implemented—and periodically review the changed business processes to verify that the realized gains are being maintained. One of the most effective ways to hold gains is to standardize the methodologies employed, because everyone can easily begin to identify with the new approach to doing work and take full ownership of it.

## Analyze Improvement Efforts

A continuous improvement/TQM program has three essential elements: measurement, evaluation, and reporting. These elements draw attention to the effectiveness of productivity improvement endeavors and recognize functional work areas for future applications.

All levels of management should be included. A fundamental requirement in all productivity improvement programs is the capacity to measure the worth of a reengineering activity in terms that are understandable and relevant. Say there were 25 customer complaints each week before the activity was altered and now there are only 3. Other meaningful quality yardsticks are suggested later in this chapter.

Behavioral change measurements aren't as scientific, but they should be observable and consistent in their application. They include:

- Executive advocacy
- Mutual trust regardless of hierarchical level
- Two-way, open communication
- Teamwork
- Recognition and reward mechanisms
- Equal emphasis on long-term as well as short-term goals
- End-to-end process rather than territorial orientation

- Full training in applying the knowledge and skills of continuous improvement and TQM
- Employee support, buy-in, and involvement in the process

There is a cost associated with quality. That cost increases not only when a product or service falls outside established parameters but also when the product or service falls within the parameters yet departs from the goal. The best approach for reducing costs is to lessen variability and increase standardization.

A few examples of frequently identified cost factors are

- Rejects
- Scrap
- Rework
- Inspection
- Warranty costs
- Lack of customer satisfaction

Figure 5-4 identifies the full range of chronic waste.

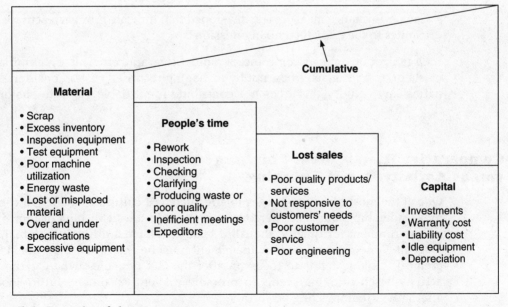

**Figure 5-4.** Examples of chronic waste.

### Review and Reemphasize the Continuous
### Improvement Process

A basic desire in a continuous improvement/TQM program is to so indoctrinate all levels of workers with the methodology and its power that the approach lasts forever. Reality and history tell us that many programs of this type tend to have a limited life if left alone. Even if an organization has great success, employee enthusiasm will wane.

Rejuvenation efforts through shared gains—resulting from suggestion awards—should assist in reinforcing the concept that the continuous improvement/TQM program is not a project but a new way of life. Day-to-day behavioral patterns must be altered, new habits must be formed, and an esprit de corps must be established that radiates self-fulfillment and pride of ownership.

Continuous improvement/TQM is an evolutionary process, not a revolutionary one. The less time it takes to complete an activity (i.e., reduce elapsed time), the greater the flexibility, the higher the quality, and the lower the cost. Look for situations that force completion of nonessential activities or cause performance to fall below expectations.

You can improve areas that matter to the customer or organization by asking these questions:

- What external factors cause high consumption of resources to perform an activity?
- What can be done differently?
- What causes waste of materials, time, space, or labor?
- Can performance measures be developed that indicate how each activity contributes to the overall company mission?

Organizations can become more competitive and efficient by eliminating waste in operating activities, not by managing recorded costs. Consider eliminating any activity that does not contribute identifiable value to customers (Fig. 5-5).

## Comparative Hierarchical Thinking
## versus Activity-Based Thinking

One of the most difficult changes to effectuate is a cultural change. If a company's leadership team is not personally committed to establishing or improving an environment for quality, the ABM team will have a difficult time realizing its goals. A new paradigm in management must be embraced. Traditional hierarchical thinking tends to focus on after-the-fact remedies, whereas the new activity-based thinking seems to promote preventive, timely, future-looking alternatives to improving performance.

A total quality management/continuous improvement approach generates opportunities to utilize financial and market data analysis, as well as process

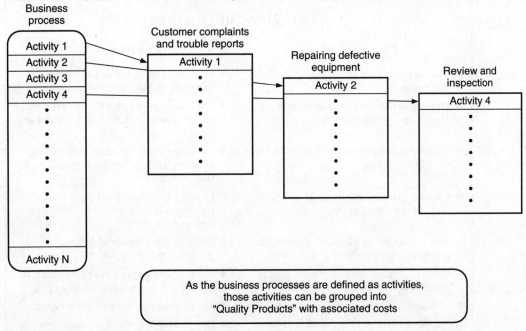

**Figure 5-5.** Quality products and activities.

and customer information, to focus attention on improvement efforts. In traditional hierarchical thinking, management doesn't always care if company values are understood and committed to by the workers. Strategic plans don't always include quantified goals or how plans will be deployed. In activity-based thinking, management understands that in order to manage and improve the business, leadership information and analysis, strategic planning, human resource management, and process management must be integrated in order to reach the desired results in the areas of customer satisfaction, customer retention, market share, and shareowner value.

Such understanding will help focus quality and continuous improvement efforts and accelerate progress.

Activity-based management provides support for total quality management/continuous improvement by assisting in the managing of business processes, analyzing all the steps within an activity—and all the activities within a business process—to eliminate certain non-value-added tasks and/or activities for improved productivity.

Continuous improvement has several objectives:

- Elimination of waste (non-value-added activities)
- Improvement of performance of value-added activities
- Improvement of quality

---

## Two Views of Quality

| *Traditional view* | *Current posture* |
|---|---|

- Productivity and quality are conflicting goals.
- Quality is defined as conformance to specifications or standards.
- Quality is measured by degree of nonconformance.
- Quality is achieved through intensive product inspection.
- Some defects are allowed if product meets minimum quality standards.
- Quality is a separate function that is focused on evaluating production.
- Workers are blamed for poor quality.
- Supplier relationships are short-term and cost oriented.

*Current posture*

- Productivity gains are achieved through quality improvements.
- Quality is conformance to correctly defined requirements satisfying user needs.
- Quality is measured by continuous process/product improvement and user satisfaction.
- Quality is determined by product design and is achieved by effective process controls.
- Defects are prevented through process control techniques.
- Quality is a part of every function in all phases of the product life cycle.
- Management is responsible for quality.
- Supplier relationships are long term and quality oriented.

---

## New Paradigm in Management

| *Traditional hierarchical thinking* | *New activity-based thinking* |
|---|---|
| ■ Cost reduction | ■ Cost prevention |
| ■ Overhead allocation | ■ Overhead control and elimination |
| ■ Static, precise information | ■ Timely, relevant information |
| ■ Historical reporting of actuals | ■ Future cost structure |
| ■ Negative finger-pointing | ■ Proactive involvements |
| ■ Functional view | ■ Business process view |
| ■ Current period costs | ■ Total life-cycle costs |

---

- Elimination of process variances by correcting the source that caused the variance
- Simplification of activities

An example of the interaction of activity performance measurement and quality can be seen with a payroll check and purchase order processing, as shown in the activity performance measurement–quality chart (Fig. 5-6).

- Establish performance measures
  -Lead time
  -Quality
  -Flexibility
  -Schedule attainment
- Monitor performance per unit

| Activity | Measurement criteria | Time | Quality performance per unit |
|---|---|---|---|
| Payroll check | Checks | 3 days | 75 voids per 1000 |
| Purchase orders | Purchase orders | 2 weeks | 125 corrections per 1000 |

**Figure 5-6.** Activity performance measurement–quality.


## Customer Satisfaction Linkages

The quality products and activities chart presented earlier (Fig. 5-5) assists in painting the ABM linkage among management, employees, and customers. This philosophy incorporates many aspects of the Baldrige criteria, whose categories "fit together" and correspond to a quality management methodology. A good quality program consists of quality planning, a human resources/human performance component, information and analysis, and a quality assurance/quality control segment.

Feedback from employees goes back to the organization's leadership. A quality achievement progress report should demonstrate how we satisfy customers in terms of

- Improved quality
- Cost reduction
- Productivity gains (e.g., reduced cycle times, reduced defects)

The organization's quality results can then be interpreted into *customer satisfaction*—the ultimate goal:

- Do you know your customer's needs and expectations?
- Do you manage your "relationship" with your customer?

Commitments to customer satisfaction may be your warranty or guarantee policy for managing customer complaints and measuring and tracking customer satisfaction. How well you demonstrate customer satisfaction should be a good indicator of your competitiveness in the marketplace.

The elements of a good continuous improvement/total quality management program are interactive and interdependent. A significant weakness in any single element can limit your ability to meet customer expectations.

## Customer Satisfaction Measurements

Customer satisfaction measurements include the following:

- Functional work area requirements
- Market share performance
- Competitive benchmarks
- Customer perception surveys
- Customer complaints
- Employee feedback

An analysis of quality improvement work drivers, as shown in Fig. 5-7, graphically demonstrates how quality improvement relates to sales.

## Human Resources Recognition

Human resources considerations must be included as a key element in any productive continuous improvement/total quality management approach. A reward system should be put in place that provides an immediate acknowledgment to the employee who suggests an operational improvement which results in a quantifiable cost reduction.

The rewards can be in privileges, cash, merchandise, trips, promotions, and so on, and should be publicized to the entire functional work area populace as

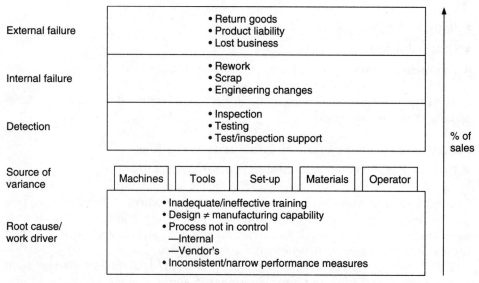

**Figure 5-7.** Quality improvement work drivers.

the benefit is implemented. When employees participate in improving the company operation, they will make sure the improvement is lasting, and not a quick-fix. An impartial committee of peers should carefully review each suggestion as to its merits, magnitude, and duration.

## Components and Significant Aspects of Human Resources Participation

| Component | Significant Aspects |
|---|---|
| Goal setting | Outputs, excellence criteria |
| Performance management | Ongoing feedback, consequences |
| Development | Present and future job focus |
| Appraisal | Performance—what and how |
| Compensation | Performance—not peer based |
| Career planning | Development, not promotion |
| Staffing | "Deregulated market" |
| Outplacement | Humane transition |
| Recruitment | Vitality, diversity |

One of the reasons self-empowered teams are successful is that they combine management, employee, and customer satisfaction into their mission. The elimination of hierarchical status and power struggles, coupled with direct rewards for accomplishment, fosters an environment in which a continuous improvement/TQM approach thrives. What are some of the quality measurements that are being used in corporations today?

# Quality Management Measurements

We must know our current and future customer requirements and expectations, and cross-compare them with other key data such as customer complaints, losses and gains of customers, and performance data that may yield information on customer requirements and expectations relating to key products or services.

The following lists of quality measurements provide a checklist that should be reviewed and adapted for implementation within a company's global continuous improvement/total quality management approach. The functional work areas to be described include:

- Accounting
- Clerical
- Product/development engineering

- Finance
- Forecasting
- Procurement/purchasing
- Production control
- Quality assurance

These lists, while comprehensive, are not the total universe of possible quality measurements and will vary by industry and organization. Utilize the measurements that best fit your circumstances and needs, since there aren't any perfect, all-inclusive measurement designations.

## Accounting Quality Measurements

- Percent of late reports
- Percent of errors in reports
- Errors in input to information services
- Errors reported by outside auditors
- Percent of input errors detected
- Number of complaints by users
- Number of hours per week correcting or changing documents
- Number of complaints about inefficiencies or excessive paper
- Amount of time spent appraising/correcting input errors
- Payroll processing time
- Percent of errors in payroll
- Length of time to prepare and send a bill
- Length of time billed and not received
- Number of final accounting jobs rerun
- Number of equipment sales miscoded
- Amount of intracompany accounting bill-back activity
- Time spent correcting erroneous inputs
- Number of open items
- Percent of deviations from cash plan
- Travel expense accounts processed in 3 days
- Percent of advances outstanding
- Percent of data entry errors in accounts payable and general ledger
- Credit turnaround time

- Machine billing turnaround time
- Percent of shipments requiring more than one attempt to invoice
- Number of untimely supplier invoices processed
- Average number of days from receipt to processing

## Clerical Quality Measurements

- Misfiles per week
- Paper mailed/paper used
- Errors per typed page
- Administration errors (not using the right procedure)
- Number of times manager is late to meetings
- Number of times messages are not delivered
- Percent of action items not done on schedule
- Percent of inputs not received on schedule
- Percent of coding errors on time cards
- Period reports not completed on schedule
- Percent of phone calls answered within two rings
- Percent of phone calls dialed correctly
- Pages processed error-free per hour
- Clerical personnel/personnel supported
- Percent of pages retyped
- Percent of impressions reprinted

## Product/Development Engineering Quality Measurements

- Percent of drafting errors per print
- Percent of prints released on schedule
- Percent of errors in cost estimates
- Number of times a print is changed
- Number of off-specs approved
- Simulation accuracy
- Accuracy of advance materials list
- Cost of input errors to the computer

- How well the product meets customer expectations
- Field performance of product
- Percent of error-free designs
- Percent of errors found during design review
- Percent of repeat problems corrected
- Time required to correct a problem
- Time required to make an engineering change
- Cost of engineering changes per month
- Percent of reports with errors in them
- Data-recording errors per month
- Percent of evaluations that meet engineering objectives
- Percent of special quotations that are successful
- Percent of test plans that are changed (changed/test plan)
- Percent of meetings starting on schedule
- Spare parts cost after warranty
- Number of meetings held per quarter in which quality and defect prevention were the main subject
- Persons/months per released print
- Percent of total problems found by diagnostics as released
- Customer cost per life of output delivered
- Number of problems that were also encountered in previous products
- Cycle time to correct a customer problem
- Number of errors in publications reported from the plant and field
- Number of products that pass independent evaluation error-free
- Number of missed shipments of prototypes
- Number of unsuccessful preanalyses
- Number of off-specs accepted
- Percent of requests for engineering action open for more than 2 weeks
- Number of days late to preanalysis
- Number of restarts of evaluations and tests
- Effectiveness of regression tests
- Number of days for the release cycle
- Percent of corrective action schedules missed
- Percent of bills of material that are released in error

## Finance Quality Measurements

- Percent error in budget predictions
- Computer rerun time because of input errors
- Computer program change cost
- Percent of financial reports delivered on schedule
- Number of record errors per employee
- Percent of error-free vouchers
- Percent of bills paid so company gets price break
- Percent of errors in checks
- Entry errors per week
- Number of payroll errors per month
- Number of errors found by outside auditors
- Number of errors in financial reports
- Percent of errors in travel advancement records
- Percent of errors in expense accounts detected by auditors

## Forecasting Quality Measurements

- Number of upward pricing revisions per year
- Number of project plans that meet schedule, price, and quality
- Percent error in sales forecasts
- Number of forecasting assumption errors
- Number of changes in product schedules

## Procurement/Purchasing Quality Measurements

- Percent of discount orders by consolidating
- Errors per purchase order
- Number of orders received with no purchase order
- Routing and rate errors per shipment
- Percent of supplies delivered on schedule
- Percent decrease in parts costs
- Expeditors per direct employees
- Number of items on the hot list
- Percent of suppliers with 100 percent lot acceptance for one year

- Stock costs
- Labor hours per $10,000 purchases
- Purchase order cycle time
- Number of times per year line is stopped because of lack of supplier parts
- Supplier parts scrapped because of engineering changes
- Percent of parts with two or more suppliers
- Average time to fill emergency orders
- Average time to replace rejected lots with good parts
- Parts cost per total costs
- Percent of lots received on line late
- Actual purchased materials cost per budgeted cost
- Time to answer customer complaints
- Percent of phone calls dialed correctly
- Percent of purchase orders returned because of errors or incomplete descriptions
- Percent of defect-free supplier model parts
- Percent of projected cost reductions missed
- Time required to process equipment purchase orders
- Cost of rush shipments
- Number of items billed but not received

## Production Control Quality Measurements

- Percent of late deliveries
- Percent of errors in stocking
- Number of items exceeding shelf life
- Percent of manufacturing jobs completed on schedule
- Time required to incorporate engineering changes
- Percent of errors in purchase requisitions
- Percent of products that meet customer orders
- Inventory turnover rate
- Time that line is down because of assembly shortage
- Percent of time parts are not in stock when ordered from common-parts crib
- Time of product in shipment
- Cost of rush shipments

- Spare parts availability in crib
- Percent of stock errors
- Percent of errors in work-in-process records versus audit data
- Cost of inventory spoilage
- Number of bill-of-lading errors not caught in shipping

## Quality Assurance Quality Measurements

- Percent error in reliability projections
- Percent of product that meets customer expectations
- Time to answer customer complaints
- Number of customer complaints
- Number of errors detected during design and process reviews
- Percent of employees active in professional societies
- Number of audits performed on schedule
- Percent of quality assurance personnel to total personnel
- Percent of quality inspectors to manufacturing directs
- Percent of quality engineers to product and manufacturing engineers
- Number of engineering changes after design review
- Number of process changes after process qualification
- Errors in reports
- Time to correct a problem
- Cost of scrap and rework that was not created at the rejected operation
- Percent of suppliers with 100 percent lot acceptance for one year
- Percent of lots going directly to stock
- Percent of problems identified in the field
- Variations among inspectors doing the same job
- Percent of reports published on schedule
- Number of complaints from manufacturing management
- Percent of field returns correctly analyzed
- Time to identify and solve problems
- Percent of lab services not completed on schedule
- Percent of improvement in early detection of major design errors
- Percent of errors in defect records
- Number of customer calls to report errors

- Level of customer calls to report errors
- Level of customer surveys
- Number of committed supplier plans in place
- Percent of correlated test results with suppliers
- Receiving inspection cycle time
- Number of requests for corrective action being processed
- Time required to process a request for corrective actions
- Number of off-specs approved
- Percent of part numbers going directly to stock
- Number of manufacturing interruptions caused by supplier parts
- Percent of error in predicting customer performance
- Percent of product cost related to appraisal, scrap, and rework
- Percent of skip-lot inspections
- Percent of qualified suppliers
- Number of problems identified in process

## Quality Activity Measurements— Quality Test Points

### Customer Satisfaction Benchmarks

1. Customer satisfaction index (e.g., price, service, quality, delivery, responsiveness)
2. Customer complaints received (number, type)
3. Customer service index (timeliness, frequency, type)
4. Customer quote efficiency (backlog, days to process)
5. Customer order entry efficiency (backlog, days to process)
6. Customer delivery efficiency (past due, early, late, timeliness)
7. Customer order to delivery (cycle time, lead time versus customer requirements)
8. Market share (dollars, units, or percent versus competitors)
9. Customer reject rates (number, type)
10. Customer invoice/billing errors
11. Accounts receivable as a percentage of sales
12. Held orders as a percentage of sales
13. Carryover

## Financial Benchmarks

Return on equity:

$$\text{ROE} = \frac{\text{earnings}}{\text{shareholder's equity}}$$

Return on assets:

$$\text{ROA} = \frac{\text{earnings}}{\text{assets}}$$

Collection period:

$$\text{CP} = \frac{\text{accounts receivable}}{\text{credit sales per day}}$$

Days sales in cash:

$$\text{DSIC} = \frac{\text{cash and securities}}{\text{net sales per day}}$$

Debt-to-assets ratio:

$$\text{DTAR} = \frac{\text{total liabilities}}{\text{total assets}}$$

Debt-to-equity ratio:

$$\text{DTER} = \frac{\text{total liabilities}}{\text{shareholders equity}}$$

Time interest earned:

$$\text{TIE} = \frac{\text{earning before interest and taxes}}{\text{interest expense}}$$

Current ratio:

$$\text{CR} = \frac{\text{current assets}}{\text{current liabilities}}$$

Earnings yield:

$$\text{EY} = \frac{\text{earnings per share}}{\text{price per share}}$$

Price-to-earnings ratio:

$$\text{PTER} = \frac{\text{price per share}}{\text{earnings per share}}$$

1. Sales growth

2. Earnings growth

3. Inventory carrying costs

4. Account receivables

5. Cost of sales

### Supplier Performance Benchmarks

1. P.O. efficiency (i.e., backlog, requisition-to-order cycle time, order-to-delivery cycle time, etc.)

2. Supplier delivery efficiency (i.e., past due, late, early, on time, etc.)

3. Supplier reject rates

4. Supplier price trends

During a work year, the content of activities in a functional work area can change for various reasons. When this occurs, you must be prepared to document the changes, update the activity by using the detailing methodology described in Chapter Four, and redesign the activity work flows. The revision to work documentation must be completed within 72 hours of the activity changing, and should not have to go through a committee.

Someone in the functional work area should be assigned responsibility for change control, and should be a member of the team that is approving and implementing the change in work content. The change control process is an integral part of every continuous improvement/total quality management effort. If a functional work area's management and employees have embraced the continuous improvement concept, they must have a mechanism to implement change.

Be aware that a change control process can turn into a functional work area manager's worst nightmare if it becomes a bottleneck rather than an enabler and catalyst for productivity improvement.

## Employee Recognition

All personnel should be given training in TQM principles, practices, tools, and techniques. This training instills in each employee the notion that successful activities do not mean contentment or maintaining the status quo, because there is always room for further improvement.

The TQM philosophy emphasizes an immediate response to problems affecting product and/or service quality by either changing the design or the activity, not by increasing inspection levels. Defect prevention should be viewed as the key to deficit control. TQM provides each employee with a method for identifying problems, determining needed corrective actions, and taking those actions. It also emphasizes that problems are owned by everyone in a functional work area, and that success or failure is a collective responsibility dependent upon the long-term and regularly renewed commitment of both employees and senior management.

Employee development is a continuous and ongoing process, and several tools are available for developing job mastery. Utilizing these tools and/or attending courses is often not enough to change behavior and improve effectiveness. Development must be focused on continuous learning.

Continuous learning is fundamental but is seldom practiced as an approach to improving one's working and/or personal life. It has often been described as a methodology in which individuals or teams continually focus on acquiring, translating, reworking, reorganizing, or integrating data, proficiencies, acumen, approaches, feelings, and behaviors which transcend circumstances and responsibilities.

Continuous learning also includes understanding the origins of other people's ideas, behaviors, feelings, and attitudes. As part of continuous improvement, it develops an employee attitude that says, "I can do that more efficiently." Not surprisingly, therefore, the continuous improvement work ethic can be used both inside and outside the work environment.

A basic underlying benefit or by-product of continuous improvement is that employees begin to understand themselves, which can serve as a baseline against which to gauge their own efforts and accomplishments. A motivated worker is usually a productive one.

Functional work area managers should be cognizant of different learning styles. An employee or team's success in learning may be dependent on the manager's understanding what style to select and then structuring various learning situations to maximize productivity and development in line with that recognized style.

## Summary

Total quality management consists of continuous process improvement activities involving everyone in an organization, from managers to workers, in a totally integrated effort toward improving performance at every level. This improved performance is directed toward satisfying such cross-functional goals as quality, cost, schedule, mission need, and suitability. The activities associated with the TQM effort are ultimately focused on increased customer/user satisfaction. The TQM philosophy,

*Doing the right thing right the first time, on time, all the time, always striving for improvement and always satisfying the customer*

provides a comprehensive way to improve quality by examining how work gets done in a systematic, integrated, consistent, organization-wide perspective. Remember that you must

- Emphasize continuous improvement and compliance with standards.
- Motivate employees to improve rather than wait for user complaints/demands.
- Satisfy the customer; do not merely conform to requirements.
- Understand the effects of variation on processes.
- Provide customers/users with products and services that consistently meet their needs and expectations at reasonable costs.

User satisfaction is the ultimate requirement for which everyone must strive, whether the user is an internal customer or an external customer. Users require products and services that satisfy their expectations for technical support (including logistic support), schedule (available when needed), and cost (within budget).

Quality is conformance to a set of customer requirements that, if met, result in a product that is fit for its intended use. Knowledge of user requirements (internal and external) is a prerequisite to satisfying them. User requirements must be defined before their specifications are identified, because blind adherence to inappropriate specifications can easily become counterproductive. It is critical that these requirements be reflected accurately in specifications for products, services, and processes. There must be an alignment between user expectations and user requirements to attain user satisfaction.

A good manager will provide resources and time for prevention activities when improving quality, because correction of problems is a more costly procedure: much of the high cost of poor quality comes from processes that are allowed to be wasteful. This waste is often chronic and is accepted as the normal cost of doing business. Chronic waste of time, material, and other resources can be driven out of the business process by implementing continuous process improvement.

A continuous improvement strategy requires sustained attention. The day-to-day application of continuous improvement to routine work is what gets results, along with infrequent innovations. Do not wait for the "Hail Mary touchdown pass" to be completed.

Structured problem-solving methodologies can help to identify opportunities for improvement. Every work activity has inputs and outputs. Critical points in the process can be selected, and measurements can be taken at the input, at the output, and within the process. These measurements help identify the most serious problems to be resolved. Then alternatives should be developed to arrive at solutions, and finally corrective action should be taken to resolve the problem and improve the business process. This cycle is repeated indefinitely, resulting in a continuous quality improvement process. A critical factor is the reduction of variances by using stable technologies and standardized parts and processes, and by minimizing the total number of parts in a product and steps in the process.

The TQM philosophy emphasizes the importance of people in the total process. Considerations such as culture, incentives, teamwork, training, and work involvement are typical. The optimum effectiveness of TQM results from an appropriate mix of the social and technical systems by enabling each employee to do his or her job right the first time.

Such a philosophy requires that top management demonstrate to all employees that it is personally committed to, and will continuously pursue, efforts to improve quality. The organization must provide an environment in which all employees will voluntarily cooperate to achieve stated objectives. Management must accept the idea that employees can and want to contribute. Employees will expend the necessary effort if they perceive that their performance will lead to desired rewards. Management thus flows ideas and goals down and encourages the flow of ideas up.

Continuous improvement/total quality management is not a program—here today, gone tomorrow. Total quality management is a practice, an ongoing way to manage an enterprise. It is a customer-oriented management concept that gives the customer what the customer wants. It is about leadership which advocates participation in problem identification and problem solving by the entire work force. This effort combines a participative management style, opportunities for improvement, and statistical measurements under a structured environment. It requires management commitment and personal involvement at every level of the organization, with a clear understanding of the mission, goals, objectives, and roles. The successful continuous improvement/total quality management operation is characterized by an organization of quality-trained and motivated employees, working in an environment where functional work area managers foster creativity, initiative, and trust; and where each individual's contributions are actively sought, and are properly recognized and rewarded.

The focus of continuous improvement/total quality management is to change the cultural paradigm of hierarchical management to a comprehensive end-to-end process approach. This approach focuses on customer satisfaction for each product or service. The objective is to analyze the value-added activities to continuously improve every aspect of the business process they are a part of, and to enhance performance in order to achieve productivity improvement gains. Error prevention, rather than error detection and rework, eliminates waste and is the guiding force behind a program of this type. These concepts were pioneered by W. Edwards Deming in Japan. However, they are not unique to Japanese culture and have been instituted in some of the largest American companies—Ford, Motorola, Xerox, Hewlett-Packard, and Westinghouse among them.

It is important to understand the precepts of continuous improvement/total quality management before specific techniques and tools are applied. Customer-oriented management requires a fundamental change in our thinking process. There are four cornerstones to continuous improvement/total quality management:

- Customer and supplier responsiveness
- Productivity improvement

- People buy-in at all management levels
- Quality centered on the customer's needs (internal, external)

Implementation of these cornerstones requires (1) education, (2) an understanding of the techniques and methodology to engage in process improvements, and (3) a change in culture. Education is crucial for TQM to be successful. Institutionalizing concepts requires an orderly and systematic grassroots education and training approach. Those directly involved with operational business processes need to be informed of and provided with the necessary skills to effectively carry out the implementation. It is equally important that leaders create an environment that promotes total, open participation by the work force. The key is to talk, feel, believe, and live quality. Those organizations that do so unlock the door to growth and survival.

In summary, continuous improvement/total quality management

- Creates and supports a culture committed to change
- Emphasizes the whole rather than the sum of the parts
- Focuses on activity-based management, in which the role of management is one of leader, facilitator, and provider of information
- Concentrates on meeting customer requirements and visions, whether internal or external
- Demands commitment, dedication, and involvement from all management levels
- Requires that every employee take control for improving his or her own activities
- Builds teamwork and cooperative interrelationships
- Acknowledges people as the most important corporate asset

## Continuous Improvement/Total Quality Management Assessment Checklist

Figure 5-8 summarizes the focal points of continuous improvement/TQM assessment. Use the following checklist as a guide.

### Senior Management Commitment

- Does senior management convey and energize its support for continuous improvement and total quality management?
- Do organizational platforms emphasize long-term quality instead of short-term solutions?

**Figure 5-8.** Focal points of continuous improvement/TQM assessment.

- Is productivity improvement included in every job description?
- Is quality a dominant perception in assembling annual business plans?

## Human Resources Considerations

- Is employee morale high?
- Is there an objective performance measurement program in place that rewards employee effectiveness?
- Are employee training requirements periodically reevaluated?
- Is there a formal productivity improvement, continuous improvement, and total quality management program in place for improving job performance and quality?
- Are employees encouraged to solicit customer and supplier feedback about the organization's product and service quality?

## Customer Satisfaction

- Do organizational products and services adhere to customer needs and expectations?
- Are customer requirements regularly evaluated?
- Are objective performance measurement criteria in place to evaluate customer satisfaction at regular intervals?
- Are organizational customer satisfaction measurements compared against industry benchmarks and competitive trends?

- Is there a customer complaint resolution desk which makes sure complaints are resolved and do not arise repeatedly?
- Does the organization have established key performance indicators that employees must meet for customer service?

## Quality Assurance Requirements

- Is there a control mechanism for ensuring that products or services are free from imperfections?
- Is there a set of quality standards against which products and services are frequently and uniformly measured?
- Is the cost of quality regularly captured, analyzed, and evaluated?
- Does the organization customarily make productivity and quality projections?
- Does the organization have established quality selection criteria for suppliers?

# 6
# Observation Process

## Introduction

The observation process is the natural follow-up to the interview and detailing process because the observer has identified the activities, classified them into primary and secondary categories, and documented the primary activities as to content. The observer can now intelligently watch the primary activities actually being performed in their natural environment.

The primary element in the observation process is the associating of units of completed work to the time it takes to perform the activity. It assists a functional work area manager in recognizing out-of-sync conditions at their earliest manifestation while work is being processed.

For example, an activity which causes either paper of some kind (i.e., invoices, purchase orders, claims) to be processed or creates, routes, and/or counts items rarely provides a functional work area manager with the appropriate data, such as:

- Item count at each work station
- Time to process paperwork through each work station
- Time frame when the paperwork will complete the work flow through its life cycle

When the observation process is completed, a functional work area manager will have an accurate idea as to how work moves through each work station and will be able to quantify the amount of work completed in each hour of the day. The manager will then be in a position to take corrective action at the earliest possible moment to alter any conditions that may be impeding work flow.

## Reasonable Expectancies

In order to develop work-to-time relationships in usable form, a functional work area manager generally needs to collect detailed data. The association of an appropriate activity unit of work to a time factor becomes significant in the implementation of a successful reengineering program.

The observer must take care to develop a uniform factor in measuring work that is consistently the same. Determining the unit of measure for nonrepetitive activities, such as investigation or repairs, becomes more difficult, but not insurmountable. If we carefully study the individual components of these types of activities, the unit of measure will generally emerge as a combination or grouping of tasks within an activity which can be performed within a prescribed period of time.

In most office and administrative activities, the unit of measure can frequently be easily ascertained—as a piece of paper, ledger entry, line item, claim, order, and so on. The controlling element for operational application is that the unit of measure should, when available, be located in a source record being used, instead of a document which can be measured only after an activity is completed.

Sometimes units of measure cannot be developed through a time study approach, but they are still valid (e.g., number of line items per purchase order). A very important point to recognize is that the accuracy of the work-to-time relationship need not be precise or scientifically determined. The term *reasonable expectancy* is often used to indicate this idea. If a number of letters are typed in varying lengths, an appropriate measure would be the number of words, especially when a personal computer has the ability to count them.

A reasonable expectancy is defined as the amount of work which an average employee can produce under normal working conditions in an hour. A reasonable expectancy is usually described in terms of a unit of measure. For example, having identified a claim as an appropriate unit of measure, the observer can establish a reasonable expectancy on the number of claims in the same amount of time, provided the mix of claims was approximately the same.

The proof of the value of the observation process is that functional work area managers learn how to measure work loads, arrive at reasonable expectancies as to the quantity of work their staff members should process, and then appropriately schedule work. Scheduling, not work measurement, is the most critical result of the process.

Different activities will have different life cycles. Clerical operations may be controlled at hourly intervals; lengthy or complex operations may require several hours. The important element is to establish realistic, reasonable expectancies.

Two rules should govern the observer's setting of work-to-time relationships:

- It should be brief enough so that corrective action can be taken in time to regulate an out-of-control condition before it adversely affects the entire process or activity.

- It should be an attainable target for the average staff member to achieve.

A large part of the gain in productivity that is realized from the observation process comes from the psychological impact it has on staff members. When an individual has a short-term goal to attain, reasonable expectancies tend to intensify the worker's sense of urgency. A good analogy might be a runner in a marathon. He or she realizes the event will take approximately 3 hours to complete. At first glance, it appears like a long period of time.

However, if the runner breaks the marathon down into four parts, with a goal of being at a certain mileage marker at the end of each quarter, the runner's stimulation to achieve the short-term goal is heightened, because it is more approximate. If the runner broke the race into two parts, his or her sense of urgency to complete each part of the race would be further magnified, because each part represented a more immediate short-term objective.

The same analogy holds true for any staff member. Assign someone a project or activity that will last several hours, and chances are he or she will accomplish about one-fourth of the activity in the first half of the time and three-fourths in the second half. In the final hours, the worker will be pushing to the outer limits, hoping to finish on schedule, and will even sacrifice quality to attain the objective.

The reality is that the work will not be completed. Assign another staff member exactly the same job, but break the activity down into specific shorter tasks to be completed. He or she will come much closer to completing the activity in equal parts. The sense of importance is energized by the immediacy of the goal to be accomplished. This result has been demonstrated many times, because short-term objectives turn into short-term demands for concentration and attention spans which are easier to control.

Many functional work area managers who have a cursory understanding of the mechanics of the observation process might consider their task complete once they have developed reasonable expectancies for the activities that make up the business process. However, this is not the case, because all the activities that make up the product or service must also be coordinated.

In order to control a particular activity, the manager must control all the work drivers that cause the activity to happen, as well as the outputs. For any business process to work efficiently, the work must flow smoothly from one work station to another, with each work station's capacity matching those before and after each operation.

Just as a chain is only as strong as its weakest link, so output can be only as fast as the smallest capacity. In a smoothly running business process, coordinating work station capacities is extremely important and if there is a mismatching of capacities, a serious situation arises.

An excellent example of this occurred in an order processing department of a distribution company which sold giftware. The order of activity flow and staffing of each activity within the process and the capacity of each activity can be seen in Fig. 6-1.

A review of the capacity of each activity made it obvious that only 150 orders per day could be processed end to end. The functional work area manager determined that 250 orders was the goal for processing each day.

| Activity | Staffing | Output/day |
|---|---|---|
| Order taking | 4 | 400 orders |
| Order checking | 1 | 150 orders |
| Order entry | 2 | 250 orders |
| Order processing | 3 | 375 orders |
| Shipping | 2 | 300 orders |
| **Total** | **12 people** | |

**Figure 6-1.** Order activity flow and staffing before activity analysis.

The order checking work station was always backlogged and regularly required overtime to become current. It was evident that only the order entry work station was staffed to handle the correct volume. Once the functional work area manager was trained to utilize the work-to-time relationships as a tool to control activity work flow on an hourly basis, the picture was altered to look like Fig. 6-2.

This basic example indicates that two people could be removed from the process, at a savings of $70,000 per year. Staff members were cross-trained so they could be shifted to any work station in case of illness, vacation, and so on. In light of incremental savings that accrue in other processes when capacities haven't been matched, the potential dollar impact becomes significant. The cross-training creates flexibility, which augments the functional work area's manager's ability to react to unexpected surges or drops in volume.

A by-product of the observation process is the creation of a platform for exercising good management control through advanced planning. If the functional work area manager finds there are excess hours in a day, what should be done with the plethora of hours? An aware manager will prepare for this eventuality. Quite possibly, additional activities can be absorbed on days when full capacity isn't required. The development of the work distribution matrix that is completed as part of the interviewing process can assist management's thinking on how to identify training needs.

| Activity | Staffing | Output/day |
|---|---|---|
| Order taking | 2.5 | 250 orders |
| Order checking | 1.7 | 250 orders |
| Order entry | 2.0 | 250 orders |
| Order processing | 2.0 | 250 orders |
| Shipping | 1.7 | 250 orders |
| **Total** | **9.9 people** | |

**Figure 6-2.** Order activity flow and staffing after activity analysis.

The manager can even rate each person in the functional work area as to competency in performing each activity. A typical example of the advantage of such flexibility is illustrated by a cash application team and a customer service team in a distribution company. Customer service representatives handled their work load routinely and without pressure until after lunch hour. Between 1 p.m. and 3 p.m., the team came under extreme pressure to respond to incoming customer telephone inquiries. Telephone calls became backlogged, customers hung up, and the team members were exhausted and became short tempered.

The cash application team's work peaked between 9 a.m. and 12 noon, during which time they opened the mail and entered cash received from customers. Historically, the teams worked independently, and each had no experience in the work of the other. A cross-training program was implemented that resulted in the cash application team being able to allocate resources from its team to the customer service team as peak volumes were reached.

The work went more smoothly; backlogs and hang-ups were eliminated, and the customer service team became relaxed. The result was an improvement in the quality of their work. This elementary idea is apparent to many, but it was overlooked by the distribution company. Create the flexibility to place staff members where the work is and schedule the work properly, thus leveling off the peaks and filling in the valleys.

When an action plan is implemented and can be monitored at regular intervals, adjustments can be made as the need arises, to avoid or minimize delays. There are always several reasons or excuses as to why productive hours are lost, but an alert functional work area manager who recognizes off-schedule conditions can eliminate the alibis. He or she can eliminate the arguments as to the causes for lost productivity and focus efforts on a closer investigation to obviate reappearances of delays in the future.

The observation process establishes the platform for recapturing lost hours which are built into most business processes. In some organizations, it will be a reduction in staffing; in others, the recapture can be accomplished by increasing productivity.

In today's customer-focused business world, many organizations find themselves competing on the basis of service rather than price. Speed of delivery is more important than price, so a company's policy of speedy delivery and exact order fulfillment on promised delivery dates will be the catalyst for generating additional business.

The day of the specialist is past, because flexibility is a key element in keeping costs down. It is becoming more important for staff members to be multifunctional, as many of the newly created positions are not full-time jobs. The activity requirements of these new jobs are such that they will normally not fill a workday. In order to prevent a staff member from making the work fill up a day, the functional work area manager should utilize the data collected during the observation process to review his or her staffing requirements.

Matching the correct number of hours to complete a job to the job can be enhanced by monitoring a work schedule in short segments so work cannot be stretched to fill up a day—that is, by preparing a work sequence plan, as discussed in Chapter Seven.

If necessary, attach a transmittal form to the claim, and as it passes through each work station record the start time, stop time, and arrival time. In-process time is usually a relatively small portion (say, 5 percent) of total time to complete the activity. The goal of the tracking process is to identify where the significant waiting time is occurring and is creating a bottleneck, so the functional work area manager can institute immediate corrective action.

Some of the most frequent reasons for bottlenecks are:

- Lack of planning
- Failure to control the movement of work
- Improper utilization of staff resources
- Insufficient work tools (e.g., PCs, printers)

A prime example of a bottleneck is when an order that is supposed to be delivered in 2 weeks takes 6 business days to reach the warehouse floor for picking. The warehouse manager is charged with the responsibility of delivering the order on time. The key is to keep the work moving by eliminating roadblocks.

The functional work area manager is responsible for planning work, implementing the action plan, and being able to measure how well it is working. If the management of activities is done efficiently, it produces a consciousness of all phases of a process, and becomes the basis for forecasting roadblocks and avoiding them. The scheduling process provides the missing elements to make the action plan successful.

The manager must ascertain that he or she has the proper resources and tools, which must then be committed at the appropriate place and time. The manager can determine if any missing or delayed ingredient will cause a time loss or prevent closure. Corrective action can be immediately taken to minimize delays and/or avoid them.

An additional benefit derived from completing the observation process, establishing reasonable expectancies, and scheduling work as it flows smoothly from work station to work station is improved customer service. This improved service is a direct result of increased productivity, better assignment of work, and reduced processing time.

The important element is to maintain these improvements on a continuous basis without sacrificing quality. Processing time as discussed here means total "time in process," which includes all elapsed time from the beginning of an activity (e.g., receiving an insurance claim) until the completion of that activity (paying an insurance claim).

Time in process equals waiting time plus "in-process time," which is when some physical action is being applied to process a given activity. Thus, if an order is received in the claims area along with a hundred other claims, it will be handled by several staff members. The mail is opened, the claim is removed, date-stamped, sorted by line of business, and delivered to a claims analyst.

Each of these tasks may take only a few seconds, yet the claim may reside at the control desk for more than an hour. The few seconds for each task represents "in-process time" and the remainder is waiting time (i.e., control desk time).

If we reduce the waiting time by organizing and scheduling our work, we can reduce total claims processing time, therefore improving customer service. There is a simple method for determining waiting time. List the activities for the claims process in their operational sequence or the way work flows, and calculate the time it takes to process a claim by using known volumes and the corresponding reasonable expectancy for each activity in the process. If there isn't an established reasonable expectancy, the observation process as described in this chapter will enable you to arrive at in-process time and a reasonable expectancy.

It can be easily documented that in many companies work standards are based on an established pace created by a staff member, not by management. Most lost time in a business process is management's doing, because it failed to provide the leadership needed to develop a proper activity work flow and allowed the staff member to do as he or she pleased.

The correct scheduling of work improves customer satisfaction, increases the demand for goods and services, and therefore creates additional jobs and makes current jobs more secure. The subject of terminations is a more emotional issue, but when terminations are an expected result of the observation process, it can be explained that lower costs make for a healthier company and the job security of the remaining workforce is enhanced.

It should also be emphasized that lower costs make the company's goods and services more competitive and could increase sales, resulting in newly created job openings. The termination initiative would most likely be a temporary situation under these circumstances.

A frequent mistake committed in the development stage of reasonable expectancies is management's failure to utilize the very people who will implement the process. Staff members should be urged to become involved from the beginning, assisting in the creation of units of measure, setting reasonable expectations, and furnishing their objective thoughts.

The functional work area manager should emphasize the importance of an individual staff member's productivity, and above all never use work-to-time relationships as a club to produce more units. Many implementations have failed because of management's misuse of this tool, thereby sending the wrong message to its staff members. Management as well as staff members will need enough time to assimilate the change in work routine with the adoption of a new philosophy before these enablers can successfully be applied to a functional work area operation.

Functional work area managers must buy in to the premise that the results of the observation process will assist them in managing their activities to ensure the achievement of their goals. The creation of work-to-time relationships is difficult enough when a company is union free, and it is understandable if management is truly scared in creating work measurements in a union environment.

A union shop primarily will complain of excessive pressure to work faster in order to increase productivity and because it fears layoffs. The most expeditious way to handle this situation is by making the union a participant early in the process and by providing a detailed explanation of how the observation process works to both union officials and union employees.

Batching of work is a commonly employed tool in utilizing reasonable expectancies for controlling activity work flows. It sometimes involves setting up a control desk but it is not mandatory to do so. When practical, the batches should be comprised of equal quantities (e.g., 50), which can be translated in equivalent time units—usually an hour. Depending on the degree of control management wishes to exercise, a sign-out, sign-in routine can be implemented, with a control desk functioning as the focal point for the distribution and collection of assigned work. However, not all work environments lend themselves to the sign-out routine.

The observation process may have its antagonists who resist anything that deviates from what they are used to doing. Prior to the commencement of the observation process, the ABM team should sell the process at all levels of the company, showing clearly how the process will enable everyone to increase productivity and control over the work performed.

Do not take for granted that establishing reasonable expectancies will be comprehended by everyone. It may require retraining of functional work area managers so they understand how their roles and responsibilities transcend the technical acumen and content of their function. They must understand that time management is as important as any other part of their responsibilities as managers. Similarly, do not assume that completion of the observation process will be a panacea and automatically bring positive results. It is a work enabler, and like any tool it must be used properly. It will be only as potent as the user will make it.

Earlier, we described a cross-training program that was extended to train customer service representatives in the cash application activity in order to make sure that cash was deposited in the bank on the same day it was received. If check volume was higher on Mondays, then extra resources could be required. The functional work area managers knew what their requirements had to be by taking the established reasonable expectancies and the volumes on hand and performing a quick calculation. Customer complaints were reduced, customer satisfaction went up, and the company's competitive position was enhanced.

More important, the field sales force gained confidence in the ability of the company to service the client base. Morale went up and so did sales.

## Work-to-Time Relationships

The past 20 years have seen a tremendous growth of clerical white-collar workers as industry moves toward a service orientation and away from a manufacturing-driven economy. Most service business relies on people, not machines, to carry out the primary activities of the organization.

A white-collar rather than blue-collar work force has become the driving influence on the national economy. Historically, manufacturing operations have drawn the attention of operating executives and industrial engineers, and they did not focus their energies on clerical or office workers in their search for cost reductions. Very little attention was paid to the methods and procedures of either how or why we do our work.

Currently, the transition to a service economy has brought more attention to the large amount of non-value-added, unproductive time that has found its way into clerical operations. More and more companies around the world are seeking ways of eliminating and improving activity work flows.

When companies establish work-to-time relationships, they are creating the foundation for effectively reducing costs in clerical areas, as well as in manufacturing areas, and recapturing lost time. The utilization of reasonable expectancies makes it possible to measure results and to quantify savings. A simple and effective way of taking the pulse of a clerical operation is through a ratio delay study. Included in this chapter is a description of a ratio delay study and how to conduct it. It is easy to detect a vibrant functional work area, but not always easy to detect a lackluster one.

There is usually a buzz of activity in a functional work area when a normal quantity of work is being produced, and a quiet, lazy, talkative atmosphere with a lack of defined rhythm and no sense of urgency in an unproductive functional work area. The ratio delay study assists management in quantifying the extent to which lost time is impacting the productive operation of a functional work area. There is obvious lost time, during which staff members are not performing any productive work (e.g., coffee breaks).

During one consulting assignment, a functional work area manager informally discovered approximately 30 percent "obvious lost time" by observing staff behavior. The normal workday was 8:30 a.m. to 5:30 p.m., with an hour for lunch, or an 8-hour effective workday. The staff would arrive at work and converse with one another until 9:00 a.m. and then go for coffee at the company cafeteria, returning around 9:30 a.m. They would congregate in one of the staff member's offices, drinking coffee until about 10:00 a.m. before truly beginning work.

The staff would go for lunch around 12:30 p.m. and return around 2:30 p.m. At approximately 3:00 p.m., the staff members would go to the vending machines for a drink and/or a snack, and hang out until 3:30 p.m. before returning to work. The functional work area manager randomly observed this behavior for several days during the month with approximately the same results being observed. The obvious daily lost time looked like the following:

| | |
|---|---|
| 8:30 a.m.–10:00 a.m. | 1.5 hours |
| 12:30 p.m.–2:00 p.m. | .5 hours (lunch extended an extra 30 minutes) |
| 3:00 p.m.–3:30 p.m. | .5 hours |
| Total obvious lost time | 2.5 hours |
| Normal workday | 8.0 hours (31 percent lost time) |

The company was paying these staff members for the time, but wasn't receiving any productive output. Some managers will argue that coffee breaks boost morale by breaking up the arduous work routine and giving staff members the opportunity to become revitalized, which in turn increases productivity. This perspective has some merit, and a happy medium should be worked out by the functional work area manager and the staff members involved.

If a functional work area manager were invisible to his or her staff, the manager might see and hear:

- Idle conversation
- Daydreaming
- Reading the newspaper or a magazine
- Group conversations and/or visiting with one another
- People missing from their work stations for no reason

Many of these types of incidents occur every day. They will never be totally prevented from happening and perhaps shouldn't be entirely eliminated. It would be impossible for most of us to work in an environment in which there was total silence, no interaction, as if we were in a monastery with a vow of silence. The goal is to question the degree to which obvious lost time subsists and recognize the fact that it exists.

A more subtle type of time loss that is less tactile, and more difficult to detect or measure, is "hidden lost time." It can be difficult to detect when there is work stretching—with staff members making work to fill the available time (i.e., Parkinson's Law)—or when wide variances occur in the speed with which work is performed.

Checking for hidden lost time requires a disparate course of action, because the wasted time occurs while a person is actually working. One approach involves observations when creating work-to-time relationships. Individuals tend to work at different rates at various times. The variation in output represents hidden lost time. A benchmark can be established by informing an individual that you will be observing his or her job: the result during the observation will be a steady output of work.

Then collect output data on other days when you are not observing the individual; convert the production to units per hour. Compare the units per hour when an observation was taking place against the units per hour under normal conditions and note the difference in output as "hidden lost time." Variances from 0 to 10 percent are insignificant. You will probably find a variance more on the order of 50 to 60 percent, and do not be surprised if the variance is much higher.

We should recognize that some variance will always exist because workers never perform at the steady pace of a robotic machine. In any functional work area comprised of a large number of individuals, there will be high performers, low performers, average performers, lethargic people, energetic individuals—in short, employees with varied work ethics.

The observation process allows us to measure individual human behavior and can serve as the basis for creating compensation programs which match ability with productiveness. The uncontrollable factor is management's inability to provide work in sufficient quantities to staff members and then to manage their time.

We cannot find fault with individuals who stretch work either because they know they will not be occupied all day (i.e., insufficient available work) or because they do not know what is expected of them. It is the functional work area manager's responsibility to clearly inform staff members of what is expected of them.

To attain the objective of smoothing out activity work flows with consistent output to eliminate the major amount of lost time, work-to-time relationships must be employed. Reasonable expectancies help eliminate unwanted backlog by removing activity work flow impediments. Individuals in a functional work area can become demoralized by seeing piles of work that never appear to get smaller, but rather seem to grow larger despite their best efforts. Such individuals totally reject any sense of urgency to get work done, and employee turnover skyrockets.

One distribution company was constantly behind in applying cash because of the arrival each day of several thousand checks from customers. It seemed that the cash application process was never up to date. In truth, it was always 4 days behind. This backlog created problems in several areas of the organization and resulted in the loss of bank interest, because cash wasn't deposited the same day it arrived. This illustration is used only to point out the psychological effect and work flow problems caused by mismanagement of the functional work area's transaction volumes.

Conversely, that lack of any backlog is also disturbing. This type of situation can foster laxity in work routines, idle chatter, and a poor work ethic. The time it takes to process work will expand to fill the day, workers will become bored, and turnover will increase.

The utilization of observation process data will provide functional work area managers with the ability to control backlog in order not to permit the buildup of too large a work load at a given work station. This proactive approach will prevent staff members from running out of work and/or having to stretch the work on hand. Work will flow more evenly and, depending upon the volume of work, will allow the manager to adjust staffing to coincide with the availability of work.

In a majority of work situations the 80–20 rule applies. That is, a few activities will constitute the major portion of the work. Primary activities are usually apparent. A typical mailroom clerk spends 75 percent of his or her time sorting and delivering mail; the remaining 25 percent is comprised of preparatory activities—opening the mail, date-stamping mail received, preparing outgoing mail, and handling special requests from operating departments. Some work activities are not as easily identified, and in some cases staff members may not know which activity or activities make up their primary work load.

The ABM team should assist functional work area managers in identifying and categorizing activities into primary and secondary groups through the interviewing process described earlier. A method for validating this data is to provide each staff member with a daily activity worksheet on which to list each activity—time started and time stopped.

After this data is collected for a month, the manager can determine which activities are performed daily and the time spent each day doing the activity. The activities on the daily activities worksheet can also be classified as to frequency—weekly, biweekly, and so on—thus establishing the primary activity first. This self-observation exercise is similar to the process an ABM team member will use in observing the work performed.

Once data is collected, an appropriate work-to-time relationship can be established. If a source document indicates variances in the makeup of the data to be processed, it should be analyzed to determine the change in the time required for processing so a uniform unit of measure can be created.

For example, an order processing group might receive customer orders that varied as to number of line items and/or pieces ordered. Thus, processed sales orders would not be easily measured, because each unit might vary as to the time it takes to process. An alternative unit of measure would be in order here, such as number of line items.

The ABM team should keep in mind that the goal in measuring activities is to attain a credible level of reliability, not precise scientific accuracy. An excellent example of this is the cash application process described earlier, which clearly demonstrates how the measuring of work can be simplified. The cash application unit handled several checks received in the mail each day. The opening of the mail and sorting of checks involved more than six cash application staff members. It was virtually impossible to count each check that was received each day. The check sorting was an expeditious activity, but it was discovered that a tray of mail 24 inches long could hold approximately 720 checks. The functional work area manager decided it was accurate enough to use the tray capacity as his count, and each inch of space equaled approximately 30 checks for an incomplete tray.

Interpolating the count as a unit of measure, the functional work area manager was able to determine how long it would take to complete processing the contents of a tray. The unit of measure was simplified to trays and/or inches, and the time necessary to apply cash was then ascertained in terms of trays and/or inches per hour. The measurement of applying cash became a simple process. In addition, the manager used a color-coding scheme for the trays, as follows:

| | |
|---|---|
| Monday | Blue |
| Tuesday | Red |
| Wednesday | Yellow |
| Thursday | Orange |
| Friday | Green |

When a functional work area manager can apply some original thinking and open his or her mind to the work-measuring process, solutions to problems become very simple. An uncomplicated technique that has a reasonably high degree of accuracy should be every functional work area manager's goal.

### Summary

The key elements of the observation process are summarized below.

- It assists managers in reducing the time it takes work to flow through the operation, improving customer service.
- It reduces time in process by minimizing waiting time.
- It identifies where the smallest capacity within an activity's work flow is located, so managers can match capacities to volume requirements at work stations.
- It finds hidden bottlenecks in order to eliminate them.
- It forces managers to be more disciplined—to plan, execute the plan, and follow up to eliminate causes of delay before they occur.
- It recaptures lost hours.
- It emphasizes the advantages of personnel flexibility and the cross-training of staff members.

We have examined the observation process at a broad level. Now let's see how each of the techniques in the process is actually applied.

## Ratio Delay Study

A *ratio delay study* is a proven method for determining idle time. As discussed in the introduction to this chapter, idle time is defined as staff members engaging in idle conversation, daydreaming, visiting with each other, and/or being absent from their work station without reason.

Idle time is an indication of a staff member's attitude, commitment, and work ethic—provided the condition wasn't created by management's inefficiency in assigning sufficient quantities of work. Once a functional work area manager and senior management acknowledge the fact that lost time exists, the ratio delay study is the tool to use in quantifying the degree to which it exists.

The study is organized into 15-minute intervals, during which the ABM team records whether a staff member isn't working (i.e., is away from the work station) or is working. Although this technique is not scientifically based, it usually presents a highly accurate snapshot of obvious lost time in a functional work area.

The study doesn't indicate where staff members go when they are away from their work station or whether the observed time at work is value added or non-value added. The calculation of idle time is simply the number of people not working and/or away from their work station divided by the total number of people observed. It is not unusual to find that a significant percentage of the people are not working at each observation. By making this test over a period of several days, and at various times during each day so as not to bias the observation, the ABM team can determine the lost time percentages quite accurately.

Obvious lost time is not hard to expose if the manner in which it is exposed is not apparent to the staff members being observed. The ABM team should approach this activity without any preconceived biases and conduct the study objectively. The observer does not want people to know they are being observed and should try to be judicious and sensible in his or her application of this technique.

The ABM team should choose a place within the functional work area from which all or most of the staff members can easily be seen. The observer should then begin doing some sort of work which doesn't require a great deal of concentration. The following steps are in order:

- Tally the number of staff members in the functional work area who can easily be observed.
- Scan the workers every 5 minutes and count the number of staffers who appear not to be working.
- Repeat this process every 5 minutes for approximately 3 hours.
- Divide the number of staffers not working at each observation by the total number of staffers observed.
- Convert the ratio into a percentage of nonworking staffers and/or obvious lost time that occurs as of that time period.
- Repeat the entire process over a 3- to 4-day period.

The results obtained will be eye-opening and will probably indicate that 25 to 35 percent of the staff members weren't working at each observation. Prior to commencing the formal ratio delay study, the observer can conduct an informal study by walking through the functional work area and casually counting those people who appear not to be working. If the process is repeated a few times at different points in the workday, the lost time will be evident. The formal study will validate these initial impressions.

## Ratio Delay Study Worksheet

A *ratio delay study worksheet* (Fig. 6-3) is used to accumulate observations of functional work area employees performing work in the course of a normal workday. If the ratio delay study is properly conducted, functional work area employees should be unaware that the observation process is going on. The observer should attempt to position himself or herself in a location that affords a clear visual path of all the functional work area work stations. The observer should utilize the floor diagram to be certain to account for all the people who are at work and to omit anyone who is not in attendance.

| Functional work area: (1) | | | Prepared by: (2) | |
|---|---|---|---|---|
| | | | Date: | |

| Time period (3) | People working (4) | People not working or away (5) | People total (6) | Percent not working or away (7) |
|---|---|---|---|---|
| | | | | |
| | | | | |
| | | | | |
| | | | | |
| | | | | |
| | | | | |
| | | | | |
| | | | | |
| | | | | |
| | | | | |
| | | | | |
| | | | | |
| | | | | |
| | | | | |
| | | | | |
| | | | | |
| | | | | |
| | | | | |
| | | | | |
| | | | | |
| | | | | |
| | | | | |
| | | | | |
| | | | | |
| | | | | |
| | | | | |
| | | | | |
| | | | | |
| | | | | |
| | | | | |
| | | | | |
| | | | | |
| | | | | |
| | | | | |
| | | | | |

**Figure 6-3a.** Ratio delay study worksheet.

| Line # | Title or Term | Is Used to Indicate |
|---|---|---|
| (1) | Functional work area | The name of the work unit in which the activity is performed. |
| (2) | Prepared by / date | The name of the observer and date of observation. |
| (3) | Time period | The 15-minute intervals in which employees are observed at work. |
| (4) | People working | The number of employees in a functional work area who are working. |
| (5) | People not working or away | The number of employees in a functional work area who are not working. |
| (6) | People total | The combination of employees working and not working. |
| (7) | Percent not working or away | The percent of the time not working in each 15-minute interval. |

**Figure 6-3b.** Ratio delay study worksheet key.

The purpose of the ratio delay study worksheet is to record each 15-minute observation period and accumulate data for completing the ratio delay study (Fig. 6-4).

## Time Allocated for Observation

The observation process is applicable to small companies, medium-size companies, Fortune 1000 companies, Fortune 500 companies, and Fortune 10 companies. The size of a company is immaterial for utilizing a sound methodology to achieve the intended result of determining how long it should take to perform an activity.

Unfortunately, there isn't a scientific calculation for determining how much time should be allocated for making observations of staff members performing their everyday activities. Some observers who don't understand the merits of the observation process believe that too much time is spent doing observations and do not see a cost/benefit relationship.

The answer is a simple one: There is no shortcut to collecting comprehensive, unbiased data upon which to establish a meaningful and accurate reasonable expectancy or work-to-time relationship. The analyzing of historical data by the ABM team provides only a current barometer of how many units *are* being produced in a certain period of time. It doesn't indicate how many units *should* be produced in that same time period.

The cost/benefit test is easily calculated once the ABM team can compare what is to what should be produced. The volume data can be transformed into

| Time period | People working | People not working or away | Total people observed | People not working or away, percentage |
|---|---|---|---|---|
| 8:15 – 8:30 | 2 | 7 | 9 | 78 |
| 8:30 – 8:45 | 4 | 5 | 9 | 56 |
| 8:45 – 9:00 | 8 | 1 | 9 | 11 |
| 9:00 – 9:15 | 7 | 2 | 9 | 22 |
| 10:15 – 10:30 | 6 | 3 | 9 | 33 |
| 10:30 – 10:45 | 6 | 3 | 9 | 33 |
| | | | | |
| Total minutes | 33 | 21 | 54 | 39 |

**Figure 6-4.** Ratio delay study data.

quantitative dollar values when units of measure and reasonable expectancies have been established. The two most common measurements are changes in staffing requirements and increases in productivity.

To calculate the amount of time that should be devoted to the observation of activities, three elements are required:

- Number of staff members in a functional work area
- Number of hours in a normal workday, excluding time for lunch
- The 30 percent factor, which is arbitrary, but has proven over time to be an appropriate guideline for determining the amount of time to be devoted to the observation process

For example, a claims area in a health-care company has 50 staff members whose normal workday is 8 a.m. to 5 p.m., with 1 hour for lunch. Take the staff size of 50 people multiplied by 8 hours (9 hours less 1 hour for lunch), to arrive at 400 hours. Apply the 30 percent factor to the 400 hours to arrive at 120 hours for observations in the functional work area. The next section, on how many observations to perform, explains why there is a need to set aside this level of time for observations.

## How Many Observations to Do

For all the identified primary activities, the ABM team should make from 6 to 10 separate observations. The observation program should proceed

- At various times during the day
- On various days of the week

- During different shifts
- With various staff members performing the activity

The purpose for widening the observation routine is to obtain a good mix of transactions, and to observe staff members whose energy levels vary at different times in a day. The observations should be made without pressure, so that the activities are performed at a reasonably steady pace under normal working conditions. Utilize the procedures developed during the detailing process and their associated activity work flows as background material to be certain not to miss a routine and/or task in the activity being performed.

The observation should be conducted without interruption by either telephone calls or questions during the performance of the activity. If there is an unavoidable work stoppage during the observation, stop the clock, and do not begin timing the work routine again until the activity is resumed. Do not use a stopwatch. Try to be discreet by utilizing a wristwatch or an easily visible wall clock as the timing tool. This low-key approach will allow staff members to complete their work from start to finish.

The observation process is a proven, fast, and low-cost way of obtaining information about the activities being performed in a functional work area. We have only to look around to see what is going on and then draw conclusions as to the productivity enhancements that present themselves.

Observations are generally fast, but they are not always easy. The process requires experience and knowledge about the type of work going on. The observation technique benefits from experience within an organization, and its success depends on the uncanny ability to draw correct and relevant conclusions from what is observed.

Observation will not be enough to obtain all the data required to reengineer a functional work area's activities, but it can prove to be a valuable supplement to data collected from other sources. Even with its proven historical ability to present objective data, there will be skeptics who will never believe the results. Figure 6-5 summarizes the multiple facets of the observation process.

During a consulting assignment for a national distribution company of industrial tools, an accounts receivable manager refused to believe that the cash application staff members could encode checks as fast as the reasonable expectancy established during the observation process. We suggested that the functional work area manager select a staff member of her choice, and randomly select a typical batch of work. The staff member was observed performing the activity, and the accounts receivable manager timed the work. When the batch of work was completed the functional work area manager calculated the units-per-hour work-to-time relationship.

The reasonable expectancy was 30 percent higher than the established one set as a result of 10 observations made by the ABM team. The manager was still apprehensive, so we suggested that she select another batch of work and a different staff member to repeat the process.

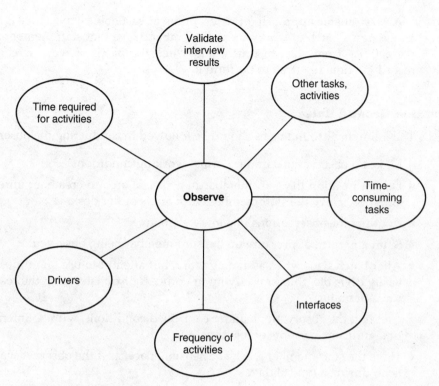

**Figure 6-5.** Side-by-side observations.

The process was repeated, and a similar work-to-time relationship was arrived at using the methodology employed during the first observation. The functional work area manager did not become a convert—as in fairy tales that begin with "once upon a time"—but she did refrain from questioning the validity of any other reasonable expectancies for the remaining activities in the functional work area.

# Determining Work-to-Time Relationships

Once you have established an appropriate unit of measure, as described in the introduction to this chapter, you need to associate that unit of measure with a unit of time required to perform the activity. This is the work-to-time relationship, or reasonable expectancy of performance, which is normally expressed in units per hour. As emphasized earlier, it is not essential to have scientifically crafted measurements, because the assignment and regulation of activities are more important elements in achieving productivity improvement.

A very reliable approach for determining a reasonable expectancy is to create and assign a batch of work to a staff member. Have that staff member perform the activity from start to finish, and when the batch of work is completed, record the time required to perform it.

## Observation Ground Rules

The following ground rules should be followed in conducting the observations:

- Make all observations under normal working conditions.
- Do not position the staff member in a special area to create an unreal work situation. Have the staff member work at his or her desk.
- Conduct the observations in a low-key manner.
- Shun any form of pressure on the staff member being observed.
- Alter batch sizes when assigning work, but attempt to use quantities that are easily divisible, thus simplifying the process of transforming the results into units per hour.
- Conduct the observations under controlled conditions, with no interruptions or significant amounts of lost time.
- Have the staff member work at a sensible pace, as if the observer wasn't present, during a typical day.
- Do not use historical data to establish a reasonable expectancy, because any inherent lost time in performing an activity will most likely be included in such data.
- Make sure you have chosen a good, representative unit of measure.

The role of the ABM team member is to stimulate a positive attitude in a staff member, employ discriminating decision making, and establish a two-way communication link by exercising high-level people skills. In addition, there is the analytical portion of separating an activity into its basic tasks, documenting the time periods to do the work, and measuring the staff member's performance. These two aspects of the ABM team member's role are equally important.

There shouldn't be any surprises. The ABM team should openly discuss the mechanics of the observation process with the functional work area manager. The manager can be helpful in providing excellent understanding as to the idiosyncracy of performing an activity and clarity as to whether a problem is a result of machine or human failure. The ABM team should keep in mind that the functional work area manager and his or her staff members are the customers, and their performance are the manager's direct responsibility.

The staff member chosen for observation should be someone whose work has been deemed to be average or slightly above average. Do not choose high performers. These types of staff members usually have positive attitudes about their job and the company. They exhibit excellent work habits and usually take direction well while following official guidelines. Staff members whose work pace is either superabundant or less than desired will be difficult to measure accurately, while the average worker's performance will be more reliable to gauge.

Prior to commencing the observation process, the ABM team should make an attempt to identify what level of performance the staff member has attained. Even the most experienced staff member will require some warmup time to gain a smooth working routine. An observation should not be undertaken until the chosen staff member is in rhythm. The education of the staff member to be observed in the techniques of observation should help promote a positive attitude for doing a good job. It is also important to find an individual who likes the work he or she is doing.

Obtaining a staff member's buy-in can never be overemphasized. Before the observation begins, the ABM team should reread the activity procedure developed during the detailing process to become familiar with the content of the activity. This refresher course will provide the observer with all the tasks to be observed so an accurate work-to-time relationship can be established.

When different staff members performing the same activity are observed, note any small variations in their routines for comparative purposes. Remember that no two individuals will perform any one activity exactly the same way. Procedures are continually being altered because of the subjective view most people have in determining what is easier or more convenient for completing an activity.

Activities should be audited at regular intervals (e.g., semiannual or annually), because changes occur. If an observation involves machinery, the machine speed should be set for maximum output consistent with quality requirements; worn-out machinery will provide inaccurate work-to-time relationships.

The ABM team should demonstrate a friendly attitude, explain the reason for the "observation process," and discuss openly any questions a staff member may have about the process. During this cordial short conference, continue to motivate staff members to offer important ideas for improving the activities performed. Caution all staff members to work at a pace they can sustain and emphasize that the observation process is neither rating their individual performance nor comparing it with others'. It is simply a technique to determine normal work-to-time relationships for primary activities.

This candor should eliminate deliberate slowdowns and individuals working at an abnormally fast pace, both of which make it difficult for an observer to establish a proper work-to-time relationship. Most individuals will work at a higher rate when they are being observed than when they are alone. The observer should always show respect for the staff member's skill and knowledge, and the staff member must have confidence that the resulting work-to-time relationship is fair and equitable.

The observer is like a baseball umpire or basketball referee: on the scene but out of the way of the players on the playing field. His or her positioning should be behind and to the side of the staff member so the field of vision is clear and so the staff member is less nervous about being constantly watched at work.

The observer should be natural and not just sit in silence, but should not engage in idle distracting conversation that either slows a process down or interrupts it with questions. Save all questions until the batch of work is completed.

The reason we emphasize a good relaxed interaction between the ABM team member who is observing the work and the staff member who is performing the work is that not even the functional work area manager can devote as much individual attention to a staff member as does the observer.

The observer should be constantly gaining acceptance, removing resistance, explaining the observation process methodology, and suggesting changes to daily routines. The emphasis should be placed on communication and interaction, with about one-quarter of the time being spent on analysis and setting work-to-time relationships.

## Work-to-Time Relationship Behavior Checklist

- Remember that you have no direct authority over staff members. You have to cajole them into cooperating with you and implementing your suggestions. If the staff member doesn't buy in, the ABM team will fail.

- Never argue or lose your temper, even in dealing with angry and sometimes unreasonable people.

- Always work with and through the functional work area manager. Inform the manager of what you want to do and how you plan to do it. You are acting as a manager's assistant and performing a function that the manager does not have the time to perform.

- Never criticize in a negative manner the way things are currently being done.

- Act warmly and humanely to a staff member. Before commencing an observation, chat briefly with the staff member to create a relaxed environment. If a staff member is upset for any reason—whether it is work related or home related—consider postponing the observation to a later time.

- When completing an observation, make sure to thank the staff member for being cooperative.

- Be open and informative. If a staff member is interested in how and why certain things are done, offer an explanation. However, do not become involved in discussions that are none of the ABM team's concern.

- Actively listen to all staff members' ideas for improvement, because the more they become involved the greater are the chances for creating a continuous improvement approach to work.

- Blend in and become an accepted part of the functional work area, demonstrating a desire to be helpful, not antagonistic.

- When several individuals perform an activity, try to observe as many of them as time allows so no one feels left out.

- Maintain a discipline to stay on target to be sure to complete the observation process on schedule.

- Maintain all confidential data (e.g., payroll data, costs) under lock and key. This data should not be discussed with the general population.

- Don't gossip and become involved in personnel issues.

- Check and validate all information to eliminate bias through opinions, emotion, and misinformation. People do not usually intend to misinform, but information does become altered as it is passed from one staff member to another (as in the game of telephone we played as kids).

- Never try to correct or improve an activity until the root cause and/or work driver is identified. Emphasize to all staff members that they do not have to accept existing conditions as required. Coach staff members to ask: "What are we doing and why?"

One of the distinct advantages of developing work-to-time relationships is that they become the basis for cost control in an organization. When work-to-time relationships are employed, individual activity costs can be quickly identified.

When operating deficiencies are corrected, two obvious cost reductions show up; achieving the same production with fewer staff members and/or achieving production gains without increasing head count. It is important for senior management and the ABM team to agree on how they will measure success or failure to avoid any future controversy concerning the success of the ABM program.

## Observation Record

The *observation record* is used to record physical observations of activities in a functional work area. The purpose of the observation record is to

- Record several observations of each primary activity in a functional work area
- Serve as the data for calculating work-to-time relationships

The observation record should be used to observe primary activities at least six times, at different times during the day, to ensure a good mix of transactions. This form (Fig. 6-6) should be reviewed for accuracy and completeness.

Once the observation record is completed, a work-to-time relationship (i.e., units per hour) should be calculated for each observation, as follows:

- Look at column 12, the number of units processed, in Fig. 6-6.
- Divide column 12 (i.e., 21 units) by column 11, the elapsed time to process the units (i.e., 21 minutes).
- Multiply the result ($21/21 = 1$) by 60 to arrive at units per hour (60).

Indicate any special comments that seem appropriate—for example, if productivity improvements were suggested or if the mix of transactions processed was good.

Activity number: _____ (16)  
Activity name: _____ (1)  
Activity type: _____ (5)  

Functional work area: _____ (2)  
Supervisor name: _____ (3)  
Unit of measure: _____ (4)  

**Activity description (15)**

| Date (6) | Value added (7) / Non-value added | Employee name (8) | Time | | | Units prod. (12) | Units/hour (13) | Comments (14) |
|---|---|---|---|---|---|---|---|---|
| | | | Start (9) | Stop (10) | Elap. (11) | | | |
| | | | | | | | | |
| | | | | | | | | |

**Figure 6-6a.** Observation record.

Activity number: 01
Activity name: Final notice letter calls
Activity type: Primary

Functional work area: Collections
Supervisor name: Ed Smith
Unit of measure: Letters

**Activity description**

To prepare letters notifying customers that this is their final notice to settle their account or it will be turned over to a collection agency and that credit bureaus will be notified.

| Date | Value added Non-value added | Employee name | Time | | | Units prod. | Units/ hour | Comments |
|---|---|---|---|---|---|---|---|---|
| | | | Start | Stop | Elap. | | | |
| 08/01/94 | VA | Susan Brown | 10:08 AM | 10:29 AM | 0.21 | 21 | 60/hr | Older batch |
| 08/01/94 | VA | Ellen Brown | 01:00 PM | 01:48 PM | 0.48 | 24 | 30/hr | Current batch, many calls |
| 08/03/94 | VA | Susan Brown | 10:53 AM | 11:35 AM | 0.42 | 21 | 30/hr | Bad debt write off |
| 08/15/94 | VA | Tony Franco | 12:30 PM | 01:21 PM | 0.51 | 21 | 25/hr | Call before final letter goes out |
| 08/05/94 | VA | Ellen Brown | 02:42 PM | 03:22 PM | 0.30 | 15 | 30/hr | Good mix, several calls |
| 08/11/94 | VA | Tony Franco | 11:35 AM | 12:12 PM | 0.37 | 17 | 28/hr | Duplicate invoice |
| 08/12/94 | VA | Fran Mayer | 03:00 PM | 03:30 PM | 0.30 | 15 | 30/hr | Good mix, contact letter |
| 08/12/94 | VA | Fran Mayer | 04:19 PM | 06:01 PM | 0.52 | 26 | 30/hr | Current batch, self observation |

**Figure 6-6a.** (*Continued*) Observation record.

Activity number: 02
Activity name: Daily follow up calls
Activity type: Primary

Functional work area: Collections
Supervisor name: Ed Smith
Unit of measure: Telephone calls

## Activity description

To telephone customer accounts for money.

| Date | Value added Non-value added | Employee name | Time | | | Units prod. | Units/ hour | Comments |
|---|---|---|---|---|---|---|---|---|
| | | | Start | Stop | Elap. | | | |
| 08/02/94 | VA | Phil Gordon | 09:15 AM | 09:45 AM | 0.30 | 30 | 60/hr | |
| 08/02/94 | VA | Phil Gordon | 09:50 PM | 10:10 AM | 0.20 | 21 | 60/hr | |
| 08/04/94 | VA | Don Corso | 12:00 PM | 12:15 PM | 0.15 | 30 | 120/hr | Did not speak with many customers |
| 08/04/94 | VA | Don Corso | 12:20 PM | 12:50 PM | 0.30 | 28 | 60/hr | |
| 08/09/94 | VA | Leslie Forte | 10:15 AM | 10:40 AM | 0.25 | 25 | 60/hr | |
| 08/09/94 | VA | Leslie Forte | 11:00 AM | 11:35 AM | 0.35 | 20 | 36/hr | Problem calls |
| 08/10/94 | VA | Abby Johnson | 01:00 PM | 01:30 PM | 0.30 | 27 | 54/hr | |
| 08/10/94 | VA | Abby Johnson | 01:45 PM | 02:15 PM | 0.30 | 30 | 60/hr | Self observation |
| 08/12/94 | VA | Lori Crystal | 03:00 PM | 03:20 PM | 0.20 | 20 | 60/hr | |

**Figure 6-6a.** (Continued) Observation record.

196

| Line # | Title or Term | Is Used to Indicate |
|--------|---------------|---------------------|
| (1) | Activity name | The name of the activity that is being observed. |
| (2) | Functional work area | The name of the work unit in which the employees being observed work. |
| (3) | Supervisor name | The name of the work unit person in charge of the functional work area. |
| (4) | Activity measure | The unit of output to measure the activity. |
| (5) | Activity type | P for primary activity and S for secondary activity. |
| (6) | Date | The month, day, and year that the observation was made. |
| (7) | Value added or non-value added | VA for value added and NVA for non-value added. |
| (8) | Employee name | The name of the employee being observed. |
| (9) | Start time | The hour and minute the observation began (9:14). |
| (10) | Stop time | The hour and minute the observation ended (10:21). |
| (11) | Elapsed time | The total elapsed minutes for the interview (67 minutes). |
| (12) | Units processed | The total number of units processed during the observation. |
| (13) | Units per hour | The units per hour processed during the interview. |
| (14) | Comments | Any special comments (e.g., good mix of transactions) that may be meaningful in evaluating the observation. |
| (15) | Activity description | A brief description of the activity observed. |
| (16) | Activity number | A sequential number for each activity observed in a functional work area. |

**Figure 6-6b.** Observation record key.

If a staff member appears to be interested in the mechanics of the observation process, and the ABM team member conducting the observations deems that individual to be objective, encourage the individual to make a self-observation. When the self-observation is completed, record it as you would any other observation, but make a note that it was a self-observation. Many staff members enjoy being a partner in the observation process, and it is a reinforcement for employee buy-in. An additional benefit is the training of staff members in the technique for future utilization when an activity is changed and/or a new activity is introduced.

Usually a secondary activity cannot be observed because it is performed infrequently. Ask the staff member to estimate the average elapsed time it takes to complete the secondary activity (e.g., 2 hours twice a month). Estimating is thoroughly discussed in Chapter Four.

Even though some functional work area managers agree in principle that work-to-time relationships produce beneficial results, they contend that many jobs depend primarily on the use of judgment and are therefore unmeasurable. However, research and detailed analysis usually indicate that what generally passes for judgment may actually be nothing more than comparison, inspection, selection, and/or classification, all of which can be measured.

In addition, the segregation of those activities deemed to be judgmental may comprise only a small portion of a functional work area's activities. Remember that personal time, fatigue, and/or unavoidable delays are excluded in the calculation to arrive at pure work time, but all three factors can account for 10 to 15 percent of a staff member's workday.

## Observation Recap

The *observation recap* is used to accumulate a series of physical observations of each primary activity from the observation record. The purpose of the observation recap is to consolidate all physical observations from the observation record and then develop reasonable expectancies for primary activities. This form (Fig. 6-7) should be reviewed for accuracy and completeness.

When the 6 to 10 observations of each primary activity are entered on the observation record, transcribe all the unit-per-hour entries to the observation recap. The recap summarizes all a functional work area's activities in one place in preparation for calculating the reasonable expectancy for each primary activity. Recall that a reasonable expectancy is the amount of work that an average staff member can produce under normal working conditions, expressed in units per hour.

In calculating the reasonable expectancy for an activity, you should

- Ignore the highest work-to-time relationship on the observation recap (e.g., Activity 2: Daily follow-up calls—120 per hour)

- Ignore the lowest work-to-time relationship on the observation recap (Activity 2: Daily follow-up calls—36 per hour)

- Calculate the difference between the second highest work-to-time relationship on the observation recap (Activity 2: Daily follow-up calls—60 per hour) and the second lowest work-to-time relationship (54 per hour). The result is 6.

- Divide the result (6) by 3 to arrive at the incremental factor of 2.

- Create an incremental scale starting from the second lowest work-to-time relationship (54) and ending with the second highest work-to-time relationship, using intervals of 2 (54, 56, 58, 60).

- Establish the reasonable expectancy in the upper-third range (58–60).

Date: (1)

Page ___ of ___

| Functional work area: (2) | | | Supervisor name: (3) | | | | | | | | | | |
|---|---|---|---|---|---|---|---|---|---|---|---|---|---|
| Activity number (4) | Activity name (5) | Activity measure (6) | Observation results (7) | | | | | | | | | | |
| | | | 1 | 2 | 3 | 4 | 5 | 6 | 7 | 8 | 9 | 10 | R.E. (8) |

**Figure 6-7a.** Observation recap.

Date: (1) 8/12/94

Page 1 of 1

| Functional work area: (2) Collections | | | Supervisor name: (3) Ed Smith | | | | | | | | | |
|---|---|---|---|---|---|---|---|---|---|---|---|---|
| | | | Observation results (7) | | | | | | | | | |
| Activity number (4) | Activity name (5) | Activity measure (6) | 1 | 2 | 3 | 4 | 5 | 6 | 7 | 8 | 9 | 10 | R.E. (8) |
| 1 | Final notice | Letters | 60/hr | 30/hr | 30/hr | 25/hr | 30/hr | 28/hr | 30/hr | 30/hr | | | 30/hr |
| 2 | Daily follow up | Calls | 60/hr | 60/hr | 120/hr | 60/hr | 60/hr | 36/hr | 54/hr | 60/hr | 60/hr | | 58/hr |
| 3 | 45 day aging | Calls | 70/hr | 96/hr | 60/hr | 60/hr | 60/hr | 90/hr | 60/hr | | | | 83/hr |

**Figure 6-7a.** (*Continued*) Observation recap.

| Line # | Title or Term | Is Used to Indicate |
|---|---|---|
| (1) | Date | The month, day, and year the reasonable expectancies are calculated. |
| (2) | Functional work area | The name of the work unit in which the employees being observed work. |
| (3) | Supervisor name | The name of the work unit person in charge of the functional work area. |
| (4) | Activity number | The sequence of the activity observed. |
| (5) | Activity name | The name of the activity that is being observed. |
| (6) | Activity measure | The unit of output to measure the activity. |
| (7) | Observation results | The units per hour for each observation made. |
| (8) | R.E. | The reasonable expectancy determined for the activity on the basis of the observations made. |

**Figure 6-7b.** Observation recap key.

■ Establish the reasonable expectancy in the lower half of the upper-third range (58) for the specific activity observed (Activity 2: Daily follow-up calls) and enter it in the appropriate column on the observation recap.

It often takes the full complement of allotted hours to make the observations in order to be certain that the most accurate reasonable expectancy is determined for each of the primary activities in a functional work area. The reasonable expectancy becomes a key element for staffing an organization, as discussed in detail in Chapter Seven.

Once all the reasonable expectancies are calculated, it is easy to group them on the reasonable expectancy data sheet. A data sheet should be created for each functional work area, categorized by business process, and placed in a binder for easy reference. The binder should be indexed to facilitate finding each sheet when needed.

The reasonable expectancy data sheet should include both primary and secondary activities to be certain all functional work area activities are accounted for. The reasonable expectancies for secondary activities will not be calculated, but accurate estimates will be acceptable for these lesser activities.

# Work Sequence Plan

The *work sequence plan* is a guide that assists functional work area managers in organizing their activity work load. It is a flexible, living tool to be altered, revised, and reconstructed as work changes and as the functional work area manager learns more about the activities performed in his or her area. It is a joint venture between staff members and functional work area management, utilizing all of the data accumulated in the interview, detailing, and observation processes. Most work sequence plans are constructed in half-hour intervals.

In constructing the work sequence plan, the ABM team must review historical volume data for each activity, including both primary and secondary activities, to be sure that 100 percent of the activity is accounted for. The review of volume data should attempt to smooth out any erratic levels which may occur on various days of the week and/or various hours in a day. In a major distribution company certain work activities had their largest volumes in the morning and others between 12:30 p.m. and 2:30 p.m. (during lunch hour periods).

The knowledge of these transaction volumes coupled with their associated work-to-time relationships provides the functional work area manager with the data needed to construct a useful work sequence plan for the area. Test the work sequence plan in a functional work area for several days to determine where any fine tuning should be made (Fig. 6-8).

When it is discovered that specific activities tend to peak at specified time periods during the day, the work sequence plan provides the functional work area manager with the data and game plan to adjust resources to handle those peaks. It also enables the staff members to perform other activities during the lower-volume and less intensive time periods. Flexibility is the key.

A functional work area manager should not worry if the work sequence plan does not always run like a finely tuned engine. There will always be times when nothing goes right no matter what is attempted. The activity dictionary (see Chapter 3) should be the guide ensuring that all functional work area activities are accounted for in the work sequence plan. Remember that the work sequence plan is not set in cement and should be continuously reviewed and revised as the functional work area manager works with it.

It is a guide whose primary purpose is to organize activities. The functional work area manager can constantly monitor equivalent units of work to work force capacity and then make a determination of the best method of completing the available work. If the manager finds that the volume of available work exceeds the functional work area's capacity to complete the work, it is his or her responsibility to

- Create a backlog of the overabundance of work
- Plan to work overtime to process all available work
- Contact other functional work areas to obtain temporary help to eliminate the potential backlog

Generally, when volume is not abundant enough to support a full day of work, a functional work area manager should investigate the utilization of his or her excess capacity by another work group. If the condition is sporadic or temporary, the aforementioned approach is relevant. However, a continuing reduction of activity volume in a work area is sufficient reason to reexamine the

Time of day

| Activity | 8:30–9:30 | 9:30–10:30 | 10:30–11:30 | 11:30–12:00 | Lunch | 1:00–2:00 | 2:00–3:00 | 3:00–4:00 | 4:00–5:00 | 5:00–5:30 |
|---|---|---|---|---|---|---|---|---|---|---|
| Daily Follow-up Calls | EVERYONE | | | | | | | | | |
| Final-Notice Letter Calls | | EVERYONE | | | | | | | | |
| 45-Day Aging Calls | | | EVERYONE | | | | | | | |
| Place Collection—Regular | | | | | | | ELLEN | | | |
| Place Collection—D&B | | | | | | | ELLEN | | | |
| Final-Notice Letters | | | | | | | SUSAN | | | |
| Bankruptcy Process | | | | | | | TOM | | | |
| Filing | | | | | | | | | ELLEN | |
| Payments from Agency | | | | | | | | | ELLEN | |
| Collection Agency Comm. Pay | | | | | | | | | ELLEN | |
| Collection Agency Bad Debt W/O | | | | | | | | | ELLEN | |
| Final-Notice Letter Mailout | | | | | | | | SUSAN | | |
| Bounced Checks | | | | | | | | SUSAN | | |
| Statement Mailout | | | | | | | | TOM | | |
| Terms Account Review | | | | | | | | TOM | | |
| Terms Account New | | | | | | | | TOM | | |

**Figure 6-8.** Work sequence plan.

functional work area's staffing requirements and, if necessary, reduce the work force to maintain the appropriate balance between volume and payroll.

In a business process comprised of several functional work areas, managers should regularly communicate with one another so they can easily determine the need to borrow or exchange resources to balance the work load. This eliminates the danger of one functional work area having excess capacity while another work area has excess volume without the possibility of matching volume to capacity.

The manager should be able to monitor the work of each staff member, to easily be alerted when a problem causes a delay in processing work so immediate corrective action can be taken to minimize that delay. In some organizations work may be grouped in one-hour batches and assigned by a work flow control desk, but this approach is not currently in widespread use. It has too many negative connotations of "Big Brother is watching you," but the approach could have selective utilization.

An interesting sidelight that can be analyzed is the calculation of a productivity percentage for each staff member. This is accomplished by dividing the actual amount of completed work by the amount of work scheduled to be completed in a normal workday.

A great deal of work just arrives at a work station. It isn't batched or assigned to the staff member, but rather is processed and forwarded to the next work station in the activity work flow sequence. In some instances, work is created but not planned for; in other instances, work is performed for which a work-to-time relationship cannot be established.

If a staff member is current in processing his or her work and productivity is low, the functional work area manager is responsible for finding additional work for that individual. Most individuals would rather have a reasonable work load rather than sit idle. The functional work area manager must exercise restraint to avoid loading a staff member with too much work.

The work sequence plan becomes especially useful when a functional work area manager has a mandate to move a set amount of volume each day, regardless of what level of volume is available. The manager must reach the objective on schedule even when staff members are absent. This is controllable with the work sequence plan, assisting the manager in shifting resources to attain the goal. If a situation arises which indicates that the scheduled work load will not be completed, the functional work area manager will know this at the earliest possible moment and can then plan overtime, borrow resources from other areas, or set aside some other work with a lower priority. The appropriate speedy action can take place without delay. The manager will be equipped with the most advanced data to take the appropriate action.

In configuring the work sequence plan, a manager can take into consideration the experience of the staff member. When the work-to-time relationships were established, they were based on the ability of an average worker working at a normal pace. A new staff member cannot be expected to perform at the reasonable expectancy immediately, but that level can be used as an objective means of measuring an employee's progress.

If statistical data is accumulated, a functional work area manager can develop a basis for forecasting how long it should take a new staff member to process work to standard. A training curve can be established and monitored so inadequate performance can be readily identified. The staff member can then obtain the required additional training he or she may need. This monitoring of work will identify and document which staff member will not make the grade, hastening the decision to make a change in staff. The learning curve will become more structured and precise.

An additional benefit of the work sequence plan is to afford the functional work area manager with a minimal strain on the ability to understand what effect changes in volume will have on productivity and staffing requirements. The manager can expand or contract the area's work force with complete faith that his or her staffing is in line with the volume of available work. Senior management can be fully assured that it is protected against overstaffing or understaffing throughout the entire organization. Also, senior management can easily identify who is both accountable and responsible for staffing levels, and can readily monitor if those responsible are attaining the goals of the organization from a cost and customer service point of view without sacrificing quality.

The historical transaction volumes that functional work area managers use should be tallied by computer rather than by hand to increase accuracy and lessen the possibility of overrecording or underrecording. If an activity is a primary one and the only source of data available is manually produced, the ABM team should use the data as a last resort.

It is preferable to use 12 months of historical transaction volume data, but if only 6 months of data is available, utilize it. Make sure to ask the functional work area manager about any seasonality factors associated with the transaction volume data.

The most appropriate information to use in order of preference is daily, weekly, and then monthly data to avoid special highs and lows (e.g., Monday—high volume; Tuesday to Friday—medium volumes). The ABM team should note special holidays, 5-week months, and/or facility shutdowns when reviewing historical transaction volume data.

## Work Sequence Summary Plan Checklist

- Utilize the activity dictionary (see Chapter Three) as the basis for creating the work sequence plan.
- Involve the functional work area manager in the construction of the work sequence plan.
- Control backlogs.
- Maintain a balanced relationship between capacity to perform work and available volume to be processed.
- Coordinate work activity with other functional work areas within a business process for staffing needs.

- Keep the work sequence plan flexible so increases or decreases in volume can be handled by adjusting requirements for resources.

- Distribute work loads evenly.

- Provide functional work area managers with the tools necessary to measure performance and assign and monitor work.

Excellent tools can be used to conduct transaction volume analysis:

- Activity volume tally worksheet
- Activity volume tally recap
- Volume sampling worksheet
- Activity analysis linkage worksheet

All the aforementioned analysis tools are not mandatory, but our experience indicates they are all used at different times, for different purposes, by different functional work area managers. We have included them so any one or all can be utilized. Our recommendation is to use tools that you are comfortable with and that yield the type of data you wish to obtain in an organized manner.

### Volume Tally Worksheet

The *volume tally worksheet* is an excellent tool for manually accumulating current transaction volume data for both primary and secondary activities. In addition, it can be used to validate computer-generated historical transaction volumes to determine if there have been any significant changes to the data. This is an optional worksheet and should be used as a last resort for primary activities and for all secondary activities. Once the volume tally data collection activity is installed, it should be maintained for several weeks.

The purpose of the volume tally worksheet is to link activities to related volume transaction data. The volume tally worksheet should be used over a 3-month time frame. The worksheet shows each activity, activity type, and activity measure. This form (Fig. 6-9) should be reviewed for accuracy and completeness.

There should be a volume tally worksheet for each staff member in a functional work area. The activities to be listed on the worksheet are taken directly from the activity dictionary prepared during the interview process, including the activity type and activity measure. Each volume tally worksheet is used for a full week and should be totaled line by line by each staff member before it is handed to the functional work area manager at the end of the week.

The functional work area manager summarizes the weekly volume tally worksheet by preparing the volume tally recap by staff member and by activity. If an activity wasn't performed during a given week, a zero should be entered on the volume tally worksheet instead of leaving a line blank. The volume tally recap is used for 5 weeks. The data source for the volume tally recap is the total column on the volume tally worksheet.

| Functional work area (1) | Date W/E (2) | | Name of employee: (3) | | | | | |
|---|---|---|---|---|---|---|---|---|
| Activity name (4) | Activity type (5) | Activity measure (6) | Monday | Tuesday | Wednesday (7) | Thursday | Friday | Total |
| | | | | | | | | |
| | | | | | | | | |
| | | | | | | | | |
| | | | | | | | | |
| | | | | | | | | |
| | | | | | | | | |
| | | | | | | | | |
| | | | | | | | | |
| | | | | | | | | |
| | | | | | | | | |
| | | | | | | | | |
| | | | | | | | | |
| | | | | | | | | |
| | | | | | | | | |
| | | | | | | | | |
| | | | | | | | | |
| | | | | | | | | |
| | | | | | | | | |
| | | | | | | | | |

**Figure 6-9a.** Volume tally worksheet.

| Functional work area | Date W/E | Name of employee: |
|---|---|---|
| Accounts receivable | 8/5/94 | Hillary Martin |

| Activity name | Activity type | Activity measure | Monday | Tuesday | Wednesday | Thursday | Friday | Total |
|---|---|---|---|---|---|---|---|---|
| Bank deposit verification | P | Deposits | 10 | 10 | 10 | 10 | 10 | 40 |
| Problem checks–telephone calls | S | Calls | 5 | 7 | 4 | 6 | 1 | 23 |
| Bounced checks | S | Checks | 3 | 0 | 0 | 4 | 4 | 11 |
| Customer credit aging | S | Occurences | 0 | 2 | 0 | 1 | 0 | 3 |
| Encoding | P | Checks | 240 | 270 | 230 | 200 | 305 | 1,245 |
| Cash application–regular CODS | P | Items | 15 | 70 | 15 | 20 | 0 | 60 |
| Bank charges–VISA, Master Card | S | Transactions | 5 | 9 | 20 | 10 | 5 | 49 |
| Bank credits–VISA, Master Card | S | Transactions | 0 | 3 | 10 | 4 | 0 | 17 |
| Freighting | S | Accounts | 1 | 0 | 0 | 2 | 0 | 3 |
| Accounts receivable research | S | Accounts | 0 | 2 | 0 | 0 | 1 | 3 |
| Cash application–checks | P | Checks | 393 | 400 | 500 | 400 | 400 | 2,093 |
| Faxing | S | Faxes | 2 | 2 | 2 | 2 | 3 | 13 |

**Figure 6-9a.** (*Continued*) Volume tally worksheet.

| Functional work area<br>Accounts payable | Date W/E<br>8/5/94 | | Name of employee: Joanne Bigelow | | | | | |
|---|---|---|---|---|---|---|---|---|
| Activity<br>name | Activity<br>type | Activity<br>measure | Monday | Tuesday | Wednesday | Thursday | Friday | Total |
| Mail sort | P | Invoices | 160 | 94 | 100 | 100 | 100 | 554 |
| Checking saves—regular | P | Saves | 50 | 154 | 60 | 70 | 70 | 404 |
| Checking saves—drop shipments | P | Saves | 10 | 20 | 37 | 25 | 15 | 107 |
| UPS/Federal Express | S | Items | 0 | 2 | 0 | 0 | 19 | 21 |
| Void—stop payment checks | S | Checks | 0 | 0 | 5 | 0 | 0 | 5 |
| Review checks—prior to issue | P | Checks | 106 | 394 | 100 | 200 | 50 | 850 |
| Accounts receivable refunds | S | Checks | 10 | 0 | 31 | 0 | 0 | 41 |
| Debit/memos | S | Debit memos | 2 | 0 | 0 | 0 | 3 | 5 |
| Filing | P | Invoices | 200 | 60 | 300 | 100 | 40 | 700 |
| Vendor statement research | S | Statements | 5 | 0 | 0 | 0 | 2 | 7 |
| Problem research vendors | S | Requests | 1 | 0 | 1 | 2 | 0 | 4 |
| Faxing | S | Faxes | 5 | 0 | 5 | 0 | 0 | 10 |
| Prepare/store invoices | P | Invoices | 57 | 30 | 23 | 20 | 20 | 150 |
| | | | | | | | | |
| | | | | | | | | |
| | | | | | | | | |
| | | | | | | | | |
| | | | | | | | | |
| | | | | | | | | |
| | | | | | | | | |

**Figure 6-9a.** (*Continued*) Volume tally worksheet.

| Line # | Title or Term | Is Used to Indicate |
|---|---|---|
| (1) | Functional work area | The name of the work unit in which the activity is performed. |
| (2) | Date/week ending | The date of the week ending that volume data is being captured. |
| (3) | Name of employee | The name of the person capturing and reporting volume data. |
| (4) | Activity name | The name of the activity for which volume data is being recorded. |
| (5) | Activity type | P for primary activity and S for secondary activity. |
| (6) | Activity measure | The unit of output to measure the activity's volume data. |
| (7) | Day of the week | The day of the week on which an activity produced volume transaction data. |

**Figure 6-9b.** Volume tally worksheet key.

Once the transaction volume data has been accumulated, the functional work area manager and the ABM team should begin analyzing the data. Volume analysis is important for identifying activities whose transaction volumes are not easily counted in order to find a surrogate which can be converted into a unit of measure. An example of an activity that could be counted by using a surrogate measure is as follows:

| Activity | Unit of Measure | Surrogate Unit of Measure | Conversion Data |
|---|---|---|---|
| Mail delivery | Letter | Weight of incoming mailbag | Letters per pound |

## Volume Tally Recap

The *volume tally recap* is used to accumulate a month of volume data from the volume tally worksheets. The purpose of the volume tally recap is to consolidate weekly volume transaction data from the volume tally worksheets. The volume tally recap should be used over a 3-month time frame. If time permits, compare Mondays with one another and/or analyze week-to-week results to determine if there is a heavier, lighter day during the week, or week during the month.

This form (Fig. 6-10) should be reviewed for accuracy and completeness. If an activity wasn't worked during a given week, place a zero on the line instead of leaving it blank.

Functional work area: (1)  Date/month ending: (2)  Name of employee: (3)

| Activity name (4) | Activity type (5) | Activity measure (6) | Date Week ending (7) | Date Week ending (8) | Date Week ending | Date Week ending | Date Week ending | Total |
|---|---|---|---|---|---|---|---|---|
|  |  |  |  |  |  |  |  |  |

**Figure 6-10a.** Volume tally recap.

| Functional work area: | | | Date/month ending: | | | Name of employee: | | |
|---|---|---|---|---|---|---|---|---|
| Activity name | Activity type | Activity measure | Date Week ending | Date Week ending | Date Week ending | Date Week ending | Date Week ending | Total |
| | | | | | | | | |

**Figure 6-10a.** (*Continued*) Volume tally recap.

| Functional work area: Accounts receivable | | | Date/month ending: 8/26/94 | | | Name of employee: Hillary Martin | |
|---|---|---|---|---|---|---|---|
| Activity name | Activity type | Activity measure | Date Week ending 8/05/94 | Date Week ending 8/12/94 | Date Week ending 8/19/94 | Date Week ending 8/26/94 | Total |
| Bank deposit | P | Deposits | 40 | 43 | 40 | 35 | 158 |
| Problem checks | S | Calls | 23 | 18 | 23 | 19 | 83 |
| Bounced checks | S | Checks | 11 | 18 | 8 | 7 | 44 |
| Credit aging | S | Occurence | 3 | 2 | 3 | 1 | 9 |
| Encoding | P | Checks | 1,245 | 542 | 1,350 | 940 | 4,077 |
| Cash—CODs | P | Items | 60 | 12 | 50 | 35 | 157 |
| Bank charges—VISA | S | Transactions | 49 | 52 | 61 | 40 | 202 |
| Bank credits—VISA | S | Transactions | 17 | 5 | 7 | 10 | 39 |
| Freighting | S | Accounts | 3 | 2 | 0 | 6 | 11 |
| A/C receivable aging | S | Accounts | 3 | 2 | 1 | 2 | 8 |
| Cash application | P | Checks | 2,093 | 1,612 | 1,795 | 1,940 | 7,440 |
| Faxing | S | Faxs | 13 | 10 | 5 | 4 | 32 |

**Figure 6-10a.** (*Continued*) Volume tally recap.

| Functional work area: Accounts payable | | Date/month ending: 8/26/94 | | | Name of employee: Joanne Bigelow | | |
| --- | --- | --- | --- | --- | --- | --- | --- |
| Activity name | Activity type | Activity measure | Date Week ending 8/05/94 | Date Week ending 8/12/94 | Date Week ending 8/19/94 | Date Week ending 8/26/94 | Total |
| Mail sort | P | Invoices | 554 | 600 | 480 | 530 | 2,164 |
| Check saves, regular | P | Saves | 404 | 440 | 395 | 415 | 1,654 |
| Check saves, drop ships | P | Saves | 107 | 110 | 50 | 135 | 302 |
| UPS/Federal Express | S | Items | 21 | 29 | 30 | 24 | 104 |
| VOID stop payment | S | Checks | 5 | 6 | 2 | 7 | 20 |
| Review checks | P | Checks | 850 | 900 | 910 | 875 | 3,535 |
| Accounts receivable refunds | S | Checks | 41 | 34 | 35 | 50 | 160 |
| Debit/memos | S | Debit memos | 5 | 2 | 4 | 6 | 17 |
| Filing | P | Invoices | 700 | 800 | 750 | 650 | 2,900 |
| Statement research | S | Statements | 7 | 10 | 8 | 5 | 30 |
| Problem vendors | S | Requests | 4 | 3 | 3 | 0 | 10 |
| Faxing | S | Faxes | 10 | 16 | 15 | 12 | 53 |
| Prepare/store invoices | P | Invoices | 150 | 160 | 170 | 130 | 610 |

**Figure 6-10a.** (Continued) Volume tally recap.

| Line # | Title or Term | Is Used to Indicate |
|--------|---------------|---------------------|
| (1) | Functional work area | The name of the work unit in which the activity is performed. |
| (2) | Date/month ending | The date of the month ending that the volume is being captured. |
| (3) | Name of employee | The name of the person capturing and reporting volume data. |
| (4) | Activity name | The name of the activity for which the interviewee performs work. |
| (5) | Activity type | P for primary activity and S for secondary activity. |
| (6) | Activity measure | The unit of output to measure the activity's volume data. |
| (7) | Date/week ending | The date of the week ending on which an activity produced volume transaction data. Some months have 5 weeks. |

**Figure 6-10*b*.** Volume tally recap key.

## Activity Analysis Linkage Worksheet

The *activity analysis linkage* worksheet is a template for summarizing and describing activity characteristics. The purpose of the activity analysis linkage worksheet is to

- Define and link activities to end users
- Identify output sources
- Define end users

The activity analysis linkage worksheet provides a complete activity listing. Ongoing enhancements might include maintaining a product dictionary—a published reference. This form (Fig. 6-11) should be reviewed for accuracy and completeness.

## Summary

The key elements of the observation process are summarized below.

- The observation process matches units of work with units of time.
- The process sets the appropriate unit of work.
- Work-to-time relationships do not have to be scientifically precise. A reasonable expectancy of performance is adequate.

- Scheduling of work, not solely its measurement, is the important factor.

- Work-to-time relationships create an environment for increased productivity and include a psychological component.

- Associating activity work flow to work station capacities is a significant element of the process.

- Cross-training that creates worker flexibility greatly enhances the effect of the process.

- The process will create added value if it is introduced and sold at all levels of the organization at the outset.

- Management can avoid labor problems by demonstrating to union officials and union member workers the benefits of such a process.

| Functional work area: (1) | Prepared by/date: (2) | Approved by/date: (3) | Page 1 of 2 |
|---|---|---|---|

| Activity | | | Activity measure | | | | |
|---|---|---|---|---|---|---|---|
| Activity driver name (4) | Activity driver source (5) | Type (6) | Name (7) | Description (8) | Basis (9) | Source (10) | End users (destination) (11) |
| | | | | | | | |
| | | | | | | | |
| | | | | | | | |
| | | | | | | | |
| | | | | | | | |
| | | | | | | | |
| | | | | | | | |
| | | | | | | | |
| | | | | | | | |
| | | | | | | | |
| | | | | | | | |
| | | | | | | | |
| | | | | | | | |
| | | | | | | | |
| | | | | | | | |
| | | | | | | | |
| | | | | | | | |
| | | | | | | | |

**Figure 6-11*a*.** Activity analysis linkage worksheet.

| Functional work area: | Prepared by/date: | Approved by/date: |
|---|---|---|
| Accounts receivable | Forrest-9/30/94 | Smith-10/3/94 |

**Activity** / **Activity measure**

| Activity driver name | Activity driver source | Type | Name | Description | Basis | Source | End users (destination) |
|---|---|---|---|---|---|---|---|
| Receive mail | Mail room | P | Bank deposit verification | Prepare bank deposit after cash is applied | Deposits | Cash receipts log | Accounts receivable |
| Receive mail | Bank | S | Problem checks | Investigate checks that can not be applied | Calls | Problem check log | Customer |
| Receive mail | Bank | S | Bounced checks | Contact customer to collect funds | Checks | Bounced check log | Accounts receivable |
| MIS | MIS | S | Customer credit—aging | Analyze report and contact customers who are past due | Occurence | Accounts receivable subsystem | Accounts receivable |
| Cash/application | Accounts receivable | P | Encoding | Encode checks and endorse for deposit | Checks | Deposit log cash receipts journal | Accounts receivable |
| Receive mail | Mail room | P | Cash applications—CODs | Enter cash to apply to customer account | Items | Accounts receivable subsystem | Accounts receivable |
| Receive mail | VISA, Master Card | S | Bank charges—VISA, Master Card | Record cash to customers account | Transactions | General ledger system | Accounts receivable |
| | | | | | | | |
| | | | | | | | |

**Figure 6-11a.** (Continued) Activity analysis linkage worksheet.

| | | | | | Activity measure | | |
|---|---|---|---|---|---|---|---|
| **Functional work area:** Accounts receivable | | **Prepared by/date:** Forrest-9/30/94 | | **Approved by/date:** Smith-10/3/94 | | | **Page 2 of 2** |

| **Activity** | | | | **Activity measure** | | | |
|---|---|---|---|---|---|---|---|
| **Activity driver name** | **Activity driver source** | **Type** | **Name** | **Description** | **Basis** | **Source** | **End users (destination)** |
| Receive mail | VISA, Master Card | S | Bank credits—VISA, Master Card | Apply credits to customer account | Transactions | General ledger system | Accounts receivable |
| Sales order | Sales | S | Freighting | Record freight expenses to customer account | Accounts | Accounts receivable subsystem general ledger | Sales |
| Telephone order | Customer | S | Accounts receivable—research | Research order problems | Accounts | Problem action report | Customer |
| Receive mail | Mail room | P | Cash application | Apply cash to customer account | Checks | Cash receipts journal accounts receivable subsystem | Accounts receivable |
| Fax-telephone call | Customer | S | Faxing | Communicate with customer | Faxes | Fax log | Customer |
| | | | | | | | Accounts receivable |
| | | | | | | | |
| | | | | | | | |
| | | | | | | | |

**Figure 6-11a.** (*Continued*) Activity analysis linkage worksheet.

| Functional work area: Accounts payable | Prepared by/date: Forrest-9/30/94 | Approved by/date: Smith-10/3/94 | Page 1 of 2 |

| Activity | | | | | Activity measure | | |
|---|---|---|---|---|---|---|---|
| Activity driver name | Activity driver source | Type | Name | Description | Basis | Source | End users (destination) |
| Receive mail | Mail room | P | Mail sort | Assign work to each staff member | Invoices | Accounts payable sub system | Accounts payable |
| Receive mail | Mail room | P | Checking saves   Regular | Record invoice to be paid | Saves | Accounts payable sub system | Accounting |
| Receive mail | Mail room | P | Checking saves   Drop ships | Record invoice to be paid | Saves | Accounts payable sub system | Accounting |
| Receive mail | Mail room | S | UPS   Federal Express | Record invoice  to be paid | Items | Accounts payable sub system | Accounting |
| Receipt of goods | Receiving | S | VOID   Stop payments | Notify bank to stop payment | Checks | Accounts payable sub system | Accounting |
| Run checks | MIS | P | Review checks prior to issue | Compare invoices to check | Checks | Accounts payable system cash disbursements | Accounts payable |
| Telephone call | Customer | S | Accounts receivable   Refunds | Return funds to customers | Checks | Accounts receivable sub system | Accounts receivable |
| | | | | | | | |
| | | | | | | | |

**Figure 6-11a.** (*Continued*) Activity analysis linkage worksheet.

| Functional work area: Accounts payable | Prepared by/date: Forrest-9/30/94 | Approved by/date: Smith-10/3/94 | |
| --- | --- | --- | --- |

| Activity | | | | | Activity measure | | |
| --- | --- | --- | --- | --- | --- | --- | --- |
| **Activity driver name** | **Activity driver source** | **Type** | **Name** | **Description** | **Basis** | **Source** | **End users (destination)** |
| Purchase order | Supplier | S | Debit memos | Prepare corrections for purchases | Debit memos | Debit memo log | Accounting |
| Invoices | Accounts payable | P | Filing | File accounts payable invoices | Invoices | N/A | Accounts payable |
| Telephone call | Vendor | S | Vendor statement research | Investigate problems on vendor statements | Statements | Investigation log | Vendor |
| Telephone call | Vendor | S | Problem research vendors | Investigate problems | Requests | Investigation log | Vendor |
| Fax  Telephone call | Vendor | S | Faxing | Faxes | Faxes | Fax/log | Vendor |
| Sales | Retail sales | P | Prepare/store invoices | Record and prepare retail store invoices | Invoices | Retail sales log | Marketing |
| | | | | | | | |
| | | | | | | | |
| | | | | | | | |

**Figure 6-11a.** (*Continued*) Activity analysis linkage worksheet.

| Line # | Title or Term | Is Used to Indicate |
|--------|---------------|---------------------|
| (1) | Functional work area | The name of the work unit in which the activity is performed. |
| (2) | Prepared by/date | The name of the interviewer and date of interview. |
| (3) | Approved by/date | The signature of the person interviewed, indicating the accuracy and completeness of the worksheet and date of interview. |
| (4) | Activity driver name | The name of the work driver which causes the activity to be performed. |
| (5) | Activity driver source | The name of the individual or functional work area in which the activity driver is activated. |
| (6) | Activity type | P for primary activity and S for secondary activity. |
| (7) | Activity name | The name of the activity which the interviewee performs as work. |
| (8) | Activity description | A brief statement of what the activity accomplishes. |
| (9) | Activity measure basis | The unit of output to measure the activity. |
| (10) | Activity measure source | The system, report, or log that gives the transaction volume. |
| (11) | End user | The individual or functional work area for which the activity is performed. |

**Figure 6-11b.** Activity analysis linkage worksheet key.

# 7
# Staffing
# Considerations

## Introduction

Once the functional work area manager and the ABM team have successfully completed the data gathering and analysis, they are ready to dedicate their efforts to determining staffing requirements for carrying on the business.

Essentially, the methodology for determining staffing needs of a functional work area has been well established for several decades. One of the key elements of an activity-based management program is to provide the objective data required to calculate and recommend appropriate staffing requirements for each functional work area within an organization.

Each functional work area's primary activities, secondary activities, activity transaction volumes, and calculated and estimated reasonable expectancies should be assembled in preparation for determining staffing requirements. Review the following with each functional work area manager:

- Activity dictionary
- Primary activity reasonable expectancies
- Secondary activity estimates
- Transaction volume data, including any seasonal or life-cycle variances
- Company policy for vacation days, holidays, optional days, personal days, and sick days as part of the 260 possible working days in a year
- The normal workday (e.g., 8:30 a.m. to 5:30 p.m., or 9 hours) minus 1.0 hour for lunch and an additional 1.0 hour as a miscellaneous allowance (e.g., for breaks)—to arrive at the available hours in a normal workday ($9.0 - 2.0 = 7.0$ hours)

Many organizations whose accounting systems are well defined, have utilized state-of-the-art technology for costing, but have no clue in associating work to staffing needs. Some managers have asked, "Why do we need performance measurements in an era of high-speed electronic data processing equipment?" The answer is easy. The impact of developing appropriate staffing requirements isn't negated because organizations still require individuals to operate their personal computers and many functions will continue to be manually driven.

The reality of the situation is that many corporations with highly technical, high-speed electronic equipment are those in which work-to-time relationships have been most effective in accurately determining staffing needs.

## Function of Staffing Requirements

The framing of staffing requirements on the basis of work-to-time relationships serves a variety of functions:

- It helps establish an objective criterion for a reasonable amount of work to be produced on a daily basis.

- It provides the basis for preparing budgets, using work-to-time relationships to identify various levels of activity. In businesses subject to seasonal variations in volume, the need for more or fewer staff members can be accurately forecast as to both the time and the numbers required.

- It provides senior management with an objective way of appraising the efficiency and productivity of functional work area managers and/or staff members. Frequently, a functional work area manager may be deemed to be a high-level performer because he or she submits reports promptly. This obvious effectiveness may simply be a result of overstaffing in the functional work area. The ABM methodology, which quantitatively analyzes activities, usually discloses those types of conditions, and provides senior and functional work area management with the tools for evaluating performance against a reasonably accurate standard.

- It serves as a structured way for reviewing and lowering staffing costs on a permanent basis. Such reviews enable senior management to choose the most cost-effective alternative, because one of the significant considerations in choosing the best alternative is staffing costs.

- It offers senior and functional work area management a method for predicting the staffing cost of each alternative. In addition, it allows costs to be stated in similar comparative terms for both the current process and the alternative processes. This eliminates a frequent mistake that managers make in attempting to compare efficiency under the current process, together with its bottlenecks, with that of the alternative, streamlined process. The result could be disappointing if the newly reengineered process falls short of expectations.

- It provides the chief financial officer with controls in maintaining staff levels required to perform company activities.

- It provides human resources with the platform for developing an objective system for staff promotions and salary increases—one that is based on performance instead of length of service or on a general subjective impression that the productivity and quality of work has been high level. When work-to-time relationships are being established, most observers find that the proficiency level of experienced staff members processing similar work will pay off greatly, resulting in increased productivity.

- It provides human resources with preemployment testing guidelines that go beyond the traditional words per minute for typists. Similar types of performance measures can be utilized for other activities (e.g., cash application, purchase orders).

- It provides senior management and functional work area management with data on which to base employment requisitions, rather than basing them on an unfounded belief that more staff members are needed.

In determining staffing considerations, several functional work area managers establish incentive programs. There is historical evidence that incentive programs can spawn increased productivity. Research has shown that productivity improvement when activities are performed in association with incentives exceeds that of activities performed without incentives by roughly 30 percent.

It is important to note that incentives do not have to be financial. Generally, the implementation of an ABM program that includes work-to-time relationships results in an increase in production because staff members realize that the amount and quality of their work are subject to continuous review and evaluation.

Some senior managers and functional work area managers will acquiesce that creating work-to-time relationships is a good concept which can yield beneficial results. They will then argue that several of the activities in their functional work areas require the application of intuitive judgment and are therefore unmeasurable.

However, historical analysis of data indicates that what some functional work area managers believe is judgmental may genuinely be nothing more than differentiating, scrutinizing, choosing, or ranking activities, all of which can be measured. With some activities involving creative concepts that do not lend themselves to being measured, true judgment must be exercised. The identification and isolation of these types of activities from those which are routine in nature will often prove to be rewarding. The segregated activities should have compensation programs based on the application of good judgment.

It has been our experience that professional workers frequently perform excessive amounts of routine clerical work which could be performed by far less educated and expensive workers. Many of these inconsistencies are brought to the surface during the interviewing and detailing processes, when activities are identified, categorized, and documented.

It is important to know this information before establishing the staffing requirements for a specific functional work area. You may find the need is for more clerical help and a smaller number of expensive managers. One large service organization had three functional work area managers directing three supposedly independent functional work areas. Careful analysis pinpointed that the activities in one of the work areas consisted of functions which could be easily dispersed to the other two functional work areas. This shift negated the need for a very expensive functional work area manager.

No single technique can be used to translate all the data collected into a performance-driven staffing action plan. Rather, a number of approaches are available, and each situation should be studied as to the complexity of the work, size of the current staff, and future growth of the organization. Three approaches deserve special mention.

1. Compare your productivity levels with those of other companies in a similar line of business. Management must be careful not to be misled by competitors' production statistics. A thorough understanding is needed of what the activities were, under what conditions they were performed, and which tools were utilized to compile those statistics. Industrywide productivity statistics usually have limited application and should not be blindly accepted; rather, they should be modified to meet an organization's specific needs. Senior management will not know if the comparative data represents what is currently being done or what should be done.

2. Compile historical work-to-time relationships on the basis of volume and payroll hours. For example, a cash application clerk may report the completion of 2400 checks during a 40-hour workweek; the historical work-to-time relationship could then be determined to be 60 checks per hour. This type of study is not scientific, but nevertheless provides meaningful data as to what is being produced, and is easy to implement. This technique is excellent for those activities which are repetitive and are not subject to a large number of exceptions (e.g., invoicing, cash application, data entry).

3. Use the detailing and observation processes described throughout this book. This approach offers by far the most thorough combination of techniques for determining what should be completed under normal working conditions.

Staffing data can be applied in a variety of ways. By utilizing daily volume reports, a functional work area manager can determine staffing requirements by associating the activity's reasonable expectancy with the activity volume on hand. The manager can decide if overtime and/or additional resources are required to complete the available work. Staffing data allows a manager to be proactive by properly directing what the staff members in the functional work area are to do, enabling him or her to manage people, not their work.

When the volume data is known, it becomes possible to shift activities from one staff member to another to fill up the workday. The cross-training of staff members, coupled with the shifting of work loads, provides the functional work area manager with the opportunity to utilize fewer people in a dynamic and flexible way. Staff members have a more diverse and interesting job content which makes them well rounded and a more productive force in the organization.

An excellent example of how proper staffing has worked can be shown in the controller's functional work area of a large distribution company. The functional work area consisted of three subgroups: accounts payable, accounts receivable, and cash application data entry. The staffing of these work groups is shown in Fig. 7-1.

The total available person hours was 128 hours per day (16 people multiplied by 8 hours per person). The staffing level indicated only a 50 percent work load, with approximately 50 percent of idle time available for additional work. When work was redistributed, a new staffing level emerged that resulted in an 80 percent workload (10 people multiplied by 8 hours per person).

The reduction of staff and the redistribution of the activities significantly increased productivity (Fig. 7-2). Senior management had the option of reassigning the available staff members or reducing operating costs because the work load could be completed with fewer resources. In a growing organization the result would indicate that fewer staff members had to be hired because the newly available staff members would be redeployed to fill the open requisitions.

This is a classic example of what activity-based management can accomplish when it is fully applied on the basis of objective and accurate data. It is important to note that the restructuring example still provides the functional work

| Group | Staff | Daily Person Hours | Total Person Hours |
|---|---|---|---|
| Accounts receivable | 6.0 | 4.0 | 24.0 |
| Accounts payable | 5.0 | 4.0 | 20.0 |
| Cash application | 5.0 | 4.0 | 20.0 |
| TOTAL | 16.0 | 12.0 | 64.0 |

**Figure 7-1.** Current staffing level.

| Group | Staff | Daily Person Hours | Total Person Hours |
|---|---|---|---|
| Accounts receivable | 4.0 | 6.0 | 24.0 |
| Accounts payable | 3.0 | 6.7 | 20.0 |
| Cash application | 3.0 | 6.7 | 20.0 |
| TOTAL | 10.0 | 19.4 | 64.0 |

**Figure 7-2.** Revised staffing level.

area manager with a 20 percent cushion, or 1.6 hours per staff member per day. This provides protection against absenteeism, which can run between 5 and 7 percent, and against the fact that most staff members do not perform at 100 percent of the established reasonable expectancies.

In this example, the dollar savings with benefits amounted to approximately $150,000 annually. The ABM team and functional work area manager should exercise extreme care in reducing the work force. One of the most common and potentially serious mistakes is to implement a spectacular reduction in the work force, suddenly and all at one time.

While such a step is the most effective way of maximizing cost reductions, it can cause a collapse in morale, frighten staff members, and send a very negative and incorrect signal across the breadth of an entire organization. This is especially true when an off-the-payroll type of reduction rather than redeployment of affected staff members is implemented.

Natural attrition will assist in staff reductions over a period of time, causing less trauma when it is coupled with a partial redeployment of staff members to other functional work areas. Historically in most clerical type of operations, attrition has accounted for a significant number of staff reductions.

Another tempering approach is to find some special projects to be staffed by excess staff members until a final resolution of what to do with the individuals is determined. It is common for projects that have been placed on the back burner to now be addressed when the excess staff members are taken off regular work. This will allow more time for natural attrition to take place.

The important element to recognize and accept is the fact that a specific volume of work in a functional work area, coupled with a reengineering productivity improvement and activity-based management program, brings a potential work force reduction. The handling of this reality should be planned for with compassion within company policy, and must involve human resources early in the program to minimize the traumatic effect.

## Taylor's Scientific Management

Frederick W. Taylor is recognized by most experts as the father of the work-to-time relationship in the corporate world, primarily in manufacturing plant operations. He developed several original concepts which are considered by many management historians to be the principles of *scientific management.*

Taylor suggested that each staff member's work be planned in advance, very similar to the work sequence plan discussed in the observation process. He further recommended that activities be delineated in detail, along with the tasks to be completed in performing those activities. Everything should be committed to paper in the form of a written procedure.

Taylor also believed that each activity should have a reasonable expectancy associated with it—based on the capacity of a high-performing staff member who was experienced and who performed the activity regularly. Every activity was broken down into smaller entities called *elements,* and their collective values were used to determine an allowed time for that activity. In activity-based management terminology, Taylor's elements are now referred to as *tasks*.

Taylor's formula for good management had three parts:

- *Define the activity.* Analyze the activity work flow sequence for a complete process.
- *Determine elapsed activity time.* Taylor utilized stopwatches to determine how much time it took to complete an activity.
- *Establish how an activity is to be performed.* Taylor selected a method for performing an activity that would fit within the time he determined was appropriate for that activity.

Like many new concepts that are pioneered by people with vision, scientific management initially didn't draw rave reviews and universal acceptance. Staff members, without appropriate training, began to establish unrealistic rates of work-to-time relationships, and ignored the important component of worker buy-in. The individuals who performed the time studies were designated as "efficiency experts." They so incensed the general public that in 1913 the U.S. Congress passed a bill stating that no government funds could be used to pay any individual engaged in time study work. It was not until 1943 that the prohibition was lifted.

Let us hope we have profited from our predecessors' mistakes. We no longer base reasonable expectancies on the best performer; rather, work-to-time relationships are established for normal staff members performing work at a normal pace. We also stress the human relations aspects throughout the observation process by copartnering with the functional work area manager and the staff member throughout the process.

Taylor's accomplishments were nevertheless of significant proportions. While working with men in a steel mill, he established that each man was averaging 38 pounds per shovel for the shoveling-iron-ore activity. He was asked to increase production, just as we are today. Taylor did some extensive research and found that men who shoveled ashes from the furnaces were handling only 3.5 pounds per shovel.

Taylor decided to try an experiment using a handpicked team of high-performing shovelers. Handling the 38-pound loads, the team produced 25 tons per day. He had the shovel blades reduced in size so they could handle only 34 pounds, and production increased to 30 tons per day. He continued to reduce the size of the shovels and production continued to rise until finally, at 21 or 22 pounds per shovel, the men were handling their largest day's production of 59 tons.

When the shovel capacity was further reduced in size to hold 18 pounds, Taylor found that production tonnage began to drop. Through his experimentation he determined that 21.5 pounds per shovel was the optimum load in order to produce maximum daily production. He then reversed the types of shovels to be used, by having a large shovel for lightweight material (e.g., ashes), and a small shovel for heavier material (ore).

The functional work area manager and the ABM team should make sure they are familiar with and understand all quality requirements of each activity. In utilizing work-to-time relationships for maximum success, every functional work area, regardless of size, should have written quality standards, and every staff member should be trained to meet those standards.

## Tools for Analysis

Only with a definite comprehension of all quality parameters can an effective change in the way an activity is performed be implemented. We must always be prepared to leave sufficient amounts of time for the normal staff member to be able to follow the methodology in performing an activity that is consistent with the organization's total quality management requirements.

One of the reasons that the observation process is so widely accepted as the basis for determining staffing requirements is that its methodology can be easily taught and readily understood by both functional work area managers and their staff members. The observation process allows the collection of objective, detailed data which can be used by management for improving productivity.

A downside to developing work-to-time relationships by using the observation process is that it is time-consuming—a single individual is required to study and observe a single staff member. Still, the results far outweigh the criticism.

In analyzing work for the purpose of establishing work-to-time relationships and then utilizing them to determine staffing requirements, there are other tools and techniques besides the observation process.

**Judgment/Experience.**   Generally, smaller organizations do not have enough resources to perform observations, and cannot afford to hire outside consultants to perform the activity. Therefore, they will base their work-to-time relationships on the judgment of one or two functional work area managers who have a great deal of experience. This process is easily enacted in a job shop oriented operation doing "one of a kind" unique custom work.

It isn't necessary to study in detail either a process or activity if it is unique and non-repetitive. This approach can be successful and is economical, but the drawbacks are numerous. You would not want to base a reward or incentive system for work performed only on good judgment because it is too subjective.

**Staff Member Activity Reporting.**   Some companies ask staff members to count the number of units of work they processed in a specific time period. If the elapsed time is divided by the number of items processed, you can arrive at a work-to-time relationship. This approach can result in a meaningful work-to-time relationship, provided the integrity of the staff member is beyond reproach and the activity to be worked on has available transaction volume to be processed.

In spite of the fact that the resultant data is accurate, it has limited application except for superficial costing purposes. An important element is disregarded:

what *can* be done, instead of the historical what *was* done. If improved activity content or work flows is management's objective, this method doesn't provide sufficient detail to accomplish this requirement.

**Predetermined Time Systems.** Predetermined time systems assign to each body motion a time element, depending on the type of the motion and the conditions under which it is made. These types of systems were developed in the 1930s and 1940s.

The most significant advantage of this technique is that it forces the observer to critically view each and every motion in the smallest detail. Activities which require eye travel, eye focus, application of pressure, alignment, and orientation must be precisely analyzed. A major disadvantage of this technique is that it requires extensive formal and on-the-job training before accurate work-to-time relationships can be developed and relied upon.

Reliable work-to-time relationships can easily be attained using a predetermined time system once staff members are thoroughly trained in its use. This is possible because there isn't any requirement to evaluate a staff member's performance.

**Sampling Techniques Applied to the Work Place.** The sampling of activities is a distinctive approach for developing work-to-time relationships. It usually begins with the functional work area manager conducting a study to determine what activity staff members are performing, not how quickly they are working. The research is devoted to obtaining a significant number of random observations over a prolonged time interval of a week or more. The activity of each staff member is recorded and categorized into predetermined entities at the instant of observation. The percentage ratio for any one category is derived by dividing the total number of observations recorded in a specific category by the total number of all observations.

This technique was developed in England by L. C. Tippett, who was investigating why weaving looms were breaking down so frequently in a textile mill. He studied the problem on four looms for several weeks before he reported his findings. Senior management at the mill was concerned about the length of time it would take to complete the assignment, because the four looms represented only 1 percent of the total number of looms at the mill.

Mr. Tippett also became concerned until he had a conversation with one of the mill's experienced supervisors. The supervisor explained that he would know if production was up to par or not by simply observing from his desk whether or not the loom operators were busy or idle. If loom operators were fixing thread breaks he knew production would be down, and conversely if everyone was at their machine, this told him production was good.

This approach is very similar to the ratio delay study that we discussed as part of the observation process. A primary advantage of this technique is that it can be readily learned and is easily applied by a functional work area manager and/or his or her staff members as a "do-it-yourself" approach. Another advantage of sampling is that it can be conducted on either staff members or their machines, with several studies being conducted at the same time. A disadvantage is that numerous observations are required to achieve acceptable accuracy and reliability. In addition, the data must be obtained over long periods of time to obtain a representative picture of the activity studied.

However, this technique is not generally used to establish production-type work-to-time relationships, because no detailed activity descriptions are obtained during a sampling technique application. If there isn't any other type of data gathering, a work-to-time relationship can be determined by dividing the number of units produced into the amount of time a staff member was working. The work-to-time relationship in this case would be expressed in minutes per piece.

Expect some disinclination by both senior and functional work area management to acknowledge that all activities can be completed by fewer staff members and still maintain a high level of quality. Sometimes functional work area managers become overprotective of their staff members, some of whom may be personal friends.

## Applications of Staffing Data

In today's business community it has finally become apparent to senior management that the principles and techniques formerly confined to factory and/or manufacturing organizations also have application in service organizations (e.g., banks, health care, communications).

The data captured from a properly conducted observation process can serve several functions.

**Productivity Performance Reports.**   The reporting frequency is often daily, but the most common time periods are weekly or monthly. The reports should indicate the performance of an individual staff member or a group of functional work area staff members. Functional work area managers can use the reports as a monitoring device to be able to take immediate corrective action when necessary. Often, unnoticed but significant events which negatively effect production can be surfaced by looking for trends as one report is compared with another report.

**Activity-Based Costing.**   Knowing the correct cost of an activity is important for the success of any company in today's competitive marketplace. A reasonable expectancy helps identify activities that are both non-value added and not cost-effective. Once these types of activities are eliminated, the organization's profitability will begin to climb, along with shareholder value.

**Determining Functional Work Area Capacity.**   Every operational area in an organization can produce just so much of a product or service. Once a functional work area's capacity is determined, informed decisions can be made to obtain more equipment, and staff resources. This knowledge provides management with realistic service dates for customers which will build customer satisfaction and quality.

**Balancing Activity Work Flow.**   When several staff members are working in a serial sequence similar to a manufacturing assembly line performing consecutive operations, it becomes more difficult to ascertain the correct number of staff members needed to complete all the operational activities within a specific process.

The slowest team member usually ends up setting the rate of production, resulting in reduced output levels for all other staff members. The establishment of work-to-time relationships for each activity within a process, and each task within an activity, enables the functional work area manager to determine how to proportion the individual staff member's work load more evenly in order to minimize idle time.

**Estimating Profitability.**   Very often a company is asked to quote a price for the manufacture of a product and/or for providing a service. Costs for material and even overhead components can usually be determined with a reasonably high level of reliability, but staff or labor costs frequently are determined by guesstimates. "How many staff members do we need and for how long?" is a principal question on the lips of functional work area managers.

The development of reasonable expectancies and composite reasonable expectancies can provide the functional work area manager with a reliable basis for costing the labor component. The guesswork is eliminated and the price quotation is more accurate, so the organization can make a fair return on its product and/or service.

**Establishing an Appropriate Reward System.**   In today's quality-focused, customer-driven marketplace, perhaps the most significant factor for establishing a continuous improvement atmosphere is the development of an appropriate wage incentive reward program. Work-to-time relationships form the platform for implementing a required program for individual and team performance. Compensation will be objective when an accurate and objective yardstick, like work-to-time relationships, is utilized.

**Quality Improvement Methods.**   There is generally more than one way to complete an activity. A primary activity may be performed by four different staff members, all of whom do the work differently and arrive at the same end point. With reasonable expectancies for the various alternatives, it is easy for a functional work area manager to choose the best method that is associated with the organization's total quality management requirements.

## Steps for Improving the Way an Activity Is Performed

When a functional work area manager uses an organized approach to solving any problem, the chances for success are enhanced. In making improvements and initiating reengineering activities, the manager should consider the following six steps:

- Select the activity to be revised after meticulous deliberation. Select an activity that will result in the most significant amount of time and/or money saved.

- Obtain and document the details of how an activity is currently performed in a step-by-step sequence. All the details of an activity must first be understood before any reengineered revisions can be made. From this base position it is then possible to develop improvements.

- Question everything about the activity, detailing potential alterations. The standard what, where, when, who, how, and why should be asked to disunite fact from rumor and opinion.

- Design a revised activity and test it out. Many activity changes are made by simply eliminating an entire task, or some of the redundant parts of it. Creating an improved way to perform an activity may require a rearrangement, combination, or disaggregation of tasks within an activity. Often the path to either simplification or improvement may be by changing a staff member, work station, or sequence in the way an activity is performed.

- Obtain the staff member's buy-in for the newly revised activity. Remember that an improvement is only a concept and incomplete until it has been installed and is in use. All levels of personnel who are involved must be thoroughly convinced of its value-added impact, and in some instances additional training may be required.

- Periodically audit the newly revised activity to see if it is being maintained per the revisions.

## Elements for Determining Staffing Requirements

One of the most important results that an organization derives from a reengineering, productivity improvement, activity-based management program is the determination and flexible utilization of resources required to operate a functional work area. A significant achievement is to ascertain the number of staff members it takes to complete all the activities at a level of quality which satisfies the customer.

In order to accomplish this goal, certain elements should be in place and specific parameters must be defined.

1. Establish a staffing time parameter (e.g., weekly, monthly).

2. Obtain company policy for

   - Vacation days
   - Holidays
   - Optional days
   - Personal days
   - Sick days

3. Define the number of working days in a calendar year (260 days).

4. Gather volume data, including any considerations for seasonal and/or cyclical fluctuations, from computer-driven historical records, and/or manual volume tally recap sheets.

5. Accumulate or extract secondary activity estimates of hours and/or minutes for each activity from the activity dictionary (see Chapter Three).

6. Utilize primary activity reasonable expectancies or work-to-time relationships from the observation recap.

7. Validate the entire universe of activities by using the activity dictionary, which indicates all functional work area activities whether they be primary or secondary. Use the data to determine that the entire universe of activities is accounted for in the functional work area.

8. Establish the productivity level that a functional work area is to achieve—say, 90 percent. It should not be 100 percent, because no staff member works at that perfect level. This determinate has a direct bearing on the level of staffing and sets the tone for the work environment (e.g., loose, tight).

When all the aforementioned elements are available, it is time to calculate the staffing requirements for the functional work area.

## Staffing Calculation

In order to calculate the appropriate staffing requirements for a functional work area, a staffing calculation worksheet must be prepared (Figs. 7-3 and 7-4).

### Staffing Calculation Worksheet—Part 1

**Activity.** List all primary and secondary activities performed in the functional work area, as indicated in the activity dictionary.

**Weekly Volume.** Indicate the transaction volume for a specific activity. The source is either computer-driven historical transaction volume or data accumulated through the volume tally worksheets. Most primary activities have asso-

| Activity | Weekly volume | R/E | Weekly hours |
|---|---|---|---|
| Place accounts for collection | 32 | 8/hr | 4.0 |
| Place accounts for collection-D&B | 10 | 32/hr | .3 |
| 60 day aging calls | – | 35/hr | |
| Bankruptcy process | 52 | 24/hr | 2.2 |
| Org. final notice letters | 490 | 86/hr | 5.7 |
| Final notice letter calls | – | 30/hr | |
| *Daily follow-up calls | 1274 | 30/hr | 42.5 |
| Bulk sales | – | 6 min/daily | .5 |
| Tracers | 15 | 24/hr | .6 |
| Write off/offset adjust | 22 | 180/hr | .1 |
| Faxes | 50 | 20/hr | 2.5 |
| Questions credit dpt. | 115 | 20/hr | 5.7 |
| Attorney payment rpt. | – | 10 min/daily | .8 |
| C/A bad debit write-off | 24 | 30/hr | .8 |
| Bounced checks | 10 | 30/hr | .3 |
| Follow-up certified letter | 7 | 30/hr | .2 |
| Nasty Gram-collection letters | 12 | 12/hr | 1.0 |
| Time card tally | – | 6 min/daily | .5 |
| Final notice letter mail out | – | 45 min/daily | 3.8 |
| Statement mail out | – | 30 min/daily | 2.5 |
| C/A commission payments | 7 | 30/hr | .2 |
| Request for invoices | 20 | 20/hr | 1.0 |
| Payments from agency | 15 | 30/hr | .5 |
| Employee review | – | – | |
| Filing | – | 30 min/daily | 2.5 |
| | | **Total** | **78.2** |

*KVI indices

**Figure 7-3.** Staffing calculation worksheet—Part 1.

ciated transaction volumes, whereas secondary activities have time-related reasonable expectancies instead (e.g., bulk sales—6 minutes daily). In addition, volume data doesn't have to be weekly. It can be daily, semimonthly, monthly, and so on. The important point is that a consistent volume time frame be utilized within a functional work area.

**Reasonable Expectancy (R/E).**   Indicate the work-to-time relationships for each primary and secondary activity. The source of the reasonable expectancy data is the reasonable expectancy data sheet discussed in Chapter Six. The primary activities will generally express the work-to-time relationship in units per hour, and secondary activities may indicate the number of minutes (e.g., statement mail-out—30 minutes per day).

**Weekly Hours.**   Weekly hours is a calculation arrived at by taking the weekly volume of an activity (e.g., place accounts for collection—32) and dividing it by the reasonable expectancy for that activity (8 per hour). In this example, the weekly hours for the activity "place accounts for collection" is

| Staffing calculation | | |
|---|---|---|
| Total hours required | 78.2 | |
| Total hours req. at work at **90%** productivity | 86.9 | $(78.2 \div 90.0 = 86.9)$ |
| Vac./personal sick time at 10% (i.e., $86.9 \times .10$) | 8.7 | 25 days/260 workdays |
| | | 10 vacation, 7 holiday, 2 optional, 6 sick days $86.9 \times 10\% = 8.7$ |
| Total hours req. on payroll | 95.6 | |
| Total people req. on payroll @ 38.5 hrs/person ($95.6 \div 38.5$) | 2.5 | 8 hrs $\times$ 5 = 40 hrs |
| | | Less break (2 at 9 min. each $\times$ 5 people = 1.5 deducted from 40 hrs.) |
| Current staffing level | 4.6 | One part-time person @ .6 |
| Variance | 2.1 | |
| Staffing level decision | 3.0 | |
| Staffing adjustment | 1.6 | |
| **Composite R/E = 12.1** | | |

**Figure 7-4.** Staffing calculation worksheet—Part 2.

4.0. If monthly or daily hours were the established unit, the same calculation would be made.

For those secondary activities that have only number of minutes in the reasonable expectancy column, a conversion to an hour equivalent is required (e.g., bulk sales—6 minutes daily would equal 30 weekly minutes, or .5 weekly hours).

**Total Hours.** Total the weekly hours for all functional work area activities, including both primary and secondary activities (78.2 hours).

**Key Volume Indicators (KVI).** Designate which activities are considered significant indicators of the work being completed in the area. These "vital few" activities are usually called *key volume indicators* (KVI). These activities should be closely monitored and identified by an asterisk on the staffing calculation worksheet (e.g., daily follow-up calls).

Key volume indicators represent the backbone of a functional work area, and by monitoring their transaction volume opening balance, received, processed, and ending balance, a functional work area manager can tell how much actual work there is at any given time. With the knowledge of how much work is available, along with the associated reasonable expectancy, a functional work area manager can determine what resources are required to process the work load, and how long it will take to complete the work. Senior management can utilize the "vital few" as a high-level monitoring tool for work, and ask appropriate questions when trends begin to appear.

## Staffing Calculation Worksheet—Part 2

When all the activities, volumes, reasonable expectancies, and hours are established, it is time to begin the formal staffing calculation.

**Total Hours Required.**    The source of this starting index is from the total hours calculated on the first part of the staffing calculation worksheet (78.2 hours).

**Productivity Level.**    The functional work area manager must establish the productivity level that the functional work area should achieve (e.g., 90 percent), recognizing that no staff member will realistically work at 100 percent capacity. The productivity level directly affects the staffing requirements, so it should be carefully discussed before it is determined.

**Total Hours Required at Work at 90 Percent Productivity.**    Divide the beginning total hours required (78.2) by the productivity level percentage (90) to arrive at the total hours required at work at 90 percent productivity (86.9).

**Vacation, Holiday, Optional, and Sick Days.**    Verify the number of vacation, holiday, optional, and sick days allowed by organizational policy. This is best done by contacting human resources. A typical number is 25 days:

- 10 vacation days
- 7 holidays
- 2 optional days
- 6 sick days

Calculate the total number of vacation, holiday, optional, and sick days (25) as a percentage of the total number of annual workdays (260). In Fig. 7-4, it is 9.6 rounded to 10 percent. Apply this figure to the total hours required at work at 90 percent productivity (86.9). The result is 8.7 hours ($86.9 \times 10\% = 8.7$).

**Total Hours Required on Payroll.**   Add the result of the vacation, holiday, optional, and sick day calculation (8.7 hours) to the total hours required at work at 90 percent productivity (86.9) to arrive at total hours required on payroll (95.6 hours).

**Total People Required on Payroll at Net Hours/Person.**   Calculate the net normal work hours by taking the gross work hours (i.e., 8 daily hours multiplied by 5 days = 40 hours) and deducting any official break time. In this illustration each staff member has two official 9-minute breaks per day, or 1.5 hours for the week. This break time should be deducted from the gross normal weekly hours (40.0 hours less 1.5 break hours = 38.5 net weekly hours).

Divide the total hours required on payroll (95.6) by the net weekly hours (38.5) to arrive at the total people required on payroll at 38.5 hours per person (2.5 people).

**Staffing Analysis.**   Compare the functional work area's current staffing levels (4.6 people) with the newly calculated staffing requirements (2.5). The overstaffing variance is 2.1 people in this illustration. The functional work area manager should recommend a revised staffing level (e.g., 3.0 people) and a corresponding staffing adjustment either up or down (1.6 people). In this example it would be to reduce staff by 1.6 people. This functional work area had a part-time worker who accounted for the .6.

Determining the staffing requirements for a functional work area is a capacity analysis tool utilized to substantiate staffing requirements based upon work loads (as determined from validated volume data). Staffing levels and/or requirements should be revisited when any of the following events occur:

- Changes in a reasonable expectancy
- Changes in transaction volumes which are significant
- Addition of new products and/or services
- Alteration in the content of an activity
- Productivity and/or methods improvement that alters activity work flows
- Significant structural reorganization
- Improved systems support that converts manual work to automated-assisted work or simply improved systems

When staffing adjustments are to be implemented in a functional work area, they should all be made at one time to minimize any trauma among staff members, especially if the adjustment is downward. All functional work areas involved should be realigned, including movement of desks, prior to the next workday (over a weekend is usually preferable).

Immediately following implementation, the functional work area manager should hold a team meeting with the remaining staff members. A representative from human resources should participate in the meeting to explain the direction that the organization is moving toward by rightsizing. It should be emphasized that functional work area managers should involve human resources early in this process to assist in redeploying the excess staff members to fill other variances in other functional work areas.

## Composite Reasonable Expectancy

A *composite reasonable expectancy* for a functional work area is a snapshot guideline to be utilized by the work area manager for forecasting staffing needs. The composite incorporates selected primary activity data which have been designated as key volume indicators (KVI). The source of data for calculating the composite reasonable expectancy comes from the staffing calculation worksheet (Part I: Volumes and Hours).

### Calculation of Composite Reasonable Expectancy

Take the total KVI transaction volume (i.e., 8906) calculated on the composite reasonable expectancy volume worksheet (Fig. 7-5) and divide it by the total

| Activity | KVI weekly volumes |
|---|---|
| Regular adjustments | 270 |
| Cash application process | 6900 |
| Cash application-COD's Reg/Detroit | 535 |
| Cash sales with order | 60 |
| Bank charges (AMEX) | 56 |
| Bank charges (VISA, MC) | 434 |
| Chicago cash application process | 101 |
| Due to/from Chicago cash application | 40 |
| Under $25 aging write-off (2195 monthly divided by 4.3 weeks) | 510 |
| **Total KVI volume** | **8906** |

**Figure 7-5.** Functional work area composite reasonable expectancy volume worksheet.

hours required, as shown on the staffing calculation worksheet [Part I (Fig. 7-6)] (145.1 hours), to arrive at the functional work area composite reasonable expectancy (61.4). Enter the composite reasonable expectancy on the staffing calculation worksheet (Part II: Composite R/E) after adjustments (Fig. 7-7).

The composite reasonable expectancy is also used for preparing the staffing master schedule and for calculating "what if" scenarios.

| Activity | Weekly volume | R/E | Weekly hours |
|---|---|---|---|
| * Regular adjustments | 270 | 160/hr | 1.7 |
| * Cash application process | 6900 | 150/hr | 46.7 |
| Encoding | 6900 | 1000/hr | 6.9 |
| Daily cash sales/Br. Bk charg sheets | 282 | 130/hr | 2.2 |
| * Cash application—CODs Reg/Detroit | 535 | 178/hr | 3.0 |
| * Cash sales with order | 60 | 25/hr | 2.4 |
| * Bank charges (Amex.) | 56 | 48/hr | 1.2 |
| * Bank charges (Visa, MC) | 434 | 86/hr | 5.0 |
| Bank charge credits | 60 | 60/hr | 1.0 |
| * Chicago cash application process | 101 | 108/hr | .9 |
| * Due to/from Chicago cash app. | 40 | 40/hr | 1.0 |
| On account adjustments | 30 | 60/hr | .5 |
| Offset adjustments | 80 | 70/hr | 1.1 |
| * Under $25 aging write-offs | 2195 | 84 hr/monthly | 6.1 |
| Regular credit memos—branches | 30 | 180/hr | .2 |
| Faxing | 40 | 20/hr | 2.0 |
| Mail sort | – | 10.5 hr/weekly | 10.5 (wk/vol = 510) |
| Duplicate invoice branches | – | 5 min/daily | .4 |
| Amex checks—cash deposit | – | 10 min/weekly | .2 |
| Rubber check—calls | – | 6.0 hr/weekly | 6.0 |
| UPS, COD research | – | 45 min/weekly | .7 |
| Bounced checks | – | 20 min/daily | 1.6 |
| Refunds | – | 60 min/weekly | 1.0 |
| Dollars, checks intercompany | – | 15 min/weekly | .2 |
| Philadelphia report | – | 45 min/monthly | .2 |
| Daily sales—billing control | – | 10 min/daily | .8 |
| Sales tax corrections | – | 10 min/daily | .8 |
| Request duplicate credits | – | 6 min/daily | .5 |
| Problem bank charge calls | – | 30 min/daily | 2.5 |
| Bank deposit | – | 10 min/daily | .8 |
| Return to vendor | – | 60 min/weekly | 1.0 |
| Freighting | – | 30 min/weekly | .5 |
| Accounts receivable research | – | 180 min/weekly | 3.0 |
| Deposit slips | – | 15 min/weekly | .7 |

*KVI indices

**Figure 7-6.** Staffing calculation worksheet—Part I.

| Activity | Weekly volume | R/E | Weekly hours |
|---|---|---|---|
| COD check batching | – | 3 min/daily | .2 |
| Bank deposits | – | 45 min/daily | 3.7 |
| Daily rpts. record & balance | – | 60 min/daily | 5.0 |
| Due from Boston—adjust | – | 30 min/daily | 2.5 |
| Leasing accounts | – | 60 min/monthly | .2 |
| Gen. ledger—Cobra, freight | – | 60 min/weekly | 1.0 |
| COD check batching | – | 20 min/weekly | 1.6 |
| Cust. ser. mail tray process | – | 60 min/weekly | 1.0 |
| Special adjustments | – | 30 min/weekly | .5 |
| Month end procedures | – | 60 min/weekly | .2 |
| Reconciliation—Boston Inter. Co. | – | | |
|   GL A/C | – | 30 min/monthly | .1 |
| Journal entries—Inter. Co. | – | 60 min/monthly | .2 |
| Cash app. batch report | – | 30 min/daily | 2.5 |
| Cash app. COD Detroit | – | 40 min/daily | 3.3 |
| Bank charges Br. statements | – | 30 min/weekly | .5 |
| Amex checks—cash rec. process | – | 20 min/weekly | .3 |
| Bounced checks—branches | – | 15 min/monthly | .0 |
| Regular credits | – | 20 min/daily | 1.6 |
| Month-end rpts | – | 60 min/monthly | .2 |
| Credits—Amex | – | 5 min/weekly | .1 |
| Stat. boart posting | – | 5 min/daily | .4 |
| Adjustment review controls | – | 5 min/daily | .4 |
| Bounced checks monthly process | – | 20 min/monthly | .7 |
| Boston payments Philadelphia/Chicago | – | 25 hrs/monthly | 5.8 |
| Bank charge aging | – | 20 min/monthly | .1 |
| Intercompany sales | – | 24 min/weekly | .4 |
| | | **Total** | **145.1** |

**Figure 7-6.** (*Continued*) Staffing calculation worksheet—Part I.

## Staffing Master Schedule

The *staffing master schedule* is a comparative chart that indicates

- Functional work area
- Current staffing level
- Recommended staffing level
- Staff level adjustment—either up or down

The staffing master schedule has a "what if" or forecasting component which enables a functional work area manager to more effectively plan his or her allocation of resources in advance. The staffing master schedule should be reviewed monthly by the functional work area manager and quarterly by senior management.

Senior management should be alert for trends that are significantly above or below forecast, and should question the functional work area manager on

| | |
|---|---|
| Total hours required | 145.1 |
| Total hours required at work at **90%** productivity | 162.2   (145.1 ÷ 90% = 161.2) |
| Vacation, personal, sick time at 10% | 16.1 |
| Total hours required on the payroll | 177.3 |
| Total people required on the payroll @ 38.5 hrs/person | 4.6 |
| Current staffing level | 8.0 |
| Variance | (3.4) |
| Staffing level decision | 5.0 |
| Staffing adjustment | (3.0) |
| **Composite R/E = 61.4** | |

**Figure 7-7.** Staffing calculating worksheet—Part II.

whether the trend is short term or long term. Trends are influenced by changes in business conditions, system enhancements, and/or changes in the product or service mix.

The functional work area manager is responsible for the timely and accurate completion of this schedule. Senior management is responsible for monitoring and analyzing the reported data at the end of each month.

The staffing master schedule is used to compare current staffing levels with recommended staffing levels and to forecast future staffing requirements before they are required. The staffing master schedule has three purposes:

- It enables senior management to quickly and easily ensure that adequate staffing is available for functional work area managers, and to meet any emergencies.

- It forecasts staffing levels for 3 months into the future on the basis of contemplated increases or decreases in transaction volumes, by applying the functional work area's composite reasonable expectancy to those volumes.

- It permits senior management to effectively allocate resources to the functional work area that requires assistance, thereby taking more timely corrective action when unfavorable trends arise.

This schedule (Fig. 7-8) should be reviewed for accuracy and completeness.

**Functional work area:** _____ (1)

**Prepared by:** _____ (2)
**Year(s):** _____ (3)

## Forecast volumes-hours

| KVI indices (4) | Composite R/E (5) | Month: (6) | | | Month: | | Month: | | Month: | |
|---|---|---|---|---|---|---|---|---|---|---|
| | | Number of work days: (7) | | | Number of work days: | | Number of work days: | | Number of work days: | |
| | | Volume (8) | Hours | | Volume | Hours | Volume | Hours | Volume | Hours |
| | | | | | | | | | | |
| | | | | | | | | | | |
| | | | | | | | | | | |
| | | | | | | | | | | |
| | | | | | | | | | | |
| Total forecast volume | (9) | | | | | | | | | |
| Total forecast hours | (10) | | | | | | | | | |
| Total hours required at work ___ % productivity | (11) | (12) | | | | | | | | |
| Personal and sick time at ___ % | (13) | (14) | | | | | | | | |
| Vacation hours scheduled | | (15) | | | | | | | | |
| Total hours required on the payroll | | (16) | | | | | | | | |
| Monthly hours worked per person | | (17) | | | | | | | | |
| Total staff required on payroll | | (18) | | | | | | | | |
| Current staff level | | (19) | | | | | | | | |
| Variance +(−) | | (20) | | | | | | | | |
| Staff level decision | | (21) | | | | | | | | |
| Staff level adjustment planned | | (22) | | | | | | | | |

**Figure 7-8a.** Staffing master schedule.

| Line # | Title or Term | Is Used to Indicate |
|--------|---------------|---------------------|
| (1) | Functional work area | The name of the work unit in which the forecast is being made. |
| (2) | Prepared by | The name of the functional work area manager who is presenting the schedule. |
| (3) | Year(s) | The year or years covered by the months being forecasted. |
| (4) | KVI indices | The KVI indices for the functional work area indicated on the staffing calculation worksheet. |
| (5) | Composite R/E | The composite R/E for the functional work area indicated on the staffing calculation worksheet. |
| (6) | Month | The month(s) being forecast. |
| (7) | Workdays | The number of working days in the specific month(s) being forecast. |
| (8) | Volume | The forecast transaction volume for each KVI index. |
| (9) | Total forecast volume | The volume column added for all KVI indices. |
| (10) | Total forecast hours | The calculation of total forecast hours by dividing the total forecast volume by the functional work area composite R/E. |
| (11) | Total hours required at ____% productivity | The productivity performance percentage factor (e.g., 90 percent) indicated on the staffing calculation worksheet. |
| (12) | Total hours required at work | The calculation of total hours required at work by dividing the total forecast hours by the performance percentage factor. |
| (13) | Personal and sick time percentage | The calculation of personal and sick time percentage by dividing the sum of the number of sick time and personal days by the annual workdays indicated on the staffing calculation worksheet. |
| (14) | Personal and sick time hours | The calculation of personal and sick time hours by multiplying the total hours required at work by the personal and sick time percentage. |
| (15) | Vacation hours scheduled | The calculation of vacation hours scheduled by multiplying the functional work area scheduled vacation days for the forecast month by the net daily hours (i.e., gross hours less lunch and less official breaks). |

**Figure 7-8b.** Staffing master schedule key.

| Line # | Title or Term | Is Used to Indicate |
|---|---|---|
| (16) | Total hours required | The calculation of total hours required on the payroll by summing lines 12, 14, and 15. |
| (17) | Monthly hours worked per person | The calculation of monthly hours worked per person by multiplying the number of workdays in the forecast month by the net daily hours. |
| (18) | Total staff required on payroll | The calculation of total staff required on payroll by dividing line 16 by line 17 and rounding the result up or down. |
| (19) | Current staff level | The current staff level for the functional work area. |
| (20) | Variance + (−) | The calculation of the variance by subtracting line 19 from line 18. |
| (21) | Staff level decision | The staff level decision for the functional work area—usually the number on line 18. |
| (22) | Staff level adjustment planned | The staff level adjustment planned—the number of additional or fewer staff members required to perform the work in the functional work area. |

**Figure 7-8b.** (*Continued*) Staffing master schedule key.

## Summary

The key elements in the staffing calculation are summarized below.

- Organize all the functional work area data obtained during the interview, detailing, and observation processes.

  Activity dictionary

  Work distribution matrix

  Observation recap

  Volume tally recap

  Reasonable expectancy data sheet

- Develop a living flow chart
- Determine staffing parameters

  Number of company vacation, holiday, optional, personal, and sick days

  Number of calendar-year working days

  Historical volume data

  Reasonable expectancies for primary activities

  Estimates for secondary activities

Full activity list
Productivity level percentage

- Perform staffing calculation.
- Prepare staffing master schedule.
- Conduct management/supervisory development needs analysis.

# 8
# Management Reports

## Introduction

The management reports and controls are the centerpiece of the management reporting phase of an activity-based management program to ensure that a continuous improvement ethic becomes a habitual part of the everyday work routine. Important elements of the management reporting process are developing a positive attitude toward a strong work ethic and utilizing structured tools to control the overall environment within a functional work area.

The design of each management report with its appropriate instructions provides the functional work area manager with an explanation of the report's purpose, who is responsible for the preparation of the report, the frequency of use, who receives a copy, and a line-by-line set of instructions for filling in each report and how to use the data. Each sample report indicates what data goes into each numbered line or box and clearly corresponds to the preparation instructions that accompany each report.

The ABM team should meet with the functional work area manager and his or her staff members to explain the reporting system, procedures, and controls that will become a permanent part of the work routine. The functional work area manager should test each management report for several days with one representative group of staff members in morning periods and a different set of staff members in afternoon periods. This will give all staff members a familiarity with the reports they must prepare, and they can provide feedback with suggested changes, if appropriate.

The staff members will be taking ownership, and their buy-in and commitment to using the reports are critical to the success of the management reporting system.

It has been estimated that ABM programs which include reengineering and productivity improvement and total quality management modules have saved corporate America millions of dollars. ABM programs have gone beyond manufacturing organizations into service-oriented businesses with large clerical populations. Business processes that have benefited from the implementation of ABM include order processing, customer service, accounting, credit, data processing, sales service, and repair maintenance operations. The return on investment is always available if functional work area managers know how to mine the gold.

Functional work area managers also need enablers—like the management reporting system described here—to allow them to effectively direct, analyze, and manage their restructured and possibly reduced work force. The tools we discuss assist the functional work area manager and senior management in making sure that all available work is processed in a timely manner.

It would be foolhardy to restructure the way work is processed, reduce the resources needed to perform the work, and then watch as quality worsens, backlogs increase for unprocessed work, and the customer base ends up dissatisfied. The speed with which change takes place within an organization also impacts the relative intensity with which empowerment and decentralized authority can grow.

Generally, in fast-growing businesses that are encountering problems that accompany enlargement, top-level senior managers tend to make the greater share of decisions that involve company policy. A majority of senior executives have found that the most common factor that limits their ability to meet rapid change is the shortage of trained staff members to whom decision-making authority can be conveyed. Utilizing ABM management reporting tools makes this transition of responsibility and accountability easier and accelerates the training of staff members.

In a mature organization, where uniform policy guidelines are in place, it becomes easier to decentralize, especially when continual customer contact and satisfaction drives the business. The topic of management reporting is a broad one, because every manager regardless of level has his or her own concepts about the information required to do the job. To complicate matters, many functional work area managers can't distinguish between the information they need and the information they want. Often, the senior management team in an organization is the work driver that creates the mountain of paperwork.

If functional work area managers and senior management are to function efficiently and effectively, they must have a meaningful, objective, brief, and timely understanding of what is happening in their organization. These four elements form the foundation for a management reporting system.

We do not intend to profile the entire universe of reports that management should generate, because all organizations have a unique culture and the task is virtually impossible to complete. We believe the information suggested in this chapter is of a significant nature and can provide both functional work area managers and senior management with the basic critical data on which to base meaningful, informed decisions.

As with any management reporting system, it is not solely the information provided that is important but also, more vitally, how it is used.

Functional work area managers and senior management can sometimes fall victim to receiving too much information. In companies throughout the world, executives are spending valuable time and thousands of dollars reading and quickly tossing out useless reports. The level of wasted time for these worthless activities compares with similar useless time executives spend in meetings discussing ways to arrive at a decision after they have already held previous meetings on a subject.

When an ABM program includes reengineering, productivity improvement, and total quality management processes, staff members at all levels of an organization are encouraged to question the existence of and/or need for every copy of each report as well as the work they perform.

Functional work area managers must be discerning in their preparation of management reports and utilize only the vital few that have value. In some organizations, administrators discourage the unnecessary generation of written reports. All levels of management must have information, but this information must be meaningful, concise, and, above all, timely. Any report must have as its purpose to offer information which enables the recipient to make an informed decision. The data contained in a report should be related to the staff member's decision-making level, because that is the individual who must read it and analyze it.

Certainly, it would be meaningless for the vice president of finance to receive a report detailing the productivity of each cash application staff member in the accounting department. However, such a report does have value for the functional work area manager, and has considerably more value to the team leader, who should be the first to know when a specific staff member's productivity is low.

A very reliable sequence can be used to construct a set of meaningful, brief, objective, and timely management reports. The entire ABM philosophy is to take a bottoms-up approach to gathering meaningful data. Developing a reporting system also begins at the lowest level of management and moves upward. The front-line manager—team leader, clerical supervisor, and so on—usually generates a report that becomes a control mechanism which is totaled at the end of each workday.

For example, a controller has three functional work areas, each headed up by a functional work area manager. At the conclusion of the workday, each manager turns in his or her completed report, which includes the following information:

- Individual staff member productivity
- Schedule attainment
- Problem action summary

The problem action summary explains off-schedule conditions that occur each day. The controller receives three such reports, which he or she critiques with the functional work area managers and discusses their correctness and content. The controller should coach each manager on achieving high-level performance.

The controller now has to report to the vice president of finance. The controller's report should contain some of the following data:

- Productivity by functional work area
- Schedule attainment by functional work area
- Finance process productivity
- Number of problems resolved

The vice president of finance reviews each of the functional work area reports, questioning any low productivity in a functional work area. The vice president must then report to the president of the company. The VP's report would contain some of the following data:

- Productivity by business process
- Schedule of attainment by business process
- Total company productivity

Generally, the president will first look at total company results, and if these are satisfactory he or she probably will not drill down for further details. If the total company results for productivity appear low, the president will scrutinize the numbers to see which business process was not performing up to par. The president would then question the vice president of finance to find out why the performance was poor.

The aforementioned management reporting example demonstrates how each level of management focuses its attention to obtain the information required to direct sound reasoning, behavior, and decision making. Exactly what type of information is needed?

Team leaders often have to develop their own work plan on the basis of transaction volumes received, backlog transaction volumes, and any planned carryover to keep the pipeline filled. To achieve production goals, the team leader must know how he or she is advancing during a given workday at designated periods in order to take timely corrective action if required.

The functional work area manager should be aware of how team leaders (e.g., front-line supervisors) are doing their jobs and at what level of effectiveness. Decision making is based on this awareness and provides the functional work area manager with information to assist the team leaders. He or she must ask:

1. What is the functional work area's available transaction volume to be processed?
2. How many staff members and other resources are available to complete the work on hand?
3. How productive are the resources used?
4. What level of backlog is acceptable?
5  Is the performance within established quality and productivity parameters?

Senior management should receive a report similar in format, though less burdened by detail. The senior manager doesn't need the information by staff member, but does need it by functional work area. The senior manager can then evaluate how well the functional work area is being run.

The creation of the database of information required at the different levels of management is significant because the intent of the information is to execute solid decisions. It is, however, no more consequential than the timeliness of providing the information. It should be emphasized that the success or failure of an ABM management reporting program may well hinge on the timely reporting of that significant information.

At the conclusion of each working day, the team leader and/or functional work area manager should summarize the production results, indicating what went well and what problems surfaced. This data should be available for review by the following morning so timely corrective action can be taken if required. Senior management should receive a report approximately once a week, delivered no later than noon on the Monday following the close of the week. An increase in the reporting frequency is acceptable, but not a decrease in frequency. A decrease in reporting frequency to senior management can grievously affect the decision-making process.

Reading any report is time-consuming, and in today's competitive, fast-paced business world, any time that can be saved for the busy executive has merit. A modern-day business technique is managing by exception. If a report can highlight any results that are out of sync with the norm, it will save a busy executive valuable time. This consideration should be extended beyond senior management to first-line management.

All management reports should be carefully crafted to make it easy for the reader to ascertain certain significant items, especially when they deviate from the norm. There are several ways to accomplish this mission. Many automated reports can be generated in which exceptions are emphasized. One distribution company highlighted inventory items that fell below the restocking point by placing an asterisk next to the appropriate inventory item. The purchasing department would examine the report and take action on those items marked with an asterisk. This type of report has the exception rule built into its architecture. Other highlighting techniques include

- Placing totals at the bottom of a report page
- Shadowing key items
- Multicolor printing
- Encircling

Functional work area managers should be concerned with highlighting those things that didn't go well rather than those that did. Any management reporting system is successful only if it is being used. As long as senior management insists on receiving this type of information, not only in words but also in actions and follow-up, the reporting system will endure.

When senior management insists that a report be delivered at a specific time and frequency, the report can be generated only if lower-level managers are doing their jobs—and so on down the line. Remember that reporting may originate from the bottom up, but follow-up must come from the top down.

## Summary Checklist

It is literally impossible to illustrate all the types and versions of management reports that can be utilized by various users. The following guidelines are helpful in developing meaningful reports.

- Develop the management report for the basic information needs of the user.
- Develop the management report for a specific level of management.
- Include only relevant information.
- Report information in a brief manner.
- Issue reports in a timely manner.
- Implement a well-structured reporting schedule so all levels of management can take timely corrective action.
- Insist on senior management's participation and follow-up.
- Highlight the important items to save the reader time.

# Individual Daily Volume Plan and Report

## Purpose

The individual daily volume plan (Fig. 8-1) is designed to assist individual staff members as well as the functional work area manager in maintaining a sufficient flow of work through each work station and, thereby, through the entire functional work area. The form achieves this objective by providing reasonable expectancy goals for primary activities along with transaction volumes processed, end-of-the-day carryovers, and notes on any problems encountered. This data enables the functional work area manager to monitor and guide the daily progress of work more effectively by taking more timely and immediate corrective action on problems encountered by the staff.

## Responsibility

Each staff member is responsible for entering all the required data, at the indicated times. The functional work area manager is responsible for monitoring and analyzing the data twice each working day.

## Frequency

The necessary data is entered by each staff member for each working day by 12 noon for the morning period and by 4:30 for the afternoon period.

Functional work area _____ (2)

Week ending date _____ (1)

Staff member _____ (4)

Functional work area _____ (3)

| Primary activities (5) | Units of measure (6) | R/E (7) | Monday | | | Tuesday | | | Wednesday | | | Thursday | | | Friday | | |
|---|---|---|---|---|---|---|---|---|---|---|---|---|---|---|---|---|---|
| | | | Units A.M. (8) | Comp. P.M. (9) | B/L unit (10) | Units A.M. | Comp. P.M. | B/L unit | Units A.M. | Comp. P.M. | B/L unit | Units A.M. | Comp. P.M. | B/L unit | Units A.M. | Comp. P.M. | B/L unit |
| | | | | | | | | | | | | | | | | | |
| | | | | | | | | | | | | | | | | | |
| | | | | | | | | | | | | | | | | | |
| | | | | | | | | | | | | | | | | | |
| | | | | | | | | | | | | | | | | | |
| | | | | | | | | | | | | | | | | | |
| | | | | | | | | | | | | | | | | | |
| | | | | | | | | | | | | | | | | | |
| | | | | | | | | | | | | | | | | | |
| | | | | | | | | | | | | | | | | | |
| | | | | | | | | | | | | | | | | | |

**Figure 8-1a.** Individual daily volume plan and report.

Functional work area _____

Week ending date _____

Staff member _____

Functional work area _____

| Secondary activities (11) | Units of measure (12) | R/E (13) | Monday | | | | | | Tuesday | | | | | | Wednesday | | | | | | Thursday | | | | | | Friday | | | | | |
|---|---|---|---|---|---|---|---|---|---|---|---|---|---|---|---|---|---|---|---|---|---|---|---|---|---|---|---|---|---|---|---|---|
| | | | Work (14) | | Not work (15) | | B/L unit | | Work | | Not work | | B/L unit | | Work | | Not work | | B/L unit | | Work | | Not work | | B/L unit | | Work | | Not work | | B/L unit | |
| | | | A.M. | P.M. | A.M. | P.M. | P.M. | | A.M. | P.M. | A.M. | P.M. | P.M. | | A.M. | P.M. | A.M. | P.M. | P.M. | | A.M. | P.M. | A.M. | P.M. | P.M. | | A.M. | P.M. | A.M. | P.M. | P.M. | |

Problems/Notes (16)

**Figure 8-1a.** (*Continued*) Individual daily volume plan and report.

| Line # | Title or Term | Is Used to Indicate |
|---|---|---|
| (1) | Week ending date | The month, day, and year for the current week ending period, which closes a Friday. |
| (2) | Functional work area | The functional work area name (e.g., accounts receivable). |
| (3) | Functional work area manager | The name of the responsible functional work area manager. |
| (4) | Name | The staff member's name who is filling in the report. |
| (5) | Primary activities | Primary activities for each functional work area are preprinted. The source of the data is the activity dictionary. |
| (6) | Units of measure | Units of measure for each primary activity should also be preprinted. The source of the data is the activity dictionary. |
| (7) | R/E (reasonable expectancy) | The R/E, or work-to-time relationship, for each primary activity is preprinted. Figures are expressed in units per hour. The source of the data is the reasonable expectancy worksheet. |
| (8) | Units completed—a.m. | The number of units completed or processed for each primary preprinted activity, up to the staff member's normal lunch hour break. |
| (9) | Units completed—p.m. | The number of units completed for each primary preprinted activity, from the lunch hour break through the end of the workday. |
| (10) | B/L units (backlog) | The number of units left over or not processed for each of the preprinted primary activities just prior to the end of the workday. |
| (11) | Secondary activities | Secondary activities have been preprinted for each functional work area. The source of the data is the activity dictionary. |
| (12) | Units of measure | Unit of measure for each preprinted secondary activity should also be preprinted. The source of the data is the activity dictionary. |
| (13) | R/E (reasonable expectancy) | The R/E, or work-to-time relationship, for each secondary activity is preprinted. Figures are expressed in units per hour. The source of the data is the staffing calculation worksheet. |
| (14) | Work | If a staff member has done any significant amount of work for any of the secondary activities, a check mark is entered in the appropriate work column (before lunch=a.m.; after lunch=p.m.). Record performance for each workday—Monday to Friday. |

**Figure 8-1b.** Individual daily volume plan and report key.

| Line # | Title or Term | Is Used to Indicate |
|--------|---------------|---------------------|
| (15) | Not work | If no significant amount of work was processed for any of the listed secondary activities, a check mark is entered in this column. If the column is checked for 3 consecutive days, the backlog for that secondary activity should be counted and the number of units entered in the B/L column. The manager should also talk to the staff member to see if there may be a problem associated with the specific activity that prevented it from being performed. |
| (16) | Problems/notes | If a staff member encounters a problem that has a negative impact on his or her ability to perform, use the spaces provided to make notes outlining what went wrong. The notes serve as a reminder so a staff member can discuss the problem in detail with the functional work area manager. Be descriptive and account for lost time. Record problem notes for each workday—Monday to Friday. |

**Figure 8-1b.** (*Continued*) Individual daily volume plan and report key.

## Distribution

Each day the functional work area manager discusses the individual daily volume plan and report with the staff member. At the end of the week, the original is given to the manager, with the staff member retaining a copy.

## How to Use the Report

The individual daily volume plan and report should be reviewed twice daily— at about noon and again at the end of the workday. A good routine is for the functional work area manager to approach each staff member at his or her work station and review the report while the staff member continues to work. The functional work area manager collects all reports at the end of each day, reviews them, and files them by individual staff member.

**Primary Activity Section.**   Review the units completed and B/L (backlog) columns. If the morning segment is from 9 a.m. to 12 noon, the functional work area manager can easily divide the R/E into the units of completed work to determine if approximately 3 hours' worth of work was processed. If the functional work area manager determines that productivity was below expectations, he or she should immediately look at the problems/notes section for a possible explanation of why work was not completed as planned.

If no problems are recorded, the staff member should be asked if any problems in fact arose. The functional work area manager should discuss the situation with the staff member.

If no problem is identified and yet a particular staff member continues to perform below expectations, while other staff members reach appropriate levels, the functional work area manager should hold a more detailed discussion with the low-performing staff member to determine the reason for the low level of performance. This one-on-one discussion should be a private session in the manager's office, not at the staff member's work station. The functional work area manager should be understanding, not accusatory, in his or her approach. Generally, the real reason for the lower production will surface during this type of quiet, uninterrupted, and relaxed interactive session.

The B/L column provides information that will assist the functional work area manager in establishing priorities for the next day's work. This may include the possibility of overtime and/or shifting resources to a functional work area that has developed a problem backlog. When staff members have been cross-trained to perform several different activities, the functional work area manager will have additional options.

**Secondary Activity Section.**  The functional work area manager should review the secondary activity section of the report to see whether the activities listed were worked on or not. If several days pass and no activity has taken place, ask staff members if there is any work building up for that activity. If there is, ask them to count the number of backlogged units and enter the figure in the B/L column. Have staff members spend some time on the activity the next day.

The individual daily volume plan and report is also an excellent tool for measuring the progress of a new staff member or a current staff member who is learning a new activity. A new individual cannot be expected to attain the R/E level immediately, but should steadily improve with time and with the proper training and coaching from the functional work area manager.

## Daily–Weekly Operating Report

### Purpose

The daily–weekly operating report (Fig. 8-2) is designed to assist the functional work area manager in monitoring key performance measures that are identified for a specific functional work area. The report accomplishes this objective by comparing actual work processed to planned levels. This data enables the functional work area manager to more effectively monitor and guide each functional work area's activities and service commitments. In addition, it allows the functional work area manager to respond in a more timely manner so he or she can take immediate corrective action when operating problems arise.

Week ending date _____

(1)

| Day/date | People on payroll | | Hours worked | | | KVI volumes | | | Backlog hours | | Service indicators | | | | | | | | |
|---|---|---|---|---|---|---|---|---|---|---|---|---|---|---|---|---|---|---|---|
| | (5) | (6) | (7) | (8) | (9) | (10) | (11) | (12) | (13) | (14) | (16) | (17) | Plan | Act. | Plan | Act. | Plan | Act. | Plan | Act. |
| (4) | Plan | Act. | Plan | Act. | Memo OT | Plan | Act. | % atn. | Plan | Act. | (15) | | | | | | | | | |
| Monday | | | | | | | | | | | | | | | | | | | | |
| Tuesday | | | | | | | | | | | | | | | | | | | | |
| Wednesday | | | | | | | | | | | | | | | | | | | | |
| Thursday | | | | | | | | | | | | | | | | | | | | |
| Friday | | | | | | | | | | | | | | | | | | | | |
| Total (18) | | | | | | | | | | | | | | | | | | | | |

**Figure 8-2a.** Daily–weekly operating report.

| Line # | Title or Term | Is Used to Indicate |
|---|---|---|
| (1) | Week ending date | The month, day, and year for the current week ending period. |
| (2) | Functional work area | The name of the functional work area (e.g., accounts payable). |
| (3) | Functional work area manager | The name of the responsible functional work area manager. |
| (4) | Day / date | The days are preprinted. The calendar dates for each day are entered by hand under the day. |
| (5) | People on payroll—plan | The number of staff members planned to be on the payroll, excluding the functional work area manager. This figure will generally not change more frequently than once a month. It comes from the staffing decision line on the functional work area's staffing master schedule. |
| (6) | People on payroll—actual | The number of people who are actually on the payroll, excluding the functional work area manager. This figure is not the number of staff members in attendance that day but rather the number of staff members who would come to work if all was well. |
| (7) | Hours worked—plan | The number of hours planned for a specific day. This figure is derived from the staffing master schedule—total hours required at work at 90 percent productivity (e.g., 86.9 hours divided by 5 days = 17.4). |
| (8) | Hours worked—actual | The total number of hours actually worked each workday. Exclude the functional work area manager's hours, but include any overtime hours. |
| (9) | Memo OT (overtime) | The number of actual hours worked that were overtime hours (i.e., beyond normal workday hours). These hours are also included in the "hours worked–actual" column. They are entered here for possible special attention by the functional work area manager. |
| (10) | KVI volumes—plan | The total KVI transaction volumes planned to be processed each day. The figure is taken from KVI transaction volumes identified in developing the functional work area composite R/E, as in an average week (e.g., 875 collections divided by 5 days = 175 per day). |

**Figure 8-2b.** Daily–weekly operating report key.

| Line # | Title or Term | Is Used to Indicate |
|--------|---------------|---------------------|
| (11) | KVI volumes—actual | The total KVI activity transaction volumes that actually were completed each day. |
| (12) | % Atn (percent attainment) | The percent attainment each day. This figure is derived by dividing the KVI transaction volumes–actual by the KVI transaction volumes–planned (e.g., 242/255 = 95%). |
| (13) | Backlog hours—plan | The total planned backlog hours for each day, from the daily–weekly backlog report plan column (see Fig. 8-3) for the specific day of the week that is involved. |
| (14) | Backlog hours—actual | Actual backlog hours for each day, from the daily–weekly backlog report (actual) column for the specific day of the week that is involved. |
| (15) | Service indicators | Each department's key service indicators (e.g., daily follow-up calls) are preprinted. There is room for up to five. |
| (16) | Service indicators—plan | The plan or goal in units, percents, etc., for each specific indicator (i.e., aging look-ups 80 per person per day $\times$ 3 people = 240). |
| (17) | Service indicators—actual | The actual units completed or percent achieved for the specific indicator from actual transaction volumes processed and/or statistics calculated. |
| (18) | Total | Total the following columns for the entire week—Monday through Friday: |
| | | ■ Hours worked—plan, actual, and memo OT |
| | | ■ KVI volumes—plan, actual |
| | | Then calculate the percent attained, utilizing total line plan/actual numbers. Do not total people on payroll figures. The figures entered for the last working day of the week are brought down to the weekly total line for the plan column. The functional work area manager should then calculate an average for the actual column. |

**Figure 8-2b.** (*Continued*) Daily–weekly operating report key.

## Responsibility

The functional work area manager is responsible for entering all required data daily and for monitoring and analyzing the data at the end of each working day. This data enables the manager to more effectively control work in the functional work area by taking more timely and specific actions when upward or downward trends and/or unplanned conditions are indicated.

## Frequency

The daily–weekly operating report should be completed and ready for review and/or distribution by 9 a.m. each working day.

## Distribution

Each day the functional work area manager discusses the daily–weekly operating report with his or her staff members. At the end of the week, the original report is given to senior management, with the functional work area manager retaining a copy.

## How to Use the Report

The daily–weekly operating report should be reviewed and analyzed at the end of each day as well as the end of each week. The functional work area manager should look for trends whether they be upward or downward, and be prepared to discuss reasons for improvement and/or a downturn. A question should be raised regarding whether a trend is short or long term, because trends are influenced by changes in business conditions, system enhancements, a change in work activity mix, methods changes, and so on.

**People on Payroll Section.**    Staffing levels are easily analyzed on the basis of the number of people planned for and/or the number of staff members actually working on a given day. If an unusually high backlog of work develops, the functional work area manager may wish to shift resources from other activities to cut into or eliminate the backlog. The manager may also wish to utilize overtime, depending on whether he or she feels the situation will dissipate by itself over time or will require more direct intervention.

**Hours Worked Section.**    Hours worked are a by-product of the people on payroll section and should be analyzed in a similar manner. The memo OT (overtime) column should be monitored to make sure it is not abused and remains a small percentage of total hours at work.

**KVI Volume Section.**    The KVI volume section highlights the key volume indicators for each functional work area (e.g., credit = total units for items reviewed and items pulled). The functional work area manager should review the percent attainment column to determine if the planned level of output was attained. This performance measurement is extremely important, since it indicates that the primary activities are being completed. If they are not, the functional work area manager should know what the problems are and what he or she has to do to correct the situation. Poor attainment is caused by operating problems, which may include such things as high absenteeism (insufficient hours worked) and low individual staff member productivity.

**Backlog Hours Section.**   The functional work area manager should review the backlog hours section to ensure that backlog levels are under control. Backlogs that are always at *zero* or at very low levels can also be a problem. Low levels of backlog could indicate lower demand for products and/or services and should be analyzed as carefully as high levels of backlog.

**Service Indicators Section.**   The functional work area manager should monitor service indicators closely, since they are important barometers of collecting receivables, servicing customers, and receiving discounts. The manager should investigate any large differentials between planned and actual levels, especially inappropriate trends, so corrective action can be taken as soon as possible.

## Daily–Weekly Backlog Report

### Purpose

The daily–weekly backlog report (Fig. 8-3) is designed to assist individual functional work area managers in monitoring activities that have unprocessed volumes at the end of a day. The report achieves this objective by providing a mechanism to plan backlog levels on the basis of desired turnaround times or service commitments. This data enables functional work area managers to more effectively plan their work for the following day, to take timely and specific action on problems encountered by their staff, and to identify and review unfavorable levels or trends.

### Responsibility

Each functional work area manager is responsible for entering all required data daily and for monitoring and analyzing the data at the end of each working day. This data enables the functional work area manager to more effectively control work flow by taking action when upward or downward trends and/or unplanned conditions are indicated.

### Frequency

The report is to be completed by 9 a.m. each working day.

### Distribution

The functional work area manager should discuss the daily–weekly backlog report each day with members of the staff. At the end of the week the original report is given to senior management, with the functional work area manager retaining a copy.

Week ending date _____ (1) _____

Functional work area _____ (2)

Functional work area manager _____ (3)

| Activity (4) | Units of measure (5) | R/E (6) | Monday |||| Tuesday |||| Wednesday |||| Thursday |||| Friday ||||
|---|---|---|---|---|---|---|---|---|---|---|---|---|---|---|---|---|---|---|---|
| | | | Volume || Hour || Volume || Hour || Volume || Hour || Volume || Hour || Volume || Hour ||
| | | | Plan (7) | Act (8) | Plan (9) | Act (10) | Plan | Act | Plan | Act | Plan | Act | Plan | Act | Plan | Act | Plan | Act | Plan | Act |
| | | | | | | | | | | | | | | | | | | | | |
| | | | | | | | | | | | | | | | | | | | | |
| | | | | | | | | | | | | | | | | | | | | |
| | | | | | | | | | | | | | | | | | | | | |
| | | | | | | | | | | | | | | | | | | | | |
| | | | | | | | | | | | | | | | | | | | | |
| | | | | | | | | | | | | | | | | | | | | |
| | | | | | | | | | | | | | | | | | | | | |
| | | | | | | | | | | | | | | | | | | | | |
| | | | | | | | | | | | | | | | | | | | | |
| | | | | | | | | | | | | | | | | | | | | |
| Totals (11) | | | | | | | | | | | | | | | | | | | | |

**Figure 8-3a.** Daily–weekly backlog report.

| Line # | Title or Term | Is Used to Indicate |
|--------|---------------|---------------------|
| (1) | Week ending date | The month, day, and year for the current week ending period. |
| (2) | Functional work area | The name of the functional work area (e.g., credit). |
| (3) | Functional work area manager | The name of the responsible functional work area manager. |
| (4) | Activity | Primary activities for each functional work area manager are preprinted. The source of the data is the activity dictionary. |
| (5) | Units of measure | The units of measure for each primary activity should also be preprinted. The source of the data is the activity dictionary. |
| (6) | R/E (reasonable expectancy) | The R/E, or work-to-time relationship, for each primary activity is preprinted. The figures are expressed as units per hour. The source of the data is the reasonable expectancy worksheet. |
| (7) | Volume—plan | Transaction volumes are established by each functional work area manager. The levels are generally based on desired work turnaround times or customer service commitments. |
| (8) | Volume—actual | The actual backlog transaction volume for each day, taken from the B/L unit columns on the individual daily volume plan and report (see Fig. 8-1). |
| (9) | Hours—plan | The planned backlog hours, calculated by dividing the planned backlog volumes by the R/E for the specific activity involved. |
| (10) | Hours—actual | The actual backlog volumes, calculated by dividing the actual backlog volumes by the R/E for the specific activity involved. |
| (11) | Totals | The columns for planned backlog hours and actual backlog hours should be totaled each day. |

**Figure 8-3b.** Daily–weekly backlog report key.

## How to Use the Report

The functional work area manager should review the daily–weekly backlog report at the end of each day and be alert to trends that are over or under plan. The manager must continually determine if a trend is self-liquidating or if some intervention is required.

The functional work area manager should utilize the data to determine whether overtime and/or extra resources are required to correct a problem backlog condition. Sometimes volume may surge and then dissipate during a week's time or less without any special intervention.

## Problem Action Report

### Purpose

The problem action report (Fig. 8-4) is designed to assist the functional work area manager in identifying and correcting operating problems encountered in his or her work area. The report achieves this objective by providing a format for staff members to record significant problems and the corrective actions they have taken to prevent recurrence. This data enables experienced functional work area managers to highlight recurring problems and to prioritize their corrective action efforts more effectively.

### Responsibility

Each functional work area manager is responsible for entering all required data each day on an as-needed basis. This activity will normally take place during the morning and afternoon follow-up routines, when the functional work area manager is making his or her walk-through in the work area. This process enables functional work area managers to more effectively control problems by taking timely and specific corrective action.

### Frequency

The functional work area manager should enter the necessary data for each working day as problems are identified on a real-time basis.

### Distribution

Any activities identified in the problem action report should be discussed as they happen by the functional work area manager and the staff member. At the end of each day the results should be summarized on the problem action report summary (see below).

### How to Use the Report

The problem action report is initiated by the functional work area manager, as required, during the morning and afternoon follow-up periods. During this twice-daily process, the functional work area manager approaches each staff member to see if he or she has any problems and/or needs help or guidance.

Problems identified are then recorded, along with the corrective action taken. The functional work area manager should investigate recurring problems to determine why they continue to occur so that a permanent method of eliminating them can be developed. Problems with an individual staff member on a recurring basis may signal that additional training is required. The critical point is to identify and solve problems as early as possible.

Date _____ (1)

Functional work area _____ (2)

Functional work area manager _____ (3)

| Staff member name (4) | Hours lost (5) | Problem description (6) | Corrective action taken (7) |
|---|---|---|---|
| | | | |
| | | | |
| | | | |
| | | | |
| | | | |
| | | | |
| | | | |
| | | | |
| | | | |
| | | | |
| | | | |
| | | | |
| | | | |
| | | | |
| | | | |
| | | | |
| | | | |
| | | | |
| | | | |
| | | | |

**Figure 8-4a.** Problem action report.

| Line # | Title or Term | Is Used to Indicate |
|---|---|---|
| (1) | Date | The month, day, and year for that specific date the report is being utilized. |
| (2) | Functional work area | The name of the functional work area (e.g., credit). |
| (3) | Functional work area manager | The name of the responsible functional work area manager. |
| (4) | Staff member name | The name of the staff member who had a problem. |
| (5) | Hours lost | The hours lost associated with the identified problem. This figure is usually calculated by dividing the volume that was not processed because of the problem by the R/E for that specific activity. |
| (6) | Problem description | A description of the problem resulting from a discussion between the functional work area manager and the staff member who identified it. |
| (7) | Corrective action taken | A brief description of the corrective action taken to prevent recurrence of the problem. Effective corrective action requires that the functional work area manager get to the real source of the problem and in some cases obtain help from other members of the management team. |

**Figure 8-4b.**  Problem action report key.

## Problem Action Report Summary
### Purpose

The problem action report summary (Fig. 8-5) is designed to assist functional work area managers in monitoring key problem categories for their individual functional work areas. The report achieves this objective by categorizing problems and the resulting hours lost. The data also enables managers to identify recurring problems and better prioritize their problem-solving efforts.

### Responsibility

Each functional work area manager is responsible for entering all required data each working day on an as-needed basis. The functional work area manager is responsible for monitoring and analyzing the data.

### Frequency

The necessary data is entered by each functional work area for each working day. The data is reviewed both daily and weekly by the functional work area manager and staff members.

Week ending date _____ (1)

Functional work area _____ (2)

Functional work area manager _____ (3)

**Lost time-categories (hours lost)** (5)

| Day/date | (6) | | | | | | | | | Totals |
|---|---|---|---|---|---|---|---|---|---|---|
| Monday (4) | | | | | | | | | | |
| Tuesday | | | | | | | | | | |
| Wednesday | | | | | | | | | | |
| Thursday | | | | | | | | | | |
| Friday | | | | | | | | | | |
| **Totals** (7) | | | | | | | | | | |

**Figure 8-5a.** Problem action report summary.

269

| Line # | Title or Term | Is Used to Indicate |
|---|---|---|
| (1) | Week ending date | The month, day, and year for the current week ending period. |
| (2) | Functional work area | The name of the functional work area (e.g., accounts receivable). |
| (3) | Functional work area manager | The name of the responsible functional work area manager. |
| (4) | Day/date | The date for each preprinted day of the week. |
| (5) | Lost time—categories (hours lost) | The category titles are preprinted (e.g., computer down) |
| (6) | Hours lost | The hours lost in each category, calculated from the problem action report (see Fig. 8-4) for each day. |
| (7) | Totals | The hours lost should be totaled across the form each day. At the end of the week, the hours lost should be totaled by category down to the bottom line. |

**Figure 8-5b.** Problem action report summary key.

## Distribution

Each day the functional work area manager discusses the problem action report summary with senior management. At the end of the week the original report is given to senior management, with the functional work area manager retaining a copy.

### How to Use the Report

The functional work area manager should review the problem action report summary at the end of each day and again at the end of each week. The manager should look for trends and continually work to eliminate those types of problems that cause the most lost time.

Problems which occur randomly and infrequently may be unavoidable. However, if lost time keeps occurring on a regular basis, a more structured action plan may be required. The main thrust is to research problems as early as possible and then take immediate and decisive corrective action.

## Individual Activity Evaluation Report

### Purpose

The individual activity evaluation report (Fig. 8-6) is designed to assist the functional work area manager in monitoring overall performance levels in his

Prepared by: _____ (1)

Activity name: _____ (2)

Functional work area _____ (3)

Unit of measure _____ (4)

Base period: (5)  From: _____  To: _____ (7)

Base volume _____ (6)  Base hours worked _____  Base ratio _____ (8)

| Week ending date | Current week | | Ratio | Hours required at base | Differ + (−) | Hourly cost w/fringe | Dollars | | 4 Wk Current week | Roll avg Annual |
| | Volume | Hours worked | | | | | This week | Cumulative | | |
| (9) | (10) | (11) | (12) | (13) | (14) | (15) | (16) | (17) | (18) | (19) |
| | | | | | | | | | | |
| | | | | | | | | | | |
| | | | | | | | | | | |
| | | | | | | | | | | |
| | | | | | | | | | | |
| | | | | | | | | | | |
| | | | | | | | | | | |
| | | | | | | | | | | |
| | | | | | | | | | | |
| | | | | | | | | | | |
| | | | | | | | | | | |
| | | | | | | | | | | |

**Figure 8-6a.** Individual activity evaluation report.

| Line # | Title or Term | Is Used to Indicate |
| --- | --- | --- |
| (1) | Prepared by | The name of the person responsible for preparing the report. |
| (2) | Activity name | The name of the primary activity. |
| (3) | Functional work area | The name of the functional work area (e.g., collections). |
| (4) | Unit of measure | The key volume indicator for each primary activity (for collections, it would be follow-up calls). |
| (5) | Base period: from/to | The base period covered (e.g., 1/1/96 to 6/30/96). |
| (6) | Base volume | The total volume generated in the selected base period. |
| (7) | Base hours worked | The total hours worked in the selected base period. |
| (8) | Base ratio | The base ratio is developed by dividing base volume by base hours worked (e.g., $14{,}043/2{,}602 = 5.40$). *Note:* All historical base periods and data should be developed with and approved by the individual functional work area manager. This ratio expresses units process per hour worked, and as such serves as a productivity measurement. |
| (9) | Week ending date | The month, day, and year for each week ending period. |
| (10) | Current week—volume | The current week's KVI volume(s) from the KVI data supplied by each functional work area manager (e.g., follow-up calls from computer). |
| (11) | Current week— hours worked | The current total hours worked, taken from official weekly payroll data (e.g., regular and overtime hours excluding holiday, sick, and vacation hours) supplied by each functional work area manager. |
| (12) | Current week ratio | The current week's ratio. This figure is calculated by dividing the current week's volume by the current week's hours worked. Carry this figure to two decimal places. |
| (13) | Hours required at base | The work hours that would have been required at the base ratio. This figure is calculated by dividing the current week's volume by the base ratio. Round this figure to the nearest whole hour. |

**Figure 8-6b.** Individual activity evaluation report key.

| Line # | Title or Term | Is Used to Indicate |
|--------|---------------|---------------------|
| (14) | Difference + (−) | The *plus* or *minus* difference between actual hours worked and hours required at the base ratio. If the hours required at the base ratio are higher than the actual hours worked for the current week, it is a *plus* condition. |
| (15) | Hourly cost with fringe | The hourly labor cost with fringe benefits (e.g., $12.00), taken from official payroll data supplied by the chief financial officer for each functional work area. |
| (16) | Dollars—this week | The total dollars this week, calculated by multiplying the difference + (−) column by the hourly cost with fringe column. |
| (17) | Dollars—cumulative | Cumulative dollars, calculated by adding the cumulative dollar total from the prior week to the dollars–this week entry. This serves as a running total from the beginning of the measurement process. |
| (18) | Dollars: 4-week rolling average—current week | The 4-week rolling average, in dollars, for the current week. This figure is calculated by adding the four most recent entries in the dollars–this week column and dividing the result by four. |
| (19) | Dollars: 4-week rolling average—annual | The annual 4-week rolling average, in dollars, calculated by multiplying the 4-week rolling average for the current week by 52 weeks. This figure represents the annual change in cost to process the total functional work area workload compared against a base period. |

**Figure 8-6b.** (*Continued*) Individual activity evaluation report key.

or her functional work area. The report achieves this objective by comparing historical base period ratios, expressed as key unit volumes processed per hour, against current levels of production, expressed in the same type of ratio. Any variance between the current ratio and the base ratio is then converted into payroll dollars, utilizing a 4-week rolling average to facilitate proper analysis.

## Responsibility

The functional work area manager is responsible for the timely and accurate completion of the individual activity evaluation report. Senior management is responsible for monitoring and analyzing the data at the end of each week. This data enables the functional work area manager to more effectively monitor overall performance of the functional work area and thereby take more timely action when unfavorable trends and/or unexpected conditions arise.

**Frequency**

The necessary data for the week must be supplied by 10 a.m. the following Monday.

**Distribution**

The individual activity evaluation report is analyzed and discussed each week by the functional work area manager and his or her staff members.

**How to Use the Report**

The individual activity evaluation report should be reviewed at the end of each week by the functional work area manager. The manager should focus on trends rather than week-to-week fluctuations. The cost dollar impact of changes to functional work area performance is rolled over a 4-week period for this purpose.

**Difference + (−).**   Analyze the difference column from week to week to see if a plus or minus trend is developing. A negative trend means that the functional work area is not operating as productively as it could or at levels it has achieved in the past. A discussion should then take place, between the functional work area manager and the staff members performing the activity, regarding identified problems and corrective action plans.

**Dollars—This Week.**   Also analyze the dollars column from week to week, since it is a by-product of the difference + (−) section. This entry will be a plus if current performance is greater than the base.

**Dollars: 4-Week Rolling Average—Annual.**   Rolling average figures represent the overall impact as an annualized labor cost of the change in functional work area performance versus the established base period. The greater the difference is, on the plus side, the more effectively resources are being managed in the functional work area.

## Functional Work Area Evaluation Report

### Purpose

The functional work area evaluation report (Fig. 8-7) is designed to assist senior management in monitoring overall performance levels in a functional work area. The report achieves this objective by comparing historical base period ratios, expressed as key unit volumes processed per hour, against current levels of production, expressed in the same type of ratio. Any variance between the current ratio and the base ratio is then converted into payroll dollars, utilizing a 4-week rolling average to facilitate proper analysis.

Functional work area _____ (2)

Unit of measure _____ (3)

Base period: (4) From: _____ To: _____ (5)

Base volume _____ Base hours worked _____ (6) Base ratio _____ (7)

Prepared by: _____ (1)

| Week ending date | Current week | | | Hours required at base | Differ + (−) | Hourly cost w/fringe | Dollars | | | 4 Wk | Roll avg |
| | Volume | Hours worked | Ratio | | | | This week | Cumulative | Current week | Annual |
| (8) | (9) | (10) | (11) | (12) | (13) | (14) | (15) | (16) | (17) | (18) |
| | | | | | | | | | | |
| | | | | | | | | | | |
| | | | | | | | | | | |
| | | | | | | | | | | |
| | | | | | | | | | | |
| | | | | | | | | | | |
| | | | | | | | | | | |
| | | | | | | | | | | |
| | | | | | | | | | | |
| | | | | | | | | | | |
| | | | | | | | | | | |
| | | | | | | | | | | |
| | | | | | | | | | | |

**Figure 8-7a.** Functional work area evaluation report.

Functional work area ___ Accounts payable ___

Unit of measure ___ Purchase and expense invoices ___

Base period: From: 5/6/94 To: 6/28/94

Base volume ___ 24,142 ___ Base hours worked ___ 2,509 ___ Base ratio ___ 9.62 ___

Prepared by: ___ Edward Forrest ___

| Week ending date | Current week | | | Hours required at base | Differ + (−) | Hourly cost w/fringe | Dollars | | 4 Wk | Roll avg |
| | Volume | Hours worked | Ratio | | | | This week | Cumulative | Current week | Annual |
|---|---|---|---|---|---|---|---|---|---|---|
| 7/15/94 | 2,626 | 360.0 | 7.29 | 272.9 | (87.1) | $12.00 | (1,045) | (1,045) | (1,045) | (54,340) |
| 7/22/94 | 2,700 | 335.0 | 8.06 | 280.6 | (54.4) | $12.00 | (653) | (1,698) | (849) | (44,148) |
| 7/29/94 | 3,179 | 339.0 | 9.38 | 330.4 | (8.6) | $12.00 | (103) | (1,801) | (600) | (31,200) |
| 8/5/94 | 2,706 | 299.0 | 9.05 | 281.2 | (17.8) | $12.00 | (213) | (2,014) | (504) | (26,208) |
| 8/12/94 | 2,676 | 306.0 | 8.75 | 278.1 | (27.9) | $12.00 | (335) | (2,349) | (326) | (16,952) |
| 8/19/94 | 2,603 | 350.0 | 7.44 | 270.5 | (79.5) | $12.00 | (954) | (3,303) | (401) | (20,852) |
| 8/26/94 | 3,153 | 344.0 | 9.17 | 327.7 | (16.3) | $12.00 | (196) | (3,499) | (424) | (22,048) |
| 9/2/94 | 2,039 | 209.0 | 9.76 | 211.9 | 2.9 | $12.00 | 35 | (3,464) | (362) | (18,824) |
| 9/9/94 | 2,326 | 208.5 | 11.16 | 241.7 | 33.2 | $13.00 | 432 | (3,032) | (171) | (8,892) |
| 9/16/94 | 2,330 | 237.8 | 9.80 | 242.1 | 4.3 | $13.00 | 57 | (2,975) | 82 | 4,264 |
| 9/23/94 | 3,200 | 239.0 | 13.39 | 332.6 | 93.6 | $13.00 | 1,216 | (1,759) | 435 | 22,620 |
| 9/30/94 | 3,306 | 264.2 | 12.51 | 343.6 | 73.4 | $13.00 | 1,032 | (727) | 684 | 35,568 |
| 10/7/94 | 2,951 | 248.5 | 11.88 | 306.7 | 58.2 | $13.00 | 756 | 29 | 765 | 39,780 |

**Figure 8-7a.** (*Continued*) Functional work area evaluation report.

| Line # | Title or Term | Is Used to Indicate |
|---|---|---|
| (1) | Prepared by | The name of the person responsible for preparing the report. |
| (2) | Functional work area | The name of the functional work area (e.g., collections). |
| (3) | Unit of measure | The key volume indicator for each functional work area (for collections, it would be follow-up calls). |
| (4) | Base period: from/to | The base period covered (e.g., 1/1/96 to 6/30/96). |
| (5) | Base volume | The total volume generated in the selected base period. |
| (6) | Base hours worked | The total hours worked in the selected base period. |
| (7) | Base ratio | The base ratio, calculated by dividing base volume by base hours worked (e.g., $14,043/2,602 = 5.40$). *Note:* All historical base periods and data should be developed with and approved by the individual functional work area manager. This ratio reflects units processed per hour worked, and as such serves as a productivity measurement. |
| (8) | Week ending date | The month, day, and year for each week ending period. |
| (9) | Current week—volume | Enter the current week's KVI volume(s) from the KVI data supplied by each functional work area manager (e.g., follow-up calls from computer). |
| (10) | Current week— hours worked | The current total hours worked, from official weekly payroll data (e.g., regular and overtime hours excluding holiday, sick, and vacation hours) supplied by each functional work area manager. |
| (11) | Current week—ratio | The current week's ratio. This figure is calculated by dividing the current week's volume by the current week's hours worked. Carry this figure to two decimal places. |
| (12) | Hours required at base | The work hours that would have been required at the base ratio. This figure is calculated by dividing the current week's volume by the base ratio. Round this figure to the nearest whole hour. |

**Figure 8-7b.** Functional work area evaluation report key.

| Line # | Title or Term | Is Used to Indicate |
|---|---|---|
| (13) | Difference + (−) | The *plus* or *minus* difference between actual hours worked and hours required at the base ratio. If the hours required at the base ratio are higher than the actual hours worked for the current week, it is a *plus* condition. |
| (14) | Hourly cost with fringe | The hourly labor cost with fringe benefits (e.g., $12.00), taken from official payroll data supplied by the chief financial officer for each functional work area. |
| (15) | Dollars—this week | The total dollars this week, calculated by multiplying the difference + (−) column by the hourly cost with fringe. |
| (16) | Dollars—cumulative | Cumulative dollars, calculated by adding the cumulative dollars total from prior week to the dollars–this week entry. This serves as a running total from the beginning of the measurement process. |
| (17) | Dollars: 4-week rolling average—current week | The 4-week rolling average, in dollars, for the current week. This figure is calculated by adding the four most recent entries in the dollars–this week column and dividing the result by four. |
| (18) | Dollars: 4-week rolling average—annual | The annual 4-week rolling average, in dollars, calculated by multiplying the 4-week rolling average for the current week by 52 weeks. This figure represents the annual change in cost to process the total functional work area workload compared against a base period. |

**Figure 8-7b.** (*Continued*) Functional work area evaluation report key.

## Responsibility

Senior management is responsible for the timely and accurate completion of the functional work area project evaluation report and for monitoring and analyzing the data at the end of each week. This data enables senior management to more effectively monitor overall performance of the functional work area and thereby take more timely action when unfavorable trends and/or unexpected conditions arise.

## Frequency

The necessary data for the week must be supplied by 10 a.m. the following Monday.

## Distribution

The functional work area evaluation report is analyzed and discussed each week by senior management personnel.

## How to Use the Report

Individual functional work area evaluation reports should be reviewed at the end of each week by senior management. Senior management should focus on trends rather than week-to-week fluctuations. The cost dollar impact of changes to functional work area performance is rolled over a 4-week period for this purpose.

**Difference + (−).** Analyze the difference column from week to week to see if a plus or minus trend is developing. A negative trend means that the functional work area is not operating as productively as it could or at levels it has achieved in the past. A discussion should then take place, between senior management and the functional work area manager, regarding identified problems and corrective action plans.

**Dollars—This Week.** Also analyze the dollars column from week to week, since it is a by-product of the difference + (−) section. This entry will be a plus if current performance is greater than the base.

**Dollars: 4-Week Rolling Average—Annual.** Rolling average figures represent the overall impact as an annualized labor cost of the change in functional work area performance versus the established base period. The greater the difference is, on the plus side, the more effectively resources are being managed in the functional work area.

# Weekly Functional Work Area Comparison Evaluation Summary

## Purpose

The weekly comparison evaluation summary (Fig. 8-8) is designed to enable senior management to quickly and easily become aware of the cost dollar impact of current performance levels in several functional work areas compared with the base performance level. The report achieves this objective by comparing historical base period ratios with current ratios, and converting the variance into dollars utilizing a 4-week rolling average to more effectively analyze the effects of changes in productivity.

## Responsibility

Senior management is responsible for the timely and accurate completion of this report. The chief financial officer and other members of senior management are

Prepared by:_____ (1)

| W/E date (2) | Functional work area name (3) | Unit of measure (4) | Base ratio (5) | Current ratio (6) | Dollars + (−) | | 4 Wk averages | Rolling dollars |
| | | | | | This week (7) | Cumulative (8) | Current week (9) | Annual (10) |
|---|---|---|---|---|---|---|---|---|
| | | | | | | | | |
| | | | | | | | | |
| | | | | | | | | |
| | | | | | | | | |
| Weekly totals    (11) | | | | | | | | |
| | | | | | | | | |
| | | | | | | | | |
| | | | | | | | | |
| | | | | | | | | |
| Weekly totals | | | | | | | | |
| | | | | | | | | |
| | | | | | | | | |
| | | | | | | | | |
| | | | | | | | | |
| Weekly totals | | | | | | | | |
| | | | | | | | | |
| | | | | | | | | |
| | | | | | | | | |
| | | | | | | | | |
| Weekly totals | | | | | | | | |
| | | | | | | | | |
| | | | | | | | | |
| | | | | | | | | |
| | | | | | | | | |
| Weekly totals | | | | | | | | |

**Figure 8-8a.** Weekly functional work area comparison evaluation summary.

Prepared by:_____Edward Forrest_____

| W/E date | Functional work area name | Unit of measure | Base ratio | Current ratio | Dollars + (−) | | 4 Wk averages | Rolling dollars |
|---|---|---|---|---|---|---|---|---|
| | | | | | This week | Cumulative | Current week | Annual |
| 9/9/94 | A/C payable | Invoices | 9.62 | 11.16 | $432 | ($3,032) | (170) | (8,840) |
| | A/C receivable | Items appld. | 29.79 | 46.31 | $1,691 | $4,804 | 1,092 | 56,784 |
| | Collections | F/U calls | 5.40 | 8.71 | $866 | $6,573 | 631 | 32,812 |
| | Credit | Reviews | 7.39 | 15.08 | $2,537 | $10,881 | 1,283 | 66,716 |
| | Customer service | New prospects | 3.28 | 8.45 | $756 | ($132) | 224 | 11,648 |
| | Weekly totals | | | | $6,282 | $19,094 | 3,060 | 159,120 |
| 9/16/94 | A/C payable | Invoices | 9.62 | 9.80 | $578 | ($2,974) | 82 | 4,264 |
| | A/C receivable | Items appld. | 29.79 | 37.95 | $719 | $5,523 | 1,054 | 54,808 |
| | Collections | F/U calls | 5.40 | 6.91 | $420 | $6,993 | 680 | 35,360 |
| | Credit | Reviews | 7.39 | 13.93 | $2,619 | $13,500 | 1,884 | 97,968 |
| | Customer service | New prospects | 3.28 | 8.91 | $834 | ($702) | 529 | 27,508 |
| | Weekly totals | | | | $4,650 | $22,340 | 4,229 | 219,908 |
| | | | | | | | | |
| | Weekly totals | | | | | | | |
| | | | | | | | | |
| | Weekly totals | | | | | | | |
| | | | | | | | | |
| | Weekly totals | | | | | | | |

**Figure 8-8a.** (*Continued*) Weekly functional work area comparison evaluation summary.

| Line # | Title or Term | Is Used to Indicate |
|--------|---------------|---------------------|
| (1) | Prepared by | The name of the person preparing the report. |
| (2) | Week ending date | The month, day, and year for the current week ending. |
| (3) | Functional work area | The name of the functional work area (e.g., accounts payable). |
| (4) | Unit of measure | The KVI base unit of measure for each functional work area (e.g., accounts payable—invoices). This information comes from the individual functional work area evaluation reports. |
| (5) | Base ratio | The base ratio from each functional work area evaluation report. |
| (6) | Current ratio | The current week's ratio from each functional work area evaluation report. |
| (7) | Dollars + (−)—this week | The dollars this week, from each functional work area evaluation report. |
| (8) | Dollars + (−)—cumulative | The cumulative dollar entries from each functional work area evaluation report. |
| (9) | 4-week rolling average, dollars—current week | The 4-week rolling average, for the current week, in dollars, from each functional work area evaluation report. |
| (10) | 4-week rolling average, dollars—annual | The 4-week rolling average annual, in dollars, from each functional work area evaluation report. |
| (11) | Weekly totals | Total the following columns:<br>■ Dollars + (−)—this week<br>■ Dollars + (−)—cumulative<br>■ 4-week rolling average, dollars—current week<br>■ 4-week rolling average, dollars—annual |

**Figure 8-8b.** Weekly functional work area comparison evaluation summary key.

responsible for monitoring and analyzing the data at the end of each week. This data enables the chief financial officer to more effectively monitor the overall performance of several functional work areas and thereby take more timely action when unfavorable trends and/or unexpected conditions arise.

## Frequency

The chief financial officer enters the data each week and performs all necessary calculations.

## Distribution

The weekly functional work area comparison evaluation summary should be analyzed and discussed each week by the chief financial officer and other senior management personnel. The original report is retained by the chief financial officer, with copies distributed to other members of senior management.

## How to Use the Report

The weekly functional work area comparison evaluation summary should be reviewed at the end of each week by the chief financial officer and other members of senior management. Senior management should look for performance trends from week to week and at the 4-week rolling average annual dollars figures.

**Base Ratio/Current Ratio.**   Compare the base ratio and the current ratio, being alerted if the difference between the two ratios widens or diminishes. The key item is the current ratio, which will always be higher than the base ratio if overall performance (cost) is better than the base period.

If the differential diminishes or goes negative, it could indicate that volume or productivity has dropped, excessive overtime or people were utilized, and/or functional work area management has not reacted appropriately to what was happening. Each of these situations should raise questions as to staffing levels, staff productivity, service levels, and work backlogs. Inappropriate trends can be isolated by functional work area and investigated further.

**Dollars + (−).**   Analyze the dollar from week to week, being alerted if a negative condition and/or lowering trend begins to appear. This column converts productivity changes into dollars, with the cumulative total showing the result from the first week of the evaluation.

The dollars + (−) figures show the potential annualized impact on labor cost by any change in performance between the current period and the base period. A 4-week rolling average is used to smooth the possible fluctuations in weekly functional work area performances. Trends are an important consideration in analyzing this column. Future trends can also be predicted to some degree by looking at the most current weekly dollar figure along with the oldest week in the 4-week rolling calculation.

**4-Week Rolling Average, Dollars.**   Rolling average figures show the potential annualized impact on labor cost by any change in performance between the current period and the base period. A 4-week rolling average is used to smooth the possible fluctuations in weekly functional work area performances. Trends are the important consideration in analyzing this column. Future trends can also be predicted to some degree by looking at the most current weekly dollar figure along with the oldest week in the 4-week rolling calculation.

## Preinstallation Backlog Review

A day or two before the scheduled installation of all management reports and staffing adjustments, it is necessary to identify and quantify the backlog of work for each activity in each functional work area. In an activity-based management program, this procedure is important to prevent functional work area staff members from saying they never had a backlog until the staff was right-sized and/or resources were deployed.

The functional work area manager should visit with each staff member at his or her work station. Have the staff member empty the contents of all desk drawers and desktop containers, including trans files. Categorize documents into similar activities, label the documents by activity, and count the number of items in the batch. Place each batch in a file folder and/or put a rubberband around it and keep the documents on the top of a staff member's desk. Do not put batches back into drawers. Prepare a list of backlog items and their associated quantities (Fig. 8-9).

Assure each staff member that the purpose of this backlog identification process is to know what work remains to be completed. It is not a means of checking and evaluating employees. This exercise often provides surprises, especially for functional work area managers who believe they have closely monitored the work in their area, then suddenly find items that couldn't be found the day before.

| Staff member name-Ann | Date count taken 9/7/94 |
|---|---|
| **Category** | **Volume** |
| Credit upgrades | 7 |
| Prospects | 20 |
| Regular maintenance | 17 |
| Customer reference calls | 1 |
| Waiting for references | 4 |
| References to be called | 7 |
| Follow-up references | 12 |
| Discrepancies to ship to | 25 |

**Figure 8-9.** Customer service—backlog count.

# Operational Installation Mechanics

## Follow-Up

The key to a successful installation is the dedicated daily follow-up process that the functional work area manager must complete. The follow-up process makes a statement to staff members that their management is in support of the continuous improvement quality process, and that their manager is a resource for them if they need assistance.

The ABM team should discuss the follow-up routine with the functional work area manager. The follow-up process should take place twice a day: once before the lunch break and once before the end of the workday. When visiting with each staff member, the functional work area manager should carry along problem action reports and record any problems that surface.

The follow-up procedure provides the functional work area manager with an early warning system for detecting problems and allows immediate corrective action to be implemented. If a usually productive staff member isn't working up to capacity, the manager should inquire, "Is there a problem?" In visiting the staff member, the manager should review the individual daily volume plan and report for that employee to determine what his or her performance level is and whether any problems have been noted.

The manager can make mental notes when more than one person is working on an activity, comparing productivity throughput among individual staff members. The follow-up process is a hands-on manager's delight and doesn't require a great deal of time to properly complete. It must be done to show staff members that the process is permanent and that their management supports the methodology.

## Preparation of Operating Reports

Senior management should emphasize the importance and timeliness of completing all the management reports discussed in this chapter, since they are an integral part of a continuous improvement quality process. This will provide senior management with an excellent opportunity to reemphasize the benefits of a continuous improvement quality process and the importance of the follow-up routine. The ABM team should explain to each functional work area manager where the source of data for each report comes from, how to prepare the report line by line, and how to use each report in managing his or her functional work area.

Senior management should designate someone on the staff to do the coaching and to be responsible for preparing the management trend report, functional work area evaluation report, and weekly functional work area comparison evaluation summary. These reports should be reviewed by senior management every week and the numbers discussed with the functional work area managers at their weekly staff meetings.

## Weekly Senior Management–Functional Work Area Manager Staff Meeting

The importance of the follow-up process doesn't apply solely to functional work area managers and their staff members. Senior management must also make the statement that it fully supports the continuous improvement process and will participate in making the process work.

Senior management should establish a set time each week to meet with a functional work area manager to discuss the operating results, problems, corrective actions, and trends of the past week. The focus of the meeting should be on the daily–weekly operating report, daily–weekly backlog report, problem action summary report, functional work area evaluation report, and management trend report.

The aforementioned package of reports presents the nucleus of operating data summarized for the prior week. The weekly one-on-one meeting with each functional work area manager should not exceed 30 minutes. Senior management should emphasize that these meetings are not group sessions but individual ones, so the functional work area manager can discuss freely whatever is on his or her mind.

The senior manager can demonstrate to the functional work area manager that senior management is not an adversary but a resource available to assist the functional work area manager when required.

## Management Reporting System Procedure Manual

The company should prepare a management reporting system procedures manual that contains a complete set of forms, procedures, reports, and additional tools to assist functional work area managers in training their staff members.

The manual reduces to writing all the tools developed and implemented during the ABM program, and becomes a future reference book for the functional work area manager and each staff member. The functional work area manager should implement a formal change process to make sure that all management reporting system procedures manuals are constantly updated and current.

### Format

The meeting should center on trends. To assist in this effort, use the management trend report, which includes the previous week's data. Also, the functional work area evaluation report can hold up to 52 weeks' worth of data along with a continuous 4-week rolling average for the annualized dollar improvement. In focusing on trends, meeting attendees must not neglect to look at the current week's data. It will tend to indicate and influence future trends. What is being done now, either to maintain a positive trend or to turn around an unfavorable one, is what's important.

## Weekly Performance Review Meetings

Senior management should hold regular performance review meetings with functional work area managers. The purpose of the meeting is to conduct a detailed analysis of the daily–weekly operating report, daily backlog report, problem action summary report, functional work area evaluation report, and management trend report.

## Meeting Times and Duration

This meeting is a key ingredient in the perpetuation of the jointly installed change, ABM, and reengineering process. The meeting should be held each Monday afternoon. Since the production week ends on Friday, this will provide sufficient time for reports to be procured, distributed, and analyzed in preparation for the weekly performance review meeting.

## Daily Backlog Report Summary
### Purpose

The daily backlog report summary (Fig. 8-10) is designed to assist the functional work area manager in analyzing activity transaction volumes that remain in the pipeline at the conclusion of a workday. The report achieves this objective by displaying the unit volumes that were available at the beginning of a day, what volume was received, how many units were completed during the day, and what unit volume is left over to begin the next morning. This data enables a functional work area manager to more effectively plan the following day's work and where to place the processing emphasis.

### Responsibility

Each functional work area manager is responsible for entering all required data each day. The list of activities can be preprinted along with the units of measure. The functional work area manager is also responsible for monitoring and analyzing the data at the end of each working day. This data enables a manager to more effectively control work in his or her functional work area by taking more timely and specific actions when an activity's ending balance is above normal levels.

### Frequency

The daily backlog report summary is to be completed and ready for review and/or distribution by 9 a.m. each working day.

Functional work area:_____(1)_____

Prepared by:_____(2)_____

Date:_____(3)_____

| Activity description (4) | Units of measure (5) | Volume | | | |
|---|---|---|---|---|---|
| | | Opening balance (6) | Received (7) | Completed (8) | Ending balance (9) |
| | | | | | |
| | | | | | |
| | | | | | |
| | | | | | |
| | | | | | |
| | | | | | |
| | | | | | |
| | | | | | |
| | | | | | |
| | | | | | |
| | | | | | |
| | | | | | |
| | | | | | |
| | | | | | |
| | | | | | |
| | | | | | |
| | | | | | |
| | | | | | |
| | | | | | |
| | | | | | |
| | | | | | |
| | | | | | |
| | | | | | |
| | | | | | |
| | | | | | |
| | | | | | |
| | | | | | |
| | | | | | |
| | | | | | |
| | | | | | |
| | | | | | |

**Figure 8-10a.** Daily backlog report summary.

| Line # | Title or Term | Is Used to Indicate |
|--------|---------------|---------------------|
| (1) | Functional work area | The name of the functional work area (e.g., accounts payable). |
| (2) | Prepared by | The name of the responsible functional work area manager. |
| (3) | Date | The date for the day of the week. |
| (4) | Activity description | The activities for each functional work area are preprinted. The source of the data is the activity dictionary. |
| (5) | Units of measure | The units of measure for each activity should also be preprinted. The source of the data is the activity dictionary. |
| (6) | Opening balance | The prior ending balance of transaction volumes for each activity. |
| (7) | Received | The current day's volume of transactions received in the area for each activity. |
| (8) | Completed | The current day's volume of transactions completed by staff members for each activity. |
| (9) | Ending balance | The total of the opening balance plus the volume of units received less the volume of units completed. |

**Figure 8-10b.** Daily backlog report summary key.

## Distribution

Each day the functional work area manager discusses the daily backlog report summary with his or her staff members. At the end of the week, the original report is given to senior management, with the functional work area manager retaining a copy.

## How to Use the Report

The functional work area manager should review the daily backlog report summary at the end of each day. The manager should look for activities that seem to be receiving a greater unit volume than is being completed. The functional work area manager must continually determine if a trend is developing by looking at several days' work. The manager should utilize the data to decide whether overtime and/or extra resources are required to correct a problem backlog condition. Sometimes volume may surge on a given day and then dissipate during a week's time or less without any special intervention being required.

## Management Report Usage and Distribution Summary

### Purpose

The management report usage and distribution summary (Fig. 8-11) is designed to assist senior management in tracking the distribution and frequency of each management report. The summary achieves this purpose by displaying a frequency code for each report that is being distributed to a specific functional work area and/or senior manager.

### Responsibility

Senior management is responsible for entering all required data. The list of management reports can be preprinted along with frequency codes and functional work area managers receiving a specific report. Senior management is responsible for monitoring the timely distribution of each report to the appropriate functional work area manager.

### Frequency

The management report usage and distribution summary should be reviewed quarterly.

### Distribution

The management report usage and distribution summary is discussed quarterly by senior management with functional work area managers for additions and/or deletions. The original report is retained by senior management, with each functional work area manager receiving a copy.

### How to Use the Report

The management report usage and distribution summary should be distributed to each functional work area manager to be sure he or she is reviewing the appropriate reports. Senior management should review the report to be sure functional work area managers are receiving all the tools they need to monitor, control, and manage their areas.

## Summary

The procedures and information contained in the activity-based management program have been specifically designed to provide all levels of management

| Management report description | Functional work area manager's name | | | | | | | | | | | | | | | | | |
|---|---|---|---|---|---|---|---|---|---|---|---|---|---|---|---|---|---|---|
| I = Initiator<br>N = When needed<br>D = Daily<br>W = Weekly<br>M = Monthly<br>S = Every six weeks<br>Q = Quarterly | | | | | | | | | | | | | | | | | | |
| | | | | | | | | | | | | | | | | | | |
| Daily backlog report summary | | | | | | | | | | | | | | | | | | |
| Individual daily volume plan report | | | | | | | | | | | | | | | | | | |
| Daily–Weekly operating report | | | | | | | | | | | | | | | | | | |
| Daily–Weekly backlog report | | | | | | | | | | | | | | | | | | |
| Problem action report | | | | | | | | | | | | | | | | | | |
| Problem action report summary | | | | | | | | | | | | | | | | | | |
| Individual activity evaluation report | | | | | | | | | | | | | | | | | | |
| Functional work area evaluation report | | | | | | | | | | | | | | | | | | |
| Weekly functional work area comparison evaluation summary | | | | | | | | | | | | | | | | | | |
| KVI volume and hours daily forecast conversion chart | | | | | | | | | | | | | | | | | | |

**Figure 8-11.** Management report usage and distribution summary.

with the information necessary to effect practical application of the various systems, methods, and concepts installed.

The procedures, controls, and reports are designed to provide both a method and a means for proper and effective use of the planning, implementation, follow-up, and reporting phases of the ABM program. It must be understood, however, that the ABM management reporting program will not alone solve any operating problems. However, if used effectively, it can and will highlight areas which require functional work area management and senior management attention and action.

A primary objective of the ABM management reporting program is to provide management at all levels with the information necessary for proper and more effective control of their operations. Taking immediate corrective action on any irregularities and identified negative trends will result in productivity improvement and help sustain overall quality operating efficiencies. In essence, the ABM management reporting program places the responsibility for direct supervision on the functional work area managers and causes them to be aware of and accountable for the successful achievement of agreed-upon goals.

At the front-line supervisory level, the ABM management reporting program is designed to provide control over all the primary activities within each functional work area. The total effectiveness of the program, however, is directly dependent upon the degree of attention and involvement by *all* levels of management. It is the responsibility of functional work area management to diligently apply the ABM methodology in its entirety, and it is the responsibility of senior management to ensure adherence to the ABM management reporting program by functional work area managers through consistent follow-up action.

In order to effectively use any methodology, all those involved must have a thorough understanding of the concepts. The procedures and controls detailed in the ABM management reporting program are designed to achieve the following:

- Operations can be predicted and controlled on a current and timely basis.

- Continuous evaluation and follow-up ensure absolute quality service to a customer.

- Functional work area managers find their jobs more meaningful once they master the techniques of the ABM methodology.

- Fewer "wrong moves" occur—because decisions are made on the basis of objective fact rather than on feel and rumor.

- The "hurry up and wait" is taken out of the workday for staff members— because they understand what is expected of them (e.g., when assignments should be completed).

- Timely recognition is given to high-producing staff members.

- Less effective staff members are easily recognized so that they can be given additional training or moved to jobs that better fit their capabilities.

The ABM management reporting program fosters a *supervisory operating technique.* It is built on proven concepts for planning and assigning work. It involves forecasting the work to be done and then translating this plan into the required person hours necessary to get the expected work accomplished. Finally, the ABM program contains tools to bring the work and appropriate capacities together in a smooth, continuous flow—with a means to know when the flow is disrupted and when help is needed.

A simple set of principles underlies the ABM program: to make the total plan happen by controlling the parts.

**Planning.**   The functional work area manager is responsible for planning work assignments in his or her area using a procedure that will determine *who* will do the job and *what* the reasonable time of completion will be.

**Implementation.**   It is the responsibility of the functional work area manager to give work assignments to employees so that each person knows *what* is to be done and *when* the work should be completed. The functional work area manager is also responsible for keeping track of assignments in process, so that he or she knows when work is not going according to plan.

**Follow-Up.**   It is the functional work area manager's responsibility to investigate promptly when assignments are not completed on time and to establish the cause for delay. The manager should then take corrective action to eliminate future interference so work can be completed as planned.

**Reporting.**   Reports are the functional work area manager's "scorecard" to let senior management know

- Whether our objectives were accomplished at the right *time* and *cost* with a high level of *quality*.
- What we must do to correct off-schedule conditions.

The ABM management reporting program provides the tools necessary to effectively operate each functional work area. It is management's judgment that is the most sound and sensible approach to the control of the work flow. The ABM management reporting program enables functional work area managers to work with objective facts as a foundation from which to exercise sound judgment.

Functional work area managers should fully understand not only the mechanics of the ABM management reporting program but also the theories and concepts behind it. In this way, as procedures change and work is revised, they can take the necessary steps to keep basic data up to date and to perpetuate the process.

Business managers generally seem to agree that the key to good management control is strong follow-up. As important as follow-up is to a productive management reporting system, the timeliness of that follow-up activity is even more critical to success. There are two types of follow-up: immediate and long range. When staff member buy-in is a reality, most staff members who want their organization to succeed will instinctively take the necessary corrective action because it makes good sense to do so.

Before funds are invested in any program in a business enterprise, a return-on-investment calculation is completed to determine if the money spent will be worthwhile. An activity-based management program, whether it is done internally or through the hiring of outside consultants, costs money to implement. Once the ABM program is installed, it will require additional operating capital to maintain.

The reality of whether or not the investment in an ABM program produces a return rests with the follow-up at all levels of management from the president of the company on down. If both senior management and functional work area management believe that an ABM program, once implemented, will not require attention and follow-up, the ABM program will fail.

A company should not make the initial investment unless its management team is willing to work at generating the savings. The dedication that is required will bring an organization a return on its investment that is several times greater than its initial investment. Activity-based management assists managers in taking normal types of actions and in avoiding abnormal reactions.

Consider the following example. The functional work area manager in one health service organization assigned batches of 50 claims to 15 different staff members, and all 15 employees were at their work stations on time to begin the workday. The reasonable expectancies that were developed indicated that these batches would be completed by the end of the first hour of work.

The functional work area manager then proceeded to each work station to see how the staff member was doing and stopped at the control desk to make sure the next batch of work was ready to be assigned. At the end of the first hour, the manager knew that 10 staff members had completed their work and were ready for their next batch to be assigned to them. Five staff members weren't finished. What should the functional work area manager's natural reaction be? "Investigate the problem so immediate corrective action can be taken" is the proper and logical approach.

The manager found that the personal computers required to process the batch of claims had become frozen, and one staff member was trying frantically to fix the problem. Does the functional work area manager call the director of claims for assistance? Not if he or she reacts normally! The manager either takes corrective action to unfreeze the PCs or, if this is not possible, tries to reassign the staff members involved to other PCs and calls MIS maintenance to unfreeze the PCs involved.

By reacting normally and taking timely corrective action, the functional work area manager was then free to continue making the rounds to check other staff members.

In dissecting the aforementioned illustration, you can readily see how ABM was the catalyst for rapid action because it provided the manager with timely data. The functional work area manager could just as easily have missed the fact that several PCs weren't working for a lengthy period of time. Only because the functional work area manager utilized the ABM management reporting tools, did he or she become aware of the problem early and therefore able to take the necessary corrective action.

Recall that the problem action report is designed into the ABM management reporting system. In this instance, the functional work area manager would indicate on that day's problem action report the history of the event. The information given in the report would show:

- Planned time for the activity to be completed
- Actual time it took for the activity to be completed (or time until the activity was halted)
- Reason for the work stoppage
- Corrective action taken

Now make believe you are the director of claims at the health service organization. You are reviewing the production numbers for the day with the functional work area manager. You note that the manager has indicated the action he or she took to unfreeze the PCs involved. You also note that the activity took an additional 30 minutes to complete. What would be your normal reaction? You want answers to the following questions:

- How long were the PCs frozen when the manager noticed the condition?
- How long did it take to unfreeze the PCs?
- What were the staff members doing during the down time?
- Should the functional work area manager have spent that much time unfreezing the PCs himself or herself?
- Was an MIS staff member available?

The responses to these queries open the door and surface the training needs of the functional work area manager. Your actions on a daily basis should be timely and focused. Certainly, if you react normally, the functional work area manager will benefit from your coaching, and the company will benefit from the functional work area manager's involvement as a result of additional training.

Let's continue with this example of the frozen PCs. What possible long-range action can result from the problem action report? As director of claims, you review these reports, and you spot a trend that indicates that this type of problem has been recurring. Why does the problem keep happening? You learn that the functional work area manager was not aware that this was happening frequently. You yourself were not aware of the condition, even though it happened several times, so you don't want to point fingers at the functional work area manager. Take action!

The various courses of action open to you are too numerous to mention, but don't procrastinate—because it is your responsibility to correct the problem. Determine the origin of the problem and fix it, using whatever methods or services are necessary.

What this example shows is that the basic ABM approach we have illustrated holds true in almost any situation. The ABM management reporting system will surface trouble spots for immediate corrective action. The reports will highlight how well each functional work area manager handles problems, and serve as a tool to be used at each level of management. The main emphasis from an ABM perspective is that control be instituted at the spot of the action in the trenches. The work-to-time relationships are only guidelines and are secondary to being cognizant of problem conditions which diminish the throughput of work.

An excellent example of this principle occurred in a large international gift-ware company. The order processing team took approximately 5 days to process an order, from receipt in the mail room to the shipping platform. The functional work area manager in charge of customer service was receiving complaints from customers and company sales personnel and finally asked, "Why is this happening?"

It turned out that each work station in the processing chain lacked any requirement to handle an order in a specific amount of time. When an ABM program was implemented, the order processing time was reduced to 2 days simply by establishing work-to-time relationships for each activity. In addition, the ABM management reporting system provided the tool to monitor and follow up the work being performed.

The functional work area manager for order processing was able to plan and make things happen. The ABM program allowed work to flow smoothly, and the number of staff members required to do the work was reduced by 25 percent. The ABM management reporting system reduced lost time and improved customer satisfaction.

The ABM reporting system discussed in this chapter indicates that reports should be easy to create and simple to read, and should highlight the areas requiring quick action. Functional work area managers are often the hardest individuals to convince that an ABM management reporting system will assist them in managing their work areas.

There are several reasons for this outlook, with the primary one being the additional paperwork involved. Their displeasure stems from the implied idea that the ABM reports are a negative reflection on their management ability. In addition, like most of us, front-line managers see the idea of change as scary and tend to resist it at all costs.

Often these front-line managers will turn away from any type of control mechanism because it gets in the way of their doing so-called real work. These psychological fears can be minimized and overcome by involving the functional work area manager early in the development of the ABM management reporting system. The ABM team should ask questions that will draw a positive response and obtain and incorporate the manager's ideas into the design of the reports. Personal involvement makes the functional work area manager feel like a significant resource for the ABM program, not just someone who has controls unilaterally imposed on him or her.

Front-line managers will come to feel that this is *their* reporting system—something they have helped to create—and they will become willing and cooperative participants. Once functional work area managers cross over the imaginary line of resistance, their job becomes simpler, and they will find that the ABM management reporting system isn't the horrible nightmare they thought it was.

As the functional work area managers come to understand how to use the ABM management reporting system, they begin to feel more in command of their work area than they thought was possible. Their jobs become simpler and more fun, and problems substantially decrease as the managers become "masters of all they survey." This type of positive result has come about over and over again in thousands of different organizations.

This simple, structured environment does not happen by accident. It occurs when senior management comes to the realization that controls can produce positive results. The ABM management reporting system is the enabler, but the utilization of this instrument, not the instrument itself, is what bears fruit.

It is important to recognize that the ABM management reporting program does *not* solve problems. Rather, the program brings problems to light and often suggests solutions, but correction depends on management's action. Unless action is taken, costs will be high, service will be inconsistent, and the fault will lie with management.

The ABM management reporting program, properly applied and followed, will achieve the desired results. The tools and mechanics have been designed as clearly and simply as possible. It is important to consider them in their proper light. They are not an addition to supervision, but are the means by which supervision is accomplished.

In summary, *all* levels of management have an obligation to diligently comply with all the procedures outlined in the ABM management reporting program in order to continually achieve and then perpetuate the desired results, meet corporate goals, and increase shareholder value. Remember:

- The significant element to the control of work is follow-up.
- All levels of management must be involved.
- Assurance for attainment begins with the support of senior management.
- The success of an ABM management reporting system hinges on:

  Proper planning

  Full implementation

  Management and staff member buy-in and utilization

  Timely and dedicated follow-up

# 9
# Activity-Based Costing

## Introduction

A global economy dictates maintaining standards of customer value through the management of activities, not costs. Activity-based costing (ABC) informs us about the work that consumes resources and delivers value in a business. This operational information facilitates making long-term strategic decisions about such things as production or service mix, sourcing, lower prices to hold market share, and buy-or-make alternatives.

In order for a company to compete in today's marketplace with quality and flexibility, it needs to utilize activity-based information to focus primary attention on underlying causes of work, called *work drivers*. The customer is "king" and demands shorter time frames while placing emphasis on quality, service, and distribution.

Traditional accounting approaches which classify cost measurements only as variable, fixed, and semivariable have *not* proved to be a source of competitive value. Only activities or work has the power to add or subtract value in a business, with the caveat that no activity adds to customer value 100 percent of the time. Thus, to achieve competitiveness, businesses must monitor and remove wasted effort, or non-value-added activities. Activity-based costing allows them to improve their productivity, shareowner value, and competitive position by eliminating waste—causes of delay (rework), excess inventory (scrap), and work unevenness (overtime)—in the performance of activities. Corporations must concentrate on improving both cash flow and profits. A disciplined approach to cost management is required to remain competitive, and it must be an ongoing process, not a one-shot project.

Activity-based costing provides the performance breakthrough for the 1990s. ABC empowers people with the information and tools to improve business performance. ABC data reveals the problems that an organization needs to correct

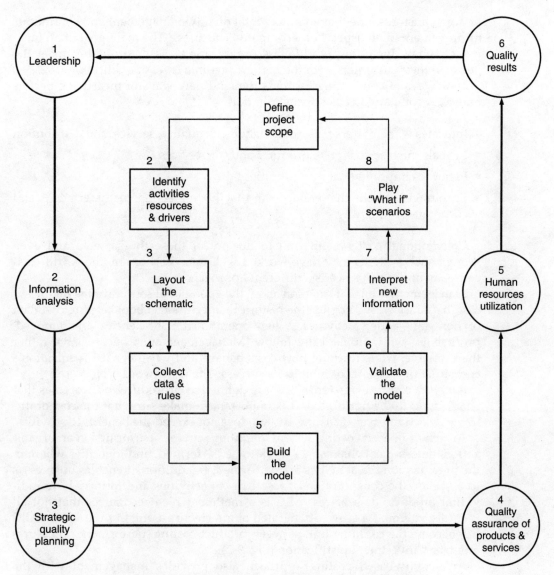

**Figure 9-1.** Activity-based costing framework—implementation model.

and the profitable opportunities that are available. Its ability to measure the true cost of business performance activities ensures that an organization can improve where it counts the most—the bottom line (Fig. 9-1).

It is clear that yesterday's cost systems don't work in today's competitive environment. This is because global competition, technological change, and information system development have radically changed the rules of the marketplace. There have been equally dramatic changes in the way companies are coping with the competitive challenge. The term *world class* defines a new way of doing business, one that embraces total quality management and continuous improvement in all aspects of a company's business. The main goal of all businesses today, including world-class organizations, is to profitably meet the needs of their customers with the highest possible level of quality.

New ways of conducting business demand new ways of measuring performance. A company needs information that

- Indicates what matters most to its customers: quality, service, and distribution
- Reveals the true cost of its products and/or services
- Identifies improvement opportunities
- Encourages actions that enhance and facilitate meeting customer needs and corporate profitability

Conventional cost systems fail to do any of these things well, and even though such systems may have worked well in an earlier era, the world-class company of the 1990s needs a different approach.

Management needs information about the operational sources of the inefficiencies that cause waste, not just the historical, after-the-fact bookkeeping cost data of non-value-added activities. When operational inefficiencies are removed, profitability will automatically follow. Management must be proactive rather than reactive, while learning how costs behave and whether the organization's cost structure supports or inhibits its success. The watchword is *vigilance*.

*Activities* consume resources and are defined as procedures or processes that enable work to be performed. It is important to make sure that the cost of utilizing an activity-based costing system does not exceed the benefits it provides.

An activity-based costing system identifies activities performed in an organization, determines what causes work to be performed, and identifies where in the organization the activities are performed. In addition, it enables businesses to associate the consumption of resources to activities and ultimately to individual products or services. ABC is a method which recognizes that not all costs are volume-sensitive—generated or affected by a unit of production. ABC has become the common link between product costing, performance measurement, and investment justification (Fig. 9-2).

An activity-based costing approach also provides management with the capability of assigning overhead support costs such as administrative, selling, and marketing costs to products or services in more meaningful ways than traditional costing methodologies. Remember that expenditures do not stop automatically because resources are made redundant by a campaign to reduce waste. People and office space do not vanish just because an organization no longer needs them to get the job done. Good organizations will either use excess resources somewhere else productively or eliminate them.

An organization should not overlook the possibility of changing its mix of activities or the mix of products and/or services which its customers require. The goal of every activity in a business should be to provide value to the cus-

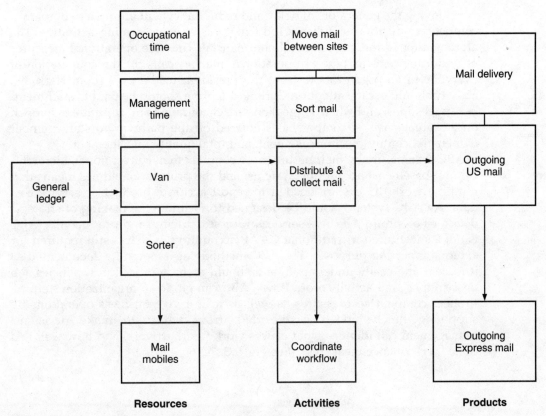

**Figure 9-2.** The mechanics of activity-based costing.

tomer at a reasonable cost. Senior managers need timely and accurate information to compare the competitiveness and cost of each activity's output with the next best alternative (e.g., zero-based budgeting) in order to make an informed decision about that alternative, whether it be inside or outside the company. Activity-based costing provides the vehicle to produce the applicable data to make an informed decision. Financial numbers alone cannot provide the appropriate insight into managing a business more efficiently.

The key is to capture the volume of each activity and the resources it must consume to produce a product and/or service. Management must zero in on work activities, asking:

- Where are they?
- How much do they cost?
- How do they behave?
- Why do they behave that way?
- What can be done to manage them more efficiently?

Removing the generators of delay and redundancy will improve a company's competitive position simply by reducing waste in performing activities. The aforementioned indicators are all nonfinancial. They are operational measures of performance. This type of operational analysis calls for the cooperation of everyone in an organization, from the president to the mail room clerk. No activity should escape attention. Serious attention should be paid to staff member suggestions, and when suggestions are encouraged and continue to happen on a regular basis, a company has entered on the pathway to staff member ownership, continuous improvement, and total quality management.

ABC systems are by their nature more complex than conventional, hierarchical unit-based cost accounting systems, and the process sometimes means that multiple work drivers are needed to report accurate product or service cost data. An ABC system should be designed to facilitate the making of strategic decisions on product design, service processes, pricing, and product mix. ABC is not a substitute for traditional GAAP accounting, which is still required for external reporting purposes. The ABC methodology should be documented so it is clear and easily understood, and should include procedures, policies, job descriptions, and activity work flows. ABC can guide an organization's efforts to meet competitive pressures as well as to improve business operations by supplying timely and objective data from which to make decisions. Management can identify what causes work (work drivers) and how well it is done (performance measures). (See Fig. 9-3.)

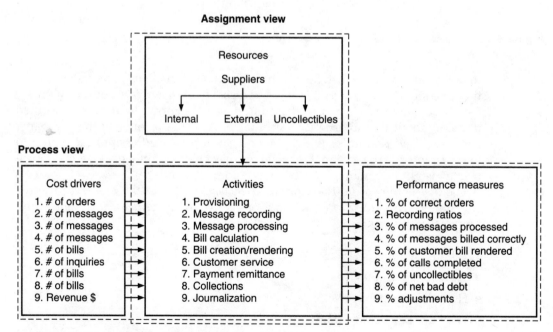

**Figure 9-3.** Assignment and process views in ABC/ABM.

Activity-based management (ABM) utilizes the data gathered by activity-based costing methodology to

- Improve the value received by the customer
- Reengineer business processes
- Improve company profitability
- Enhance activity performance by identifying productivity improvement opportunities in functional work areas
- Identify the factors that cause waste
- Measure the activities that are doing well (value-added activities)
- Determine which activities are not essential (non-value-added activities)

Essential activities have value to the customer and the functioning of an organization, with all other activities being classified as non-value-added. Non-value-added activities should be candidates for immediate elimination.

## Purpose of Activity-Based Costing

Activity-based costing provides corporate management with the knowledge of how costs behave and why. Its application assists an organization in attracting customers by being the low-cost quality supplier. The methodology emphasizes common sense, logic, preparation, planning, research, and objectivity.

Conventional cost accounting systems that collect costs by cost element (e.g., labor, travel) distort product costs, because they consider only the total financial cost of an activity without regard to its operational output and do not highlight how each cost element is used to implement productivity improvement opportunities. Traditional cost accounting methods do not provide adequate operational information to management. Further, such systems ignore the interrelationship of activities, thereby fostering competition between functional work areas rather than cooperation and promoting poor and selfish, turf-protective business decisions.

The key to improving a corporation's productivity and quality while fostering continuous improvement is to understand the interdependence of activities. This knowledge will tear down the barriers that tend to exist between corporate business processes. Operational coherence must be based on activities (actions), not hierarchies. Activities should be managed to minimize waste and to eliminate non-value-added work.

Activities are a powerful basis for managing an enterprise. An activity-based management program that is built on activities ensures that plans can be transmitted to management level. It enhances a manager's ability to take timely action in order to improve a business process and/or activity.

Activities describe what organizations do. To make operational changes meaningful and permanent, organizations must change what people do. The costs associated with developing an activity-based costing system must not outweigh the benefits to be derived from it, and the system should be structured so it supports change. Activities provide a uniquely effective medium for meaningful communication between accounting and operational personnel. In activity-based costing, performance is measured as the cost per output (i.e., time to perform the activity), and an understanding of the inputs and outputs of activities clarifies the linkage among activities. One activity's output could be another activity's input.

An activity's life cycle must be understood in order to accumulate the cost for that activity over its life cycle. A key to effective cost management is the implementation of changes that improve multiple dimensions of business performance simultaneously. (*Example:* Reduce the cost of an activity and/or the time to complete an activity.) One method of reducing cost is to increase output by using the same amount of resources. This method should not be accomplished at the expense of quality. The cost reduction in one functional work area should not be offset by additional activities and/or cost increases in downstream functional work areas. Overall company performance should not be diminished.

Resources consumed by activities (i.e., materials, labor, and technology) can be purchased externally or obtained internally from other departments with the prime objective being to convert them into outputs (i.e., services or products). The activity-based costing accounting process reshapes the way companies think about and manage their costs.

The formula for a successful activity-based costing program is a combination of people, technology, raw materials, methods, and work flow that produces a given product or service of excellent quality.

An activity-based costing system relies on the costing of significant activities to

- Provide a natural baseline for describing a manufacturing or service process
- Provide visibility and highlight non-value-added activities
- Understand underlying cause-and-effect relationships between the operational factors of production, distribution, service, and the manufacturing business processes
- Identify, evaluate, and implement new and improved activities
- Capture both budgeted and actual costs
- Measure the efficiency and effectiveness of the performance of an activity

Fully exploiting the power of ABC as a guide to productivity improvement requires a conceptual break from the traditional cost accounting systems and a willingness to act on the insights that ABC analysis provides. Managers must refrain from allocating all expenses to individual units and instead separate the expenses and match them to the level of activity that consumes the resources. Very simply, managers should separate the expenses incurred to produce individual units of a particular product from the expenses needed to produce different products, independent of how many units are produced.

Consider a purchase order activity which is not volume-sensitive. Suppose it costs $100 to process all purchase orders for the total output of an automobile manufacturing plant—say 10 cars. If each car requires the same direct labor, the traditional accounting methods would distribute the $100 cost to all units, at $10 a car. However, one of the cars might be a custom-built model in which half the parts are nonstandard and have to be ordered individually. Under the new methodology of ABC, that custom-built car might be assigned $50 in purchasing overhead costs, with the remaining $50 allocated to the other 9 cars.

After the ABC methodology is applied, managers must be prepared to act. First, they should explore ways to reduce the resources required to perform various activities. In order to transform those reductions into profits, they must either reduce spending for those resources or increase the output that those resources produce. These timely actions allow management to utilize the data gathered from ABC to be transformed into increased profits, which go directly to the bottom line of the company.

ABC highlights for functional work area managers where their timely action will most likely have the greatest impact on profits or costs. Managers have two types of actions they can take after gathering ABC data:

1. They can attempt to reprice products: raise prices for products that make heavy demands for support resources and lower prices to more competitive levels for the high-volume products and/or services that have been subsidizing the low-volume products and/or services. If the repricing strategy is successful, the company should arrive at a new product mix that either creates lesser demands for resources or generates more revenues for the same consumption of resources.

2. They can search for ways to reduce overall resource consumption. This approach, fundamentally more important than repricing, requires either decreasing the number of times activities are performed to achieve the same output or reducing the resources consumed to produce and/or service the existing mix of products and customers. This could mean implementing productivity and continuous improvement programs to enhance quality, reduce setup times, and improve factory layouts, or utilizing information technology to facilitate the processing of batches, products, and customer orders.

Steps to reduce resource consumption are, however, just the beginning. Even the most ambitious improvement programs won't show up automatically and fall to the bottom line unless the company follows up by dealing with excess resources. When fewer of their resources are being demanded, functional work area managers must either eliminate the freed-up resources or redeploy them in other functional work areas.

When functional work area managers recognize that they have reached the point at which they can obtain the same output with either fewer staff members or fewer machines, they can simply reduce spending on those resources. Management can reduce spending and reduce the levels of resource consumption. Resource consumption usually falls evenly across a period of time, but spending lags in a staircase pattern. Alternatively, management can use the freed-up excess resources to increase output if customer demand warrants increased production.

Activity-based management methodology utilizes the data collected by activity-based costing techniques to provide company management with operational data, not traditional accounting information. ABC reveals unexpected peaks of profitability and craters of losses in a company's operations. Functional work area managers should use this information as a guide to perform activities more efficiently. If managers fail to follow up on staff reductions and the reduced demand for organizational resources, improvements will only create excess capacity, not increased profits. Managers might then conclude erroneously that operating expenses are fixed and not variable. The expenses could appear to be fixed, however, only because managers did not take the collective action required to make them variable.

Costs are not intrinsically fixed or variable. ABC data permits managers to understand the sources of cost variability and to take the necessary corrective actions to reduce demands for organizational resources. Having reduced the demands, managers can then increase throughput or reduce spending to convert the savings into increased profits.

## What Is Activity-Based Costing?

Activity-based costing (ABC) is a methodology for understanding the activities, processes, services, and products of a business. This technique identifies activities and the work drivers that cause work to be performed, and then associates these activities to products and/or services to be delivered to the customer. Activity-based costing is a management tool as well as a financial tool (Fig. 9-4).

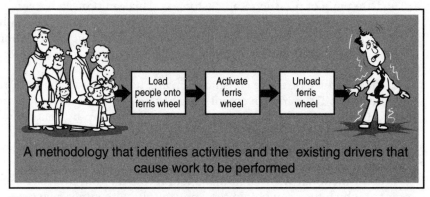

**Figure 9-4.** What is activity-based costing?

Thomas H. Johnson, author of *Relevance Lost: The Rise and Fall of Management Accounting,* notes that "to succeed in today's global economy, companies must begin by articulating a customer-focused mission statement, and then encourage employees to help map out and systematically improve the processes in which they work." ABC offers a structure and methodology that enables management to understand

- What causes work
- When work is completed
- Where work comes from and where it goes
- How work is performed
- Why work is performed

Management can utilize this data to commit and optimize resources and to manage the work load efficiently.

Activity-based costing focuses on the relative differences in assigning support costs. It uses the experience of operations people, and quantitative information where available, to develop causal relationships between work drivers (what causes work to be done) and work to be done (activities). It allows the value of each activity to be assessed, identifies the factors that cause the activity to happen, and gives a true representation of the unit of measure of those activities (Fig. 9-5).

The total cost in each functional work area can be traced to activities by identifying why each activity is performed. ABC demonstrates that activities consume resources, and products or services consume activities. ABC emphasizes the total quality management elements of

- Total focus on the customer
- Continuous improvement
- Employee ownership and empowerment
- Waste elimination by identifying non-value-added activities
- Prioritization of improvement efforts
- Delivery of decision-making information to all employees

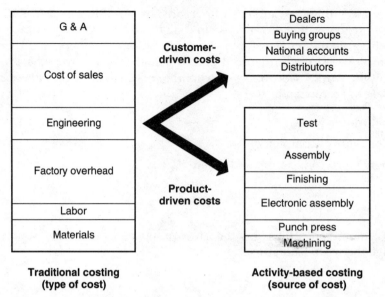

**Figure 9-5.** Activity-based costing looks at what really drives costs.

ABC places emphasis on the operational understanding of all activities in the business.

1. It identifies key activities and resources consumed:
   - What do people do?
   - What resources are consumed and how?
   - Establish appropriate nonfunctional activity work drivers.
2. It establishes inputs and outputs to and from each activity:
   - Inputs to one activity may be outputs from another.
   - Understand the interactive relationships among activities.
3. It documents activity work flow using activity work flow diagrams:
   - Create a network of interrelated activities.
   - Identify any multistage activity relationships.
   - Graphically represent business process.

## Elements of an Organization's Activity-Based Hierarchy

The primary function in developing an activity hierarchy (Fig. 9-6) is the aggregation of activities that are related by a common purpose or business process (e.g., selling a product).

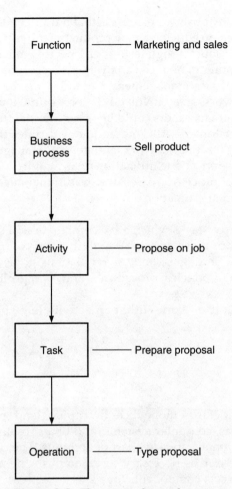

**Figure 9-6.** The activity hierarchy.

**Business Process.** Determine how individual activities are connected. Activities should be grouped into a business process and may cut across traditional hierarchical organizational lines. A *business process* is an orderly arrangement of related activities operating under a set of procedures or business rules in order to accomplish a specific objective, such as marketing products or processing customer orders. The activities are related because a specific event initiates the first activity in the process chain, which in turn triggers subsequent activities. Costs of these activities are aggregated into a business process cost.

By controlling the initial triggering of a primary activity, a company can reduce and/or eliminate the cost of all subsequent activities. This approach will identify redundant, non-value-added, and unnecessary activities which tend to increase cost without a corresponding benefit to either the company or its customers. An important feature of any business process is that it transcends organizational boundaries. For example, introducing a new product requires marketing analysis, R&D, product design, product design testing, engineering, manufacturing, quality planning, process planning, financial analysis, and recording.

Business process alignment focuses management's attention on the interdependency of all the functional work areas involved. It forces functional work area managers to realize that their customers could be other internal functional work areas as well as external customers. ABC methodology dictates the inclusion of activities like supervising, secretarial work, and general management in the costing of a product and/or service. The utilization of an activity work flow clearly depicts how a business process crosses the traditional hierarchical departmental structure within an organization.

**Activity.** An activity is a group of tasks which are a combination of elements of how work is performed (e.g., propose on a job). Activities are controlled by business rules that define goals, strategies, and/or regulations governing the activity. Rules can take the form of policies, procedures, and/or algorithms.

**Task.** A task is the smallest unit of work within an activity (e.g., prepare a proposal).

## Determination of an Activity's Cost Basis

The cost makeup of an activity includes money, credit, capital, land, property, people, machines, travel, supplies, computer systems, and other resources that are defined as cost elements within a standard chart of accounts. The cost of an activity is the sum of all the resources necessary to accomplish the activity's objective. The aggregation of the cost components for a specific activity includes all resources. The activity unit cost is then calculated by knowing both activity volume and activity cost.

| Activity | Resources for aggregating cost |
|---|---|
| Sell car | Car, sales rep, showroom |
| Service car | Skilled mechanic, tools, service manual, garage, materials |

Costs are considered traceable directly to an activity when the resources used by an activity can be shown to be directly consumed by that activity (e.g., processing purchase orders). If costs are not directly traceable, they should be allocated. Measuring an activity's effectiveness requires knowing the volume of output as well as the cost assigned to the activity. Knowing the cost per activity (e.g., $15 per purchase order $\times$ 10,000 purchase orders = $150,000 to process purchase orders) will allow functional work area management to take corrective action to reduce their cost per unit.

Cost reduction can be accomplished either by increasing the number of purchase orders processed to 15,000 instead of 10,000, thus reducing unit cost to $10 instead of $15 per purchase order, or by reducing some of the cost elements that are consumed in processing a purchase order (e.g., eliminate some steps, automate the manual procedure).

The functional work area manager should review an activity's entire life cycle, since it provides the road map for managing cost and performance over that activity's lifetime. Understanding an activity's life cycle is important for controlling cost because of the interdependence of activities in different time periods. A life-cycle review facilitates the evaluation of alternative organizational structures and groups staff members and equipment into natural associations like business processes and/or information flows.

When costs are not properly matched with time periods, product and/or service cost can be distorted (e.g., capitalized, not expensed). The assessing of factors that control activity volume is an important element for marshaling the various types of resources necessary to perform an activity.

There are five preferred methods for determining the cost basis for an activity: budgeted cost, standard cost, planned cost, engineered cost, and actual cost. Most activity-based systems use a predetermined cost method such as budgeted, standard, or planned costs.

**Budgeted Cost.**   Budgeted cost reflects functional work area management's opinion regarding future financial expenditures and profitability. This application should be used with discretion as a basis for an activity-based costing system because costs under this method represent what management wants to happen rather than what does actually happen.

**Standard Cost.**   Standard cost is a predetermined cost based on normal conditions of efficiency and volume of production. This method utilizes controlled costs at an elemental level and does not portray an activity's actual life cycle or business process in a relationship to the way operations function. Real-life business situations don't always function under normal laboratory-controlled conditions. The standard cost method does not capture abnormal everyday occurrences.

**Planned Cost.**   The output from a planned cost approach is a set of theoretical, what-if assumptions providing the basis for computing activity cost in an effort to achieve a predetermined goal. If the attainment of the goal becomes endangered, this approach enables functional work area management to take immediate corrective action. Costs are derived from the actual operational data. The planning process usually provides for off-schedule alternatives.

**Engineered Cost.**   Engineered cost is derived from an industrial engineering study that provides insight into how an activity is performed and whether any method and/or work flow improvements can increase performance and/or reduce cost. Engineered data is more reliable than subjective estimates but is more costly to develop.

**Actual Cost.**    Actual cost is the exact cost paid for a factor of production or service. Actual cost is not a recommended method because it is too sensitive to short-term fluctuations in activity volume. In addition, capturing actual cost at the activity level can be expensive and cumbersome. However, it is often necessary to selectively develop precise data of this type for repair and maintenance activities so the cost can be directly attributed (on the basis of actual usage) to a specific piece of equipment being serviced.

Once a cost basis for an activity-based costing system has been chosen, costs must be developed at the activity level by identifying and separating out any non-value-added components of cost. The functional work area manager should proceed to aggregate activity costs to the business process level, and then upward to companywide costs. All the work performed should be determined and isolated.

Stability and accuracy of data are important. It is advisable to use quarterly data or yearly data and to continually adjust the data for any changes in the operating environment. Take into consideration any seasonal fluctuations, organizational reorganizations, and modifications to the way activities are performed.

The classification of activities and their associated costs into life-cycle segments is critical to activity-based costing. It enables the functional work area manager to determine whether a cost is a current cost to be expensed in the current financial accounting year or a period cost to be capitalized and amortized over several financial accounting periods.

## Identification of Work Drivers and Non-Value-Added Activities

 Certain activities influence the cost and performance of subsequent activities and are considered work drivers. By reducing or eliminating an event that triggers the first activity to commence in the work process chain, a functional work area manager may be able to eliminate the need for all subsequent activities in that chain (e.g., defective-part rework scrap), thus creating an opportunity for reducing costs. A thorough analysis of activity work flows through functional work areas, business processes, and/or supplier operations can be useful in identifying the most efficient way to process work and/or perform an activity.

Work drivers are factors that cause the consumption of resources in performing activities. Clearly defined corporate goals enable functional work area managers and senior managers to determine if the activities being performed relate to those corporate goals. Inadequate control and structuring of company activities can lead to missed deadlines, unfinished projects, disappointed customers, and increased non-value-added costs.

The unmasking of non-value-added activities through an effective operationally oriented management system is the basis for an effective continuous improvement program. The analyzing of activities and how work is done provides functional work area management with information to identify redundant, duplicate, and wasteful activities and the factors that drive cost. Understanding how activities are performed provides a functional work area manager with a comparative rationale for determining whether to continue to perform (or not perform) specific activities or to restructure the way the activities are done.

The performance of non-value-added activities results in unnecessary expenses of time, money, and resources, thereby increasing the cost of a company's products and/or services. Elimination of these profitless activities should lead, not to a deterioration of enterprise performance (cost, function, quality, perceived value), but to a definite reduction in expenses and an increase in the organization's competitive market position.

Senior management should identify those activities that are important to the decision-making component of a business process. Management should then break down work drivers by class of activity. It is crucial that a set of activities and work drivers reflect the physical activity flow within an organization and make it easy for others in an organization to recognize those activities.

Functional work area managers should be able to identify a work driver that associates the consumption of activities by a product and/or service. The type of work driver selected affects the number of work drivers needed to achieve a desired level of accuracy. The work driver enables functional work area management to assign cost by activity. The work driver measures the frequency of performing activities and demands placed on activities at both the activity and product/service levels. ABC requires that all expenses be associated with activities—even if that means subjective, surrogate, or best-judgment estimates for some infrequently performed activities.

The difficult part of designing a good ABC system lies in achieving a system that is economical to maintain yet does not introduce excessive distortions. The minimum number of work drivers an ABC system uses depends on the desired accuracy of product and/or service costs, management's required level of detail, and/or the complexity of the product and/or service mix. As the number of work drivers increases, the accuracy of product and/or service costs increases.

The complexity of the product and/or service mix plays a more subtle role. In determining whether costs of two activities can be aggregated and assigned by means of a single work driver, the functional work area manager must guard against introducing unacceptable levels of distortion.

Products and/or services are considered diverse when they consume activities in different proportions. The higher the relative cost of an activity, the greater the distortion caused by using an imperfectly correlated work driver to assign costs to the activity and ultimately to associated products and/or services. Batch size diversity must also be accounted for in analyzing the relative cost of activities.

In practice, identifying how many work drivers to use in an ABC system calls for both judgment and thorough, detailed analysis. Management should

- Identify inputs having large dollar values
- Determine how diverse the organization's products and/or services are and in what batch sizes they are produced
- Analyze smaller dollar value inputs to determine which of them can be aggregated with major inputs and which of them need to be assigned separately

The interviewing process will assist the functional work area manager in developing a detailed understanding of what his or her work area does, what has caused costs to behave the way they do, and what is driving them, by asking the following questions:

- How is a functional work area organized?
- What activities and tasks is a functional work area responsible for?
- How is the output of the functional work area measured?
- What is the distribution of costs to and from the functional work area?
- Is the distribution of cost logical?

Activity-based cost systems use more types of work drivers than do conventional cost systems. Typical work drivers are setup hours, number of parts, number of times ordered, and number of times shipped. Less common examples of work drivers include:

- *Number of receipts*—measures receiving and inspecting incoming components; updates the inventory database
- *Vendor effort by part number*—measures time in hours that the purchasing staff devotes to vendor relations
- *Number of production runs*—measures overall demands on production scheduling and how frequently individual products are run

## Factors to Consider in Selecting a Work Driver

- Are reliable data easy to obtain?
- Can a surrogate work driver be utilized if required? (For example, when each inspection takes about the same amount of time, shipments processed and inspections performed could be used in place of inspection hours.)
- Can available data within the company (e.g., transaction volumes, official payroll data) be utilized?
- Examine the company general ledger system to ascertain

  How costs are currently developed

  How costs are currently classified

  How costs have behaved recently (e.g., in the last 3 years)

  How adequate is the cost classification system

  Whether the current costing system conforms to the real world

  Whether costs are too aggregated

  How accurately the cost data are assigned to activities for all the support functions

- Does the actual consumption of resources by an activity correlate to the planned consumption of resources by the work drivers? (For example, if inspections vary as to the time it takes to complete, actual inspection hours would be a more applicable work driver than the number of inspections.)

■ Does the work driver capture actual consumption of an activity by a particular product and/or service?

■ Do the quantities of activities assigned to a product and/or service correlate with the actual quantities of activities consumed by that product and/or service?

■ Does the work driver induce positive behavior? (A work driver can affect behavior if individuals feel their performance will be evaluated in some way on the basis of the work driver. Be careful not to induce harmful behavior.)

A frequent question that is raised early in the design of an ABC system is "How many work drivers are optional?" The answer is easy: It depends on what an organization intends to use the ABC system for. If it intends to use the data only for costing its products, then the number of work drivers can be small. When management increases its demands for more drill-down and a high degree of accuracy, greater detail is required and, therefore, more work drivers.

If total quality management and continuous improvement programs are implemented, it is usually necessary to have multiple work drivers in order to properly support them—particularly to assist in identifying non-value-added activities like setup or changeover costs. The greater the detail in providing costing data, the better chance a functional work area manager has for improving his or her operation. He or she should ask:

■ Is one purchasing agent more efficient than the others?

■ Is one customer more profitable than another?

■ Which product and/or service is more costly to produce?

■ Which channel of distribution is the least costly?

The more complex and/or diverse an organization is, the more work drivers are required.

## Determination of Activity Measures

An activity measure can be an input (e.g., purchase requisition), an output (purchase order), or a physical attribute of an activity (e.g., number of line items). The activity measure for the purchasing activity discussed earlier in the chapter can be expressed as a per-purchase requisition or purchase order. The selection of an appropriate activity measure is critical to an activity-based costing process (Table 9-1).

If production of a complex product requires an average of 20 purchase orders and production of a simple product requires 1 purchase order, the complex product should absorb a greater proportion of the purchase order activity's costs, with the simple product absorbing a lesser proportion. Suppose the purchasing department spends $120,000 processing 6000 purchase orders at $20 per

**Table 9-1.** Activity Measures

| Activity | Activity measures |
| --- | --- |
| Accounts payable | Invoices<br>Checks |
| Accounts receivable | Customer orders<br>Number of customers |
| Inventory control | Number of part numbers |
| Material planning and control | Number of part numbers |
| Purchasing | Number of purchase orders |
| Receiving and component stores | Number of purchase orders |
| Incoming inspection | Number of inspections |
| Quality control | Number of inspections |
| Vendor evaluations | Number of vendors |
| Vendor certification | Number of vendors |

purchase order. The activity cost of the complex product is $400 ($20 × 20 purchase orders), while that of the simple product is $20 ($20 × 1 purchase order).

The greater the desire for accuracy, the more difficult it will be to obtain activity data. A simpler approach is to determine the total number of purchase orders rather than the number of line items on a purchase order. A cost can be either traceable to a specific activity or not traceable to a specific activity. A *traceable cost* is defined as a cost that can be associated directly to an activity. For example, a purchase order clerk's salary can be directly related to the purchase order activity.

When a resource supports several activities, it should be split into its components and each component should be assigned to the specific activity that it supports. Thus the purchasing department's activities can be segregated into procurement, planning, vendor selection evaluation, vendor negotiation, purchase order preparation, and vendor coordination. An activity dictionary (see Chapter Three) can be used to identify all activities within a business process and the quantity of each resource consumed by and assigned to a specific activity, thereby providing the cost elements for determining that activity's total cost (including all support costs).

By identifying traceable activities, functional work area management can determine how much of each activity's output is to be assigned to a specific product and/or service. This approach also provides functional work area managers with the direct link to the customer who consumes the output. Typically, 80 to 90 percent of a functional work area's costs should be traceable to the activities performed in the work area and therefore should be easily controlled and minimized. For the remaining 10 to 20 percent—costs which are not traceable directly to activities—a surrogate method may need to be used to associate these costs to activities.

Utilizing an activity work flow that specifies the sequence of activities and the quantity of each activity measure consumed assists in managing all activities over the life cycle of a given product and/or service. It is essential that the activity work flow represent the actual way work moves through a business process. If it doesn't, incorrect activities may be charged with costs for a product or service. When an alternative work flow is used, the activity work flow should be updated to reflect the alternate routing.

The primary costs that usually comprise a product or service include material, direct labor, technology, quality, engineering, manufacturing engineering, R&D, material handling, marketing, production support, customer support, and finished-good distribution.

After the selection of the aforementioned activity measure, the functional work area manager must determine the frequency of its occurrence. Two common sources of activity volume information are data processing historical transaction volume statistics and functional work area records. For example, if production orders are numbered sequentially, by subtracting the beginning number from the ending number the functional work area manager can arrive at an approximation of the number of production orders.

An activity measure should be homogeneous. If a company has both simple and complex purchase orders, the functional work area manager may not be able to use purchase orders as the appropriate activity measure. Instead he or she may choose to use the number of lines on a purchase order as a more appropriate activity measure. If the impact of an activity on total cost is insignificant, a surrogate activity measure can be used.

Primary cost data can be derived from the company's general ledger, from detailed industrial engineering analyses, or from estimated relationships among similar activities. Generally, the general ledger is the recommended source, since it is the official financial record of an organization and can be used to reconcile an activity-based costing system to the outside financial reporting system. Engineering studies can be used to supplement the general ledger data. The preparation of graphs to portray historical relationships is insurance against any seasonal influences that may have been overlooked. Management, training, general meetings, and administrative secondary activities that support primary activities should be allocated using the same factors as those used for the primary activities (head counts, initiatives, contracts, and so on).

Once the functional work area manager has traced all assigned costs to an activity, he or she should incorporate the volume data associated to the activity measure with cost data in order to calculate the cost per activity, or unit cost.

## Cost Reduction Guidelines the Activity-Based Way

There are five basic guidelines for reducing costs the activity-based way.

### Reduce the Time or Effort Required to Perform an Activity. A key element of improvement is reducing the time or effort needed to perform an activ-

ity. This reduction can come from either process flow or product improvement. For example, the time to set up a machine can be reduced by improving training methods, eliminating conflicts in employee assignments, and placing tools and dies in convenient locations. Practicing the setup routine can create the manufacturing version of a "Grand Prix pit stop team." Reductions of up to 90 percent in setup time are not unusual.

Reductions in setup time can also come from changes in product design. Engineers at a plastics manufacturer, for example, changed the specifications for the vinyl weatherizing material used in extruded window frames. The change eliminated the need to add a weather-resistant coating to the frame. As a result, setup time was reduced because a simpler die could be used and a second extruder wasn't required.

Reductions in time and effort may come, not from the activity in question, but from the preceding activity. For example, the defect rate of parts received by a machining activity is a work driver for that activity. Improving quality in the preceding activity reduces the quantity of this work driver and the effort required by the machining area.

In another case, a retail distributor used ABC to highlight breaking up packages as a high-cost activity. This cost was decreased by asking suppliers to reduce the size of the packages and to design packages for easier breakup.

**Eliminate Unnecessary Activities.**    Some activities are candidates for elimination because they aren't valued by customers or aren't essential to running the organization. It's possible, for example, to eliminate material handling activities through changes to the process flows of products.

There are a variety of possibilities here. Steps can be taken to ensure that all incoming materials and parts are fit for use. The parts can be delivered directly to the shop floor as needed. Changes can be requested in the vendor's production process to improve quality and increase responsiveness. And parts that cause quality problems can be redesigned to eliminate those problems.

Once these changes have been made, it's no longer necessary to inspect parts when they're delivered, or place the parts on the shelf in the stockroom. Eliminating these activities reduces overall cost and the cost of products that no longer use those activities.

**Select Low-Cost Activities.**    Designers of products and processes often have choices among competing activities. This latitude offers a means of reducing cost by picking the lowest-cost activity (zero-based mentality). A designer of an electronics product, for example, may be able to specify the type of activity required for inserting components into circuit boards. Components such as resistors, diodes, and integrated circuits (ICs) may be inserted either manually or automatically. Depending on the design of the component, several automatic activities can be used to insert components, including axial, radial, and IC insertion. There may also be an option to place the components on the boards using surface-mount equipment.

Each of these activities has a different set of resources associated with it. Manual insertion is predominantly a direct labor activity. Automatic insertion, however, requires equipment, software, and a setup operation for each batch of circuit boards that receives components, and additional processes of engineering and training. Each type of automatic insertion or placement also differs in the resources required.

Because each of these activities has a different cost, the designer's selection has an important impact on costs.

Process designers face similar choices. For example, a part designed for machine insertion might also be inserted manually. A process designer may choose to have the part inserted manually because a drop in the batch size makes it uneconomical to program and set up an insertion machine.

The solution may be to shift production to an automated machine more suited to the design and volume of the product. This shift reduces the number of operations required. It also reduces the need for batch activities, such as scheduling and moving, and lowers the cost. Although the change represents a small loss on the product, the customer is now profitable overall.

**Share Activities Whenever Possible.**   If a customer has unique needs, it's necessary to perform activities specific to that customer. However, if customers have common needs, it's wasteful not to service those needs with the same activities.

For example, product designers can use common parts in new product designs. A common part is one that's used in several products to perform the same function (such as a gasket used in several car models). The only parts that need to be unique are those that add product-differentiating functions valued by customers.

The activities associated with common parts—such as part number maintenance, scheduling, and vendor relations—are shared by all products that use them. This sharing increases the volume of parts each time an activity is carried out, thus reducing the cost per part.

**Redeploy Unused Resources.**   In the final analysis, cost can be reduced only if resources are either eliminated or redeployed. Reducing the work load of an activity does not, by itself, reduce the equipment or number of people dedicated to that activity. There must be a conscious management decision to deal with the freed-up resources. Resources can be redeployed by growing the business to take up the slack, diverting the resources to other activities, or removing them from the company.

ABC can help calculate the type and amount of unused or underused resources. Resource plans based on this information then become the basis for redeployment.

Not long ago, it was commonly believed that improved quality meant higher cost. This seemed reasonable: didn't improved quality mean more inspectors, more rework, more costly warranties, and the like? How wrong we were! It's *poor* quality that costs money (and loses customers). Poor quality is doing a job more than once. It's wasting resources. It's having costly systems to keep track of defective parts. It's paying salaries for hordes of inspectors. It's incurring the cost of warranties and customer returns, and it's suffering the anger of disgruntled customers.

Improving quality is a sure way to reduce cost. *Do it right the first time.* Work on reducing work drivers that cause errors (such as frequent schedule changes, excessive process variability, and poor product design).

Paradoxically, reducing cost the activity-based way almost always improves quality. Eliminating unnecessary work, for example, reduces opportunities to "get it wrong" and tightens the linkages between activities. Activity-based costing fits well with any quality improvement program. It encourages the actions that improve quality, and directs attention to quality improvements with the greatest cost-reduction potential.

## Key Steps in Establishing an Activity-Based Costing Program

**Activity Analysis.**    Activity analysis is intended to assist in identifying a company's significant primary and support activities in order to establish a clear and concise basis for describing the company's business operations and for determining the cost of these activities and how well they are performed. Activity analysis leads into activity-based management, which is the tool used to effectively and consistently organize a company's activities in order to use its resources in the best possible way to achieve its objectives.

Activity analysis allows management to reallocate time and resources in order to select alternate work methods that improve both quality and effectiveness of activities—even in a dynamic environment. The analysis process is an orderly way to decompose a large, complex organization into elemental business processes (grouping of activities) and to define the outputs of these activities into understandable, manageable, and measurable entities. It is an audit process of the way a company functions and determines the resources (skills, equipment, staffing levels) required to support a given level of service and quality while eliminating redundant and wasteful activities and thereby increasing company profits.

There are two different directions a functional work area manager can take in using activity analysis. One is the *aggregation,* or the combining of activities into business processes. The other is *decomposition,* or the breaking down of an activity into tasks. Performance improvement is best achieved by decomposing activities into tasks and then reengineering those tasks and rebuilding them into productive activities and then business processes.

Activity analysis focuses on objective, measurable facts and activity work flow effectiveness, not on individual staff members. There should be established performance measures like quality of output, timeliness (ability to deliver output at the scheduled time), and flexibility (ability to cope with changes in volume, scope, mix, and technology). Consider an activity to be a black box and activity analysis to be the technique that is concerned only with what the box does, not how it works.

*Determine Functional Work Areas to Be Analyzed.* Senior management should review an organization chart and head count summary as a starting point in the activity analysis process. This will ensure that the basic structure of the current organization is fully understood and that the whole organization has been covered. Senior management should validate the organization chart and staffing levels with each functional work area manager to ensure that they are current and accurately reflect existing operational structures.

Review activity work flows, fixed-asset registers, official transaction volume data, official sources of financial data, functional work area layouts, and availability of any functional work area detailed procedures. In order to qualify for analysis, a functional work area should consist of 5 to 20 people, with an expense level of at least $100,000. Analyze only areas of potential improvement.

*Identify All Functional Work Area Activities Performed.* The shorter the activity list, the easier it is to manage and positively influence business decisions. An overly extensive list of activities to be analyzed could invalidate many of the benefits of an activity-based costing system. Do not aggregate dissimilar activities (e.g., advertising and promotion should be kept separate), and decompose a single activity and/or multiple activities only if they are part of a decision-making process. Do not decompose an activity if it is a repetitive one that cannot be modified. Determine whether activities could be subcontracted to an outside company—because an activity that does not add value to an organization is not worth doing.

Review the organization's historical records for a full year, if available, to determine what the transaction volume for a specific activity in a functional work area has been. Analyze functional work areas by speaking directly with the manager involved to identify currently performed activities and the resources that must be allocated to accomplish them. This approach could include interviews, questionnaires, and observations.

Five major functional work areas may be identified and considered as prime examples.

1. *Marketing and sales.* The marketing function determines who the consumer is and what the consumer's needs are, and informs the market of the organization's products. The sales function consummates the transaction with the customer and tells manufacturing what to manufacture as well as when and where to ship. It also provides the necessary customer service to resolve any problems with the product and/or service delivered.

2. *Manufacturing and quality control.* Manufacturing involves procuring the necessary materials, transforming materials into finished goods, and shipping the finished products to customers. The quality control functions ensures that all materials entering the plant and all finished goods leaving it conform to predetermined customer specifications (Table 9-2).

**Table 9-2.** Activities—Manufacturing/Quality Control

| Activity | Decision |
|---|---|
| *Material management* | |
| Production planning | Equipment scheduling |
| Coordination of change | Operation sequencing |
| Receiving | Determination of economic lot quantities |
| Production control | Inventory checking |
| Routing | Requesting materials and supplies |
| Scheduling | Scheduling material receipts |
| Inventory control | Managing physical inventory and inventory records |
| | |
| *Material and supplies procurement* | |
| Plan procurement | Analyzing material specs |
| Vendor selection and evaluation | Value engineering |
| Negotiation of price, delivery, and quality | Assessing and selecting vendor |
| Purchase order (PO) completion | Negotiating with vendor |
| Vendor coordination | Quality control of vendor |
| | PO issue |
| | PO tracking |
| | PO receipt |
| | Vendor coordination |
| | Expediting |
| | |
| *Distribution* | |
| Finished-goods management | Controlling finished manufactured part |
| Transportation and shipping | Selecting method of transportation to customer |
| Packaging | Packaging finished goods |
| Field support | Maintaining product at customer location |
| Spares management | Providing spares |
| Equipment maintenance | Maintaining distribution equipment |
| Dealerships | Selecting dealerships |
| | |
| *Manufacturing engineering* | |
| Industrial engineering | Specifying labor content |
| Determining time standards | Determining best methods |
| Method selection | Evaluating and selecting capital equipment |
| Investment justification | |
| Completing special projects | |
| Preparing customer quotation proposals | |
| | |
| *Production engineering* | |
| Make or buy analysis | Subcontracting |
| Process planning | Routing |
| | Machine and process selection |
| | Tool and fixture selection |
| | |
| *Plant engineering* | |
| Plant and office layout | Allocating floor space |
| Environment control | Designing plant |
| Grounds and building maintenance | |
| Equipment setup | Lot size |

**Table 9-2.** Activities—Manufacturing/Quality Control (*Continued*)

| Activity | Decision |
|---|---|
| *Machine design* | |
| Tool, fixture, and equipment design | |
| Tool room design | |
| *Quality control* | |
| Quality specification | Determining that parts meet specification |
| Incoming inspection | Controlling quality of incoming material |
| In-process inspection | Establishing in-process inspection points |
| Final inspection | Controlling quality of final product |
| Tool and gauge control | Controlling quality of tools and gauges |
| Maintenance and operation of inspection equipment | Setting maintenance policy |
| Evaluation of vendor quality and qualification | Selecting vendor |
| Product certification | Determining cost and time to obtain product certification |

3. *Research and development and engineering.* Research and development is responsible for developing new ideas for products and services. The engineering process designs new products and modifies existing ones. These areas provide the link between marketing and manufacturing (Table 9-3).

4. *Finance and administration.* The role of finance and administration is to gather and process financial and performance data for the activity-based costing program. The finance business process provides the financial planning required to manage the cash flow to meet company financial obligations; issues all recurring financial reports; manages payroll, accounts payable, and accounts receivable; and prepares profit plans for senior management.

**Table 9-3.** Activities—Research and Development/Engineering

| Activity | Decision |
|---|---|
| New product development | When to introduce new products<br>Pricing |
| Existing product modification | Number of products<br>Number of product modifications<br>Pricing |
| Basic research | New product requirement<br>Pricing |
| R&D processing | New process requirement<br>Pricing |

5. *Logistics and field support.* Most organizations call this function customer service—product problems are non-value added because they result from manufacturing problems—and field testing.

Activity analysis creates a map which identifies the relationship between business processes and/or their associated activities. Creating an activity work flow is the first step in analyzing business processes and identifying the necessary activities to be performed to meet customer needs. Activity-based costing helps describe the cost structure of these activities in terms of activity consumption.

After activities are mapped to business processes, the next step is to map business processes to products and/or services. An activity is either required or discretionary (optional), depending on the functional work area manager's judgment. Activities can be influenced by external factors (weather or regulatory requirements) or internal factors (company policy and procedures). Activity classifications are important considerations in determining what elements should be included in an activity-based costing system.

*Activity Analysis Checklist.* An activity analysis checklist serves as a guide for functional work area managers to ensure that all critical information is analyzed.

1. Verify the organizational structure and current staffing.
   - Request a current staffing chart.
   - What are the major classifications of people?
   - Identify direct and indirect products.
2. What are the major activities of your functional work area? Request any activity work flow charts or pictures that help illustrate how work is performed.
3. Review product lists.
   - Are all the products and/or services included? If not, please add.
   - Rank products and/or services in terms of their importance.
4. What are the most labor-intensive, costly, and time-consuming operations or products?
5. What are the bottlenecks? What are the causes of the bottlenecks?
6. How do you currently keep track of the amount of activity in your area?
7. What is the current work load?
8. How do you currently keep track of costs and labor?
9. Do you have a work load forecast?
   - How was it developed?
   - How does it vary from time to time and why?
10. Is there a staff member loading and forecast? How was it developed?

11. What computerized reports and databases are used? What information is input into the system, and how is it done?

12. What information and other support do you need from other functional work areas that would help improve your operations?

13. Provide feedback.

The activity analysis process provides an initial list of significant activities performed by job category. The staff member's occupation is a key indicator of the types of activities performed. For each occupation the key activities and percentage of total time spent on those activities can be determined. The percentage of total time spent on a given activity varies primarily when the activity changes or the level of transaction volume changes.

**Identification of Staff Member Costs.** Once activities have been identified and analyzed it is time to associate people-related costs to activities. The time expended by staff members on activities is an excellent basis for assigning staff member costs and is usually best accomplished by using a positive time-reporting technique.

The company organization chart and its corresponding activity descriptions provide an excellent starting point for assigning staff member costs to activities. The activity analysis process has already determined which activities a staff member supports. There are three methods for accumulating staff member costs.

*Percentage of Total Functional Work Area Labor Method.* The total labor method multiplies total functional work area cost (i.e., salaries and related expenses) by the percentage of time the staff member spent in performing an activity in order to arrive at that activity's cost (Table 9-4). A drawback to this method is that it uses an average wage rate. Thus, activities requiring more experienced senior staff members are often undercosted. Specific staff member hours spent on each activity could be an alternative resulting in more accurate cost assignment.

*Occupational Code Method.* Under the occupational code method, salaries and other staff member costs are distributed to a functional work area's activities by multiplying the total staff member cost in each occupational code by the corresponding percentage of time spent on the activity (Table 9-5).

**Table 9-4.** Total Functional Work Area Labor Method

| Activity | Time, % | Cost | |
|---|---|---|---|
| New product design | 25 | $83,750 | (335,000 × 0.25) |
| Product design testing | 35 | 117,250 | (335,000 × 0.35) |
| Market analysis | 10 | 33,500 | (335,000 × 0.10) |
| Management and administration | 15 | 50,250 | (335,000 × 0.15) |
| Other | 15 | 50,250 | (335,000 × 0.15) |
| Total | 100% | $335,000 | |

**Table 9-5.** Occupational Code Method

| Activity | Occupational code | Number of staff members | Average salary | Hours worked | Hourly rate | Total activity cost |
|---|---|---|---|---|---|---|
| New product design | 003 | 5 | $40,000 | 5,000 | $20.00 | $100,000 |
| Product design testing | 003 | 5 | 40,000 | 3,000 | 20.00 | 60,000 |
|  | 004 | 3 | 20,000 | 4,000 | 10.00 | 40,000 |
| Market analysis | 003 | 5 | 40,000 | 800 | 20.00 | 16,000 |
|  | 004 | 3 | 20,000 | 1,200 | 10.00 | 12,000 |
| Management and administration | 001 | 1 | 60,000 | 1,400 | 30.00 | 42,000 |
|  | 002 | 1 | 15,000 | 1,600 | 7.50 | 12,000 |
| Other | 001 | 1 | 60,000 | 600 | 30.00 | 18,000 |
|  | 002 | 1 | 15,000 | 400 | 7.50 | 3,000 |
|  | 003 | 5 | 40,000 | 1,200 | 20.00 | 24,000 |
|  | 004 | 3 | 20,000 | 800 | 10.00 | 8,000 |
| Total |  |  |  | $20,000 |  | $335,000 |

The *first step* in the occupational code method is to determine the occupational codes within the functional work area. The occupational codes provide insight into the types of activities the staff members perform. The functional work area manager (or an engineering study) identifies, for each occupational code, the key activities and the percentage of total time spent on each activity. An hourly rate for each occupational code is computed by dividing the total cost for a specific activity in the functional work area (e.g., $10,000) by the number of productive hours available (e.g., 2000) to arrive at an hourly rate ($20.00) per staff member classification. This method is considered the best compromise of the three alternatives because it eliminates the problem of undercosting senior staff members, as just described in the percentage of labor method.

The *next step* is to multiply the hours worked for each activity or occupational code (e.g., 5000) by the hourly rate ($20.00) to arrive at total activity cost ($100,000).

*Specific Staff Method.*   Under the specific staff method, all functional work area managers and staff members are interviewed—and/or a full-range engineering study is conducted—to understand staff member activities and responsibilities within a functional work area. Then the functional work area manager determines the time spent by each staff member on primary activities. Let us assume that the manager's analysis reveals the following breakdown: a staff member whose salary is $60,000 spends 70 percent of his or her time on a management and administrative activity ($60,000 × 70% = $42,000 cost). The drawback of this method is that it is cumbersome and expensive and might require the implementation of a positive time-reporting system. However, the specific staff method is the most accurate of the three alternatives. All nontraceable costs (e.g., administrative) should also be allocated to primary activities on the same basis as the primary activities.

# Benefits of an Activity-Based Costing Program

There are several benefits to be derived from an activity-based costing program (Fig. 9-7).

## Support for Strategic Decisions

More accurate and objective information provides improved strategic decision-making support for

- Pricing strategies
- Product line management
- Make-or-buy decisions
- Product rationalization
- Own-or-lease decisions

## Assignment of Work Driver Information to Activities

A work driver is a measure that generates activity and begins the process of consuming resources by the activity it puts in motion. Examples of work drivers include:

- Number of orders
- Number of inspections
- Number of setups
- Number of accounts

Activity-based costing uses work drivers to identify what causes work to be performed and to assign consumed resources to activities and activities to products or services.

## Operational Effectiveness

Knowing how work is performed through the careful analysis of activities assists functional work area management in improving operational effectiveness through

- Prioritization of improvement efforts
- Identification of value-added versus non-value-added work

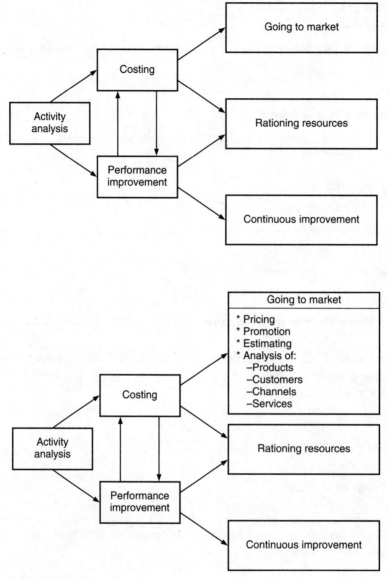

**Figure 9-7.** Benefits of ABC.

- Process redesign
- Performance measurement
- Work flow realignment

Activity-based costing encourages continual improvement and total quality management conventions because planning and cost control are directed to the

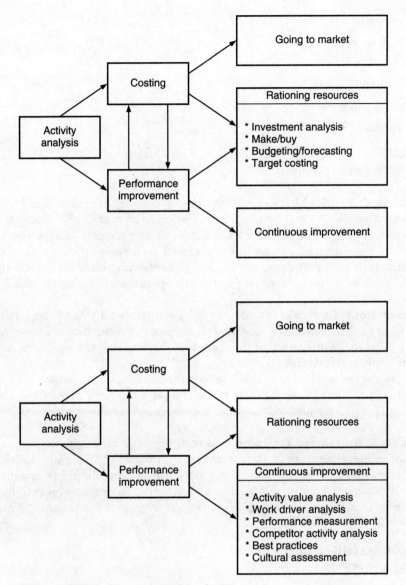

**Figure 9-7.** (*Continued*) Benefits of ABC.

business process level. The methodology also improves the budgeting process by identifying and focusing cost/performance relationships to service levels.

**Objective Information.** Activity-based costing informs functional work area managers about their work areas by providing objective and timely information on

- Processes
- Work drivers
- Activities
- Products
- Product lines
- Customers
- Services
- Staff member performance

**Improved Profitability.** Activity-based costing provides senior management with objective and accurate information to choose which products and/or services to produce and indicates which of these products and/or services will be the most profitable. In addition, it assists in managing cash flow more efficiently. It pinpoints the sources of cost by identifying the work drivers that generate work and links corporate strategy to operational decision making.

**Better Cost Control.** Waste cannot be tolerated in any size business. In order to establish effective cost-control methods, the functional work area manager must focus attention on the source of the cost, regardless of the organizational unit in which it is incurred.

A negative work driver (e.g., a customer complaint) causes unnecessary work and reduces profitability because it creates the need to redeliver the product and/or service and to have staff members also perform field service.

**Timely Management Decision Making.** Functional work area managers and senior management can use accurate cost information to facilitate decision making (e.g., make or buy, pricing, design). Costing data should be available in a timely manner to arrive at a decision on whether to perform an activity and to conform to monthly financial book-closing conventions for accounting purposes.

## Aggregation of Activities into End-to-End Business Processes

Many actions or tasks can be aggregated into a single activity, and many activities into business processes, thereby eliminating the need to measure several individual actions. It is then possible to utilize one or more work drivers to assign costs to activities. Remember that as more and more activities are aggregated into business process, the ability of a work driver to accurately assign the resources consumed decreases. Therefore, it is important to determine the level of detail to be used in reporting the resources consumed by each activity. In some instances the process should be reversed. That is, business processes should be disaggregated or split apart to uncover differences in how resources are being consumed by those activities that comprise a specific process.

Activities that are aggregated into groups of related activities for a common purpose (e.g., order fulfillment, marketing) frequently do not conform to an organizational unit and do cross hierarchical lines to form an end-to-end business process. A *business process* is defined as a network of related activities linked by the output they generate. A business process (e.g., marketing, sales) is what gets done in an organization. An activity (propose a job) and a task (prepare a proposal) describe what the company does to accomplish the business process of marketing and/or sales.

### Organization of Activities into Functional Work Areas

A functional work area is a segment of a business process for which management wants to separately report the cost of the activities which are performed there. The first step is to determine the cost of each activity within the functional work area. Each cost within the functional work area should indicate how resources are consumed. Each work area should have a clear physical interpretation that corresponds to managing a business process. A receiving and shipping department may be considered one business process, but it may be appropriate to separate them into two functional work areas within that business process. This drill-down provides senior management with comparative information so that when a problem arises management can focus on the source in an effort to eliminate the intervention quickly.

## New Paradigm in Cost Management

The most overlooked aspect in comparing activity-based costing with traditional accounting is the cultural change that must take place. New techniques and methodology must be taught as new types of tools to aid in performing daily work. A new paradigm in cost management turns upside down many years of ingrained management principles (Table 9-6).

**Table 9-6.** New Paradigm in Cost Management

| Traditional thinking | New thinking |
| --- | --- |
| Cost reduction | Cost prevention |
| Overhead allocation | Overhead control and elimination |
| Static, precise information | Timely, relevant information |
| Historical reporting of actuals | Future cost structure |
| Negative fingerpointing | Proactive involvements |
| Functional view | Business process view |
| Current period costs | Total life-cycle costs |

Managers who are used to simply comparing budgeted costs against actual costs on a monthly schedule will have to begin looking at costs differently.

Reducing cost is only one of several focal points of ABC. It is the first major difference between ABC and the old-fashioned accounting way. Improving quality, flexibility, and service—the importance of which varies from one business to another—is also central to ABC. A second major difference is the way costs are reduced. Cost reduction is best achieved by changing the way activities are performed (managing the activities first), then redeploying the excess resources identified by the improvement.

Under traditional cost accounting methods, accountants have used cost data to value inventories because it was a significant component in the preparation of financial statements for external reporting purposes. The data was largely historical, with a narrow focus, and for the most part was ignored by operational people.

## Comparison of Activity-Based Costing with Traditional Accounting

The traditional costing information wasn't used in running a business. ABC, on the other hand, affords functional work area managers with usable product and/or service costing data with which they can make informed business decisions. It is a forward-looking methodology that provides managers with alternatives for managing an organization in the future, not just for reporting what has already taken place and cannot be changed.

ABC methodology is applicable in all functional work areas of a company, including marketing and planning, not just in the financial and accounting areas. Costs can be incurred in several business processes that are involved in preproduction/service activities, manufacturing/service activities, and postproduction/service activities. The costs are calculated for an end-to-end process even if the activity flow crosses hierarchical lines.

Most costs that are calculated for external reporting purposes are frequently ignored in managing a business. Under traditional costing systems, managers often make an error in judgment by assuming that work is driven by volume only. ABC focuses its attention on the activities that cause work to happen and the activities performed in processing transactions which may or may not be volume-sensitive. The cultural transformation from hierarchical structures to an activity-based end-to-end processing business environment can be categorized as follows:

- Mission
- Customer requirements
- Objectives
- Improvement

- Problem solving
- Jobs and people
- Management style
- Role of manager
- Rewards and recognition

A comparison of each of these categories under both the traditional and ABC cultures clearly delineates the difference between the two cultures (Table 9-7).

In a manufacturing organization the incorrect allocation of overhead, if it were an insignificant part of the total cost of a product and/or service, wouldn't have any relevance. However, in today's high-technology, quality-driven, and service-driven environment, overhead and support costs are an important portion of total cost.

**Table 9-7.** Activity-Based Costing Requires a Cultural Transformation

| Category | Hierarchical culture | Activity-based culture |
|---|---|---|
| Mission | Management by objectives. | Ethical behavior and customer satisfaction. Climate of continuous improvement. |
| Customer requirements | Incomplete or ambiguous understanding of customer requirements. | Use of a systematic approach to seek out, understand, and satisfy internal and external customers. |
| Objectives | An orientation to short-term objectives and action with limited long-term perspective. | A deliberate balance of long-term goals with successive short-term objectives. |
| Improvement | Acceptance of a certain margin of error and subsequent corrective action as the norm. | Striving for continuous improvement in meeting customer requirements. |
| Problem solving | Unstructured individualistic problem solving and decision making. | Participative and disciplined problem solving and decision making on the basis of substantive data. |
| Jobs and people | Functional, narrow scope, management controlled. | Employee involvement, work teams, integrated functions. |
| Management style | A management style with uncertain objectives that instills fear of failure. | An open style with clear and concise objectives, encouraging group-derived continuous improvement. |
| Role of manager | Plan, organize, assign, control, and enforce. | Communicate, participate, and promote mutual trust. |
| Rewards and recognition | Pay by job; few team incentives. | Individual and group recognition and rewards; negotiated criteria. |

In traditional costing systems the financial team in an organization would apply support costs on the basis of some volume indicator. Today, however, many costs are not volume related. To illustrate, suppose a company produces two like products. One of the products requires 5 different parts, and the other is made up of 30 different parts.

When the parts arrive at the assembly plant, they must be received and inspected before they can be placed in inventory. The product that requires 30 parts will need more receiving and inspection activity than the product that requires only 5 parts. The volume of both products could be identical, but even if they weren't the costs associated with receiving and inspection are not volume sensitive and should be treated differently for each part.

One of the key factors in ABC is determining what drives specific costs, assigning those costs to activities, and then associating activities to products and/or services. Traditional volume-driven costing systems usually undercost low-volume products and/or services and overcost high-volume products and/or services because of the disproportional allocation of support costs (engineering, receiving, inspection, quality assurance).

An important application of ABC that is often overlooked is that the methodology is useful in service businesses as well as manufacturing organizations (Table 9-8).

ABC methodology can assist a functional work area manager in choosing what product and/or service will provide the largest profit margin for the com-

**Table 9-8.** Traditional Costing Systems versus Activity-Based Costing

| Traditional costing | Activity-based costing |
|---|---|
| Material costs are assigned to services. | Material costs are assigned directly to services. |
| Direct labor expense is traced to services, where possible. | Direct labor expense is traced directly to services. |
| All other indirect costs (e.g., overhead) are usually allocated to the products on a single volume-based relationship (such as direct labor dollars). | All other indirect costs are traced to services according to the usage of required activities. |
| Costs are accumulated by budget line items. | Only those costs associated with each activity are directly related. |
| Savings typically are buried without identifying the source of the cost reduction. | A management focus concentrates on underlying cost causes and effects. |
| Traditional costing systems "smear" overheads across all products and units. | Activity-based costing uses appropriate drivers to trade resources to activities and activities to cost objects (e.g., purchasing driver = number of purchase orders). |

*Note:* Information provided by traditional costing can be "precisely inappropriate." ABC prefers to be "approximately correct"!!

pany. In a customer-driven marketplace, marketing, selling, and distribution costs can comprise over half the total cost of a product and/or service. However, not much energy is expended by senior management either to comprehend them or to control them.

Once managers understand that the distribution activity is a significant cost—not sales volume—they can begin assigning cost on the basis of number of orders. Each customer will be charged a price that reflects both the number of units purchased and the number of deliveries a customer needs. If the customer requires frequent small deliveries of goods and/or services, it may be that costs exceed revenues and the company can't afford to do business with that customer.

ABC concepts can be utilized early in the product design activity. Reducing the number of parts needed to manufacture that product should lower receiving, inspection, and quality assurance costs such as testing. Inspection costs can be shifted to the vendor, and management can insist that the vendor inspect all products prior to shipment and that the quality fall within predetermined parameters. If the number of authorized vendors is decreased, there will be less paperwork and fewer instances to work with. Fig. 9-8 compares traditional accounting versus activity-based costing approaches in a mail department and an engineering department.

Traditional costing systems provide information that indicates only where costs are incurred; they do not link what caused those expenses to be spent in the first place. They do not address these key questions:

- What business function do I support?
- What work activities do I do?
- What resources will I use?
- What causes my work?
- How do I measure work activities?
- How well do I perform my work activities?
- How do I cost my work activities?
- What does an activity cost?
- How much work do I do?
- Who will pay for the work?
- How does operational performance relate to affordability?

Activity-based costing answers these questions so that senior and functional work area managers don't have to rightsize their organizations on instinct (Fig. 9-9). If purchasing increased the size of vendor orders, accounts payable's work load would be reduced because the number of purchase orders and vendor invoices would go down. This approach would result in available hours which could lead to staff reductions because activity levels were reduced by driving work out of the business.

**Chart of accounts view**
**Mail department**

| | |
|---|---|
| Salaries | $265,000 |
| Benefits | 132,000 |
| Rents and contracts | 31,000 |
| Supplies | 22,000 |
| MIS charges | 6,000 |
| **Total** | **$456,000** |

**Activity view**
**Mail department**

| | |
|---|---|
| Deliver mail | $70,000 |
| Deliver packages | 70,000 |
| Sort mail | 147,000 |
| Send outgoing express mail | 97,000 |
| Meter outgoing mail | 72,000 |
| **Total** | **$456,000** |

**Traditional chart of account view**
**Engineering department**

| | |
|---|---|
| Salaries | $500,000 |
| Technology | 100,000 |
| Travel expense | 50,000 |
| Supplies | 20,000 |
| Facilities | 30,000 |
| **Total** | **$700,000** |

**Activity based costing**
**Activity view**
**Engineering department**

| | | |
|---|---|---|
| Develop BOM | $29,500 | V |
| Maintain BOM | 118,000 | NV |
| Develop routing | 37,500 | V |
| Maintain routing | 112,500 | NV |
| Special orders | 75,000 | V |
| Capacity studies | 132,500 | NV |
| Process improvement | 27,500 | NV |
| Tooling design | 27,500 | V |
| Training | 41,000 | V |
| Mgmt. & admin. | 99,000 | NV |
| **Total** | **$700,000** | |

V = Value added        NV = Non-value added

**Figure 9-8.** Traditional accounting versus activity-based costing.

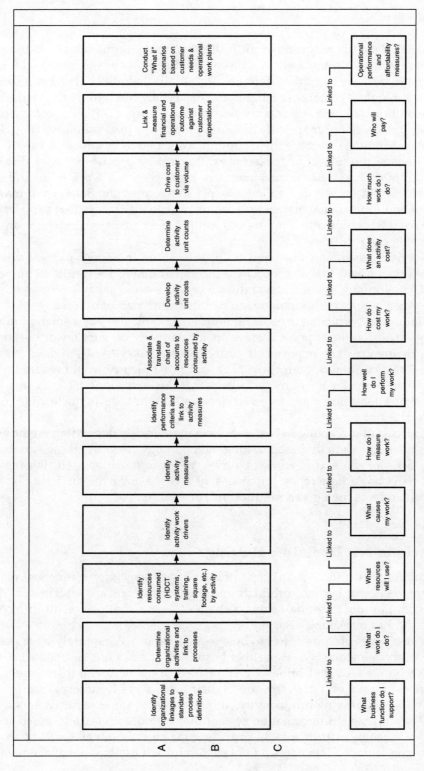

**Figure 9-9.** Key questions addressed in activity-based costing.

When a staff is reduced by gut feeling without eliminating work, the result generally is that some work is not processed and/or the remaining staff members are overworked. In addition, costs usually increase either because overtime is required or because temporary workers are hired to fill the void.

Traditional costing systems are able to view an organization's cost at a macro or overall level, but frequently ignore support costs (e.g., administration, R&D, and distribution). Because these support costs tend to be allocated evenly to all customers, products, and/or services, the costing picture becomes distorted. As all of us know, some customers are more costly to work with, and some products and/or services are more expensive to provide. Both senior management and functional work area managers mistakenly believe that support costs are fixed when in reality they are some of the most capricious expenses an organization can consume.

Servicing customers that have multiple locations in various parts of a distribution region and that also purchase in limited quantities results in numerous orders, shipping documents, and invoices. The order entry and warehousing activities require additional time to handle the myriad of orders.

By contrast, when an organization orders in bulk and has a small number of large facilities, the support costs drop substantially because fewer bills of lading or invoices are required. If support costs were evenly divided between these two customers, an incorrect servicing cost picture would result. In addition, senior management might believe that the least profitable customer is the most profitable and make incorrect decisions on the basis of misleading costing information.

The cost of marketing to customers can vary greatly depending on the activities involved. Activity-based costing methodology considers these variables on the basis of the actual work involved, whereas traditional costing methods often overlook these types of items—which could make the difference between profit and loss for a given product and/or service.

## New Directions for Decision Making

Traditional costing systems have the ability to engender erroneous management decisions, because products and/or service costs are inaccurately determined. Improper costing begins a chain of events that can result in incorrect pricing and marketing decisions.

These types of approaches to business decision making rarely have positive operational impact, because neither business processes nor individual activities are improved. Organizations are compelled to operate with insufficient, inaccurate information which misdirects their focus away from reengineering their activities, improving productivity, and meeting customer requirements.

A well-designed information system that includes an activity-based costing module can be instrumental in providing management at all levels of an organization with the data needed for a successful activity-based management program. The ABC program developed in this book elevates performance measurement and operational control to a higher level to allow manufacturing and service organizations to manage their businesses at substantially lower risk. In addition, it opens the door for wider empowerment, by allowing managers the freedom and comfort to make independent decisions.

The combined methodologies of reengineering, productivity improvement, total quality management, continuous improvement, and ABC begin a new direction for managing a business: ABM. The utilization of ABM can assist in restoring competitiveness for many organizations that have become reactive rather than proactive in operating their businesses.

Traditional costing systems are primarily concerned with the bookkeeping aspects of a business enterprise, whereas ABC is focused on controlling the circumstances that cause activities to happen. This costing approach is managerial in nature, not just reflective, and emphasizes planning as an integral part of controlling costs.

ABC puts to rest the approach taken by many accountants that costs which are difficult to explain should be classified as fixed costs and allocated by some mysterious metric. ABC allows managers to identify what activities and/or occurrences drive costs and provides them with the data needed to attack those events.

A company can excess tens of thousands of staff members, but unless the work these individuals performed is also eliminated, a permanent cost reduction can't possibly take place. Unlike traditional costing systems, ABC permits managers of businesses to take control over their costs and fate.

Traditional costing systems usually are based on the concept that direct labor and/or direct material generates overhead. ABC assumes that products and/or services incur overhead costs (e.g., inspection, scheduling, warehousing) by stimulating certain activities. Products and/or services are assigned overhead costs on the basis of how much of these activities they consume and/or use. The greater the amount of activities a product and/or service needs, the larger amount of cost it produces.

## Developing an Activity's Cost

An ABC approach provides the data to develop an activity's cost so that management can determine which activities are the most expensive, and then take corrective action to lower or eliminate them. For example, ABC can tell a functional work area manager how much it costs to produce a repair order. ABC then associates the cost per repair order to each machine on the basis of the number of repairs it required.

There are many measures that can be used to portray resource consumption and some are related to volume. Under most applications of a traditional costing system, managers believe that volume is the cause of all costs. ABC methodology recognizes that many activities are not related to the number of units produced.

A good example is the accounts payable functional work area that processes purchase orders. Traditional costing systems generally assign costs to a product on the basis of material cost, but this approach doesn't mirror the way a purchasing agent works. The work load in purchasing is determined by the volume of purchase orders processed, no matter how many items were purchased or dollars expended. ABC would allocate purchasing costs to products on the basis of the number of purchase orders processed.

The number of line items per purchase order may vary, but the observation process that determined the work-to-time relationship would have considered this variable.

Traditional costing systems distort costs when there are high- and low-volume products and/or services, because costs are distributed on the basis of labor hours. Generally, lower-volume products and/or services are undercosted and higher-volume products and/or services are overcosted—in many cases, by a significant amount.

This erroneous costing can evoke improper determinations about which products and/or services are profitable and which are losing money. Marketing management may then decide to drop viable products and/or services and retain those which are money losers. This same inconsistency can be seen when dealing with simple or complex products.

Complex products and/or services require a larger amount of a company's support activities than do simple products and/or services. Most traditional costing systems ignore this requirement and allocate overhead costs on the basis of director labor or machine hours. ABC methodology usually can identify and separate this type of subtlety and isolate true product costs. Inappropriate data can negatively affect the decision-making process.

ABC methodology strives to assign every activity cost to the proper product and/or service that causes the activity to happen. Each customer is unique, and when a customer causes activities to be performed the costs associated with those activities should be attributed to that specific customer.

Most traditional costing systems overlook the fact that customers vary depending on

- Type of customer
- Service requirements
- Size of order
- Distribution methods

## Differentiating the Customer Base and Determining Customer Profitability

ABC grasps the concept that all customers aren't alike and therefore provides managers with an accurate picture of how much it costs to service a specific customer. A chain of 1000 individual stores is more costly to service than a company with 5 major distribution centers in strategic locations.

Some customers may require frequent visits, expensive advertising programs, and/or specialized packaging. If managers can easily identify a customer's costing profile, decisions can be made that provide a competitive advantage by tailoring special services. For example, by

- Creating special marketing promotions
- Adjusting the number of units included in an order to reduce the number of orders but increase the volume shipped per order.
- Tracking the number of defects and/or service calls
- Reducing distribution points by consolidating shipments

By associating costs to customer needs, an organization can craft its pricing process to best satisfy a customer while receiving a reasonable profit for its product and/or service. When management has the proper data, it can eliminate costly services (e.g., overnight shipping) to customers who do not require and/or haven't asked for them.

Accurate costing information makes a business enterprise more flexible. For example, an international giftware distributor found its delivery expense increasing at an alarming rate. Upon investigation, the company determined that the sales department was shipping increasing numbers of customers their orders by air express. The president of the company asked the marketing vice president if customers were asking for this extra-fast service.

The marketing vice president researched the matter and learned that the majority of customers neither asked for nor required this expensive form of delivery. This non-value-added practice was immediately ended, resulting in several hundreds of thousands of dollars being saved. The company changed its unwritten, informal policy in order to eliminate a costly service that its customers didn't require. The organization continued its customer satisfaction research initiative to better grasp customer ordering patterns and tailored its service to customer needs while keeping delivery costs low.

When ABC methodology is implemented, an organization can easily determine which customers are profitable and which are money losers and can adjust its methods of operating the business accordingly (e.g., raise minimum order quantities, reduce field representatives, increase telemarketing capability). By slashing expenses for transportation and order handling, and restructuring channels of distribution to reach smaller, less accessible customers, any business can raise its annual net profit substantially.

ABC is more accurate than traditional costing systems because it can mirror more complex cost patterns. It is the second phase of ABC—the assignment of costs from business processes to products and/or services—that truly separates the methodology from traditional costing systems. ABC identifies various costs that belong to diverse customers and sets of customers.

Under traditional costing systems, the assignment of costs from business processes to products and/or services is usually based on measures of volume (e.g., direct labor hours, machine hours). In an ABC environment, this second phase of cost assignment mirrors how costs are consumed by products, services, and/or customers.

An important distinction between traditional costing and ABC is the idea that costs are by nature hierarchical because they are incurred at various levels (parts, units, batches). ABC does not overlook this uniqueness, and separates costs to facilitate informed decision making by functional work area managers. Costs like design and engineering are related to products, not individual parts or batches or units produced. These costs can be incurred whether you produce a quantity of 5 units, no units, or 10,000 units.

The most significant difference between a traditional costing system and ABC is the utilization of work drivers, because drivers are what gives ABC its accuracy, its integrity, and in some cases its intricate architecture. The total cost of each business process is assigned to products and/or services by their activities.

In a traditional costing system, either direct labor or machine hours is the work driver used, with the assumption that resources are absorbed in direct proportion to the transaction volume completed. Generally each business process has only one work driver. Under ABC methodology a business process often has multiple work drivers, because all the costs of a business process are not absorbed in association with units produced. Some expenses, such as planning and setups, are incurred whether or not large or small batches of work are processed.

When surrogates and/or metrics have to be used instead of work drivers, the true and accurate measure of an activity is not attained. Surrogates are used to mirror cost patterns, but they do not represent a true picture of how the product and/or service consumes an activity. They provide only a measure for unit consumption. Generally, surrogates are useful when so many varied tasks are associated with an activity that it would be too expensive to try to comprehend all the nuances involved.

The functional work area manager is able to simplify the tracing of costs by using some surrogates and some activity work drivers.

## Identification and Quantification of the Cost of Quality

A subtle but important difference between traditional costing systems and ABC is identification and quantification of the cost of inferior quality (e.g., scrap, rework). Traditional costing systems pay little attention to this significant requirement in today's competitive environment. However, ABC recognizes the meaningful attribute of assigning all costs to products and/or services even if those costs are scrap and rework. In addition, ABC understands the significance of tracing these types of non-value-added costs back to the source that created them.

The tracking of these costs is as easy as accounting for raw materials, parts, services, and/or products that had to be scrapped or reworked and assigning them to the associated product and/or service. This recognition of non-value-added cost is meaningful in order for functional work area managers to be able to take immediate corrective action.

ABC not only reports the costs of quality, but identifies where they are coming from and allows management to focus attention on the products and/or services that have a problem. Traditional costing systems, even if they somehow are able to identify these types of costs, offer little assistance for predicting where such unwanted costs will surface in the future, and why these costs are generated in the first place.

ABC, on the other hand, has the ability to forecast various scenarios and provide management with alternative courses of action to avoid costs. ABC prognosticates poor-quality costs, and this early warning system assists management in making intelligent decisions.

A total quality management (TQM) program and an ABC system must be linked in an organization to be effective. If these are designed as separate modules, they must be able to interface for exchanging data. The identification of the quality work drivers (e.g., number of defects, rework, inspections, repairs) and the associated products and/or services (e.g., machine number, problem types) is data that must be available in any ABC system in order to accurately calculate actual costs.

Remember that an ABC system is a planned system that emphasizes change, that forecasts, monitors, and reports on a functional work area's operation. The bottom line is to improve competitiveness.

## Measuring Corporate Profitability and Performance

Much has been written about the business community's shift to a customer-driven environment and the need to anticipate trends and change. Many senior executives have become so comfortable in doing things the same old way that they are unwilling to foresee change. They remain in a state of denial until the problem becomes so uncontrollable that all that remains is to escape the situation by transferring to another area.

Some organizations contribute to this type of behavior through a job assignment policy that allows these blinded executives to walk away unscathed from the storms they created. All of us find change unsettling at times, but without it there isn't any improvement. The most significant obstacles to reaching the full potential of ABC are the cultural issues, not the technical ones.

In today's competitive business world, an important consideration for senior management is to focus attention on the building of shareholder value. ABC is the mechanism to accurately analyze and maximize shareholder value. The revenue side of business has traditionally been given a great deal of management attention, but very little recognition has been placed on forecasting cost. If costs were forecast, they usually were based on erroneous historical records that misrepresented overhead costs.

In most traditional organizations, measuring corporate performance is based on earnings per share, return on investment, return on assets, and/or return on equity. Could these be misleading indicators? These types of standards neither forecast nor associate with the foundation of shareholder value. These indicators are reflectors of history, not predictors of the future, and represent reporting mechanisms rather than planning devices.

In forward-thinking organizations, cash flow analysis is considered to be as important as net income calculations. If a company's senior management is evaluated on shareholder value, cash flow becomes more significant as capital investments become more closely scrutinized. Inventory turnover becomes more important than balance sheet presentation of a higher asset value for inventory. Inventory value can increase as well as product cost, and net income may go up, but unsold inventory ties up company cash and doesn't show a return on the investment in that inventory.

Unlike traditional costing methods, ABC is closely linked to shareholder value, because it recognizes product-associated overhead costs. This linkage is one of the powerful forces of ABC. The increase in shareholder value is closely tied to an activity methodology.

ABC promotes the analysis and understanding of how all costs behave and interact with activities. Future expenditures for marketing, promotional, and/or advertising initiatives can be linked to a specific activity performance measurement:

| Traditional business management | ABC business management |
| --- | --- |
| Budgets | Activity work drivers |
| Products | Business processes |
| Markets | Customer requirements |
| Efficiency | Business process value analysis |
| Profit and losses | Cash flow |

This type of business analysis is supported by ABC methodology, because senior managers view their operations as a grouping of activities that consume resources in order to satisfy their customer base. This new culture forces a senior manager to think and link decisions, investments, customer needs, and costs in operating a business.

Shareholder value becomes the thread that binds and focuses a company on one objective: to create corporate value. Because it is a bottoms-up approach from activity to business process, ABC associates the work to be performed to attain that overall corporate goal of creating shareholder value. ABC provides the data to management for examining alternative directions in order to meet corporate goals in the most cost-effective manner.

ABC is not foolproof, and senior management must adopt a zero-based mentality by assiduously questioning premises underlying a business process's financial predictions, especially future revenues. ABC provides the senior management of a company with a more true-to-life cash flow because it accurately assigns support costs to products and services, and ultimately to a business process based on the activities performed. It portrays a mirror image of the life cycle of a business.

Traditional costing systems cannot inform senior management about which products and/or services are profitable, and which are losing money. In addition, conventional costing approaches do not fairly present accurate decision-making alternatives. ABC can assist in identifying cash-consuming products and/or services which become candidates for elimination. ABC facilitates the separation and identification of variable and fixed costs and accurately assigns support costs to appropriate products and/or services in order to provide superior customer value.

Customer satisfaction is a cost-preventive measure in an area that senior management often overlooks. We all understand that satisfied customers will continue and/or expand their business relationship. A by-product of this positive force is that sales and customer service staff members encounter less stress and enjoy their jobs more. This type of happy environment tends to assist the company in retaining experienced staff members, reducing training costs, and escaping the errors and rework of new employees. The result is a reduced cost of doing business.

It is widely known that it is less expensive to retain a customer than to find a new one. Many times an organization will not know that a customer is dissatisfied because the customer doesn't complain, but reacts by not buying any more of the company's products and/or services. Study after study shows the negative impact that dissatisfied customers can have. A $50 piece of faulty equipment not quickly serviced or exchanged might cost the company over $150,000 in future lost sales.

Within various industries, the negative pass-along comments to friends, neighbors, and business colleagues have the ability to negate major advertising programs. People often rely on other people for information before buying a product and/or service. Further, not all customer dissatisfaction results from defective products. Other root causes stem from improper instructions for a product's use, customer service practices, and/or overmarketing of what a product can do that fails to live up to expectations.

The VCR is a case in point. Most VCRs are cost-prohibitive to fix, especially after 10 or so years of loyal service. New units are sold, not with a minimum 1-year warranty, but only with a manufacturer's 90-day warranty. Salespeople will be quick to try to sell you an extended warranty for an additional charge. It's obvious that VCR manufacturers really don't care about the quality of their products and believe in putting profits before customer satisfaction. This attitude can have a negative effect on a company's long-term financial condition. Concentrating only on profit, while disregarding customer satisfaction, generally results in lost customers.

To create a customer-oriented approach requires a culture change for a traditionally managed company. Senior management cannot pay lip service to a customer-comes-first strategy. Management must mix with customers, communicate, and most important listen to customers. When the leadership of a company demonstrates a serious dedication to this philosophy, all levels of staff members from marketing to order entry will buy in. Many staff members interact with customers, with each one of them representing the company and communicating an impression of what their organization is like. As these personal relationships mature, important marketplace intelligence is being gathered, buyer loyalty is being developed, and customer requirements are being identified and collected.

## Importance of Interactive Relationships between Customers and the Corporation

These interactive relationships between staff members and customers are a very important channel for learning what the competition is proposing. The channel works only if senior management establishes the mechanism, demonstrates its commitment, and encourages all staff members to listen to their customers.

The president of a major distributor of industrial supplies used to put on a headset in his customer service functional work area one day a week and speak with customers about their problems. He did so on a periodic basis, just to stay in touch with his customers, and his action proved to be an excellent tool for building customer loyalty. He refused to insulate himself from the very people who were significant contributors to the company's success.

How do we measure customer loyalty and worth? By measuring company performance in meeting customer needs, an organization can better coordinate customer expectations and the ability of the company to perform in order to meet them. Benchmarking is helpful in comparing an organization's performance against its competitors' for on-time delivery, telephone response time, and customer service problem correction turnaround. It isn't acceptable for a company to believe it is shipping on time unless the customer also perceives this to be true. An organization cannot be happy with its performance unless that perception is validated by their customers.

A major distributor of giftware thought it was performing at the highest level in shipping to customers. It had installed a newly automated order processing and tracking system under which all orders were received, entered, picked, packed, and shipped within 24 hours. Customers started complaining that they weren't receiving their orders in a timely manner. Why the divergent perceptions?

The company researched the matter and discovered that its internal operation was indeed very efficient, but the trucking company it was using took 5 to 7 days to deliver products to customers. The company switched carriers and established a performance measure for the new carrier. This change aligned the customer's perspective and the company's into a shared view of high-level performance.

This example emphasizes the need for an organization to look outward, not inward, in developing performance criteria, by viewing the world through the eyes of its customers. A proven method of monitoring customer satisfaction is the use of customer feedback surveys to determine what the customer thought was important:

- Product and/or service innovations
- Delivery time
- Value received
- Price
- Warranty
- Repair service
- Determinants for buying a product and/or service

The survey must be carefully crafted using a language that both the customer and the company will understand. This establishes a common ground that will reduce misinterpretations and the erroneous collection of data. Once the data is collected, it must be organized into categories of importance to the customer. Surveys should also rate a company's products and/or services against the competition.

It is also useful to compare senior management's view of customer expectations against that of the customer base. This will assist senior managers in understanding their customers' needs, especially if they find a wide disparity between what they perceived was true and reality.

This eye-opener is very similar to what functional work area managers learn, after completing the interview and detailing processes, about what they thought staff members did and what activities were actually being performed. Both data collection and data analysis activities, seemingly with totally different purposes, try to translate perception into a reality that can be controlled. In addition, performance measurement at a detail level provides the basis for maintaining a TQM/continuous improvement program.

A company must make it easy for a customer to communicate in a timely manner so it can make informed decisions for taking corrective action. The customer/company relationship must be interactive, not reactive, for the association to be mutually beneficial. Remember that communication is a two-way process. The objective should be to satisfy customer requirements 100 percent of the time, because failure to do so could result in a lost customer.

An accurate performance measurement that can identify and highlight discrepancies between a customer's perception of performance and the company's actual performance furnishes management with the opportunity to rectify any misconceptions. This interaction must be continuous, so an organization can synchronize its activities with those of its customers. ABC can do this while traditional costing approaches cannot, because they neither map linkages nor consider a customer's viewpoint.

A customer-based focus utilizing ABC methodology naturally extends into activity-based management. A customer's requirements and expectations can be satisfied by activities that add value in delivering products and/or services. In supplying measurable data for ABM, ABC bypasses a narrow traditional product-driven and market-driven focus to view a business as a set of activities that meet customer expectations. This change in culture acts as a catalyst for creating mutually beneficial partnerships with longstanding customers instead of having to find new ones at a greater cost (e.g., higher marketing and selling expenses).

A closer relationship with customers may result in customers frequently asking their supplier for advice, and the supplier can respond in a positive manner by satisfying the customer's new wants. By analyzing how much a customer is willing to pay, an organization can adjust its activities to satisfy the customer at the most economical cost.

By properly managing activities and understanding what activities meet customer expectations, a company will experience increased profits. Senior managers will migrate away from managing output to an ABC methodology when they see consistently positive results. Some rules to follow:

- Be easy to do business with.

- Describe products and/or services clearly.

- Make ordering a pleasurable experience.

- Train and empower customer service representatives to answer questions and satisfy customer needs.

- Update catalog order forms regularly.

- Solicit customer feedback through surveys.

- Learn more about your customers' business in order to develop products and/or services to meet their needs.

- Conduct exit interviews with lost customers to learn how, why, and where the organization missed the boat.

The loss of a customer has a ripple effect. The company not only loses future revenues, but also forfeits the investment made in developing that customer relationship. Generally, customers don't care why a transaction was mishandled or by whom; they only want a speedy resolution, they want action. Senior management hasn't any choice other than to empower staff members who have customer contact with the authority and responsibility for satisfying the customer.

One health services organization handled several hundred member adjustments per month. The organization analyzed the dollar amounts of these adjustments and found that it would be less expensive to resolve transactions of $500 or less directly with the customer than to investigate them in detail.

This policy and procedural change not only reduced costs; it improved customer service staff morale and enhanced customer satisfaction.

The customer felt listened to, and the staff members felt fulfilled in doing their jobs. A successful organization:

- Influences customer needs
- Identifies potential customer needs
- Meets customer expectations
- Remains flexible
- Acts as a change agent

Traditional costing systems do not account for missed chances, and this type of omission can have negative long-term effects. Only through persistence and a commitment to innovative change can a company expect to stay competitive. Opportunity is transient and often doesn't knock twice, and a competitive advantage today could be gone tomorrow.

Every decision has a time-dependent element associated with it. The traditional costing system has a built-in penchant for inaction because old-line financial thinking believes a decision can always be made at a later date. Inaction can result in lost market share and/or not satisfying customer needs. Decisions cannot be made solely through a financial justification activity at the expense of keeping customers satisfied and maintaining one's competitive edge.

If a program substantially increases customer value, it shouldn't require a complete financial review. The company should move forward and implement it. A policy that curtails the development of improved products and/or services can lead only to an eroding competitive position. An activity-based approach to both costing and management prevents the usual sales and marketing projections and forecasts that don't take into account customer expectations. The activity-based methodology tends to result in more substantive forecasts.

Once senior management is committed to placing customer satisfaction ahead of whatever is second, all business decisions should be made on the basis of how much customer value is increased. Unlike traditional costing systems, ABC identifies a plethora of information that provides a company's management with alternatives which can be turned into a competitive advantage. Traditional management philosophy concentrates on marketing a product, while in an ABC environment the functional work area manager focuses on controlling the activities being performed and in determining how they are consumed and why they are consumed. Senior management can analyze alternatives and evaluate the cost of an activity versus its benefit and the level of significance in the customer's eyes.

ABC provides choices even if the best alternative means outsourcing some activities instead of providing the product and/or service internally. This approach maximizes each activity's value-added properties while increasing shareholder value. Senior managers can construct a business strategy by the way they choose activities to perform—activities that either increase customer satisfaction or make the company a low-cost supplier.

ABC presents to management a clear understanding of what it will take financially for a company to satisfy various customer requirements and allow management to make an informed decision. That decision may be a lower or premium price, superior customer service, and increased automation through electronic data interchange (EDI). Perhaps the decision will be to compete not on price, but on product and/or service differences. There isn't only one correct answer because each company must choose the path on which it can prosper.

ABC provides the data to allow management to make these types of decisions. The integration and linkage of supplies and customer activities creates a bond and dependency that should result in reduced costs for both parties. ABC can

- Pinpoint organizational weaknesses that prevent meeting customer needs
- Identify outsourcing advantages
- Surface inadequacies in distribution channels for future marketing penetration.
- Provide market segmentation data to better focus company selling efforts
- Identify costly alternatives that do not add value to customers and should be avoided
- Maintain a company's focus so that management doesn't take its eyes off the targets
- Help to keep a company from becoming vulnerable to competition because it has lost its direction
- Report on customer profitability and trends to make sure management remains alert and focused

Generally, a business strategy can neither be created nor be successful unless customer base considerations are an integral part of that strategy. Strategic plans designate how customer requirements will be met and in doing so how the company will achieve its operational objectives by distinguishing itself from the competition.

These points of distinction drive marketing, manufacturing, distribution, and customer service activities to support the overall corporate plan. ABC provides the data so that compromises can be made that will not negatively affect quality and customer value. As we have discussed, ABC can severely alter senior management's view of the business, resulting in a reevaluation of its business strategy.

The data collected by the customer survey contributes important elements to this rethinking exercise. It eliminates making crucial marketing decisions on the basis of improper assumptions about the customers who purchase products and/or services. Research in several industries has validated a divergence between a company's perception of what its customers value and what those customers truly find important. Typically, customers are concerned with basic services like delivery time, product quality, and price. Most successful organizations pay close attention to detail for maintaining these basic requirements, and identify other performance capabilities that might set them apart from their competitors.

ABC methodology assists management in determining how to prioritize an activity's consumption of resources for those customers that are worthy of special treatment. When a company seeks to service unprofitable customers, it misses other chances for profit while needlessly dissipating valuable resources.

A good example of excellent marketing strategy is Ralph Lauren's Polo Player cotton shirt. He limited the number of styles, but presented a large variety of colors for the consumer to choose from. Japanese auto makers followed a similar strategy by manufacturing a quality car that comes with predetermined equipment. The car buyer cannot order this extra or not order that extra. The car comes as is and reduces manufacturing costs considerably.

This example illustrates the importance of a well-orchestrated business strategy based on accurate and complete information. If a company's work force is highly trained and dedicated, and if resources are plentiful, the company still may fail if it hasn't developed a focused business strategy.

## Summary

There are several reasons that a company should utilize an activity-based costing approach as a tool for improving its business:

- Activities are actionable, because they describe the work that is done within the organization.

- Activities are easily understood by diverse groups of people and transcend hierarchies.

- Activities link together planning and control elements, and integrate financial and nonfinancial performance measures.

- Activities highlight functional work area interdependencies.

- Activities facilitate an understanding of the work drivers that cause work to be done.

- Activities provide the basis for continual improvement, reengineering, productivity improvement, and total quality management.

Activity-based costing links investment opportunities to strategic objectives in order for management to evaluate whether an investment should be made. Traditional methods of collecting costs by chart-of-account classifications within an organizational structure provide insufficient visibility of key activities and of the economic cause-and-effect relationships between activities in order to make intelligent decisions.

## Critical Success Factors

There are several critical success factors for realizing the benefits of an activity-based costing program:

- Senior management and functional work area management commitment
- Determination in managing organizational resistance to change
- Staff member buy-in
- Business process focus, not hierarchical
- Identification and evaluation of value-added and non-value-added activities
- Stable business process, not evolutionary
- Data gathering

  Define allocation assumptions.

  Identify an appropriate and representative historical time period.

  Focus on and understand the technique and methodology first, before data gathering begins.

  Verify availability of historical transaction volumes.

  Verify availability of historical work hours data.

  Avoid overkill.

## ABC's Main Ideas

The main ideas of ABC may be summarized as follows:

- Activities consume resources.
- Products and services consume activities.
- Events cause activities.
- Multiple variables determine cost.

# 10
# Conclusion

Activity-based management aims directly at two targets, both common to all companies:

- Improve the value received by customers, whether they are internal or external.
- Improve profits by providing this value.

Activity-based management, activity-based costing, reengineering, and productivity improvement methodologies are made for one another. ABC, reengineering, and productivity improvement techniques supply the information that is required to manage activities in order to operate a business. ABM uses this information in a variety of ways to improve the business.

ABM derives its force from the databases created from the other methodologies. Both of the aforementioned targets are attained by focusing on the management of activities. This philosophy begins with the basic premise that customers have simple but essential needs. They want high-quality products and/or services that fit a definite need at an affordable price and with timely service.

"And they want it now." Meeting customer requirements generally is not a difficult assignment, but meeting them *profitably* is quite another matter. It is not enough to inform shareholders that a company's products and/or services have the highest-quality standards in the industry, or that customer surveys consistently rate the company at the highest levels in customer satisfaction. An organization must also provide an adequate return on shareholder investment.

On the surface these may appear to be conflicting missions, but a closer look reveals there's really no conflict. In the business community a company's profitability is important to customers, because customers want the relationship to continue for "the long haul." That will not happen if an organization is unprofitable.

ABM adheres to the principle that managing activities is the route to profitably improving customer value. Each activity contributes in its own way to this overall goal. Each makes a measurable contribution to its customers—be it quality, timeliness, service, reliable delivery, or low cost. It is important to realize, too, that managing activities is not a custodial task. Rather, it's a process of relentless and continuous improvement of all aspects of a business. The process involves an ongoing search for opportunities to improve. That search, in turn, involves a careful and methodical study of what activities should be performed, how those activities should be carried out, and how customer value is defined.

## Defining Customer Value

The definition of customer value will vary from business to business, but one of the primary rules of ABM is to "improve what matters to the customer," whatever it is. A second important rule is to deploy resources for activities that yield the maximum strategic benefit to the organization. If quality is what matters to the customer, management needs to understand the customer's criteria for quality, asking

- What are the trends for key indicators?
- What activities are responsible for the indicators?
- How much cost is associated with poor quality?

ABM can point out which functional work areas have large detection and/or connection activities, because these usually indicate the presence of a quality problem.

Information collected on work drivers and performance measures reveals opportunities for improvement and helps monitor progress. There are many costly activities associated with documenting and correcting quality problems (e.g., inspecting, appraisal, rework).

*Customer value is about what customers get, and what they give up to get it.*

Value comes in various packages. Included in the package are the features of the product or service. For a car, features include interior space, engine size, type of transmission, front-, rear-, or all-wheel drive, and so on. For a checking account, features include electronic bill paying, access to automatic teller machines, and 24-hour verification of the account balance.

But customer value goes well beyond just features. Whether buying cars or checking services, customers also value good quality and service. In some cases, quality is the primary purchase consideration. In all cases, quality affects the cost of using the product or service. Customers sometimes buy future costs when they buy a product or service. Future costs are incurred by using and servicing a car. Fees are incurred for services associated with a checking account. Some products (such as nuclear fuel) have disposal costs.

There isn't any value received without some sacrifice. Many products and services require time and effort, both in the initial purchase and in learning how to use the product. It takes time, for example, to master a new software program.

Remember that ABM is a bottoms-up process so that staff members can take ownership of the program. Ownership also increases the likelihood that they will use it to improve productivity. The bottoms-up approach allows all staff members to share in the creation of the program and serves to eliminate roadblocks so that customers and suppliers can work together harmoniously. ABM should belong to the functional work areas so they can increase their ability to accept responsibility, which then brings them both empowerment and accountability.

A focused organization team has everyone pulling the wagon in the same direction. A strong and clear focus is critical for TQM and continuous improvement to flourish. ABM assists functional work area managers in converting a staff member's attitude from entitlement to accountability. Empowered staff members have a sense of ownership, satisfaction, and control over how activities are performed. This gives them self-esteem and a feeling of accomplishment. The greater their feeling of belonging, the stronger their connection to an organization and its goals. Staff members begin to understand more clearly how their actions and performance affect the success of a business.

## Underlying Principles of ABM

ABM is a modern-day term, but some of its principles have been around since the end of the nineteenth century. When rapid advances in technology began to appear, people started becoming interested in efficiency. Scientific management was born, and research commenced using a technique called *time-and-motion studies* to understand how long it takes to complete an activity.

From this humble beginning, many types and forms of management techniques evolved, and these concepts have all been influenced by economic, social, technological, and political events. The technological revolution has affected our planning and control functions. Recessions and inflation have had enormous impact on human resources and organizational design segments and have changed forever the way both corporations and staff members view the workplace.

No longer will employees feel that the company they work for has a social responsibility to provide a job for them, and this attitude affects motivation, morale, and values. Is there such a concept as a permanent staff member, or are we all just temporaries in the new downsizing and/or rightsizing business world?

ABM also brings many changes in the traditional roles and responsibilities that managers have had for many years. The more information that is shared with staff members, the less a functional work area manager has to be the central decision-making body. The manager has to become more of a coach, facilitator, enabler, and communicator to staff members, and this cultural change is not always an easy transition.

Under ABM, decision making becomes dispersed to many levels in an organization; it is not retained solely by functional work area and/or senior managers. The effect can be dramatic, with the decision-making process becoming quicker. Overall company productivity goes up because more and more staff members are being trained to accept responsibility. Under ABM, a manager doesn't look just at costs but rather at the actions that caused them. Since activities consume resources and create costs, the most logical approach to controlling costs is to eliminate the triggers for those activities.

Companies that have reduced staff without eliminating work are only scratching the surface of the problem, because having fewer resources means only that less work can be performed. This circular thinking also means that an organization is satisfying fewer customers, which in turn will result in lower revenues.

Managing a business enterprise becomes a game of chance. Without functional work area managers and senior management comprehending which costs are created by specific activities, or which costs are caused by certain customers and/or suppliers, costs cannot be permanently reduced.

Eliminating non-value-added activities in line with customer needs can significantly lower costs while revenue remains stable. ABM tries to match customer needs with activities performed. It views all business processes as a series of activities required to satisfy customer needs. A company can decide which activities it wishes to perform and which can be outsourced. This approach provides a company with a basic plan to construct a competitive advantage and offer its customers only those activities which add value to the customer.

ABM allows management to compare the costs of taking a certain course of action with how much a customer is willing to pay. By controlling the frequency of performing an activity, a company can also control the costs of that activity. (For example, shipping larger but fewer orders can save billing, shipping, and freight costs.)

A company must structure its activities in such a manner that customers are willing to expend resources for them; at the same time, the company needs to increase shareholder value. Utilizing the data provided by ABC, reengineering, and other sources, ABM can assist both senior management and functional work area management in attaining this level of coordinated effectiveness.

By analyzing its own activities, any organization can relate better to the customer and understand more fully the customer's activities. The productivity portions of an ABM program enable management at all levels to expend resources more efficiently, because those resources will be assigned to value-added activities.

The realization that today's managers are coming to is that they must balance the tradeoffs between customer satisfaction and reductions in cost. An ABM program clears the haziness by making costs traceable to actual activities, not to some profit-and-loss-statement line item, and by identifying what causes an activity to be performed. Eliminate a root cause and an activity will be discontinued, resulting in reduced costs. Even traditional managers will recognize that when enough activities disappear, people will follow—because they will not have any work to do.

The overall methodology espoused in this book forces managers to focus on activities that have significant costs associated with them, and to ask the question, "Why?" By refocusing priorities from hierarchical structures to end-to-end processes, ABM emphasizes to managers that costs are only symptoms and that work, policies, and equipment are the root causes of cost.

Controlling costs becomes possible only when an organization alters the way it does business. ABM surfaces the interrelationship between various functional work areas, and the interdependencies in performing activities smoothly and efficiently. We have shown how work-to-time relationships can assist managers in determining how much an activity costs, what staffing requirements are needed to perform that activity, and how to benchmark and/or compare themselves with their competitors.

Activities are the fuel that drives a company and causes it to incur costs, and the analysis of activities identifies improvement opportunities. Managers can then set about finding ways to evaluate whether a functional work area is becoming more or less efficient. A manager must know what causes an activity to happen, and how to measure it, before determining how to ameliorate the activity. By knowing what tradeoffs are acceptable to both management and the customer, a functional work area manager is better able to negotiate contracts that result in increased shareholder values.

If a supplier is reliable and has acceptable quality standards, it will save a significant amount of money, because that organization no longer needs a receiving, inspection, and warehousing process. ABM gives a company the productivity measures for each activity, the cost to perform an activity, and the ability to eliminate the activity if it is non-value added.

ABM identifies what actions, policies, and systems generate costs. Once the cost of an activity is determined, a functional work area manager can drill down to analyze the components of costs (e.g., 10 separate forms to process a purchase). When some of the forms, tasks, and required approvals are eliminated, the procurement process becomes faster and costs less.

An underlying premise in adopting ABM methodology is "A job not worth doing is not worth doing well, and if an activity cannot add value to a product, service and/or customer it should not be performed." What is the advantage of being proficient in performing an activity if it isn't required? Managers should continually question whether an activity is necessary, whether it is costly, and what caused the activity to be performed.

When a determination is made as to the root cause of an activity, an investigation should be undertaken to understand if the cause was a result of internal policy or customer actions. This investigation will surface any non-value-added work. The analysis should involve the data collected during the detailing process—including the activity work flows, which can be very helpful in identifying redundant activities and/or tasks.

The ABM team with the cooperation of functional work area staff members can evaluate each task, searching for a more proficient way to perform the work. Fewer activities and/or tasks mean reduced cost, because each time a piece of paper or item is handled, the greater the cost and the slower the process. If, as a result of some additional training, a task can be completed or a decision can be made all at one work station instead of having to move a part or a document to another work area, the process becomes more efficient and less expensive.

Look to eliminate inspections, movement, counting, scrap, and rework activities, because they are roadblocks to an efficient process. In one large distribution company, the order processing area handled brand-new orders from first-time buyers exactly the same way as it handled repeat orders from existing customers. An analysis of the activity showed that almost all the information was already in the system for existing customers. The processing protocol for repeat orders was altered, saving order processing and data entry time and also reducing entry errors. Customer satisfaction improved because orders were processed faster at a higher-quality level.

There is an unusual but important ancillary benefit derived from an ABM program. Management can determine how much a specific decision costs, because the activities involved in a decision can often be traced directly to it. The dissecting of a costly activity often proves to be the tip of the iceberg. Generally, a ripple effect can be found that creates a series of inefficiencies that were not obvious in a cursory look.

One service business found that the cost of a customer inquiry was high. An investigation revealed that more than half the inquiries were under $250. Each customer service inquiry required a form to be filled in. The form was sent to another functional work area for investigation and resolution and returned to customer service. The customer was then telephoned about the decision.

Why did the company receive so many customer service telephone calls? It was determined that the customer called as a result of processing errors in the initial handling of the transaction. The company's management took corrective action to reduce this type of problem. It clarified the guidelines for the staff member processing the transaction, and empowered the customer service representative to approve adjustments under $500 on the spot. The number of inquiries dropped drastically and the paperwork shuffle was eliminated while customer satisfaction increased.

Identifying the high cost of this activity led the ABM team to investigate the problem, track its source, and correct it in a timely manner. Only through utilizing ABM methodology could someone start questioning the root cause of the problem activity. The search for what started the activity led the ABM team to the real cause of the activity.

In the past, each functional work area would have accused the other of being at fault without anyone taking ownership of the entire problem. The ABM approach fosters a teamwork environment among functional work area managers. ABM provides the means to upgrade the entire budgeting process, because it can be completed as a bottoms-up approach activity by activity.

Staffing requirements can be evaluated with a greater degree of accuracy, because work-to-time relationships associated with transaction volumes provide a secure determination of resource requirements. Once resource requirements are identified, costs can be developed for each activity, all activities aggregated into a business process, and all business processes aggregated into a business unit or organization. ABM is a tool and if used to its fullest is a change agent for improvement.

Traditional managers become nervous because they are used to basing their decisions on past experience, not activity analysis. This culture change cannot occur overnight and can be attained only through education. It shouldn't have to take a disaster or crisis to alter the way managers work, even though there is a degree of risk involved. Executive egos should be laid aside, and instead of reacting to the demands of shareholders or the board of directors, managers should be proactively bold in their actions.

ABM methodology adds another dimension to the management of a business organization. The reward systems that are an integral part of TQM and continuous improvement utilize the data that is collected during the observation process. Reward systems come in various formats, but all such systems must rely on quantitative performance measurements. Reward systems can be a positive motivating force, but only if the established standards have been based on objective criteria that are applied uniformly and consistently throughout an organization.

If every staff member in an organization receives similar pay incentives, a situation will arise in which staff members do not see any meaningful relationship between excellent and/or average performance and their reward. In establishing work-to-time relationships for primary activities, ABM provides functional work area managers with the objective data needed to construct a reward platform. In addition, managers must understand the needs of their staff members in order to tie those needs to corporate goals.

If a staff member or functional work area continually demonstrates exceptional performance, the functional work area manager should recognize that achievement. A reward program generally invigorates and induces staff members to maintain their high level of performance. Recognition can come in the form of a citation, an item in the company newsletter, financial compensation, show tickets, and so on.

Rewards do not always have to be extensive and involve monetary gains. Intrinsic rewards that emphasize self-esteem, self-actualization, and an inner sense of accomplishment can be just as effective as a bonus check. Positive motivation can act as a catalyst that stimulates and maintains morale, personal behavior, and improved productivity.

The cost of the reward is not the important element; the awareness of a job well done is a key that reinforces quality and productivity. People should be rewarded because they are productive, not because they have seniority. Work-to-time relationships should be revisited periodically to make sure they are not unrealistic, either because they were originally set up improperly or because the content of the work has changed.

## Necessity for Enhanced Information Systems

It has become more difficult for senior management to motivate staff members because of organizational downsizing, which often results in an excess of functional work area managers and fewer workers. Rewards must meet individual needs for behavior to be altered and must be repeated to satisfy that need. If performance doesn't materialize into an expected reward, the individual will most likely not repeat the performance level.

In order for an ABM program to run smoothly, it must be supported by a well-architectured infrastructure, because all levels of management require reliable information in a timely manner to be effective and competitive. A plethora of nonintegrated data can negatively impact productivity, reengineering efforts, and ABM, because informed decision making becomes nonexistent.

Under ABC, information systems are considered a resource, just as a staff member is a resource. An ABM program is heavily dependent on information resources for planning, directing, organizational structure, and control. Senior management cannot effectively operate an organization without information about customers, competitors, staff members, and business processes.

All roads lead to MIS, and the collection of reliable data that is structured and transformable into useful information is a must if better decisions are to be made. We have discussed the importance of computer-generated transaction volume data in establishing reliable work-to-time relationships. Inadequate information starts a chain reaction of error-prone decisions that cause non-value-added activities to be performed. Converting raw data into expressive information isn't generally a simple or apparent process. Each functional work area manager may have a different definition of what meaningful information is.

Many of our larger corporations have gone to such lengths to establish information credibility that they have created a new senior management position, chief information officer (CIO). This executive is not your traditional MIS type who reports to the chief financial officer (CFO); rather, the CIO's responsibilities move beyond monitoring computers to designing the operation of advanced information and communications systems. The CIO is often on the same reporting level as the CFO.

Information must be tailored to meet the needs and purpose of the user, and the characteristics of the data should be structured to meet those specific needs:

- Preciseness
- Timeliness
- Completeness
- Relevance
- Conciseness

Information in a business environment is rarely perfect, but the closer information comes to the aforementioned standards, the more valuable it is for making informed decisions. When accurate, objective information is provided to senior managers, the more readily will they utilize it in making critical decisions. Information that is organized properly can lower staffing levels and increase quality. Accessibility to reliable external information could present an organization with a distinct competitive advantage, assist in identifying customers and markets, and improve product loyalty.

Information can be used to find new marketing territories for existing products or new products for current customers. Information is a significant element in every phase of management, from planning and organizing to leading and controlling. Throughout this book we have emphasized how important data is in the interviewing, detailing, and observation processes, and how that data must be collected and transformed into useful information for the ABM program to be a success.

During the planning process, functional work area managers benefit from timely, accurate information to generate objectives and to assign the resources required to meet those objectives. Reliable information increases confidence and credibility in management from outside sources such as banks, shareholders, and suppliers. Information can also be useful in launching new products and/or services if the information intelligence is discriminating.

Unreliable information can have a negative impact on an organization's decision making and strategic planning. If the sales functional work area projects revenues unrealistically, other areas of the company could make inappropriate staffing decisions to support that sales program. Traditional, hierarchical managers thrive on exercising managerial power by withholding information under the guise of need to know. Generally, when information is withheld or appropriate information is not provided, reduced quality, lower productivity, and uninformed decisions result.

One manager defined the parameters of an exercise poorly and withheld some critical information. Four staff members spent 2 days preparing the requested analysis and presented it to the manager. The manager began criticizing the staff members for missing the point and final result, and simultaneously had in his possession the final number he was looking for. When the staff members asked why the manager had failed to give them the objective and tie-in number, the manager replied that they didn't need to know it.

The work had to be redone to tie into the number the manager withheld. If the staff members had been given this piece of information, they could have used it as a check to make sure they weren't missing some of the pieces of the puzzle in completing the analysis. Experience has shown that the more informed staff members are, the better decisions they make.

Information can be used to create reward programs and is a pivotal element in applying an effective management monitoring program. Once work-to-time relationships are established and a management reporting structure is implemented, information becomes the key to measuring performance, comparing actual results against predicted results, and then making decisions on the basis of the results.

A functional work area manager cannot take corrective action if he or she doesn't realize that there is a problem. A major international giftware company had a customer service group that handled customer complaints in a reactive manner, but the group's access to information was limited. The customer service representative could not answer a majority of the inquiries immediately, had to take down information, research the problem, and then call the customer back—sometimes days later.

When the organization was reengineered and an ABM program was implemented, the entire scenario changed. A new information system (IS) module was created using the customer representatives' input as to the types of information they needed to satisfy the customer and feel good about doing their jobs properly. The new module provided the customer service representative with a proactive protocol for informing a customer as to where an order was—order entry, picking, packing, shipping, carrier.

In addition, the customer's complete order history was available to the service representative so he or she could encourage some impulse purchasing and/or request an on-account payment. The significant benefit was that all this flexibility was put to use while the customer service representative was on the telephone. This eliminated taking notes, researching an activity, and calling the customer back. Another significant benefit of this information enhancement was the improvement in customer satisfaction.

ABM methodology provides the approach to create a platform for an information system to be enhanced or to develop a new one. Information systems can be expensive to construct, but even more costly to maintain if they are not configured properly. All the processes involved in an ABM program participate in gathering the significant data required to convert intelligence into useful information. If done properly, the IS configuration will be made flexible and responsive to the user's needs, and should have room to expand at a later time.

ABM uses a bottoms-up approach which greatly reduces the risks involved in developing new or enhancing older systems. There are some key elements needed for a supportive information system to be responsive.

- An information system should respond to the needs of the user.

- Ask the six basic questions of the way work is currently performed before automating the system: *who, what, when, where, how, why.* Automating a flawed activity will only permit more efficient errors, not make work more effective.

- The information system must have the support and buy-in of functional work area managers if significant operational improvements are to be realized. Staff members will take their cue from their manager's attitudes, and the sending of an inadvertent message that is not supportive will have negative consequences with the rank-and-file worker.

- The information system must be configured with provisions for growth and flexibility as an organization matures (e.g., new markets, increase of customer base).

An information system should have an architecture that allows it to function at various levels of management as needed:

- Transaction processing
- Management information:

  Decision support for routine line management matters that may require drill-down capability

  Executive utilization for senior management with high-level comparative information

The impact of a reliable and timely information system is multifaceted and forever changes the way a business operates. Computer technology provides a company with a means to initiate new external associations as well as to enhance existing ones. A company's infrastructure offers more information to a wider universe of people who can become empowered to solve problems, reducing the need for a number of management layers.

Information can be assembled and then flow more efficiently and effectively so response time can be improved for making decisions and correcting problems. Everything in life has a downside as well as an upside. With all the technological advances comes a dependency that a week at a rehabilitation clinic can't cure.

With downtime, computer viruses, and hackers who can interrupt and steal information from a computer system, organizations become vulnerable to not being able to bill, apply cash, ship orders, and so on. Organizations have also been crippled by fire, power outages, and—as we have seen recently—earthquakes. Most companies are taking steps to minimize these types of problems, but senior management cannot completely eliminate circumstances of every dimension. An important point that outside auditors insist upon is that a disaster recovery plan and procedures be in place before a catastrophe occurs.

Most of us are caught up in a vicious cycle of demanding more speed, increased on-line real-time capabilities, more storage capacity, and greater flexibility from our computer systems. We even attempt to reduce travel expenses by utilizing teleconferencing at meetings. Our business lives are becoming more impersonal, and less and less frequently can we look people in the eye or shake their hand.

There is a significant management requirement to be sure that computer systems are being used properly. In order for this to happen, management must educate staff members on how to utilize the working system fully. One service organization received several internal complaints from staff members about its computer system. An investigation revealed that indeed the computer system needed some enhancing to meet user requirements. However, equally enlightening was the discovery that many staff members weren't trained to utilize the system fully. Many of the complaints would have been nonexistent if the staff members had been trained, guided, coached, and supported adequately by the IS staff.

Another obstacle is computer phobia, or the fear or mistrust of computers—particularly among older staff members who are used to handling pieces of paper. Training programs should be developed for various levels of experience and classes of users, such as senior managers, line managers, staff managers, professionals, data entry personnel, and system operators.

## Establishing Controls

ABM methodology emphasizes effective control through the monitoring of work being performed. The activities and performance measures to accomplish the required control process are established through the observation process and management reporting protocols. Management must

- Establish work-to-time relationships (reasonable expectancies)
- Measure performance
- Compare reasonable expectancies with actual performance
- Identify problems
- Take corrective action

The control element encourages staff members to work toward meeting company goals, and provides functional work area managers with feedback from their staff members. This two-way communication allows organizations to alter courses of action when business conditions change.

Managers communicate corporate goals by establishing work-to-time relationships for primary activities and then assigning those activities to staff members. This approach provides a twofold benefit: (1) an objective measure of staff member performance and (2) a catalyst for motivating staff members to be more productive. Performance should be monitored regularly and, as suggested in the chapter on management reports, the frequency will vary depending on the reporting level and the type of work being performed.

Functional work area managers should exercise care when analyzing variances from standard, whether the variances be higher or lower. Variances can often be a wake-up call signaling that a more serious problem has surfaced. Functional work area managers should employ their diagnostic skills in understanding what caused the variance before attempting corrective action. Correction action should be taken with one goal in mind: to alter activities in an attempt to allow a staff member's performance to attain the expected productivity level for a specific activity.

Successful companies are able to meet their defined objectives because they utilize an effective control process to detect marketplace changes and to monitor internal organizational performance. An important point to remember is that having a control process doesn't mean a company can run on auto pilot, because an improperly functioning control process can be a negative influence and deterrent to realizing corporate goals.

Improper signals can move senior management in the wrong direction, causing grave consequences for an organization. The most common problems result from an extreme such as overcontrol, undercontrol, or fluctuating control. Functional work area managers should periodically review the control process to evaluate whether the routine is either too rigorous or too tolerant. Overcontrol negates empowerment, curtails innovation, and is demoralizing because it restricts individual action, whereas undercontrol may open the door to misinterpretation, lack of cohesion, and wasteful use of resources.

Neither extreme is acceptable, and the task of both senior and functional work area managers is to find suitable levels of control to enhance performance. To be effective, a control process must be applied consistently to prevent sending mixed messages to staff members. To be successful in the long term, control systems should be structured to elicit positive behavior patterns, not just to end a short-term crisis.

In establishing controls, functional work area managers must be aware of the distinct needs of a work area and the way it operates. A chain of stores that are mirror images of one another (the Gap stores are an example) can operate one control system. An operation that varies because its business is based on size and/or location might have to vary its controls from site to site.

Key characteristics that seem to pervade effective control systems are:

- Consistency with organizational goals and planning
- Accuracy for gathering and dispensing dependable and correct information
- Timeliness in order to react to problems
- Appropriateness of data to monitor work
- Objectivity in reporting operating conditions
- Measurability to determine if corrective action is needed

Control processes aren't any different from other operational activities, in that a common language is required to properly evaluate functional work area performance.

Competition has become so fierce that many products are surprisingly similar, price differentials are nonexistent, and everyone knows how to meet customer requirements. How do organizations separate themselves from the herd? The main focus in business today for differentiating one organization from another centers on three concepts:

- Quality
- Productivity
- Customer satisfaction

Quality has been discussed as part of TQM and continuous improvement. Remember that when an organization makes quality a significant goal, its functional work area managers and staff members usually do not have rework and do not scrap materials. This emphasis on quality speeds up throughput, reduces errors, and utilizes resources more judiciously.

The improvement in quality directly increases productivity, because errors go down along with per unit costs as sales and market share increase. Improved quality and productivity leads to increased customer satisfaction by fulfilling customer needs and expectations as to product quality, service, and price.

If customers remain satisfied, they order more products and/or services and may even be willing to pay a higher price, which in turn increases an organization's profitability. A successful company can then reinvest some of its profits to further enhance quality and productivity. Customers then tell friends and family how exceptional their supplier is, and a positive chain reaction begins.

In service firms of all types, the sudden concern with quality has led senior management to make quality everyone's job regardless of level within the organization. Several elements characterize what quality really means in practice from a customer's perspective:

- Operational execution, which includes a product and/or service performing in the way it was described to a customer
- Characteristics of the product and/or service that augment normal functionality
- Dependability, which means that a product and/or service will function for a reasonable amount of time before repairs become necessary
- Adherence of a product and/or service to the quality standards of design and operation
- Functionality, whereby a product and/or service lives up to its basic claims
- Service response time that is fast and polite
- Intangibles that give a product and/or service an aura of being special and unique
- Perception by customers of a high level of quality (perception becomes reality, as we all know)

All these elements play a part in a customer's evaluation of a product and/or service, but they all do not have to be present at the same time. Each organization must determine for its purposes what significant elements it wants to emphasize, and must deliver those elements consistently to customers.

Most organizations establish quality assurance functional work areas to monitor quality against established standards. TQM, which is an integral part of ABM, emphasizes that quality is the responsibility of every staff member and should be a part of every activity that relates to customer satisfaction. TQM instills quality in every activity involved in the life cycle of a business process. It emphasizes that each staff member is accountable for providing each succeeding staff member in the process with a quality output or input.

Generally, when quality improves so does productivity, because costs are reduced and performance becomes more efficient. As discussed in establishing work-to-time relationships as part of the observation process, productivity is often expressed in terms of revenues per employee. Improved individual productivity is the basis for building organizational productivity. Productivity should not be improved at the expense of quality and customer satisfaction; otherwise, the organization runs the risk of forfeiting both customers and profits.

Given the emphasis on productivity, we believe the methodology outlined in this book becomes, not a luxury, but a necessity in order to compete in business.

Functional work area managers cannot just cut head count; they have to structure their performance measurements for specific activities. Each manager can establish productivity goals for primary activities that are challenging, attainable, measurable, and time defined. We believe strongly in the bottom-up approach to increasing productivity, because staff members and functional work area managers are the people closest to the operation. They are generally the most knowledgeable about how to improve efficiency and are ready, willing, and able to offer their suggestions. Senior management must be ready to listen.

In an empowered environment, the difference between a high-performing team and an average team can be traced back to the difference between management that facilitates, motivates, and coaches  and management that hierarchically impedes performance. When staff members feel they are making a significant contribution, they are invigorated to continue to perform at a high level.

The ABM program is designed to identify all activities within a business process, classify those activities into primary and secondary categories, detail all the tasks within each primary activity, develop activity work flows, observe each primary activity being performed, determine reasonable expectancies for each activity (including secondary activities), determine which activities are value added and non-value added, reengineer business operations, calculate staffing requirements, and encourage TQM/continuous improvement philosophies.

Many experts treat reengineering, productivity improvement, TQM, continuous improvement, and ABC methodologies as totally independent of one another. We have tried to show how all the aforementioned disciplines are interdependent in executing an effective activity-based management program.

We believe that anyone who understands and follows the step-by-step methodology we have devised will quickly understand how any business process operates, and can then take action to improve that operation. The methodology should provide those who embrace it with the tools and assurance that this detailed approach is powerful and objective, and in the long run the quickest way to understand a business environment.

We hope that as practitioners and business executives you agree.

# Index

*Entries appearing in figures are indicated by f after the page number.

## About the Author

Edward Forrest, CPA, is president of Productivity Consulting Limited in Roslyn, New York, and is considered a leading expert in activity-based costing and management. As a senior executive with over 20 years of broad-ranging experience with companies both abroad and in the U.S., he has gained expertise in a variety of areas, including systems integration, general management, financial management, operations, turnaround management, mergers and acquisitions, and consulting. Among the honors he has received are membership in Who's Who in America East and Who's Who in Global Business. Mr. Forrest is an active member of the American Institute of Certified Public Accountants, where he has given courses on activity-based costing, activity-based management, and reengineering productivity. He is also on the faculty of the AT&T School of Business. He holds an MBA from New York University's Stern School of Business.